DEFENDING THE REPUBLIC

DEFENDING THE REPUBLIC:

CONSTITUTIONAL MORALITY IN A TIME OF CRISIS

Essays in Honor of George W. Carey

edited by

Bruce P. Frohnen & Kenneth L. Grasso

Wilmington, Delaware

Defending the republic : constitutional morality in a time of crisis : essays in honor of George W. Carey / Bruce Frohnen, Kenneth Grasso, editors. —1st ed. —Wilmington, Del. : ISI Books, c2008.

    p. ; cm.
    ISBN: 978-1-933859-43-9

    1. Carey, George Wescott, 1933– 2. Political science—United States. 3. Federal government—United States. 4. Constitutional history—United States. 5. Political science. I. Frohnen, Bruce. II. Grasso, Kenneth L. III. Carey, George Wescott, 1933– IV. Title.

JC251 .D44 2008   2007941670
320/.011—dc22   0808

Published in the United States by:

    ISI Books
    Intercollegiate Studies Institute
    3901 Centerville Road
    Wilmington, Delaware 19807
    www.isibooks.org

Contents

EDITORS' INTRODUCTION / vii

PART I
Foundations of Political Order

Making Sense of Majoritarianism / 3
      Paul Edward Gottfried

George Carey on Constitutions, Constitutionalism, and Tradition / 17
      Bruce P. Frohnen

Locke, Our Great Founders, and American Political Life / 37
      Peter Augustine Lawler

PART II
The American Republic: Origins and Intent

George Carey and the Roots of America's Basic Liberties / 57
      Donald S. Lutz

Federalists, Antifederalists, and the Philadelphia Constitution / 79
      Gordon Lloyd

James Madison and the Extended Republic / 99
      Quentin Taylor

The Virtue of Education: The Founders' Vision / 121
      Jeffry Morrison

No Presidential Republic: Representation,
Deliberation, and Executive Power in The Federalist Papers / 139
    Gary L. Gregg II

Rights in a Federalist System / 153
    Francis Canavan

PART III
The American Republic: Derailment and Crisis

Religious Pluralism and the American Experiment:
From Articles of Peace to Culture Wars / 177
    Kenneth L. Grasso

Horizontal and Vertical Consolidation of
the United States into an Administrative State / 201
    John S. Baker, Jr.

The Rule of Men: How Caring Too Much about
Important Things Is Destroying Constitutional Law / 221
    William Gangi

The Crisis of the American Political Tradition / 245
    E. Robert Statham, Jr.

Neo-Jacobin Nationalism or Reponsible Nationhood? / 263
    Claes G. Ryn

NOTES / 283

ABOUT THE CONTRIBUTORS / 331

INDEX / 335

Editors' Introduction

For over four decades, George W. Carey has engaged students, scholars, and educated laymen in a searching conversation regarding the nature and right ordering of public life. He is perhaps best known as an expositor of conservatism, not because most of his writings have addressed that philosophy and persuasion but because his method and his vision of the good capture what is best therein: prudence in the service of the tradition of natural-law thought that lies at the heart of Western civilization. Whether discussing the workings of American political institutions, the nature and roots of social and political traditions, or the moral underpinnings of constitutionalism, Carey consistently has argued for a practical understanding of politics and its limits, along with an integrated vision of human sociability and its historical, political, and moral constituents.

Born in 1933 as the son of a well-known professor at the Northwestern University School of Law, Carey grew up in the Chicago suburb of Wilmette, Illinois. As an undergraduate at Northwestern he first encountered Charles Hyneman, one of America's most prominent political scientists, who is remembered today primarily for his writings on American political thought. Hyneman's commonsense approach to the study of politics, his openness to serious discussion of varying philosophical viewpoints, and his concern to understand self-government, the rule of law, and ordered liberty had a far-reaching impact on Carey. Through Hyneman, Carey met another thinker whose work would profoundly affect the evolution of his own thought: Willmoore Kendall, the combative conservative icon. Taught by Kendall to question the liberal platitudes offered by most of his professors, Carey began to challenge them in print even before entering graduate school.

In 1957, after graduating from college Phi Beta Kappa with high honors and serving a stint in the Marine Corps, Carey commenced graduate work at the University of Illinois, where he studied municipal government and intergovernmental relations under Charles Kneir. He transferred to Indiana University, where he worked informally with Hyneman, who was teaching there. In 1961, Carey completed his doctoral dissertation, which examined the implications of political equality in theories of democratic government and pointed out the potentially destructive nature of equality when held as an ideal. Carey then immediately took up teaching duties in the government department at Georgetown University—a position he has never left, despite several offers. He did spend the 1964–65 academic year as a Visiting Associate Professor at Indiana, where he worked with Hyneman in putting together *A Second Federalist: Congress Creates a Government* (1967).[1] With contents taken from congressional debates during the early years of the republic, this volume fleshes out the original understanding of the Constitution by showing how that document was interpreted in the course of establishing the actual institutions of American government.

During the early 1960s, Carey developed a close working relationship with Willmoore Kendall. The collaboration, continuing until the latter's death in 1967, bore fruit in several cowritten articles, including "Towards a Definition of Conservatism,"[2] "The 'Intensity' Problem in Democratic Theory,"[3] and "The 'Roster Device': J. S. Mill and Contemporary Elitism."[4] Carey and Kendall also coedited a volume, *Liberalism Versus Conservatism: The Continuing Debate in American Government* (1966),[5] and an interpretive introduction to a new edition of *The Federalist*.[6]

Although he declined to assume the directorship of the program in politics and literature that Kendall had founded at the University of Dallas and was directing at the time of his death, Carey accepted the invitation of Kendall's widow to expand into a book a series of lectures Kendall had delivered at Vanderbilt University in 1964. The result, *The Basic Symbols of the American Political Tradition* (1970), is one of the very few truly essential works in the study of American political thought.[7] Consisting of edited versions of four Kendall lectures and four additional chapters written by Carey (one of which incorporates material from an additional Kendall lecture), *Basic Symbols* employs the methodology developed by Eric Voegelin in his exploration of the historical unfolding of the American political tradition.

Carey is a prolific writer. In the decades since the appearance of these works, he has published several books, including *The Federalist: Design for a Constitutional Republic* (1989),[8] *In Defense of the Constitution* (1995),[9] and *A Stu-*

dent's Guide to American Political Thought (2004).[10] He has edited or coedited more than a half-dozen others—including *Community and Tradition: Conservative Perspectives on the American Experience* (1998),[11] *Freedom and Virtue: The Libertarian/Conservative Debate* (1998),[12] *The Post-Behavioral Era: Perspectives on Political Science* (1972),[13] *The Political Writings of John Adams* (2000),[14] and *The Federalist: The Gideon Edition* (2001).[15] His many articles have appeared in such major political science journals as the *American Political Science Review, Journal of Politics,* the *Western Political Science Quarterly,* and the *Review of Politics,* as well as in more popular publications including *National Review,* the *Wall Street Journal, Modern Age,* the *Intercollegiate Review,* the *American Spectator,* and the *University Bookman.* A longtime member of the board of trustees of the Intercollegiate Studies Institute and Liberty Fund, Inc., he also served as a member of the National Council on the Humanities from 1982 to 1988.

From 1971 until 2005, Carey served as editor of the *Political Science Reviewer (PSR),* where he continues as editor emeritus. Published annually, the *PSR* consists of article-length reviews of classic and contemporary works in political science, broadly conceived. It has sought in particular to foster in-depth examination of works that the contemporary discipline of political science has largely neglected. In the late 1960s and early 1970s, the same concern for the state of the discipline of political science that had inspired Carey's work at the *PSR* motivated him to join forces with Theodore J. Lowi, a prominent political scientist and outspoken social democrat. Together they led a successful effort to force the American Political Science Association to open its meetings to presentations by scholars who did not share the commitment to the statistical approaches that dominated the profession at the time.

I

While Carey's work is far ranging, at its heart is a central, overriding concern: the origin, development, and derailment of the American political tradition. From the very outset, Carey's writings on the American political tradition have taken issue with what he has sometimes called "the official literature"—that is, with the account of that tradition which has dominated academic scholarship during the course of his career. *Basic Symbols,* for example, challenges the widely held views that the American tradition's highest commitments are to "'freedom' and 'equality,' the tradition of 'rights of the individual,' or, if you like, the *natural* rights of the individual," and that its intellectual origins are to be sought in the thought of John Locke and the French *philosophes*—or, in sum, in the secularism of "the so-called enlightenment."[16]

Basic Symbols also takes issue with interpretations (whether emanating from the left or right) asserting that the American political tradition was created *de novo* by the Declaration of Independence. On the contrary, it argues, the Declaration as well as other key documents of the founding era such as the Constitution and Bill of Rights cannot be understood properly if they are read through the prism of one or another interpretation of Western intellectual history. Rather, these documents must be read in their natural context of the organic unfolding of a distinctively American political tradition, a tradition that was already "old . . . when the Declaration was written."[17]

Basic Symbols, which Carey has explicitly stated reflects both his own and Kendall's thought, offers Carey's most extended critique of the "official literature" and his most complete account of the American political tradition as a whole. Here he employs the methodology pioneered by Eric Voegelin. Voegelin had argued that a people expresses its self-understanding (in other words, its "political *tradition*") in public documents through "symbols" or key concepts such as self-government. The people thus expresses its "own understanding of its place in the *constitution of being* and its *role* in history, of what it calls itself to be and do as it lives its life as a political society." It expresses its own understanding of its members' "relation . . . to each other, then to the political authority whose commands they obey, and then, finally, to that . . . which is above and beyond all human beings."[18] These symbols, Voegelin argues, "develop." They tend to become progressively more complex—in Voegelinian terminology, they are "differentiated"—over time. Over the course of history, moreover, a break in a people's self-understanding is always possible. Such a break means that a society has repudiated or radically reinterpreted its old symbols, thus bringing into being a new political tradition. To understand a people's political tradition, therefore, it is necessary to explore its public documents and to trace the evolution of the symbols these documents articulate.

From this starting point, *Basic Symbols* contends that the American political tradition can be understood only by a return to its beginnings. Both historically and theologically, these beginnings lie in Puritan politics and reformed Protestantism. To be properly understood, the Declaration, Constitution, and Bill of Rights must be read against the backdrop of earlier documents such as the Mayflower Compact, Fundamental Orders of Connecticut, and Massachusetts Body of Liberties. When read in this context, *Basic Symbols* argues, these documents make it clear that the central commitments of the American political tradition are not to individual rights and equality but to self-government under God: to *"self-government* through *deliberative* processes" under "a *higher law* . . . which can be used as a standard by which to judge . . . the determinations of . . . law-making authorities."[19] Thus understood, the American tradition is not individualist or egalitarian but organic and communitarian; its supreme values are not individual rights and equality but justice and the general good. The freedom it celebrates is not the freedom of the autonomous individual but the corporate freedom of the people to govern themselves through representatives of their own choosing.

Nor, it should be stressed, is this tradition in any sense utopian. Recognizing the limitations and imperfections of human nature, it harbors no illusions of "possessing final truth" but instead understands us as "searching for . . . transcendent Truth," of "groping for it across the gulf of transcendence." Refusing to set man up as God, it harbors no illusions about remaking human nature or building "the Promised Land" in this world and "spreading it over the face of the entire earth." On the contrary, rejecting "fanaticism," the American political tradition is animated by a spirit of "conciliation," "moderation," and "persuasion." It seeks to establish a political system in which we—through our elected representatives—"think *together*" about what laws will best promote the general good, a system that puts a premium on "deliberation," "consensus," and "unanimity."[20]

Over the course of American history, however, an alternative self-interpretation has emerged. This alternative has hardened into a kind of rival tradition with a new and revolutionary reading of the Declaration of Independence at its heart. Growing from seeds planted "sometime between the very early years of the Republic and the Civil War" and receiving its classic expression in the thought of Abraham Lincoln and "the so-called progressivist historians and political scientists," this account of the American political tradition is rooted in the intellectual abstractions of the Enlightenment. It insists that America's highest commitments are to freedom and equality.[21]

In sharp contrast to the original American tradition, moreover, one of the hallmarks of this tradition is its messianism. Setting "man up as God" by cutting him off "from anything and everything higher than himself," its proponents "are terribly sure that they are right and everybody else not only wrong, but wrong because of their wickedness and perversity." Believing that the ideal society can be built in this world and that it can be remade, the later tradition produces a fanaticism that rejects the consensual politics championed by the original tradition. Knowing that they are right, certain that they know the answers to the questions that have plagued societies throughout recorded history, its proponents have little use for persuasion and deliberative processes.[22]

In this view,

> our national genius expresses itself, not so much in the Constitution and *The Federalist*, but in an apostolic succession of great leaders: George Washington, Thomas Jefferson, Abraham Lincoln, Roosevelts I and II, and John Kennedy, each of whom sees more deeply than the preceding leader into the specifically American problem, which is posed by the "all men are created equal" clause of the Declaration of Independence. America will build a New Jerusalem which will be a commonwealth of free and equal men.

In sharp contrast to the first tradition, this vision appoints America as "the arbiter of all mankind, the supreme judge of the world."[23]

Although widely accepted today, this account reduces the American political tradition to the Declaration and reads the Declaration outside of its proper historical context. The result is a distortion of our political tradition that has corrupted our self-understanding as a people. Contemporary America has become "somewhat schizophrenic"[24] because it has become home to two different and incompatible "traditions"—one genuinely American and "rooted in the history and practices of the people, the other rooted in a perfectionist ideology inimical to our inherited way of life."[25]

In the decades since the publication of *Basic Symbols,* Carey has written about many different aspects of the American political tradition, including about the thought of individual founders[26] and the political theory of the Declaration of Independence.[27] Not surprisingly, however, given his insistence upon the importance of structures and his conviction that practical realities are more important than disembodied ideology, Carey's most systematic and best-known work on the American political tradition centers on a detailed exegesis of the Constitution and *The Federalist*—in whose light, he tirelessly argues, the Constitution must be understood. It is here, in the statecraft of the founders, he suggests, that we can locate the critical center of the founding itself. The importance of the founders consists not in their ruminations on human nature or the principles of right political order in the abstract but in their efforts to establish a framework for self-government and ordered liberty in the American context—within the particular and concrete matrix of practices that constitute America.

Perhaps the most important of his voluminous writings on this subject are *The Federalist: Design for a Constitutional Republic* and the collected essays of *In Defense of the Constitution*. In these volumes, as elsewhere, Carey vigorously defends both the coherence of *The Federalist* and the constitutional order it explicates as well as the centrality of *The Federalist* to a proper understanding of that order. In response to scholars like Douglas Adair, who contend that Publius suffers from "a split personality" and that Hamilton and Madison's very real differences of opinion make it impossible to extract a consistent teaching from *The Federalist*, Carey argues that the difficulties modern scholars have had in determining the authorship of various essays illustrates the coherence of *The Federalist* as a whole. The very collaboration under the common *nom de plume* of Publius, he argues, suggests that Hamilton and Madison subordinate their individual personalities and opinions (including their personal political philosophies and pet constitutional ideas) in *The Federalist*. Their main task here is to expound the plan of government devised by the Philadelphia Convention, to articulate the consensus that emerged from the deliberations of the framers.[28]

Likewise, appreciation of the coherence of *The Federalist* allows us to appreciate the coherence of the constitutional order it champions. While it is true that the Constitution reflects many compromises and exhibits profound internal tensions, it is not simply a random collection of compromises. By offering "the most comprehensive defense and explication of the Constitution" available to us, by affording us "a theoretical understanding" of the plan that issued from the Philadelphia Convention, *The Federalist* enables us to see the principles that informed those deliberations and the structures they established.[29] It enables us to discern "a hierarchy of values and sense of priorities relative to its goals and operations, which are not readily comprehended . . . from reading the Constitution with an innocent eye."[30]

The Federalist is essential to an understanding of the American constitutional order. Not only does it enable us to see the coherence of the Constitution itself, it also provides us with what Carey terms a "constitutional morality," namely, a set of rules over and above those explicitly articulated by the Constitution. These rules then govern operation of the political equipment the Constitution establishes. In other words, they urge "upon the rulers and ruled alike [certain] standards of behavior" necessary to the proper functioning of the institutions established by the Constitution. Examples of this constitutional morality, according to Carey, include the practice of judicial review (which the founders conceived in very limited terms) and the responsibility of the legislature to display restraint and forbearance toward the other branches.[31]

Carey's work on the Constitution and *The Federalist* revolves around the four themes of republicanism, separation of powers, federalism, and limited government. At the heart of his treatment of the first two topics is a concern to show that, contrary to the contentions of many modern scholars, the American constitutional order is neither rooted in nor reflective of a hostility toward popular government. It is true, Carey readily acknowledges, that this order reflects an animus against plebiscitary democracy; it is not designed to translate every impulse of public opinion immediately into law. But this does not mean that it rejects the ideal of popular government. On the contrary, the founders were explicit in stating that every branch of republican government must be chosen directly or indirectly by the people and be answerable to them.

Carey shows that the founders' intent was to develop a republican remedy to the pathologies that historically had afflicted republican government. More specifically, they were attempting to establish a republican system of government that could address two perennial but very different problems: the abuse of power by public officials, and faction. Indeed, Carey argues, one of the primary causes of contemporary scholars' pervasive misunderstanding of *The Federalist*'s teaching has been their failure to appreciate the distinction between these two problems—and thus between Publius's respective solutions to each.

Neither the separation of powers nor the checks and balances the founders established were intended to thwart majorities or even to prevent the rule of majority factions. Rather, the system was instituted to address what Carey terms the problem of "governmental tyranny."[32] "Publius," Carey writes, "did not regard" public officials "as being above the pursuit of their own institutional self-interest distinct and apart from interests shared by the general society." Absent the separation of powers and checks and balances, officials would be free to "legislate to promote their own interests over those of citizens" while exempting themselves from its provisions.[33] The purpose of the Constitution's system of separation of powers and checks and balances was not to frustrate government by the people. Rather, in Publius's famous formulation, it was to guard "society against the oppression of its rulers"[34] by insuring "that the lawmakers are subject to the laws they promulgate . . . and that the citizens are subject only to known and fixed laws applied impartially, i.e., uniformly, equally and predictably."[35] Rather than thwarting majorities, the Constitution's system of separation of powers and checks and balances was designed to safeguard the rule of law, to protect society from capricious and arbitrary government.

Likewise, *The Federalist*'s celebrated theory of the extended republic does not seek to prevent popular rule but rather to protect democratic government from faction—a disease that had to that point been mortal. "The primary ingredient" in Publius's solution to the problem of faction, Carey contends, is not a set of "formal institutions or procedures." Rather, it is a "'natural' as opposed to man-made" aspect of America's extended republic—of its very extensiveness and "the multiplicity and diversity of interests that are concomitant with" it.[36]

To begin with, the size and pluralism of the extended republic will pose serious obstacles to the formation of majority factions. At the same time, by affording a greater number of "fit characters" from which to choose their representatives and by posing obstacles to the successful use of practices like bribery, these factors will facilitate the election of representatives who possess "a wisdom and virtue that will enable . . . [them] to comprehend and pursue the 'common good of the society.'" By the same token, insofar as "it is far less likely that the representatives from large constituencies will be beholden to one or a few dominant interests," they increase the likelihood that representatives will have the independence necessary to bring their wisdom and virtue to bear on the issues of the day.[37]

Finally, in the legislature itself, the size and pluralism of the extended republic act "to distance, on any given issue that may come before the legislature, a significant proportion of the representatives from" any particular conflict before it. This distance in turn will create "a sufficient degree of detachment from the contending interests" to allow representatives "to bring reason and impartial judgment to bear in the resolution of the issue at hand."[38] It will allow them, in other words, "to serve more or less as a jury to judge the relative merits of the arguments and proposals advanced by the interested and contending parties."[39] Thus, while factious views undoubtedly will find expression in Congress, they will seldom carry the day in that to do so "they would have to convince" a body of representatives who "do not share the same attachment to their interests" and are for this reason equipped to approach the issue at hand in a more impartial manner. Beyond this, the representatives of a large, plural republic also are distinguished from their countrymen by their exceptional knowledge, intelligence, and character.[40]

Concerning what we have come to call federalism, Carey rejects the view that the Constitution and *The Federalist* seek to erect an impenetrable wall between state and federal power or even to delineate the precise boundaries between the two. To begin with, Carey maintains, Publius's treatment of the necessary and proper clause makes it clear that he held a broad interpretation of the powers of the new national government. In Publius's own formulation, "wherever a general power to do a thing is given, every power necessary for doing it is included."[41] At the same time, where, in Publius's words, "it is impossible to foresee or define the extent and variety of national exigencies, and the correspondent extent and variety of the means which may be necessary to satisfy them," it follows that "the powers of the national government are incapable of definition"—that is, incapable of precise specification. "To promote the national defense," for example, the national government may have to "reach out and take over" what had "traditionally" been regarded as state functions.[42]

This in turn suggests that the "line" between the jurisdictions of the state and federal governments is "blurry and wavy" and that "in Publius' confederate republic" even "the residual powers of the states are not sacrosanct" but are "potentially and perpetually subject to national assimilation." When all is said and done, Carey concludes, Publius regarded the proper division of powers between the state and federal governments—unlike the question of the horizontal distribution of powers between branches of the federal government—as less a constitutional than a political question. Thus, "the line between the two jurisdictions" was to be determined by their "common constituents," by "the people," based on their judgment of which government would "provide better administration."[43]

Specific constitutional limitations on the authority of the national and state governments would be enforced through what we have come to term judicial review. Important as judicial review was to the framers' design, however, their understanding of it was far different from what prevails in contemporary American constitutional theory. For one, as *Federalist* 78 insists, judicial review does not imply a superiority of the judiciary to the legislative power, much less a superiority of the judiciary to the people. Even when "popular majorities" are "the impetus behind unconstitutional measures" in striking down such measures, the Court is simply asserting that "the constituent will of the people as expressed in the Constitution is superior to the political will of the people" as expressed in the ordinary lawmaking process.[44]

Finally, Carey maintains that Publius's understanding of judicial review takes its bearings from empirical and normative assumptions that are today widely ignored or denied. Publius assumed that the provisions of the Constitution have an intelligible meaning; that the intentions of the framers can be discerned; and that judges are to be guided in constitutional interpretation by the "manifest tenor" of the Constitution rather than by its "spirit." Judicial review ought to be employed only for laws that violate the "manifest tenor" of the Constitution—only in cases of an "irreconcilable variance" between a law and the clear meaning of the Constitution. Judges, furthermore, should be bound by strict rules and precedents; and in utilizing their powers courts should exercise judgment rather than will.[45]

The latter distinction, Carey contends, is crucial to understanding Publius's conception of judicial review. "WILL," he writes,

> connotes at least a choice among alternatives or goals with the concomitant capacity to . . . move toward the attainment of the choice. JUDGMENT would seem to have a more passive connotation because implementation or attainment are not so closely associated with it. . . . JUDGMENT and WILL do involve elements of choice. The exercise of WILL may or may not involve JUDGMENT but merely preference. . . . In this sense an act of WILL can, and often does, partake of arbitrariness. . . . [In contrast,] JUDGMENT . . . is a considered opinion or decision that is the outgrowth of a ratiocinative process in which the relative factors . . . are juxtaposed, assigned priorities, and carefully weighed.[46]

The role of the courts was thus to be rather limited and passive.

None of this should lead us to believe that, for Carey, American government is exhausted by the national government or that other levels do not play a central role in the American political tradition. Nor should it lead us to believe that he absorbs all of human life into the polis. For Carey, the roots of public order are ultimately not specifically political but cultural. He invokes Tocqueville in insisting that self-government in America has traditionally been local; the national government resulted from a "process" of "organic growth and development" whereby townships and municipalities "united into ever larger political associations, thereby creating the layers of government that are with us today." Higher levels of government were created not to absorb or replace lower levels but to assume responsibility for ends whose "scope or nature" made it impossible for them to be pursued "effectively and efficiently" by lower levels.[47]

Here again, Carey stresses the pragmatic character of America's tradition of federalism, decentralized government, and local self-rule: federalism was not an *ex nihilo* creation of the Constitutional Convention but something that evolved organically out of the American political experience. Rather than establishing a final and definitive division of powers between the state and national governments, American federalism set down a broad principle whose application was to be argued over and worked out in the course of American historical practice.[48]

Self-governing states, municipalities, and towns not only represented a counterweight to the power of the national government, Carey contends; they also played a critical role in securing the social and cultural foundations on which democratic political institutions depended for their vitality. As he reminds us, Publius believed that republican government presupposes more virtue than any other form. At a minimum, Carey notes, it presupposes "that the people possess sufficient virtue to identify and elect fit characters."[49] Publius assumes that delay and deliberation will further the cause of justice rather than merely providing "the opportunity for more resourceful scheming." To this extent, Publius also assumes that "the people . . . possess a morality sensitive to the demands of the common good and the principles of justice." They possess "the capacity and inclination to act virtuously."[50]

The obvious question would then be where the required virtue is to be cultivated. Carey maintains that, as Tocqueville recognized, the answer of the American political tradition is that "the responsibility" for its cultivation rests with "state and local governments" and "intermediate associations" such as "the family, church, and [local] communities." Quasi-autonomous localities provided the soil in which the latter could grow and flourish. Our whole constitutional system thus rested ultimately "on the common values, beliefs, and morality . . . nourished and refined within the local constituent units"—in other words, within self-governing townships, counties, municipalities, states, and other corporate groups.[51] The constitutional order established by the founders endured and flourished until recent decades, Carey concludes, only because it was rooted in practices and beliefs nurtured in local communities.

II

Unfortunately for our constitutional republic, our local communities no longer can provide—or are allowed to provide—the necessary basis for our constitutional morality. Carey argues that over the course of the past century the American constitutional order has experienced a far-reaching deformation. This deformation has been so profound as to raise the question of whether we now live under a "new regime" that is fundamentally different from the one established by the founders.

A number of factors have converged to cause this transformation. For one, there has been the simultaneous "expansion of governmental powers and their centralization in the national government." Carey argues that, "with the coming of the New Deal," government "permanently and unalterably . . . assumed a positive role." Americans now look to the national government to address virtually every imaginable social problem and human need or want. Thus, the central government has assumed a wide array of functions that had traditionally been discharged by state and local governments as well as intermediary groups. At the same time, the Supreme Court has intruded into the affairs of states, localities, and communities, depriving them of their ability to order their affairs and address social problems in the way they deem best. [52]

The expansion and centralization of governmental powers have undermined Publius's solution to the problem of faction. That solution, as Carey notes, depends on the existence on any issue of a "group of decision-makers sufficiently detached from the immediate interests of a given controversy" that it could "serve more or less as a jury to judge the relative merits of the . . . proposals advanced by the interested and contending parties." The consistent availability of such groups presupposes "a low-key or relatively passive government." [53] The reason why is not mysterious. By becoming "the mechanism through which interests . . . could achieve differential and favored treatment" and thus "the object of capture and domination," a positive government acts to "arouse the people." Involving "a form of bribery in which only a few can afford to remain neutral," positive government creates a situation in which society becomes "increasingly polarized." Under these circumstances virtually every interest would be "drawn" into a "political vortex," writes Carey. "'[H]orse-trading' and coalitional politics, all with the end of securing a needed majority, would become common practice." [54] A positive government of the type that emerged in the twentieth century would thus greatly diminish the prospects of the sort of independent force Publius presupposed.

In addition, "the shrinking role played by primary associations and institutions"—both public and private—"at the local or basic levels of human interaction" has rendered the cultivation of the virtue presupposed by Publius's solution increasingly difficult. As we have seen, cultivation of the virtue necessary for orderly and decent republican government had traditionally been entrusted to local governments and such nongovernmental institutions as families and churches. "Bound together by ties of loyalty, affection, and purpose," Carey contends, such communities emerge and prosper in political orders that "allow 'space' for their functioning and development." This space "is a function of the scope of powers vested in government and the degree to which these powers are centralized or dispersed."[55]

By simultaneously absorbing the functions that had been historically discharged by local governments and communities and severely curtailing the autonomy of those levels, the expansion and centralization of governmental powers has deprived local institutions of the space they need to flourish. And by undermining local institutions, this expansion and centralization has made it impossible for those institutions effectively to inculcate the morality the constitutional system needs to operate as it should.

Carey calls our attention to yet another factor in the deformation in our constitutional tradition: the transformation in the role of the judiciary, or the rise of what is often termed judicial activism. The signs of this transformation are numerous. One of the most important has been the ascendancy of the view that the courts, in interpreting the Constitution, are "entitled to look beyond the text of the Constitution"—beyond its "manifest tenor" in Publius's phraseology—"to its spirit and to its inherent unarticulated values." Another sign has been the courts' tendency to assume a "positive" role in the policy-making process. Drawing on Hyneman's work, Carey argues that over the last century the courts have increasingly refused to limit themselves to restoring the *status quo ante* by striking down unconstitutional innovations in public policy. They now require the enactment of new and revolutionary legislation: legislation that involves a profound departure from long-standing customs and traditional social relationships.[56]

Still another sign of the judiciary's new role has been the emergence of the idea of "judicial supremacy," of the view that "one branch—that is, the judiciary—is more equal than the others." In sharp contrast to the traditional understanding wherein "each branch was entitled to interpret the Constitution according to its best lights and then act accordingly," it has come to be widely accepted "that the Constitution means what the [Supreme] Court says it means and that its decisions are constitutionally binding on the other branches."[57]

Carey points out that this transformation both contradicts and undermines fundamental principles of the American political tradition. It is incompatible, for example, with republicanism. Likewise, insofar as it involves the concentration of executive and legislative as well as judicial powers in the hands of the judiciary, it violates the fundamental constitutional principle of the separation of powers. In the founders' terms, therefore, this transformation of the judiciary establishes a tyranny.[58]

As troubling as the governmental effects of this transformation are, its effects on American political culture are no less unsettling. Because the new role assumed by the judiciary remains highly controversial, Carey contends, it leaves us without "a consensus . . . concerning fundamental constitutional questions relating to the relationships between the branches, the locus of power, the intended restraints on government and the people, or even the proper relationship between the national and state governments." At the same time, there is the question of the "legitimacy" of the judiciary's new role. Rejecting the claim that such legitimacy is established by the "tacit" acquiescence of both the other branches and the people, Carey argues that the legitimacy of this new regime presupposes at a minimum popular acceptance of its principles, goals, and operations.[59]

Yet no such acceptance has taken place. In part, this is because the proponents of this transformation, fully cognizant of the fact that "the American people still revere the Philadelphia Constitution," have sought to obscure its revolutionary character.[60] They have refused to lay out in any systematic fashion the nature of the new regime they advocate. They have refused, in other words, to justify the powers they attribute to the judiciary, to identify the limits of these powers, and to explore the place, functions, and powers of institutions other than the judiciary in the new "constitutional cosmos" they champion—let alone to examine the relationship of these other institutions to the judiciary.[61]

A third factor in the deformation of our constitutional order has been the ascendancy of an ideology Carey designates as "secular liberalism" or "secular, scientific humanism." Rooted in modern "natural rights theory," this ideology seems at first glance to be characterized by two commitments: to a plebiscitary vision of democracy reflecting an animosity toward the very different vision of republican government embodied in the Constitution and championed in *The Federalist*; and to a regime of "egalitarianism mixed with virtually unbridled [individual] liberty." In recent decades, however, it has become clear that "ends" take precedence over "means" for this ideology. Secular liberalism's commitment to equality and individual rights trumps its commitment to "majority rule." Its adherents' "commitment to majority rule" is "contingent" on whether they like "what the majority wills."[62]

Radically individualistic, secular liberalism denies both the person's nature as an intrinsically social being and his subordination to "any higher or transcendental order not of his own making." This, combined with commitment to equality of condition, produces in secular liberalism "an absolutism with respect to the state's functions." Having no place in its philosophy for other social institutions—or what are generally called "intermediate groups"—a state informed by secular liberalism will expand endlessly in order to protect an ever-expanding array of "new, more elaborate, and unheard-of" individual rights, both negative and positive.[63]

Yet secular liberalism's reduction of the goals of political life to the protection of rights, establishment of an egalitarian social order, and promotion of material gratification also give its politics a radically elitist bent. Secular liberalism delegitimizes substantive political discussion as it elevates the role of judges and administrators who are supposedly wise and politically insulated. The insistence of secular liberalism that individual rights always trump social goods greatly reduces the need for the kind of decision making that characterizes legislatures. Indeed, insofar as the political task is reduced to the protection of individual rights, it might well be argued that judges—who are unelected and insulated from popular control—are better equipped than legislatures to undertake this task.[64]

The elitist bent of secular liberalism is intensified by its insistence on the possibility of a refined form of Bentham's "felicific calculus," which holds that "human wants and needs" can "be determined on a more or less universal basis" and that "various levels of need can be established to insure optimum collective . . . satisfaction." This calculus simplifies political decision making, eliminating the need for the type of deliberation engaged in by legislatures. It is only a short step from an insistence on the possibility of such a calculus to the conclusion that "the best state . . . is one run for the people by those best able to calculate optimum material gratification"[65]—in other words, one run by professionally trained and democratically unaccountable administrators rather than by elected legislators.[66]

Secular liberalism's narrow concern for equality, individual rights, and material gratification, Carey maintains, threatens constitutionalism, self-government, and ordered liberty. It also gives short shrift to justice, domestic tranquility, and the other goods identified in the preamble to the Constitution. And it fails to take into account either the complexity and fragility of society or the extent to which secular liberalism undermines the "intermediate institutions and associations that are essential to the cohesion of the state" and the cultivation of the virtues on which orderly and decent republican government depends.[67] Its "shallow," "barren," and "baseless" vision of the human person "leads . . . straightway into the morass of moral and ethical relativism."[68]

Against this backdrop, it is not surprising that Carey has sought restoration of the older American political tradition. Such restoration, he argues, will be no simple matter: it can take place only through the reinvigoration of American morality, but such reinvigoration will be extremely difficult to achieve given the breakdown of a moral consensus. Nevertheless, he believes that the essential first step toward any such restoration is the recovery of some meaningful understanding—on the part of both academics and the populace at large—of what our original tradition was and how it came to be eclipsed through the ideologically distorted readings of our founding documents by progressivist intellectuals. It is in this light that Carey's work on the American political tradition must be understood.

III

If the American political tradition has been Carey's primary concern, it has hardly been his only concern. Other subjects that have figured prominently in his work include the meaning of democratic government, the nature and state of political science as a discipline, and the nature of conservative thought and the challenges confronting it.

At the heart of Carey's work in democratic theory is a challenge to the dominant contemporary model of democratic government—a model Carey terms "populistic" or "plebiscitary" democracy. This model has several "essential characteristics":

(a) it treats *elections* (in which *all* the citizens cast equal votes) as the be-all of democracy; (b) it conceives of elections as a means through which the voters express their "preferences" on matters of policy; and therefore (c) it understands elections as having no other function, properly speaking, than to eventuate in policy [mandates] . . . because they express the *will* of a majority of the voters.

Only to the extent that a political system conforms to these principles, the proponents of this model insist, can that system be said to be democratic.[69]

Contrary to what its proponents suggest, however, Carey contends that populistic democracy cannot be equated with democracy as such. An alternative model of democratic government exists. Differing dramatically from those of its rival, the hallmarks of what might be termed the Madisonian or *Federalist* model are the following:

(a) It treats deliberation, that is, dialogue back and forth among the members of the assembly and among the "branches" of the government, as the be-all-end-all of the democratic process, and claims for it that it will produce the "sense" (not the will) of the people as a whole. (b) It regards elections as means through which the voters express not their (preferences) on issues of policy or their will . . . but their considered judgment . . . as to which is the "best" man they can send forward to participate in the deliberative process. . . . (c) It postpones actual decisions concerning policy issues until a relatively tardy moment in the process of deliberations. (d) It places no premium upon an all-inclusive electorate. . . . And (e) while it does not prohibit capture of its governmental machinery by a bare majority of its electorate, or . . . policy decisions imposed by a bare majority of its bicameral assembly, it discourages both and . . . seeks decisions by "consensus."[70]

Whereas populistic democracy equates democracy "with direct popular rule and equality," Madisonian democracy understands it as "government by the deliberate sense of the people, acting through their elected representatives."[71] These two models offer us radically different conceptions of the nature and organizing principles of democratic government—radically different criteria for determining what constitutes an authentically democratic political system.

The Madisonian model, Carey argues, offers us not merely a different model of democracy but a better one. Its far-reaching influence notwithstanding, populistic democracy is fundamentally flawed. Its understandings of the constitutive principles of democratic government preclude a solution to the problems of faction and governmental tyranny. A democratic government built in accordance with this model would be inherently unstable because it would be unable to handle "the intensity problem."

"What makes a democracy workable," Carey explains, is its ability to combine "the majority-principle" with the "unanimity-principle"—in other words, its ability to have "decisions made by the majority, but in such fashion that these decisions elicit" the "acquiescence" of the outvoted minority.[72] By encouraging voters to consult only their own preferences and seeing in elections clear mandates that must be executed at all costs, the constitutional morality implicit in populistic democracy discourages accommodation and compromise. It tends to foster a "more or less angry determination on both sides to have one's way and, at the margin, a fanaticism that is only too willing to let the chips fall where they may." To the extent that its constitutional morality fosters polarization of the polity "into warring camps committed . . . to irreconcilable positions,"[73] populistic democracy tends to culminate in confrontation, in imposition of the majority's will and enforcement of its decisions "by bayonets."[74]

In sharp contrast, the Madisonian model seeks to address the problems of faction and governmental tyranny and is well equipped to handle the intensity problem. Through both the procedures and structures it establishes and the ethos of moderation, deliberation, and conciliation it instills, this model facilitates conversation, deliberation, and compromise between the majority and the minority. Rather than viewing itself as entitled to impose its preferences without regard for the views and wishes of the minority, the majority of this model is called upon to deliberate and negotiate with—indeed, to accommodate the concerns of—the minority. Madisonian democracy seeks to produce decisions that reflect not the will of the majority but the deliberate sense of the people as a whole. Unlike populistic democracy, it tends neither to divide the populace into "warring camps" nor to create "pockets of irredentism that produce crises."[75]

Through its single-minded focus on populistic democracy, contemporary democratic theory obscures the alternatives that are available to a self-governing society and precludes a serious conversation regarding the respective merits of the rival conceptions of democracy. Its single-minded focus on political equality and its corollary of majority rule ignores other social goods (such as stability, justice, and domestic tranquility) as well as a host of important problems (such as governmental tyranny) that confront democratic polities.

Carey's concerns about contemporary democratic theory have been paralleled by his concerns regarding the state of his own discipline, political science. He has, for example, criticized political scientists for their smug and unreflecting prejudice against religion and their tendency to read the (almost universally left-liberal) political views they happen to hold into the American political tradition.[76] He has noted political scientists' equally distorting pretensions to possess scientific knowledge concerning human behavior. At least as problematic is their propensity to choose to answer only those questions which are supposedly scientific—the effects of various characteristics on partisan voting patterns, for example—but of no lasting significance.

Contemporary political scientists mistakenly believe themselves to be engaged in an empirical investigation of political behavior that will produce accurate predictions of future conduct. Against this belief, Carey maintains that the true objective of the study of politics is increased understanding of the institutions, beliefs, and practices that constitute public life. Recognizing that we are social beings influenced by religious as well as economic and political norms, he argues that political science must understand human beings not as atoms crashing into one another in political space but as participants in ongoing, though often conflicted, traditions. In a sense, all of Carey's work can be seen as an effort to understand the interaction of man and society within the specific, concrete tradition that is Carey's own and that he knows best—namely, the American tradition. Carey has prodded political scientists to leave aside their parochial concerns with pet policy preferences and their methodologies, more suited to parlor games than to public discourse, in order to engage in reasoned investigation concerning the sources of order and discord in public life.

Carey's consistent concern has been to preserve the American political tradition and to understand it as deeply rooted in the mores of the people—that is, in the moral habits immanent in their relationships, social structures, and other elements of culture. These elements render his thought deeply, traditionally conservative. It is not surprising therefore that he has written for avowedly conservative publications from the start of his career and that his major interests have included the nature of and challenges confronting conservative thought. He has made his conservatism abundantly clear in these writings—not through any narrow, ideological bias, but rather through a consistent integration of practical methods and concerns with a moral understanding rooted in natural law. His essays on Kendall's thought[77] distinguish a conservatism rooted in the historically grounded pursuit of virtue from the various ideologies that are rooted in individualism and progressivism—which some observers attempt to "fuse" with conservatism.[78] Carey's essays also emphasize the localist, communitarian character of conservatism. They have sought to clarify what conservatism is and the vision of human flourishing it embodies.

Carey has been particularly careful to distinguish conservatism from libertarianism, an ideology that shares the conservative aversion to a large, centralizing national government. Whereas libertarians value freedom above all, conservatives pursue a rational, ordered liberty rooted in tradition and natural law. Republican government, Carey notes following Publius, is possible only for a people possessing a high degree of virtue. Yet such virtue is not possible without both the solidifying power of tradition and the transcendent standards found in religion and made fully normative in the institutions of local life.[79]

Dismayed at the violent destruction wreaked on our society and civilization by the radicalism of the 1960s, Carey holds out little hope for a full recovery of our tradition.[80] But the very fact that it could suffer such a swift decline at the hands of uneducated ideologues shows our dependence on something higher and more fundamental even than the tradition itself. Its rapid decline shows the need to adhere to standards rooted in the nature of the universe—in the transcendent goods made evident through natural law—in order to lead decent lives. In the end, he concludes, we limited, selfish, and sinful human beings can hope to do little more than conform our own conduct to higher standards of morality and virtue, and hope that our example may prod others to do the same.

IV

We cannot conclude this introduction without making a few brief observations regarding George Carey's character as a scholar. As the status of the professoriate continues to decline, scholarship increasingly has fallen prey to two prevailing dispositions: that of the ideologue and that of the gamesman. The former follows and seeks to impose an orthodoxy on his fellows, compelling the works and phenomena he examines to fit the procrustean bed of some set of ideological preconceptions. The gamesman, viewing scholarship merely as an opportunity for personal advancement, bends his analysis to suit the fashions of the moment and opinions of the currently powerful; or he presents intentionally shocking and perverse readings of the works and phenomena he studies in order to provoke controversy and attract attention.

Eschewing any such easy out from his scholarly responsibilities, Carey exemplifies the humility that is the precondition of authentic scholarship. He exercises a meticulous attention to both text and context as well as a willingness to enter into—to "get inside," as it were—the intellectual universe he is engaging. He is committed to allowing the thinkers he interprets to speak for themselves rather than insisting on seeing them through the prism of some framework of his own devising; and he is open to the insights of a wide array of scholars and intellectual traditions. In this context, Carey's observation is perhaps worth noting: "the most interesting, informative and heuristic accounts of [the?] foundations of our political tradition . . . are to be found in works outside" the schools of thought that dominate contemporary academic discourse—in "works whose approaches are far more eclectic."[81] The orthodoxy in question has varied: from the revisionist interpretation of the founding championed by progressivist historians and political scientists to the Lockean reading espoused by proponents of the official literature to the alternative reading championed by the "classical republicanism" school or the accounts put forward by various groups claiming to present the genuine thought of Leo Strauss. Regardless of the orthodoxy, Carey has resisted surrendering his judgment to any set of ideological preconceptions for the simple reason that such preconceptions distort our understanding of the American political tradition.

Unconcerned with intellectual fashions or the trappings of academic success, Carey has refused either to be a part of any "school" of thought or to attempt to forge one of his own. And he has steadfastly refused to engage in the gamesmanship that so pervades the contemporary academy. As a result, his work is less well known than it should be outside that rather narrow circle of those academics and laymen who are open to nonideological discussion of human nature, constitutional order, and the American political tradition. Within this circle, however, his impact has been profound. Over the course of his career, Carey has produced a significant body of work that stands on its own merits—and that will so stand for generations to come. Indeed, his work establishes him as one of the preeminent interpreters of the nature and history of the American experiment in ordered liberty and self-government.

Unlike too many in the contemporary academy, Carey is a dedicated teacher as well as a scholar. This dedication comes in part through written works such as the "student edition" of *The Federalist*. Edited with his friend James McClellan, the edition includes an interpretive introduction, reader's guide, constitutional cross-reference, index, and glossary.[82] *A Student's Guide to American Political Thought* provides nonspecialists with an introduction to the concepts and arguments that have shaped our political tradition.

Despite his love of teaching, the corruption and politicization of the contemporary academy have caused Carey to discourage his students from seeking academic careers. Instead, he has encouraged them to seek other careers where they might secure decent and honorable lives for themselves and their families while pursuing the life of the mind when time allows. Yet those students who have persevered in academic life have found him a kind, selfless, and conscientious mentor.

This book is intended as a testimonial to Carey's importance as both a scholar and a teacher. Through his teaching and research, George Carey has sought to educate young and old alike on the nature and importance of the American political tradition. He has stressed the need to recover that tradition, or at least honor it through patient study rather than destroying what is left of it through self-indulgent attempts at revolution or utopian efforts to remake the world in our own image. As anyone who has conversed with him regarding topics of the day will know, he approaches all subjects of public import from the same vantage point: that of a deep concern for moral conduct that is consistent with the requirements of the fundamental institutions, beliefs, and practices constituting the American tradition. He has pursued a good life through his family, his passionate love of good music, his hard, careful scholarly work, and the personal and professional conduct befitting a man of kindness, courage, and principle. Showing what it means to be both a gentleman and a scholar, he has provided a model through which we can understand something of the moorings and nature of right conduct.

The contributors to this volume are friends, colleagues, and students of George W. Carey. What unites them is less a shared profession of some set of doctrines than a common admiration for George and his work. If relatively few actually have had the privilege of studying under him, many have found in him a friend and a sure and welcome guide through the wasteland of contemporary academic life. Conservatives have a tendency to lament the corruptions of our time and the passing of better days. But they also recognize that whatever the nature of the times our duties remain the same. In terms of the scholarly life, we can think of no better example of how to approach those duties than that of George Carey.

Part I

Foundations of Political Order

Making Sense of Majoritarianism

PAUL EDWARD GOTTFRIED

The work of George Carey as a constitutional scholar stands on its undeniable merits. As a subtle interpreter of *The Federalist Papers,* as an exponent of congressional supremacy, and as a qualified critic of a particular conservative reading of the Constitution—as having been designed to frustrate the "popular will"—Carey will long be remembered as a thinker to be reckoned with. In conversation and debate, Carey has exhibited a distinctive style—lulling his opponents with his quiet, unassuming manner before overwhelming them with text proofs drawn from the Constitution and its authors.

Carey's scholarship and interpretive angle have a point of origin that is grounded historically as well as textually. This statement is true in two senses. One, like his mentor Willmoore Kendall (1909–67)—whom he came to know well when the two of them spent a semester together teaching at Georgetown in 1962—Carey makes the case that the Constitution came out of an evolving political tradition. It presupposes the "basic symbols" of a "virtuous people," going back at least to the Mayflower Compact.[1] While the Constitution itself may have been, in Carey's deliberate understatement, "a procedural commercial document," its authors assumed a necessary backdrop for their work.[2] According to Carey, they assumed not only an Enlightenment idea that useful constitutions could be crafted but, even more significantly, a preexisting community of like-minded citizens. The youthful Carey coauthored *The Basic Symbols of the American Political Tradition* with the then-ailing Kendall. Published in 1970, this work emphasized the cultural and political assumptions that underlay early American governing documents—particularly colonial and state constitutions. The argument offered is that the practice of self-government in early America was seen to depend on a general will, which was recognizable and served as a guide for public life.[3] Kendall did not shy away from this Rousseauean term but in fact eagerly embraced it, together with his own interpretation of Rousseau's social contract.[4]

George H. Nash, in *The Conservative Intellectual Movement in America Since 1945,* provides a graphic sketch of Kendall's stormy personality and career, pointing to his odyssey from socialism to right-wing majoritarianism and, finally, to his simultaneous conversion to Catholicism and the Straussian conception of the "Great Tradition." In my view, the final stages of this odyssey are far less interesting than the intermediate stage, when Kendall laid the theoretical groundwork for a populism of the Right by adapting both Locke's majoritarian—not his conventionally emphasized libertarian—teachings and Rousseau's discussion of civil religion to a critique of the "open society." What Kendall had to say on these subjects was intellectually provocative and textually defensible, whereas his adulation of Strauss, particularly in the essay "John Locke Revisited" (1966), is both mechanical and far more vehemently anti-Lockean than Strauss or his students have been in writing on the same topic.[5] Nash notes that Kendall's turn toward Leo Strauss coincided with a slowdown in his work: "Under Strauss's influence, Kendall modified his view of John Locke and in fact became so affected by the 'revolution' that his scholarly standards 'changed drastically' and the pace of his own scholarship slowed down. He felt the duty to combat what Strauss called the 'illegitimate' (that is, behaviorist, relativist, 'value free') branches of political science."[6] Without putting too fine a point on this matter, it seems that Kendall was a more distinctive and exciting thinker when he was reading texts as a right-wing majoritarian. Further, this critical side of his interpretive work was the one that influenced Carey and is most evident in their fruitful collaboration.

Neither Kendall nor Carey argues that the Constitution mandates giving vast reservoirs of power from the people to any branch of the federal government. Since both insist that presidential and judicial powers are strictly circumscribed by the founding document and were intended to take backseats to the legislative one, these scholars criticize the increased reach of what were to be subordinate branches of the federal government. But even Congress—as they understand that institution—is to exercise enumerated powers as stated in Article One; and it would have to do so within a bicameral structure. In his discussion of the separation of powers in *The Federalist: Design for a Constitutional Republic,* Carey underlines the centrality of bicameralism for Publius, the voice of the authors of *The Federalist Papers*, in blocking factional interests and keeping impetuous majorities from getting what they think they want. "Such is a republican remedy for the problem of factions," which requires the majority "to restrain themselves after delay and deliberation"[7] by their representatives. Moreover, Carey expresses nothing but scorn for "positive government" in the modern sense—that is, for a consolidation of power by a highly centralized state that reaches beyond the founders' limited goals of "order, self-government, rule by law, stability, and ordered liberty."[8]

One factor that helps to explain Carey's allergy to "filter" theories of the Constitution is his emphatic disapproval of judicial review. The beginnings of this concept, he tells us, are to be found in John Marshall's claim to protect American citizens by giving the high court broad power to judge the constitutionality of actions taken by other branches of the federal government. Notably, Carey does not deny that a close reading of *Federalist* 78 would suggest that the Supreme Court does have the power "to declare acts of the legislature unconstitutional." Nonetheless, it is also apparent that such a power is to be exercised only in very special circumstances, when legislative acts "are contrary to the 'manifest tenor' of the Constitution, and this only after determining that there is an 'irreconcilable variance' between the statute and the Constitution."[9] Such a limited power of intervention is different from judicial governance: the increasing tendency of judges, particularly since the 1950s, to impose their will on elected officials. Judges have, according to Carey, substituted their counterfeit majoritarian rule based on a passive citizenry for the one provided for by the Constitution. Judicial power-grabbers have not softened the rough edges of popular government but are supplanting elected bodies instead.

Even more relevant, the "people" who would govern themselves in Carey's interpretation of the founding would be more alike than different. Alluding to John Jay's praise in *Federalist* 2 of cultural, linguistic, and religious solidarity as the basis of the new federal union, Carey goes on to discuss Madison's prescription for an extended republic in *Federalist* 51 in this light. Madison's hope that "a multiplicity of religious sects would be able to live and govern together" assumed a high degree of uniformity among those who would coexist:

Certainly he could not have written so confidently to this effect if the country had contained substantial numbers of, say, devout Muslims and Hindus. The basis for religious liberty in the context in which he writes seems to derive from the fact that the sects are, in the main, Christian, and that the differences between them which would cause their divisions are not of sufficient magnitude or degree to constitute grounds for a restrictive or prescriptive majority coalition. Put otherwise, it is the absence of disagreement on fundamentals that allows for their peaceful coexistence, as well as for a genuine dialogue about what constitutes their general or collective welfare.[10]

Near the end of the same work, Carey drives home his message by asking rhetorically: "Does the increasing ethnic, racial, cultural, and linguistic heterogeneity of the society, taken together with the expanded role of the national government, render the original concerns of the Antifederalists to the extended republic highly relevant?" That is to say, had the localist critics of the proposed federal union been right in their judgments, given where the Federalist project has led over time? Lest I overlook this gloomy retrospective view, Professor Carey explained his authorial purpose in a copy of his volume that he gave to me "as a right thinking friend" in 1989. That purpose was to furnish "a glimpse of the original design that has run amok."

At that time I too was working on what became a critique of mass-democratic pluralism—a critique that would inspire my intellectual biography of the German legal theorist Carl Schmitt. Like Professor Carey, I drew the foundations of this critique from Kendall's attacks on John Stuart Mill, among other sources. But unlike George, what I learned from his teacher only came to me secondhand—from Kendall's explosive polemics against the "totally open society."

This brings me, as Kendall might have said in one of his jerrybuilt paragraphs loaded with qualifiers, to point two: Kendall expressed his contemptuous reservations about a society that fawns on its gravediggers in the course of battling Communist sympathizers and Communist tolerators, at Yale in the 1950s. That same institution, which I later attended, made Kendall feel unwelcome before it acceded in 1961 to his offer to have his contract bought out. At Yale, he honed his rhetoric against those who would bring American Stalinists into the political conversation.[11] Although Kendall may actually have been too indulgent of these supposed civil libertarians, ascribing to them a self-destructive tolerance rather than a hatred of Western society that had made them eager to practice selective hospitality, he did make sound points about the requirements for self-government. Like Schmitt, he justifiably mocked those who equated republican or constitutional rule with a debating society in which all views would be equally accepted. Whence his "conservative affirmation" that

> all political societies, all peoples, but especially I would like to think, our political society, this 'people of the United States,' is founded upon what political philosophers call a consensus; that is, a hard core of shared beliefs. Those beliefs that the people share are what defines its character as a political society, what, above all perhaps, expresses its understanding of itself as a political society, of its role and responsibility in history, of its very destiny.[12]

A threat to this consensus, Kendall made clear, strikes directly at the political society that it helps define. Carey would bring new light to this concern, the fragmentation of consensus, by restating it as follows: what eats away at self-government is not sharply dissenting opinions so much as the progress of pluralism itself, the disappearance of a culture bearing the "hard core of shared beliefs" that had shaped what once had been a "political society." As Christopher Lasch observes in a similar vein in *Revolt of the Elites* (1995), Americans are avoiding debate on what used to matter to them and have come to accept the "nice" views that the media and the political class insist that they hold.[13] What they are told to "celebrate" is multiculturalism, a set of administratively controlled social arrangements that is alien both to their ancestral culture and to the political traditions that culture once sustained. Instead of Kendall's target of an unrestricted debating club liberal relativists invite the totalitarian Left to join, an imposed moral confusion has taken over, rendering self-government all but impossible.

An update of Kendall's critique of pluralism can already be found in the thoughtful study "Majority Rule Revisited," which Carey published in *Modern Age* in 1971. In this examination of the conditions in which majority rule can be made relevant to contemporary American politics, Carey brings up the "raft model"—what Germans used to characterize as a *Schicksalsgemeinschaft,* a community partaking of a shared fate. "We shall seek insofar as possible to insure that those who participate equally will be affected equally by the decisions made. Only those within these confines shall, in our view, have an equal voice." But what renders this model unworkable at present is the impossibility of "localizing" disputes in a welfare state. Here, issues are always made—or are made to appear—to "transcend the involved parties" and the government presents itself as "the guardian for and promoter of various notions of 'social justice.'" Most ominously, according to Carey, the majority–rule principle has been subverted by "groups which are making demands upon government which involve collective sacrifices wherein the problem of determining the affected parties becomes extremely difficult, the more so as the demands by their nature involve the contention that the whole of society owes something to a minority portion of it."[14]

In this description of the simultaneous rise of victim claimants and the managerial state as an instrument of "social justice," one might notice at least intimations of my own later critiques of mass managerial democracy. These intimations, however, are less apparent in Kendall's criticism of majority rule—a process he thought to be degenerating because of the loss of an overarching "American orthodoxy." Kendall's preoccupation with relativism on the Left may have made him disregard other sources of revolutionary disturbance, such as the further radicalizing effects of the civil-rights movement after 1964. Astoundingly, Kendall thought that the passage of civil-rights legislation in the mid-sixties had signified a 'No' answer to the "Civil Rights leaders' demand for a revolution." The Civil Rights Act's "impact will be felt almost exclusively in the South; even there it will affect the lot of Negroes marginally at the very most; and in its handling both of Mrs. Murphy's boarding house and jury trials in contempt of court cases, it bears the marks of a built-in Conservative bias."[15] The most likely outcome of the black movement would be its recognition that it would have to "step down its demands." Whether or not these demands were just, they did not correspond to what white people were willing to concede.[16] It is hard to imagine Carey writing so blithely even at that time on what became an escalating succession of organized victim claims advanced by progressive judges and government bureaucrats—claims that would wreak havoc on the American constitutional framework. But then, Carey had also expended less energy on the struggle against communism; and as a constitutionalist, he was more aware than his teacher of the new forces being released into American jurisprudence in the sixties. His observations about the dangers of pluralism address the role of the government in creating social chaos. By the eighties, Carey was writing about the incompatibility between meaningful self-government and the passion for cultural exotica.

Another point that merits attention is that, unlike the spiritually questing but mercurial Kendall, Carey did not build strong ideological ties with the Straussians. Although he cultivated friendly contacts among this group and had them write for the *Political Science Reviewer,* his connections to them were almost entirely pragmatic. Some Straussians, particularly the late Martin Diamond and Herbert Storing, conducted research that overlapped with Carey's work on the founders. Furthermore, Diamond held the un-Straussian view that the Constitution prescribed congressional supremacy: a belief that closely paralleled the traditional American conservative one. But beyond these ties and overlaps, there is no affinity in worldviews between the editor of the *Political Science Reviewer* and the Straussians he has sometimes featured. Carey, unlike them, does not pay homage to the American present for instantiating an eternal democratic essence. And unlike the Straussians, Carey points to the gulf between the conception of popular government that prevailed among the founders and its mass democratic derailment in the twentieth century. Indicative of the distance he has kept from the group that Kendall ran to embrace is a statement in a letter of July 22, 1990, that Carey sent me concerning *The Federalist: Design for a Constitutional Republic:* "The Straussians are displeased, or so I've been told, that I ignore them."

The way to avoid the downward course toward a degenerate majoritarianism, according to Kendall-Carey, would be to accept a quintessential Rousseauean assumption: namely, that republican self-government can work only where widespread consensus exists. In a seminal discussion of organic democracy cited at length in Kendall's essay "The Two Majorities," Rousseau, in book 4, chapter 2, of *The Social Contract,* explains:

> Since several men who come together consider themselves as a single body, they have only a single will that relates to their common preservation and general well-being. When all the springs of action for the state are vigorous and simple and its maxims are clear and luminous, there are no interests, squabbles, and oppositions; the common good reveals itself everywhere in an evident way and requires only good sense to be perceived.[17]

Moreover,

> a state thus governed has need of very few laws. When one sees among the most fortunate people in the world bands of peasants tending to their

affairs under an oak and conducting themselves wisely, can one prevent oneself from despising the refinements of other nations, which render them illustrious and miserable with so much artifice and mystery?

Indeed, "only when the social bond [*noeud social*] begins to come apart, and the state grows weak, do small groups and factions come to influence the whole" and turn their particular interests into laws.[18]

This Rousseauean interpretation of self-government as dependent on cultural homogeneity and expressing itself in political accord is pivotal for Kendall-Carey's understanding of the original American design. Factionalism could not become destructive even in the presence of religious pluralism; nor would there be the need for a managerial class to teach "diversity" if citizens agreed on what Kendall called "first principles" and Rousseau "custom [*les moeurs*]." Nor was there a need, in the view of either man, to fear censorship, as long as it was wielded in defense of the "great truths" upon which a particular society rested. In the mid-sixties, Kendall and Carey collaborated to produce some of the studies included in *Contra Mundum*, in the edited anthology *Conservatism versus Liberalism*, and in *Basic Symbols*. Working together, they made efforts to uncover the consensus that was then under siege through a study of eighteenth-century American documents. Looking at these documents carefully in their cultural context, one could supposedly see no fit between them and the "war of aggression" and "Liberal Revolution" that had come to threaten the American regime.[19]

The problem with such efforts at arriving at a majoritarian consensus may be that whatever is sought is necessarily subject to change. Thus Lincoln, the "executive tyrant" Carey and Kendall attack for having distorted the original design and having pushed his country onto the road toward a permanent egalitarian revolution, eventually became the progenitor of a new consensus.[20] And might some of our current self-styled conservatives not equally have been able to appeal to a broad, receptive public about the need for "global democratic revolution" because of a new moral consensus? Most Americans apparently believe that there are "human rights," exemplified by our steadily improving government, which we should help others acquire. Perhaps the same kind of consensus is now also extended to multiculturalism, however distasteful this thought might be to Professor Carey.

Another problem with the changing majoritarian consensus impressed itself on me while reading what may be Kendall's most graceless polemic, "The

Benevolent Sage of Mecosta." The attacks unleashed against Russell Kirk here are for the most part grossly unfair—particularly the charge that because Kirk "declares all traditions equal" he "reduces the American tradition to the level of, say, the tradition that will obtain in the Soviet Union once the latter has succeeded in getting the Russian family and the Russian churches into the business of transmitting Communist doctrine."[21] Kirk is also accused of not taking seriously enough "the teaching of constitutional morality, a continuous and never-ending task" and for speaking of the "ferocious intoxication of power" as Americans soldiered on against world communism. Kirk is taunted for daring to "link the destruction of Hiroshima and the ambitions of world Communism." This is alleged to show that "he is not the theorist contemporary conservatism requires in its hour of need."[22]

These charges are unsettling. For example, in *The Conservative Mind,* Kirk never treated all traditions as being equally worthy of respect; moreover, the critical view that he occasionally expressed about American expansion overseas was not in any substantive way different from that of Bob Taft, whom Kendall had enthusiastically supported for president in 1952. Yet even more striking is the Cold War–liberal value-consensus that permeates Kendall's polemic. The notion of "consensus history" came out of the anticommunist Left in the 1950s and was associated with such explicitly nonconservative historians as Arthur Schlesinger, William Leuchtenberg, and Eric Goldman.[23] It also found a fateful home among the Straussians, who viewed Lincoln, Wilson, Franklin Delano Roosevelt, and Truman as the promoters of an American moral mission that had already been adumbrated by the Declaration of Independence. Not surprisingly, the Straussian language that pervades Kendall's invective against Kirk and his followers would be turned against those who held Kendall's opinions concerning Lincoln, Wilson, and FDR.[24] These heretics would soon be driven out of the reconstructed consensus pushed by the mutating American Right as well as the American Left. And the attempt to read the Declaration into the Constitution—something Kendall thought was a good idea—would become another aspect of Cold War–liberal hermeneutics, although Kendall would not interpret the "self-evident truths" the same way the liberal consensus interpreters would.[25]

My intent in this excursus is not to speak ill of a departed political thinker whom I admire or to defend one departed conservative against another. It is rather to underline the difficulty of building a conservative argument on the basis of "consensus" where the content of that supposedly constant frame continues to change. When television pundits announce, for example, that there are "things that the American people have agreed to place beyond discussion," we can be sure that a new consensus is being bent into shape.

Carey and Kendall might respond that consensus designates the "deliberative sense" of a body of citizens, the quality that makes it able to govern itself. It is therefore irrelevant how many times the popular will undergoes alteration. That will ceases to be majoritarian in Kendall and Carey's sense of the term as soon as the "people"—who sets out to govern itself in a particular way and in accordance with its conception of virtue—has ceased to exist. This is the point of such essays as "The Two Majorities" and "The 'Intensity' Problem and Democratic Theory," the second of which Carey and Kendall produced together. In "The 'Intensity' Problem," we are made aware of the deficiencies of "populistic democracy," which sacrifices intense deliberateness in self-government to equality.[26] Unlike the majoritarian concept Kendall and Carey defend, populists are accused of showing an "exclusive concentration on the 'sources' of decisions rather than on the quality of their 'content.'"[27]

The *ethos tes politeias,* as Aristotle styled the disposition of a regime, cannot survive this "shift from counting to weighing." Therefore, the normative character of a people—what Carl Schmitt referred to as the *Seinsgrund,* the grounding of the constitutional order—would be lost in a system that merely counts heads.[28] The point to be stressed is that the majority to which Carey and Kendall refer is a formed, homogeneous one, not a collection of self-actualizing individuals or American minority groups being given differential victim considerations.

This last point emerges with some clarity in Kendall's essays on J. S. Mill—either those he wrote by himself or the ones cowritten with the young George Carey. Although the view presenting Mill as the advocate of an open society in which all core beliefs are subject to challenge has now been effectively disputed, the critical observations remain valid as a description of normative majoritarianism. "The man or woman who wishes to exercise a right to be heard has a logically and temporally prior obligation to prepare himself for participation in the exchange and to prepare himself in the manner defined by the community," argued Kendall. Thereafter, the exchange must "go forward in an atmosphere of courtesy and mutual self-respect," and the entrant must behave so as to show his "humble recognition that the ultimate decision as to whether to change [the received judgment] lies with the community."[29] If the entrant calls a long-standing "orthodoxy" into question, "he must expect barriers to be placed in his way." Notably, Kendall and Carey do not provide such caveats to equip diligent innovators with the tools needed to overthrow communal tradition. Rather, they consider these barriers necessary in order to preserve the "deliberative sense" that is characteristic of those governing themselves. Nor do they hesitate to recommend communal hierarchy in conjunction with communal solidarity. What they associate with *their* majority rule is collective virtue and stability, which is opposed to an abstract and individual equality.

Undergirding this majoritarianism, moreover, is a view of constitutional government that is normative as well as procedural. If properly applied, the constitutional design would "operate in accordance with the refined and deliberate will of the nation."[30] Carey is especially concerned to drive this point home in his interpretation of Publius; he reaches for Platonic and Neo-Platonic images to set mass expressiveness or fleeting caprice apart from restrained thoughtfulness filtered through moral agreement. Carey expresses anxiety that the courts, intended to render "judgments," now exercise "will"—something that was originally meant to be the "prerogative of Congress." Furthermore, they do so in a way that would be inappropriate even for congressional decision making. Looming over this critical commentary is the Platonic separation of *thumoeides* from *logistikon*, of willfulness from the reflective disposition necessary for making and interpreting sound laws.[31] Greed and ambition, which may be evident in the popular demand for redistribution of earnings and the alacrity of politicians to accommodate this demand, involve another hindrance to reflective government—namely, appetite (*epithumia*). While Plato viewed appetite, together with *thumos,* as what *logos* must master, Neo-Platonists relegated appetite to a status lower than willfulness. The appetitive man was driven entirely by passion and stood farthest removed from philosophical restraint.[32]

Although Carey never puts his classical disposition on display, a Platonic line of division runs through his constitutional conceptions. What he calls "centralized authority" exists to further a "newer morality," something that deeply concerns him as an advocate of moderation. The newer morality aims to satisfy appetites and accommodate the expressive freedoms that Carey disdains and whose gratification should not be connected to political force in any case.[33] Majority rule is an exercise in reflective virtue; and collective restraint, where it does require will, must accompany application of the will.

This attempt to draw out the classical elements in Carey's interpretation of Publius might strike some as strange, given Carey's pointed reference to "Publius's inattention to the problem of virtue." According to Carey, obviously addressing his Straussian critics, the founders did not construct the federal union because of insufficient virtue among their countrymen: "The principle shortcomings of the existing confederation were attributable to the defects of its structure and processes and not to unique underlying conditions relating to the moral character of the people." Moreover, "Publius embraces a distinction between society and government, a distinction that by itself signifies that there is a separate, somewhat distinct, and limited political realm in which government is to operate."[34]

But these warnings against an overreaching central government should not be equated with an endorsement of moral relativism—or an attribution of this stand to the founders. "The Constitution and the government it establishes is a creature of the society over which it operates." In this case, it is the creature of what was intended to be a virtuous republican society. When Carey insists, "for Publius, society, not government, is the source and generator of values," he does not argue against the need for a moral consensus but only against locating its source in a disciplined constitutional regime.[35] Transfer of the task of moral instruction from the society to the state, particularly during the twentieth century, has exacted a high cost in terms of diminished constitutional liberty and traditional civic virtue.

In the late-modern West there is no plausible possibility of a return to classical models of governance. It is in fact the pseudoclassical temptation of "erotic politics"—that is, of the elevation of administrative control to the role of generator of communal solidarity—that now threatens the traditional social bonds standing in the way of government-imposed fraternity.[36] The choice we face is one Carey is acutely aware of when he reminds us: "The Constitution created a commercial republic; and there's nothing wrong with that." One cannot get back to a virtuous polis by empowering public administration to socialize individuals. The position ascribed to Publius is at least as suited to our times as it was to the late eighteenth century.

In closing, let me point out that the majoritarian reading of American constitutional history presented above will undoubtedly irritate the law faculties at distinguished universities. It may be hard to believe that the two scholars discussed taught at such institutions—and indeed, one still does. Before the recent reconstructions of Western societies, they were taken seriously as political-constitutional thinkers. Let me stir the pot further by insisting that these figures may have been correct to assume that a preexisting consensus was necessary for self-government of the kind the framers had in mind. We now have a government that is vastly different in character, albeit one those who prefer a managed mass democracy might call "inclusive." But this updated regime is not the one that George W. Carey has devoted his life and energies to explicating. He has focused on the constitutional order that was there at the beginning: the one that now survives in memory as the original design that "has run amok."

George Carey on Constitutions, Constitutionalism, and Tradition

BRUCE P. FROHNEN

The nature and purpose of the American Constitution have been topics of heated debate from before its adoption to the present day.[1] Part
of the reason is ideological. Often those seeking particular policy ends find
one reading of the Constitution more convenient than others and, valuing
utility more than truth, either choose or create the view they find most useful. Another reason for continued debate is our lack of consensus regarding what constitutionalism (and our Constitution in particular) actually is:
whether "living" or fixed, substantive or procedural, majoritarian or aimed
at protecting individual rights. Thus, Americans bandy about constitutional
terms quite freely, no doubt in large measure because we define ourselves as a
people bound and shaped in significant measure by our Constitution. But as
the word "bandy" suggests, there is little clarity in regard to the terms under
discussion.

One might have thought that such debates would have died out in the
contemporary era, infused as it is with legal-positivist assumptions. After all,
in the legal-positivist view, law is merely the will of the stronger—to which
we attach the title "sovereign." Accordingly, our theory of law seldom rises
above assertions of power and practical expediency. That is, given that the
sovereign has the power to do whatever it wills, what would be most useful for
it to do? In contemporary discourse the American Constitution is little more
than a convenient verbal device, a god term on which to rest (or to impress)
one's own ideological goals.

George Carey has spent his career opposing this new anticonstitutional consensus. He has built a substantial reputation as an expositor of our Constitution and of its role in the American political tradition. Generally focusing on explanations found in *The Federalist Papers,* Carey often concentrates on specific structural issues that are important to our understanding of the founders' design. For example, he notes the founders' aversion to the concentration of powers in any one branch of government—on the grounds that such concentration establishes a rule that, whatever its putative aims, is arbitrary and capricious, without effective checks against it, and therefore the very negation of the rule of law.[2] But Carey's greater importance arises from his recognition that questions of constitutional structure are critical to broader issues of political philosophy; his recognition that constitutional interpretation is closely linked to political theory, broadly conceived as the study of the relationship between human nature and political arrangements. Constitutional interpretation is linked, in other words, to our understanding of what makes for a good society, given the nature of the person. Carey argues that the loss of our original constitutional structure and morality has produced—as it has in turn been produced by—an intemperate ideology placing material equality and a radically expansive reading of individual rights above ordered liberty and virtue. The result has been the moral impoverishment of our nation and people.

Here I will look at Carey's work in order to throw light on the nature and purpose of our Constitution, and of constitutions more generally. I will examine the proper or natural role of a constitution in shaping good government—which, following Carey, I define as ordered liberty. This entails examination of both the benefits and the limits of constitutions in shaping the character of a free people.

CONSTITUTIONAL NATURES

The kernel of truth in legal positivism is that constitutions, as laws, are creatures of politics; they are shaped by political institutions, characters, and culture even as they shape these in return. For example, Carey argues that our Constitution has been altered fundamentally by judges who have expanded the proper meanings of constitutional terms in order to augment their own prestige and power—all in the name of egalitarian progress.[3] Correlative to this is Carey's conviction that the Constitution itself has a proper nature: a nature set down at its origins and defining its proper scope and character, and one to which we must recur if we are to recover our polity's proper character.

But what is our Constitution's nature? Is it substantive or procedural? Does it aim at producing a specific set of policies, achieving specific ideological goals such as increasing equality? Or does it rather concern itself principally with establishing governmental structures—the mechanisms of politics?

Carey argues that our Constitution once was procedural but has been transformed into one that is substantive. Following Michael Oakeshott, he differentiates between the original view of our Constitution as "nomocratic in character, largely concerned, that is, with providing rules and limits for the government through which the people express their will" and the contemporary view, which sees our Constitution from a "teleocratic perspective, as an instrument designed to fulfill the ends, commitments, or promises of the Declaration [of Independence]."[4]

Carey seems to be arguing that our Constitution has been transformed from one concerned with the mechanisms of politics to one designed for the fulfillment of certain abstract principles—equality in particular—found in the second paragraph of the Declaration of Independence. But it is important to note that Carey does not refer here to the Constitution alone. Rather, he refers to the Constitution, "consistent with the basic symbols" of the American political tradition. Moreover, these passages are from Carey's preface to *The Basic Symbols of the American Political Tradition*. This book, written with traditional conservative political theorist Willmoore Kendall, examines foundational American documents in light of their religious and cultural roots to show their actual, socially embedded meanings. It was not the Constitution per se that was transformed from nomocratic to teleocratic. The American political tradition as a variegated whole was transformed from one concerned principally with establishing the structures of republican self-government to one aimed principally at realizing certain abstract ideals.

Any constitution is concerned primarily with the structure of government. Constitutions, whether written or unwritten, involve the distribution of political powers to particular institutions; they involve the mechanisms of politics. As a document, a constitution can be written with relatively little reference to theories of human nature, the good of man and society, or closely held values. Such is the case with the original United States Constitution. A constitution also can be written with significant attention to the proper rights accruing to individuals, groups, and institutions—and even to the central values of the community. Such is the case with earlier American state constitutions, with their long prefatory, generalized bills of rights, and also with the German Basic Law. But in all cases it is in the nature of a constitution *qua* constitution to focus on spelling out the rights and duties of the sectors of government.

A central theme of Carey's work has been the "derailing" of our (fundamentally procedural) Constitution by progressive ideologues seeking to break what they saw as the "deadlock of democracy" inherent in its decentralized structure. Beginning in the early decades of the twentieth century, academics and politicians seeking greater political centralization, more immediate implementation of the majority will, and increasing political and economic equality began attacking the Constitution. These men portrayed the Constitution as an intentional betrayal of the principles of the Declaration of Independence, as an elitist document designed to thwart the natural American drive toward individual rights and equality. Only by establishing the ideal of human equality putatively set forth in the second paragraph of the Declaration, they argued, could we salvage our nation from corruption and deadlock and put it on the path of righteousness.[5]

The progressives built their argument in part on Abraham Lincoln's successful portrayal of the Constitution as properly constituting a means by which to accomplish the promise set out in the Declaration—and in particular in the phrase "all men are created equal." In this Lincolnian reading, the Constitution is a mechanism that should be judged (and if necessary, reformed) according to its performance in transforming the Declaration's ideological statements into concrete realities.[6] By enshrining in our public consciousness the faith that we are dedicated to increasing human equality; by establishing a civil religion according to which the Constitution is sacred because of its dedication (along with that of the people) to the proposition that all men are created equal, Lincoln made it possible for the progressives to replace our nomocratic political tradition with a false, teleocratic vision that bends the Constitution to suit its needs and desires.

The progressive "derailing" of the Constitution was achieved not through amending the Constitution but rather through a reinterpretation of its purpose. Thus, even those who see the Constitution in a "substantive" way at some level recognize that it is, in essence, a structural document; they merely wish to mold its structures to make them suit their particular substantive goals. The Constitution cannot provide the substance of social, public, or even specifically political life. Such substance, such purpose, must be found deeper within a polity: in its culture and traditions.

CONSTITUTIONAL PURPOSES

An obvious objection to the line of argument presented thus far is that constitutions in the past have gone far beyond the mere definition of political institutions and powers. Ancient Greek city-states in particular were known for their all-encompassing constitutions. Sparta's constitution, for example, spelled out how its people would live, right down to their places and modes of eating. Modern constitutionalism, as some would call it, presumes a separation of the governmental sphere from the rest of public and private life. As the term "modern" indicates, many would ascribe this change in understanding to the modern ideological separation of the public from the private. Yet that undeniably modern development was quite separate from the much more deeply rooted understanding of the distinction between governmental action and the spheres of action and autonomy properly belonging to social life. Society, with its stunning variety of institutions, associations, and authorities in family, church, guild, and so on, has been the focus of most people's daily lives since at least the Middle Ages; and it has been recognized as having its own reality and dignity. Particularly in Christian natural-law thinking, with its emphasis on the natural law's proper role in guiding all aspects of life, the political has long been regarded as only one sphere of moral action among many.

What, then, is a constitution, particularly a *written* constitution, for? Why does Carey bother defending it? What good does it serve? The easy answer is that all governments must have some kind of structure and that a constitution makes clear just what that structure is. This clearly is the bulk of the answer for Carey, who defines constitutionalism in America as "following the decision making paths marked out in the Philadelphia Constitution."[7]

Even the most vocal proponents of a malleable, "living" Constitution would recognize the utility of a certain modicum of stability in the structure of government. Even if one wishes to change the fundamental character of the American political regime, one wants to be able to count on the permanence of one's victories, if only to move beyond them. Thus, for example, one hears frequently from abortion-rights advocates that the Supreme Court's decision in *Roe v. Wade* is "settled law." That is, however unjustified and simply wrong a decision *Roe v. Wade* may have been in terms of interpreting any actual language of the Constitution or the history of the common law with regard to abortion, one "must" allow it to remain as prescriptive law in order to serve the "conservative," precedential nature of American law. In this view, a bad decision made a few decades ago must be allowed to stand and to spread its influence through our legal and political structures, even when it undermines a much longer, deeper tradition.

Carey presents a more meaningful view of the purposes of our Constitution. He defines the four fundamental principles of the American political system as republicanism, separation of powers, federalism, and limited government.[8] These are self-evidently structural principles. They are set forth in the Constitution's descriptions of America's central institutions and the mechanisms for their functioning.

This emphasis on structure reenforces a procedural understanding of the Constitution. And such procedures may influence or delay substantive policy-making—hence the progressive criticism of the Constitution's decentralized structure as an elitist program preventing the quick application of the majority will. But such criticism confuses the goal of structure (order) with that of ideology (a specific policy, such as greater equality or the frustration of majority will). Indeed, as Carey notes, in *The Federalist Papers* Publius expresses pride in the fact that under this Constitution the deliberate sense of the community would rule.[9] Publius assumes republican government to be the only form appropriate for the American people and thus supports majority rule. The problem for which the Constitution was designed to be the answer was: how could that majority rule be made ordered and just?[10]

In essence, then, Publius's Constitution aims at republican government consistent with ordered liberty.[11] Publius emphasizes that the government ultimately should follow the majority will—although perhaps more slowly than its progressive critics would like. Why more slowly? To prevent rash, self-interested acts that would bring government oppression. Freedom from government oppression means stability, liberty, and a steady and impartial execution of the laws with regard to both ruler and ruled.[12] It brings good government, whose benefits Publius—and Carey—identifies in large measure with the rule of law: uniformity, legal equality, and predictability.[13]

The American Constitution embodies a specific purpose or value; it has a goal toward which its structures are intended to aim. Intrinsic to its structure—indeed, intrinsic to its *having* a structure—is the value of order. It should be emphasized that the value is more than "just" order: it is ordered liberty.

Its republican structure provides for rule by the people. Republican self-government is the essence of the Constitution, an intrinsic value its structure would maintain by keeping it ordered. Popular rule would be kept from producing oppression through the separation of powers, federalism, and the very fact that it grants only limited powers to the central government. Even the sovereignty of the people has proper limits, and those limits are served by a decentralized constitutional structure. They are served by a consensus-building deliberative process that allows opinions and interests to be refined and kept in accordance with the rule of law.[14]

Order is no small thing. It is in fact necessary for all social goods. Clearly, however, it is not enough. Even when aimed at ordering liberty, the resulting self-government does not constitute the good life in and of itself. Structure alone cannot provide for a good life, a good people, or even good government.

CONSTITUTIONAL MORALITY

At its most basic level, constitutional structure is insufficient for the simple reason that it may not be respected. As Publius recognized, mere paper barriers will not of themselves keep political actors within the boundaries set in the Constitution. Political actors in particular must have appropriate motivations and characteristics if the constitutional system of ordered liberty is to survive. In part, the proper motivations can be supplied by structure and self-interest. Ambition can be made to counter ambition so that political actors defending their institutional prerogatives keep one another in line. But these are only auxiliary precautions. As Carey notes, our Constitution principally rests on virtue. Much of this virtue is moral in the broader sense: as I will discuss later, it is rooted in general human nature as concretized in a particular culture. But much of this morality is structural in nature; it is literally a constitutional morality. Carey defines this constitutional morality, set forth in *The Federalist Papers,* as a set of standards of behavior conducive to maintaining the coherence of the Constitution.[15]

Carey summarizes the elements of this constitutional morality:

> the public's tranquility ought not be disturbed and its confidence in the regime undermined by unnecessarily submitting constitutional questions to it for resolution; the people should not tolerate representa-

tives who exempt themselves from the operations of the laws they pass; the courts should exercise "judgment," not "will," which is the prerogative of the legislature. Sometimes this morality is presented more obliquely in the form of assumptions or presumptions central to key aspects of Publius's argument—e.g., that given the opportunity, the people's votes will center on "fit" characters; that sympathetic bonds between representatives and their constituents will serve to deter the representatives from betraying the public trust.[16]

In presenting a constitutional morality, Publius does not provide a vision of the good society. He offers no complete explication of human nature and the human good, let alone a blueprint for utopia. Publius could assume consensus on the part of his readers concerning the value of ordered liberty and so did not need to develop a full political philosophy in order to explicate and defend the Constitution.[17] Rather, he provides an explanation of the values and habits of conduct necessary to maintain the coherence of the constitutional system. He provides an instrumental morality—one made truly moral by its connection to a valid, authoritative document and a political structure serving a society that provides its members (individual and communal) with the opportunity to pursue good lives. The good of this constitutional morality is not in itself liberty; it is not even the rule of law, let alone the progressives' much-vaunted equality. Its good rather is the maintenance of a constitutional system that in turn serves to maintain ordered liberty.

By following the constitutional morality, political actors would keep themselves and other political actors from undermining the constitutional structure in pursuit of any particular public policy. They would not necessarily thereby produce the most beneficial public policy imaginable, because the goal is not any particular public policy. The most the Constitution could provide would be the opportunity for the people to deliberate on public policies in an atmosphere providing time for consideration and debate.

The constitutional structure would tend to produce policies that accord with the public interest. Thus, for example, Publius argued that disinterested parties could control factions within the constitutional structure. In dealing with any particular policy debate, portions of the people's representatives would have no particular interest. This portion of disinterested representatives, in most instances sufficiently large to tip the balance in any political struggle, would be in a position to look to the public good rather than to private advantage.[18] But the system was not designed to produce any particular legislation aimed at any particular ideological goal such as equality. Moreover, a breakdown in the constitutional structure would mean the loss of its benefits for policymaking. For example, should the principle of limited government be violated, the government would no longer be relatively passive. And an activist government would change the motivations of political actors, who then would institute logrolling and other legislative techniques undermining the role of disinterested legislative actors.[19]

Those wishing to enact a political ideology in America first had to violate the existing constitutional morality in order to undermine its fundamental structure. Had they chosen to abide by the constitutional morality in their efforts to achieve particular policy goals—increased material equality and significantly broader definitions of rights and their proper spheres—they would have had to appeal to political majorities for constitutional amendments allowing for more direct majority rule, and then for the particular policy positions they favored. But this would have involved much time and effort. Indeed, the British constitution was altered, taking on its current highly centralized form of parliamentary supremacy, only after seven hundred years of constitutional struggle among its royal, aristocratic, and more popular elements. The progressives did pursue a number of majoritarian amendments—the direct election of senators, for example—but had no intention of waiting seven hundred years for an altered Constitution or an altered political tradition to direct it.

CONSTITUTIONAL SELF-GOVERNMENT

Political actors could look to the Constitution itself only for a limited, constitutional morality. Important as this morality was to the maintenance of the original structure, it clearly was not intended to produce any specific policy ends. To what, then, ought political actors look in crafting public policy? The clear answer for Carey—and, I would argue, for all concerned with the role of our Constitution in public life (though some less explicitly than others)—is the American political tradition.

Carey writes of "the unique and defining principles and practices central to the tradition of our Founding Fathers: those associated with self-government by a virtuous people deliberating under God."[20] The American political tradition clearly was deeply religious in character up to and long after the drafting of the Constitution. Indeed, *Basic Symbols* is dedicated in large measure to setting forth the religious nature of this tradition, as well as the "derailing" of it by radical egalitarian and progressive ideology. Even the much-vaunted diversity of American culture, as well as the extensive republic Publius looked to in order to control factions, must be seen in light of a common religious, specifically Christian, consensus. Many sects were influential in early America, but they operated within a Christian religious, moral, and social context. Without this moral consensus—this set of horizons within which majoritarian debate could take place—ordered liberty could not be sustained.[21]

This does not mean, however, that early America was politically millenarian. There was no concerted attempt at, no widespread belief in, the establishment of heaven on earth through political means. Rather, the American political tradition, like the Constitution it produced and supported, was essentially process-oriented.

Progressives knew we had a nomocratic Constitution, but they wanted a teleocratic one. They set about changing the Constitution by reinterpreting it through the lens of their particular reading of a particular phrase in the second paragraph of the Declaration. They read into the Declaration a particular political philosophy: one emphasizing the importance of individual equality and the limits placed on government by the inalienability of individual rights. They asserted that the Constitution must be made to serve implementation of this political philosophy lest it violate the American political tradition, which they asserted was encapsulated in the Declaration. Carey points out that this progressive reading not only misinterprets the Constitution, it also misinterprets the Declaration and, with it, the entire American political tradition.

The Declaration "was almost universally viewed by the colonists as, first and foremost, a proclamation and justification of independence."[22] It had for its principle purpose and impetus the need to make a formal break with Great Britain. Such a break was necessary for very practical reasons. French assistance would wane should the war continue as a mere internal rebellion aimed at reestablishing the colonies/mother-country relationship on more favorable grounds. Military enlistments and morale, moreover, along with the capability to plan coherently for the future, were all factors that pointed toward the need for a formal break. A formal document also would be in keeping with British traditions relating to constitutional struggles. At least from the time of Magna Carta through the Glorious Revolution of 1688, constitutional conflicts in the Anglo-American world had involved formal declarations of the constitutional tradition. Opponents of royal power in particular had set forth, generally in formal declarations, the long-standing, customary rights that the king had violated; henceforth, they demanded, these rights must be more formally recognized and better respected.

The Declaration was different from previous documents in that it had to appeal to foreign allies (the French) as well as to colonists and potentially sympathetic Britons. Thus, the opening of the Declaration needed to be rhetorically powerful and to provide a general statement of relevant political principles in order to make the American cause coherent and convincing. But the Declaration was neither intended by its drafters nor interpreted by its contemporaries to encapsulate the principles of American political philosophy. It was not intended to be a "crib," to recur to Michael Oakeshott's terminology, to sum up in highly simplified and abstract form the political customs of the people or to provide a blueprint for future conduct aimed at some specific policy end. Rather, as Carey argues, the Declaration is

> part of a continuous American political tradition of deliberative self-government that emerged and flourished during the colonial period. This is to say, the Declaration does not prescribe the ends or goals which government is obliged to realize; it does not assert rights that are inviolable, rights which cannot be modified or altered by deliberative majorities for society's well-being. Rather, consonant with the principles of the prevailing contractarian theory, it asserts that when a government violates natural rights and contravenes or ignores the natural law, "the People" have "the Right . . . to institute new Government . . . as to them shall seem most likely to effect their Safety and Happiness."[23]

Not even the Declaration itself, in Carey's view, should be read as a disembodied philosophical statement of political ideology. The Declaration, like the Constitution and many other documents within the American and British constitutional traditions, is an outgrowth of centuries of thought and practice aimed at protecting deliberative self-government under God. The Declaration, like the Constitution and the American political tradition itself, is nomocratic. Like them, it did not treat particular policy goals, even those of equality or individual natural rights, as the supreme ends of self-government.

Self-government, particularly in the Anglo-American context, has significant affinities with the social-contract theory that is so often associated with the American founding. According to that theory, the people have a right to rule themselves and to institute a new government when the old one violates the terms of its establishment; and this clearly is an integral part of the tradition behind the Declaration. But one should not confuse social-contract theory with secular-democratic thinking. In the colonies, as in the early republic, the social contract approach "also reflected and integrated Christian teachings," largely by reference to natural law.[24] The majority, even as it governed itself, owed obedience to an authority higher than itself. In any fair reading of the Declaration, its purpose was "that of establishing popular self-government in which majorities rule in conformance with the natural law."[25]

What applied to majorities applied to individuals as well. Rights, even "natural" individual rights, were "bounded, regulated, or controlled by the natural law. In other words, it was understood that these rights inherently embodied or contained within them the restrictions and caveats of the natural law. Obscenity, slander, and defamation, for instance, were not part of the right of freedom of speech."[26] In a self-governing polity, rights would be limited in their exercise by majorities seeking to determine their proper limits in light of natural law and the duty to serve the public good.[27] This control by majorities over the particular definitions of rights and their proper sphere of exercise is necessitated by the logic of constitutional, republican self-government under God.

Republican self-government is inherently majoritarian. If the people cannot enact its will—either through simple legislation or, if necessary, constitutional amendment—it is not being governed in a republican manner. And if the legislature is not the most powerful branch in its constitution, the people's republican self-government is at the very least in peril. Finally, should constitutional means such as elections and the amendment process prove inadequate to bringing the government framework into line with the demands of the natural law, revolution may be called for.[28]

The true connection between the Constitution and the Declaration is rather limited. The Declaration was a necessary means for the establishment of the United States. Within its confines we find a short—even perfunctory— restatement of a broad understanding of natural law. More important is that in keeping with the American political tradition, the bulk of the document consists of a list of charges against the British king. These charges relate his violation of long-held, customary rights—many rooted explicitly in the common-law tradition, others rooted in American charters and practices. Thus, the Constitution serves or fulfills the Declaration only in the sense that both were written with the intention of establishing self-government in accordance with the natural law. Beyond this, self-government is a matter of prudence, of meeting particular circumstances through the power of reason, with the aid of tradition, and within the context of constitutional political mechanisms.

VIRTUE AND CONSTITUTIONAL LIMITS

No constitution worthy of the name can "enact" a particular ideology. No constitution can serve as a blueprint for utopia or as a tool for achieving it. But what, then, can and must a constitution do? It must allow those in power to carry out their tasks without allowing them to usurp powers that properly belong to others. In an antagonistic world of potential internal and international conflict, the central government will always play a significant role. But it is a limited role, defined by a constitution with the inherent purpose of defining and limiting the particular powers of particular political actors and institutions.

Ironically, however, while a constitution is a schematic, utilitarian document, it relies on human virtue for proper functioning—indeed, for its very existence. This virtue must go beyond the instrumental virtue that is inherent in constitutional morality. Carey points out the fallacy of any reading of *The Federalist Papers*—or of the founding generation more generally—that emphasizes the role of mere political mechanisms over good character in maintaining peace, order, and freedom. For example,

> [c]rucial positions and arguments in *The Federalist* are based on the presumption of a people sufficiently virtuous for self-government. At one point Madison even acknowledges that "Republican government" depends to a greater degree "than any other form" on those "qualities in human nature" that "justify a certain portion of esteem and confidence." He also recognizes that those backing the Constitution are assuming a "sufficient virtue among men for self-government."[29]

Regardless of how cleverly a constitution is constructed, only a virtuous people can be free over the long term. But whence comes the people's virtue? The American Constitution cannot, any more than any other constitution, provide the people with virtue, and the founders knew this. They were convinced that character formation, the shaping of individuals into virtuous citizens and members of society, is by nature the task of local associations. Evincing an instinctive understanding of the principle of subsidiarity,[30] the founders acted on the belief that as much responsibility as possible must be left at the local and social levels rather than at the overtly political one. Only thus would local associations be able to form and shape their members' moral character. According to Carey, the founders acted on the tacit assumption

> that the private sector—e.g., the family, churches, schools, communities—would cultivate and nourish the virtue necessary not only for the perpetuation of the regime, but for the pursuit of the collective good. In short, the intellectual and moral development of individuals falls primarily to society, with government assuming only that role which society assigns to it.[31]

Key to the founders' vision of the Constitution and the nature of good government was the distinction between government and society. "To put this otherwise, in Publius's view constitutions do not create a people or society, but rather they establish governments." A government can be reformed or replaced by the people should it no longer meet the needs of the society. But the society itself abides: both in time and in importance, it predates the structures of government. This, according to Carey, is why "the notion of limited government is embodied in the very notion of constitutionalism" in the founders' universe of thought and practice.[32] It is also why "society, not government, is the source and generator of values." And because the government is not the proper source of people's values, its role in moral education is properly extremely limited; where deemed necessary by the people, such education is best left to state and local governments.[33]

This is not to say that moral education was unimportant to the founders. On the contrary, while mere constitutional morality might be sufficient to perpetuate the regime, the Constitution was intended to provide goods beyond simple self-perpetuation. As Publius argued, the Constitution was to provide for a republic that would protect and promote the "permanent and aggregate interests of the community" and "justice and the general good." Indeed, "the public good, the real welfare of the people, is the supreme object to be pursued."[34] And these great goods would be provided not by the government or by the Constitution establishing it but by the same communities that both were intended by nature to protect.

But what might a constitution—or indeed, the central government—do for communities? As Carey points out, "communities fare best and enjoy free and spontaneous development under political constitutions that allow 'space' or 'room' for their functioning and development, as well as for their adjustments to the social, economic, and technological factors that affect them."[35] Furthermore, he explains,

> [c]onstitutions play a limited role in fostering and nourishing communities. This role, moreover, is largely passive. Genuine communities evolve naturally; they are complexes of voluntary associations bound together by ties of loyalty, affection, and purpose. Consequently, constitutions, no matter how well crafted, play little, if any, role in their origins and growth.[36]

No matter how conservative in nature, no matter how well crafted to fit a people's character and culture, a constitution is by nature an abstract document. It sets down general rules intended to shape the behavior of those in positions of government power. For their part, the rules are the products of rational considerations, of a reasoning process that—at its best—integrates the results of rational study with the bare facts of human experience. Because a constitution is a set of rules rather than an embodied model of behavior, it can provide only a partial vision and guide for conduct; it is no substitute for vital, character-forming communities.

By providing "space" for local associations and communities to form and develop, the Constitution does all it can to promote not only freedom and the survival of republican government but also the source of both: a decent, virtuous character in the people. Because limited, decentralized government is best for community it is also most likely to perpetuate the people's virtue and freedom. "The reasons for this seem clear enough: the more confined the scope of the central government, the greater the need and opportunity for the spontaneous growth of communities and associations at the local level—the only place, after all, where they can grow."[37] A constitution can neither replace nor create vital, character-forming communities. As Carey notes, "communities can be created, but to be vital and functional, and to operate in conformance with their goals, they must have their origins in some shared and genuine human interest or need, not the dreams or aspirations of social planners."[38] Politics is too divorced from daily life, too abstract a concept, and too blunt an instrument to form living, functioning communities. The obverse is not true, however: good politics—in a phrase, ordered liberty—requires a proper grounding in a healthy, vibrant, and ordered culture.

COMMUNITIES, CONSTITUTIONALISM, AND THE GOOD LIFE

Local cultural institutions are necessary not only for the perpetuation of liberty. Nor are they merely the progenitors of virtues that are useful for the perpetuation of the regime—for it is in these institutions, in these communities, that any decent life is formed and lived. Centralization is not merely unwise. It both makes human beings unfree and dehumanizes them.

> Centralization in violation of the subsidiary principle not only leads to the degeneration of society but also eventually weakens (if not destroys) the individual's inherent and distinctive capacities as a human being. Specifically, unnecessary centralization deprives the individual of meaningful participation at those levels most important for developing a sense of initiative, obligation, and responsibility. The feelings of achievement, the sense of reward or accomplishment, would not be his, nor would he develop friendships through cooperative enterprises. His growth as a human being with creative potential, free choice, and dignity would be stunted. This situation, in sum, would not be unlike that of children whose parents have continually protected and coddled them at every turn throughout their lives, making all decisions for them, providing for their every want, thereby depriving them of the opportunity to develop and assume the responsibility of adults.[39]

Here Carey takes a consciously Tocquevillean tack. He specifically cites Tocqueville in arguing that local communities are not only necessary bulwarks against administrative centralization and the growth of a morally enervating soft despotism but also—perhaps most importantly—the seedbeds of human virtue. It is in our daily interaction with fellow members of local associations, townships, and other forms of face-to-face community that we learn virtue. Through interaction with the people with whom we live, we learn how to win their approval, to maintain good relations. And these means of gaining approval are inherently moral, for they involve doing many small good deeds, giving of one's self, and forming habits of mutual service. We develop good habits of the heart by seeking to make life pleasant with those with whom we share significant portions of our lives. As more distant relations are less constant and important, they are less capable of influencing our conduct in significant ways. We care much more about what someone with whom we must live or work every day thinks of us than about the opinions of someone we see only on occasion. Where localism breeds concern for the feelings of others, centralization, with its impersonal bureaucratic structures, breeds both individualism and ideological thinking aimed at changing the world to suit our own fancies.

A DERAILED TRADITION?

Today, unfortunately, centralization is a fact of political and cultural life in America. The Supreme Court in particular has imposed its ideological vision of a national community on states and localities, stripping them of their proper functions, undermining their ways of life, and forging a centralized tutelary state.[40] This is doubly problematic in that, while a good constitution cannot form the good communities on which it relies, a faulty political system can undermine even a fundamentally sound culture. The result is a loss of freedom and virtue.

This is not to say that political events alone are to blame for the corruption of American society and evisceration of local communities. Carey notes that communities must respond to "social, economic, and technological" as well as political factors.[41] "[T]he reasons for our problems today are numerous and go well beyond politics as normally defined."[42] The political factors themselves are part of a wider-ranging degradation of American culture, then, although the Supreme Court's hostility toward local communities has been devastating. It has taken issues of morality, religion, and even daily self-government from the associations people traditionally have joined to address them, depositing these issues with the federal government and more specifically with the Court itself. By nature, Supreme Court decisions involving local concerns are rooted in ideology. From the beginning, the principles guiding the Court's decisions were ideological; they were not

> developed over the years through the trials and tribulations of com-
> munities, local governments, or private associations in dealing with
> concerns closest to them. On the contrary, the creed to which the
> Court subscribes in dictating to communities and local governments
> . . . bears a close affinity to the standards and morality that attach to
> the progressive vision of a national "community" marked by "enlight-
> ened" norms and principles whose inherent worth should be evident
> to all.[43]

Whereas community development is by nature organic, the Supreme Court has rejected this form of growth and continuity—along with the diversity of local customs it spawns—as insufficiently rational and too likely to allow forms of behavior it dislikes. It has thereby squelched the independent life of communities, subjecting them to the abstract, universal standards of legalistic form and egalitarian substance that have been deemed fair by progressive ideology.

> As a consequence, one of the major difficulties in our present constitutional order can be put as follows: Whereas in the past the breeding ground for virtue and morality was the family, the church, voluntary associations, and the community, the source is now to be found at the national level, principally in the institution, the Supreme Court, that is most removed from an understanding of local concerns and problems.[44]

The new constitutional disposition is anti-organic. It devalues communities and their customary means of functioning. Carey criticizes the Court's ideology for its abstraction from any organic tradition, but the Court's actions are in fact part of a tradition of sorts—truncated and culturally barren though it may be. That tradition is the same one that has derailed our Constitution, our political tradition, and our culture. And it has deep roots:

> [T]he present conflict over the character and the destiny of our nation is principally an extension of the basic divisions that separated Burke from the *philosophes* of the French Revolution. Whereas Burke could see the vital and indispensable roles of traditions for the society to become an organic "partnership in every virtue, and all perfection," the *philosophes* were antagonistic towards traditions, convinced that society could be torn apart to be built anew by the use of "reason."[45]

Over the course of more than two hundred years, even the hyperrationalism of Enlightenment ideology has hardened into habits of thought and action that properly are termed a tradition. As Carey explains, the *philosophes'* positions have been

> differentiated and refined, their major elements now constituting well-established traditions in their own right. Modern American progressivism, with its quest for equality, its view that more and bigger gov-

ernment is the cure for whatever ails us, its propensity for blaming society for the wrongs or shortcomings of individuals, and, *inter alia,* its anti-traditionalist stance in the name of freedom, progress, and tolerance, is unmistakably the outgrowth of the Enlightenment.[46]

The Enlightenment-based tradition of progressivism is inherently opposed to the tradition that informed the American founding. Not surprisingly, attempts to further the progressive tradition have included revisionist attacks on our understanding of the founding era. Although overt attempts to delegitimize the American founding as inherently unjust and best discarded have met with little success, antitraditionalists have made great advances on a front that is no less adverse to traditional institutions and their influence. They have been extremely successful in convincing people to reinterpret the American founding as a radical event that established the liberal, progressive values of equality, toleration, and freedom unconstrained by virtue.[47] They have glossed the American tradition of active participation in close, local communities out of American history, rendering that tradition all but irrelevant as a norm and model of behavior.

The question we must face, then, is whether the American political tradition has become fundamentally progressive itself; whether we are now members of a society as well as citizens of a country; whether an ideological commitment to material equality and individual rights rules our thinking about justice and the common good. If this is so, it is difficult to see how we can hope to revive the constitutional and social moralities necessary to reviving our Constitution and the ordered liberty—the self-government under God—it was designed to protect.

Locke, Our Great Founders, and American Political Life

PETER AUGUSTINE LAWLER

My purpose here is to consider the place of John Locke in American political life. I will follow the wisdom of George Carey in explaining why Locke forms the foundation of part of us, but not all of us. Our founders had a complex view of human nature, in which Locke played his part. But we—especially our intellectuals—have become more Lockean over time, coming to believe in effect that our founders lacked our theoretical greatness because their view of liberty was not as expansive or individualistic as ours. We have come to accept too uncritically the view that our nation has progressed historically by embracing principled individualism more consistently over time.

Carey writes as a conservative American, and he distinguishes his conservatism from the progressivism he finds in neoconservatism. This does not mean that he is simply a traditionalist. He is one of the most astute and meticulous defenders of *The Federalist Papers*, a set of essays that, among other things, defends the innovation that was the American Constitution.[1] He sees that the American solution is strong on institutional remedies for destructive factional strife and is in some ways, in the interest of success, a bit weak on virtue. But that weakness is mitigated by our federalism; the cultivation of virtue, according to our founding thought, was to be left to our states and churches, and the scope—including the moral reach—of our national government was originally quite limited. For Carey, a free and healthy society is constituted by a mixture of tradition and innovation that is determined through prudence; and for the most part he would trust the good judgment of the American people. For him, the political centralization of our time—especially through judicial activism—is above all a crisis in self-government. The people have been seduced into surrendering the power the Constitution had given them to govern themselves.[2]

Carey's account of the intellectual influences on our founders is shaped by an antitheoretical or at least antireductionist impulse. True enough, the founders were avid readers of John Locke; but they also owed much to Christianity, common law, and a variety of thinkers both ancient and modern. The greatness of our framers, from this view, lies in their lack of theoretical "greatness." They differed from the French in not having attempted to impose a consistent theoretical vision on their nation. As Tocqueville explained, the Americans were fortunate enough to have acquired democratic institutions without having undergone a revolutionary social upheaval; and our founders had no intention of applying Lockean or individualistic principles to every area of life. So the greatness of America—our ability to reconcile democracy or equality with liberty and to avoid the apathetic withdrawal of individualism that is the prelude to despotism—depends on our fortunate inheritance of aristocratic or relatively traditional institutions. Our political founding did not level such foundations as free, local political institutions, religion, the habit of voluntary association, and the family.[3] Part of our good fortune is that we Americans do not think of these inheritances as aristocratic: we see localism, churches, the nuclear family, private philanthropy, and so forth as not only compatible with but indispensable for the flourishing of democratic life.

BROWNSON AND MURRAY

Close, at least, to Carey's view of the founding is the great tradition of American Catholic thought that begins with Orestes Brownson's *The American Republic* (1865) and ends with John Courtney Murray's *We Hold These Truths* (1960).[4] According to Brownson, our framers were Lockeans in theory; and he criticizes their theory for its unfettered egoism and "political atheism."[5] Their theory offers no adequate account of the citizen's loyalty to his country—indeed, no adequate account of human duties or responsibility at all. And so, in theory, our framers held no argument against the Southern states' assertion of the same "right of secession" that caused the Civil War. They had in fact no argument against the individual's "right of secession" from all the ties that bind him to other human beings and to God.[6]

Brownson admits that our framers did not think the states possessed a right to secede from the union, but he adds that they gave no compelling theoretical argument against that right. They did not in fact give any compelling argument for the individual's loyalty or responsibility to anything higher than himself. According to Locke, sovereign individuals are like sovereign states—and so government is a treaty or compact among sovereign individuals. Sovereign states can withdraw from treaties without expecting to be invaded, just as sovereign individuals can withdraw their consent from the ties that bind them when these no longer serve their self-interest. The argument used by the Confederate states to withdraw from the union is based on our framers' Lockean theory. And the argument is in fact destructive not only of all government but of all social life. Brownson sees clearly what Lockean theory would do to marriage, the family, friendship, and churches, not to mention to nations and citizens.

According to Brownson, Lockean theory produces an abstract being having few of the social qualities that characterize real human beings. That theory cannot do justice to the phenomenon of human loyalty, especially to that of our gratitude to all the sources of our being. As Roger Scruton explains, the priority of multifaceted familial or communal loyalty over individual liberation is the basic conservative insight.[7] Brownson contends that American liberalism—the liberties protected by our written Constitution—depends on the prior existence of our unwritten or providential constitution, of our invincibly conservative tradition. Providence, in this view, is what we've been given. As our various debts and inheritances, it is something we can change only by doing destructive violence to our particular identity as a people.

Our framers, Brownson observes, were less theorists than they were statesmen. As statesmen, they built well upon what they were given; they consulted human nature, our history, and our particular circumstances in constructing our political institutions. So they relied less on Lockean theory than on common law, our Christian and classical inheritances in thought and political experience, and the particular democratic genius of the American people. Their practice was better than their theory because of its complex mixture of diverse elements; this mixture, according to Brownson, produced a result better than any of these elements considered alone. Brownson affirms the framers' conclusion that the American Constitution—both written and providential—was the unprecedented result of undeniable political progress. But he denies that that progress can be explained solely or even mainly in terms of the individualistic theoretical innovations of Locke.

Murray echoes Brownson by noting that our framers were "building better than they knew." It was providential that they were more indebted to the Christian natural-law tradition than they knew.[8] They thought they were liberated Lockeans but in fact they did not really grasp the nerve of Locke's thought, which returns all human relationships to questions of power. The absence of an appeal beyond the sovereign power of the state was the theory of the French Revolution; on its basis, those revolutionaries attempted to transform all human reality. Religion, for example, was to become merely civil religion, and any human claims to be free from or transcend political sovereignty in the direction of God and the good were dismissed as illusions.

The French, Murray acknowledges, were better—or at least more consistent—theorists than the Americans. They brought political modernity closer to its logical conclusion, which he holds to have turned out to be twentieth-century totalitarianism. But the Americans, because of their inadequately acknowledged debt to pre-Lockean thought, separated state and society or state and church in a way that recognized and effectually protected the freedom of the church. Murray admits that our leading framers, particularly Madison, tended to be rather anti-ecclesiastical for Lockean or individualistic reasons. But they still acknowledged that human beings are free from political duties because they are free by nature to discover their duties to their Creator. For their part, political leaders are incompetent to direct or control any religious institutions that would come into existence in response to those duties. Our framers, finally, agreed with St. Thomas Aquinas that we are inclined by nature to know the truth about God as social beings, not as isolated individuals relying only on our idiosyncratic consciences. Murray finds our framers' inheritance of this basically Christian understanding of the limits of government and the purposes of human life to be most providential. The idea of freedom of religion—in order to sustain itself over time—has to be understood as freedom for religion, for acknowledging the responsibilities of beings that exist most fundamentally not as sovereign individuals but under a transpolitical, providential, and judgmental God.

Brownson and Murray agree that our framers understood themselves primarily as Lockeans but also that their work was less guided by the individualist's thought than they believed. Brownson pays them the compliment of having been theoretically radical as thinkers but prudently conservative as statesmen. Murray sees them as sort of Thomistic Lockeans; their understanding of Locke's modern thought was more compromised by traditional debts than they knew. They built so well because they averted their eyes from the voluntaristic and nihilistic depths of modern thought. Their providential—or we might just say lucky—theoretical confusion or in-betweenness, their lack of theoretical greatness, is the cause of our nation's practical greatness.

Carey reaches more or less the same conclusion: *The Federalist Papers* are rarely praised for "metaphysical insights or theoretical coherence," and "those concerned with the 'deeper' questions concerning the origins and purposes of the state, the limits of law, the meaning of justice, and the like, find even the major works of the American tradition wanting." Theoretical types who study our founding, Carey adds, often fill its theoretical "void" with Locke, but they always do it at the expense of simplifying the complex and contradictory currents of thought that really informed our founding statesmen.[9] For example, Louis Hartz's "single-theory explanation of the American political tradition" as "a tradition that embraces as its 'civil theology' the principle tenets of Lockean liberalism—rationalism, secularism, and individualism" uses the philosopher's theory to dismiss as unreal genuine historical continuities, contradictions, and ambivalences.[10] The truth, Carey contends, is that the most "confusing" accounts of the founding era are the ones that are "also probably more faithful to reality." That means that our founders were almost completely unaffected by the French "radical enlightenment" and that they lacked the zeal for "ideological" consistency that fueled the French pursuit of a "radical reordering of society."[11]

Because our founding cannot be reduced to a single theory, Brownson and Murray conclude that our affirmation of the work of our framers today cannot be merely or even mostly traditional. We cannot appeal to their theoretical wisdom because their theory lacked coherence, and we cannot appeal uncritically to their word as that of "our Fathers" because they themselves based their authority more in reason than in tradition. They dismissed as unworthy of a free people anything beyond a secondary reliance on what *Federalist* 49 calls "the veneration which time bestows on everything." We must come to terms with the truth or falsity of Lockean theoretical claims precisely because we live in such untraditional times. The American tradition is too attenuated and too confusing for us to avoid being in some sense theoretical men and women. When we affirm the political wisdom of our founders against theoretical individualism we must have some realistic or true view of human nature in mind.

THE STRANGENESS OF OUR THEORETICAL WORLD

Brownson and Murray add that the sense in which we live in a theoretical time is strange. Nobody—or almost nobody—believes that Locke teaches the truth any more. Since Rousseau, nobody really has believed that human beings might exist freely and independently in some state of nature or that government, the family, and all social life are merely products of rational, self-interested consent. As Murray explains, the partial truth of Darwinianism is the recovery of the Aristotelian insight that we are by nature gregarious, social animals and that our extreme efforts to replace the natural world with one consciously constructed for individuals makes us more miserable than anything else.[12] Commonsensically, nobody who thinks that sociobiology is true could also think the Lockean idea of the autonomous individual is true. But our world is filled with sophisticated libertarian sociobiologists, Darwinian feminists, and so forth. We are more theoretical in orientation—or less political or statesmanlike—than our leading framers, but this does not mean that our thought is deeper or less confused.

The reason our libertarians quite incoherently claim to be sociobiologists as well is because they refuse to acknowledge, or at least to reflect on, the fact that human sex or *eros* is quite different from chimp sex. They refuse to accept the evidence that our *eros* or love is one of the basic points of human distinctiveness, because then they would have to admit that we are more than individuals. Our erotic longings—our longings for completion—point us beyond ourselves toward other humans, the truth, and God. But the individual, as individual, claims to be complete in himself (or itself). And so he (or it) connects to others in terms only of self-interest, not of instincts or longings that would cause him to forget his interests, to forget how free or autonomous he thinks he is.[13] The libertarian sociobiologist actually *exaggerates* our difference from the gregarious chimps. But the strongest argument for libertarianism is that we are not able to take the advice of the sociologists and become more content with being animals, abandoning our self-centered rebellion against nature. The reasons for the incoherence of libertarian sociobiology actually show us that neither libertarianism nor sociobiology, neither Locke nor Darwin, could possibly teach the whole truth about being human.

Brownson and Murray both observe that the history of America is marked by a gradual but real infusion of seemingly true Lockean principles or self-understandings into all areas of human life.[14] The tendency of conservatives today, including George Carey on occasion, is to blame turn-of-the-century progressive reforms for betraying our Constitution with an alien injection of German historical thought.[15] And a few conservatives, including George Carey on occasion, blame Abraham Lincoln for "derailing" the rather atheoretical sobriety of our framers by redefining our nation in terms of a permanent reform toward egalitarian perfection.[16] In these two views, our Fathers' devotion to natural rights or natural law was changed into a rather gnostic effort to transform the world according to an imaginative vision. But Murray and Brownson see this change as having been less radical: the Lockean theory that informed our framers has had the uncanny power to liberate itself from its various non-Lockean constraints. Our framers, we can see in retrospect, may have been naïve in believing that the full practical impact of Lockean theory could be contained over time just as it had been contained in their own complex—if not theoretically "great"—thought. They thought, in effect, that they had put Locke in a Locke box. But in no respect had they contained effectively the right of secession.

How could our lives be progressively informed by a view of the human being we know to be abstract or incomplete or, in the most important respects, not true? Locke's description of the human individual was less an account of what we really are by nature than a project to free us from our natural and social limitations. It was Locke's intention to make his view of the human individual true, to reconstruct human life with that liberation in mind.[17] He wanted the abstract human being to become real, to become the basis for the description of human life, even of religion, marriage, and the family. He seems to have been almost as optimistic as our pragmatist Richard Rorty in his belief that human life could be improved slowly but, eventually, quite dramatically—could be made freer, more prosperous, and less cruel—through the right kind of redescription.

Who can deny that with every passing generation Americans understand themselves more and more as individuals—and not as friends, parents, children, creatures, and citizens? Those other understandings do not disappear of course, but they are increasingly compromised by individualism or, as Harvey Mansfield and Carey McWilliams have put it, by "creeping libertarianism."[18] Justice Kennedy expressed this view clearly in his opinion justifying the striking down of Texas's antisodomy law: limitations on liberty that one generation finds tolerable the next finds tyrannical. It would have astonished even Jefferson, the most libertarian of the founders, that anyone would regard laws against sodomy as tyrannical. Our sophisticates no longer regard the march of our history as one toward equality but as one toward individual liberty. And the mainstream consensus in our political life—the one joining Clinton Democrats and Schwarzenegger Republicans—is an increasingly comprehensive libertarianism in both our economic and our social or cultural lives.

Based on Kennedy's argument for autonomy or individual liberty in his sodomy decision, the reasonable assumption is that the Court will soon declare laws prohibiting same-sex marriage unconstitutional. Our framers and political leaders for almost our entire history did not imagine for a moment that such laws were tyrannical. But perhaps we really might regard Kennedy's activism as the result of unveiling the unintended but real implications of the Lockeanism embedded in our constitutional principles. For us, judicial review has become a mechanism for deducing the consequences of a purely individualistic self-understanding, of "liberty" defined as the viewpoint of the liberated individual. "As the Constitution endures," Kennedy concludes, "persons in every generation can invoke its principles in their own search for greater freedom."[19]

The Court, as Carey observes, uses the idea of the "living constitution" to transform our fundamental law in accordance with "a regime quite different from that established by the Constitution." The Court aims, gradually for the most part, to impose on our way of life a consistency that our founders did not choose and would not have imagined to be good. According to Carey, the Court's mandate arises from an interpretation of the Declaration of Independence that is both Lockean and "teleological." That statement of American principle is seen to embody "promises" and "goals" that can be advanced effectively only through judicial review. The Court's unique task consists in "leading the American people to a greater awareness and realization of the values that gave birth to the nation."[20] The Court leads us to improve ourselves by advancing in the Lockean project of redescribing ourselves as sovereign individuals with progressive perfection. The Court aims at the theoretical greatness our Constitution and its framers themselves lacked.

LOCKE AND MARRIAGE

But the federal courts alone are not responsible for our nation's Lockean "progress." Consider what this expansive, teleological understanding of our Lockean principles has done to marriage over time. Marriage surely is not a liberal or individualistic institution. The 1787 Constitution is not concerned with it. Indeed, that Constitution does not even distinguish clearly between men and women, just as it does not treat human beings as members of races, classes, or religions. We consent to government, the implication is, as individuals or persons rather than as men or women. But marriage occurs between a man and a woman or even, if gay activists are right, between a man and a man or a woman and a woman. It emphatically does not occur between two de-sexed persons or individuals. Because human beings are more than abstract, independent individuals, marriage—with its sex, love, distinctive responsibilities, and permanence—is possible.

According to the original understanding of federalism, the states were empowered to deal with us to the extent that we are more than individuals: that is, to the extent that we are men, women, and even creatures. And so the institution of marriage was reserved to them. Federalism, as Carey argues, was one obvious and fundamental limit the framers applied to the Lockean dimension of the work. The government described in the Constitution was originally limited largely to "those . . . functions that the states could not exercise individually or effectively."[21] One reason, for example, that "the Framers were largely silent on the issue of virtue" is that they "believed that the states, churches, local associations, and other groups would serve to nourish the virtue necessary for an orderly and decent republican regime."[22] The limits of the national government correspond roughly to the limits of the framers' acceptance of the Lockean description of the human individual. They did not doubt for a moment that we are more than that, as beings fitted by God and nature to practice virtue and be happy as a result. They did not, contrary to the Antifederalist charge, want the states and virtue itself gradually to be redescribed out of existence.

But who can deny that our understanding of marriage has become more liberal or individualistic over time? Women have become ever more consistently free and equal persons under the law and ever less merely dependent spouses. The result has been liberating for individual women, but the divorce rate has soared. Divorce laws have become progressively more permissive and we no longer associate divorce with shame or even major disappointment. Few believe any longer that all premarital or extramarital sexual activity is immoral; nor do they believe that the primary purpose of sex is procreation. Contraceptive sex and abortion are now constitutional rights for both married and unmarried persons, as is homosexual sex. People no longer expect heterosexual couples to have children, nor even that women will seek to have children only when they are married. There may be more child-obsessed marriages than ever before, but there are also more that are child-free by choice. There are virtually no legal duties and very few social expectations for married people—at least those without children—anymore. And we have, in truth, more or less separated parental duties from spousal duties.

Only because liberal individualism has almost eroded marriage out of existence can same-sex marriage seem plausible. Gay-marriage proponent Jonathan Rauch claims that liberal progress has allowed him "to pare marriage to its essential core." That core, it turns out, has nothing to do with sex or children, with the reasons we have had for treating married people as either men or women. Marriage is in essence "two people's lifelong commitment, recognized by law and society, to care for each other."[23] Marriage ensures that in our lonely, liberal society each of us has a reliable, lifelong caregiver. It is true enough that caregiving is in short supply today because we liberals tend to disparage all human activity that is not productive. It is also true enough that we are going to need it more than ever as more and more of us—spared from early death by heart disease and cancer—fade away over a decade or so with Alzheimer's. Surely there are few scarier prospects than to be alone for years as an Alzheimer's victim, and nobody denies that homosexuals need and deserve caregiving as much as heterosexuals.

But a contract between two individuals for lifelong caregiving could be between any two individuals. Two sisters could get married, or a young man could marry his mother. A gay man could even marry a woman! It turns out that when we detach marriage from procreation, we end up detaching it from sex altogether, and the violence we thereby do to the institution makes it unrecognizable. (Leave it to gays to show us that we have taken the sex out of marriage!) No married man or woman with children could say that sex is not part of the essence of his or her marriage. The shared long-term responsibilities the man and woman share as parents are so clearly its result. Parents as parents are not just individuals! And neither are reliable caregivers.

So maybe a bigger problem is that Rauch does not show that a virtually toothless marriage license would do much—if anything at all—to secure life-long care for all who need it. He stirringly proclaims his belief that same-sex marriage "will close the book on the [gay] culture of libertinism and liberation and replace it with a social compact forged of responsibility."[24] But the truth is that marriage does not have anywhere near that ennobling an effect on most childless heterosexual couples today. Their experience alone suggests that divorce among same-sex couples will be rampant. David Brooks, in his most famous column, says that we should insist on same-sex marriage in order to rescue homosexuals from "the culture of contingency" by gaining them admission to "the culture of fidelity."[25] But liberal individualism—in a process that ends with making same-sex marriage plausible—has already pushed heterosexual marriage into the culture of contingency. I say all this not to disparage caregiving, including the care of one homosexual for another, but to emphasize how little our law and custom now support it.[26]

Marriage supports the reliable care of one spouse for the other, and for the children they share less than ever. We now live in a world where each individual is more on his or her own than ever before; the powerful downside of my liberation is that nobody has to like or care for me. As the libertarian Virginia Postrel explains in her perky way, the pressure to be "smart and pretty," to deserve to be cared about and liked, is on each of us constantly.[27] Due to the diffusion of Lockean principles into all areas of life, we live in more of a meritocracy than ever—and there is a lot to be said for the resulting freedom, prosperity, and justice. But it is more than a little disquieting to think that one result is that even marriage and the receipt of care have become more purely meritocratic. A bad performance evaluation and the contract is terminated; it was bound only by the self-interested consent of all parties involved in the first place.

THE TRUE MEANING OF LOCKEAN PROGRESS

Our Lockean progress takes us toward meritocracy far more than toward big government. Tocqueville's fear was that we individuals would become so apathetic and withdrawn that we would surrender concern about our futures to a schoolmarmish soft despotism. Government would take control of the details of our lives because we would no longer care enough to govern ourselves.[28] Individualism, in Tocqueville's view, puts us on the road to serfdom; and the tendency of liberal democracy is to slouch toward socialism. But this view, I think, is wrong: sophisticated, middle-class Americans are more obsessed with the future, more full of "anticipation-induced anxiety," than ever.[29]

The individual works harder for him or herself than ever and relies less and less not only on others but even on government. Our various social safety nets, and not only the one supplied by government, are collapsing. The more we think of ourselves as individuals—and so vote against producing our natural replacements and for staying around as long as we can—the more big government becomes demographically untenable. Americans, as Brooks explains in *On Paradise Drive* (2004), are both great and miserable in their unprecedented future-obsession, which produces all sorts of transcendent or distinctively human behavior.[30] Each of us believes more than ever that the whole world came into being when I did and will disappear when I do. More than ever, we live accordingly. Brooks is right to add that we are too optimistic—too enthralled, as Tocqueville says, by the future's apparent lack of definition[31]—to become existential and melancholic about the provisional and contingent character of existence. The American individual's focus on his own mortality is blurred enough not to discourage his efforts. We Americans, as our social critics say, are particularly anxious *and* particularly hopeful pragmatists; and we use that mixture of energy and hope to dominate the world. Further, we American individuals are evidence that history or humanity are not about to end; we are evidence that, if Locke is right, then Hegel, Marx, and so forth are wrong.

To say that America has become a progressively more Lockean society is not to agree with Murray's suggestion that we have eradicated the distinctions between our own revolution and the French revolution over time. Locke was not a French Enlightenment atheist who warred openly against religion. He did not share the French revolutionary opinion that the progress of human freedom would produce human happiness in this world and so make religious longing obsolete. Locke thought we free beings would remain religious because we would remain unhappy. Thus, for Locke and our framers—unlike for the French and their revolutionary successors—freedom of religion is freedom for religion.

Our Lockean experience should keep us from taking too seriously Tocqueville's fear that our democracy will culminate in soft subhuman despotism, just as it should alleviate the concern of those Nietzschean conservatives who believe that the "last man" or the Brave New World is just around the corner.[32] Locke allows us to see that America will always be the land of human alienation and religious revivals. Those who speak of inalienable rights mean to say, among other things, that we human beings will never free ourselves from our alienation through our own efforts. In some ways, the more we liberate ourselves from what we have been given by nature, the more alienated or strangely homeless in this world we will be. We do not have it within our power to create a world in which we will be fully at home.

Locke is an advocate of human beings using their freedom to transform nature in the pursuit of happiness. We have liberty, as our Declaration says, in order to pursue happiness. But the pursuit of happiness is not to be confused with happiness itself. Locke privileges freedom over happiness because he does not seem to think that happiness itself can or should be a goal of free beings. "Locke," Michael Zuckert observes, "emphasized the pursuit of happiness rather than its achievement, for it is a goal that can never be achieved in this life. All happiness is temporary, every satisfaction soon followed by a new unease by which 'we are set afresh to work in the pursuit of happiness.'"[33] Our condition as free beings is to be restless or uneasy, not happy. If we became happy in any way other than quite temporarily, we would become like the other animals or like God. This is the paradox that constitutes our freedom: "Even though human beings are doomed to frustration in their pursuit of ever-elusive happiness, they are nonetheless unalterably committed to it."[34] To be free is restlessly to pursue what always eludes us and to be aware of the futility of our efforts. This awareness points us, sometimes, in the direction of otherworldly religion—toward mirages that sometimes spare us both the greatness and the misery of being an individual.

Locke distinguishes clearly between the illusory transcendence of the otherworldly religious imagination and the real human transcendence we achieve through our work in pursuing happiness in this world. As Zuckert explains, it is "[t]he idea of happiness" that "supplies humanity with freedom, or the nearest thing to free will that is attainable." Our ability to work in response to that idea "removes human beings from the stimulus and response to which other animals are bound" and is responsible for "the human transcendence of mere survival as an end."[35] The evidence of our transcendence is our ability freely to choose and to change the world in pursuit of happiness—even against mere survival. We are not like the other animals because we are not satisfied with simply being alive.

Our singular pursuit of happiness, therefore, makes sociobiology untrue. It makes the Christian insight—in secular form—of the special freedom of the human being true. For Locke, the only thing God ever really gave us is our freedom: our singular ability to transform all the other worthless stuff he gave us in view of our diverse and incommensurable ideas of happiness.[36] A Lockean can certainly believe that God mysteriously made human beings— and human beings only—free, transcendent individuals. Locke does not quite write as an atheist and certainly not as a materialist. But his idea of transcendence is incompatible with the biblical idea of a living, giving, redeeming God, just as it is really incompatible with the indispensable Christian idea of free will: an idea depending, among other things, on the possibility that we can really know what happiness is. For Locke, it is reasonable to believe in a Creator but not to experience ourselves as creatures—as gratefully dependent on a Creator for the goodness of our being.

AMERICA'S DIVIDED SOUL

There is no denying the strong discontinuity between the personal experience of oneself as a creature and the experience of oneself as a modern or Lockean individual. But there is also no denying that Americans are a singular people because we have been and still are strongly moved by both experiences. Tocqueville noticed that our genius consists in our ability to understand ourselves differently on different days of the week. Most days Americans are largely self-reliant individuals in restless pursuit of happiness. But on Sunday they engage in a "sort of solemn meditation." That is because "the soul finally comes back into possession of itself and contemplates itself." At times, especially on Sunday, "the American is torn away from the small passions that agitate his life and the passing interests that fill it, he at once enters into an ideal world in which all is great, pure, eternal."[37] On Sunday, Americans are at rest because they believe that God provides and so all is well with them as beings that are essentially souls. They believe, contrary to Locke, that their transcendence is not really in their own hands—even as during the week they provide plenty of evidence of their transcendence as middle-class beings, as free beings that work. We see this sort of complex or divided thinking, for example, in the very philosophic *Little House on the Prairie* books. Pa usually torments the women in his life with his restless desire to be on the move; but on Sunday the little girls don't even get to play.

The greatness and misery of the divided soul of the American Lockean Protestant might be one reason that American Protestant Christianity has

characteristically not been very leisurely or playful. It may be why our Protestants have believed that the Bible is against drinking not only on Sunday
but on every other day too. They have believed that moderation is impossible
for sinful mortals. That belief may be the result of mixing two unrealistically
extreme views—Lockean individualism and Augustinian Calvinism—of human nature or the human condition.[38]

But it is also true that that mixture has done us much good. As a result of
our Lockean pursuits, we have achieved unprecedented health, wealth, and
freedom. It would be a Lockean exaggeration to believe that our success has
not made us happier in some ways. Locke may be as responsible as anyone for
the fact that American government and American technology are the envy
of the world. People still flock to the nation where free beings can and must
work not merely for survival but in pursuit of happiness, and where people
always seem to be becoming more and less Christian.[39] And our ability to
understand ourselves in different ways at different times has been our way of
dealing with the problem of pursuing happiness but never actually enjoying it.
Insofar as we pursue happiness, we understand ourselves as individuals defined
by calculation, consent, and anxious unease about the future. But we have
then been able to use the good things we have acquired as individuals to enjoy
happiness as citizens, family members, friends, lovers, and creatures. When
we are successful we think that Locke teaches us the truth about ourselves,
but when we are happy we understand ourselves in some other way. There is a
lot to be said for this plan—although not from the perspective of harmonious
self-understanding. However, it seems to be working less and less well.

For example, few people seem to take the distinctiveness of Sunday seriously anymore. Our creeping libertarianism—the fact that the Lockean self-
understanding is informing our lives more and more—means that we are less
able to be happy, to engage in soulful self-contemplation, or to be in love in
the present. Our sophisticates demand that Sunday be treated like every other
day of the week; they even believe that the Constitution demands the end
of all such faith-based privileging. Yet what we think of as our enlightened
secularism or secular humanism is really promiscuous Lockeanism. The big-
gest intellectual error of our time is too readily to identify a genuinely rational
view of human nature with the view of the Lockean individual.

Meanwhile, as Locke and Tocqueville predicted, the unhappy excesses of
our secular individualism have generated an impressive Christian response.
Religious Americans, especially but not only our evangelicals, are becoming

increasingly "whole life" or more assertively countercultural Christians. They do not look for God's guidance only on Sunday but every day and about all things. The family's whole life centers on the church, which is the foundation of both human responsibility and human happiness. These evangelicals wholly support our political guarantee of religious liberty. But as much as our libertarians, they use their freedom to work to heal the divided soul Tocqueville describes. As Christians they do not feel alienated in America because they believe most deeply that ours is a Christian nation. Our evangelicals' most important error is the same as that of our libertarians: both identify enlightened secularism with promiscuous Lockeanism. Thus, both contribute to the quite misleading impression that our culture war plays out between secular humanists and fundamentalists and that it is a war to the death, because no principled compromise is possible.

Neoconservatives often say that the true American conservatives are Lockeans. They defend the regime according to nature against relativists and historicists on the Left and traditionalists on the Right. James W. Ceaser and Daniel DiSalvo have even concluded that the Republicans should no longer call themselves neoconservatives but rather members of the "neo–natural right" party.[40] In my view, the truly conservative response to this one-sided thinking is not merely to affirm Christian or traditional America but to wonder who in America really lives according to nature.

A nation lives contrary to nature, surely, if it is unable to perpetuate itself by bringing a sufficient number of new citizens into the world. The European nations are endangered by their strangely unnatural dearth of births. We Americans are still replacing ourselves in sufficient numbers. But as Phillip Longman explains, our fertility rate is dropping or remaining low among all our ethnic groups. Immigrant groups, it seems, cannot be relied upon to have lots of kids for more than a generation or two. "Fertility rates," Longman goes on, "correlate strongly with religious conviction. In the United States, fully 47 percent of people who attend church weekly say that their ideal family size is three or more children. By contrast, only 27 percent of those who seldom attend church want that many kids." If Americans were not more religious than the Europeans, our demographic facts would also be dangerously contrary to nature. "High fertility rates," Longman continues, "correlate strongly with support for George W. Bush." Looking back to 2000: "if the Gore states had seceded from the Bush states and formed a new nation, it would have the same fertility rate, and the same rapidly aging population, as France."[41] Our religious conservatives are the reason we are not fading away like France. That fact is as important for our national security as any. Surely there is some deep connection between our nation's singular acceptance of its global military responsibilities, our singular acceptance of familial responsibilities, and our singularly strong religious beliefs. Conservatives defend America as a place where the human being in all his or her complex natural distinctiveness can flourish, where we can be free, rational, familial, social, political, and religious beings. Liberals, conservatives believe, too readily view our freedom as freedom from the responsibilities that correspond to our natural purposes. From that standpoint, conservatives defend human nature against the unrealistic, unnatural, and ultimately self-destructive abstractness of the Lockean individual.

We need an understanding of liberty that incorporates what is true and rejects what is false in both libertarianism and evangelical Protestant Christianity. That comprehensive understanding cannot come from Locke: he cannot serve as the referee, because his principles are too closely associated with one of the teams. It cannot even come from the thought of our founders: they had the wisdom of statesmen, but it was based to some extent on theoretical confusion. An appeal to our tradition by itself cannot cure the excesses of our all-too-theoretical time. Murray and Brownson suggest that our founders built better than they knew because they were more influenced by the Thomistic or natural-law tradition than they knew. But that possibility has to be defended theoretically. Our healing American task may be show that Thomism is the true realism, that it reconciles reason and revelation through a realistic account of the whole human being.[42]

Part II

The American Republic: Origins and Intent

George Carey and the Roots
of America's Basic Liberties

DONALD S. LUTZ

This physics major first encountered George Carey in January 1963, as a student in Professor Carey's course on American political theory at Georgetown University. The course was fateful in at least two respects. First, I would leave the course as a political-science major with a focus in political theory. Second, as a student and later a professor of political theory, my research and publication agenda would be an extension of what George Carey taught me in this course and in his publications. It is not too strong to say that George Carey set me to my life's work. That life's work can be summarized as follows: to recover American constitutionalism from its enemies and to represent that constitutional tradition as accurately, as completely, and as clearly as possible in order to help rescue it from the misrepresentations of ideologues, whether Left or Right. As George Carey would have it, the fulcrum of that constitutional order is the attempt to marry republican government (defined as popular control) with constitutional restraint—yet without abandoning popular consent.[1] Now, 104 publications and seventy-three semesters of teaching later, I can look back and see how it all came about.

Professor Carey asked us to write a paper on the topic, "Is the U.S. Constitution the result of a compact among thirteen states or an organic act among the American people?" Blithely unaware of either the full implications of the question or the difficulties attendant on my methodology, I set out to answer it through a close textual analysis of the U.S. Constitution. The evidence I found on that reading was almost evenly balanced in supporting both proposed possibilities. Professor Carey observed wryly in his comments that my Solomon-like conclusion of "both" failed to answer the question. Undeterred, I began to read everything I could find that was possibly related—no matter how remotely relevant—to the topic, beginning, implausibly enough, with Aristotle's *Politics*. It took two years of work for me to realize that a sensible answer to the question could have averted a civil war and calmed most of the political conflicts in our history. As I wrote some forty years later,

> American history has at its center a federal design, an indestructible Union, composed of indestructible States, a federal design that serves as the tightly coiled mainspring of American history that drives institutional development and political processes, generates the major political controversies, tests its best leaders, defies definition, and leaves the dagger of possible state secession lurking at the center of American constitutionalism, all of which make the U.S. political system unique.[2]

"Unique," and, I might have added, endlessly fascinating for former physics majors. About a decade after graduating with a degree in government, I learned where to begin to look for the answer from *The Basic Symbols of the American Political Tradition*, a book Professor Carey cowrote with his friend Willmoore Kendall. One should begin with American colonial documents, using categories of analysis developed by Eric Voegelin. But before I could read these documents I had to collect them and learn how to be a historian. These documents, in turn, led me to study the state constitutions adopted between 1776 and 1787. An analysis of these state constitutions became my first book, and the collected colonial documents eventually became my tenth book in 1998. Other publications on colonial documents, state constitutions, and American constitutionalism intervened.

No one has more reason than I to honor George Carey as a teacher and scholar. Many of us owe him a debt for his abilities not only to state precise, thought-provoking questions but also to point unerringly in the right direction for useful answers to these questions.[3] He also helped provide a high-quality, disciplined outlet for our answers in the *Political Science Reviewer* and badgered us to move beyond the commonly accepted views, especially as presented by historians. As for the question asking whether the U.S. Constitution is a compact or an organic act: after all these years I have to say that, precisely because the American constitutional system is so profoundly federal, the answer is still *both*.

Less ambiguous is the rootedness of basic American rights. As I sought these roots long ago, I could hear Carey's voice in my head. It was aided by his continuing publications, which I was always careful to read. It is impossible even to begin to list what he has taught me, although it is striking that his scholarly writing is so consistent with his classroom messages, where the voice is even clearer and more persuasive. Professor Carey taught me how to do close textual analysis, how to handle texts carefully and respectfully. He taught me the fruitless dangers of ideology, including disciplinary ideologies that seek hegemony for a particular methodology or perspective. For George Carey, the things that matter in American politics are contingent and emergent—much as Michael Oakeshott would have it. Rights especially must be so viewed. As important as they are, they must not be reified and turned into a rights ideology, as Europeans so often try to do. Instead we must seek their origin, development, and usage in the cumulative experiences of a people.

And that is where I found rights, as George Carey and Eric Voegelin said I would: in embryonic form as the American people organized for action in history as a people. From 1620 to 1760, rights were not used as a defense against government but as statements of shared commitments and values around which colonists could organize themselves as a people for action in history. During the 1760s and 1770s this people would learn about the utility of rights as a protection against a possibly tyrannical government; but even as it retained its original use of rights in declarations of rights prefacing the first state constitutions, a lengthy, complicated debate would be required to move the people to use rights as a theory for combating encroachments from London.

Regardless, let us ask where the rights of Americans are rooted. First, because of federalism, Americans have all been granted dual citizenship. Every American is simultaneously a citizen of the United States and a citizen of the state wherein he or she resides. As citizens of the United States, our rights can be found in four related texts. First, the text of the U.S. Constitution contains approximately eighteen rights, such as the right to *habeas corpus,* prohibitions against bills of attainder, *ex post facto* laws, and the tainting of blood. Second and most famously, the Bill of Rights lists twenty-six discrete rights in the first ten amendments. Third, in the U.S. legal code, beginning with the Judiciary Act of 1789, Congress periodically reorganizes and approves a considerable number of rights that define the judicial process in federal courts, such as rights pertaining to plea bargaining, incarceration, and parole. Fourth, a considerable body of case law based on decisions by federal courts interprets the precise meaning of the first three lists of rights. These, then, are the repositories of our rights as American citizens.

Then, as citizens of a particular state, we have four equivalent repositories of rights: a state constitution, a state bill of rights, a state code of law, and the case law of the state courts. These eight repositories have not just popped into being but are each rooted in a history. To provide an example, we will examine the text of the U.S. Bill of Rights, which contains twenty-six separate rights, such as the right to assemble and the rights to free speech and freedom of the press. The voluminous and continually expanding literature on the Bill of Rights generally posits one of four hypotheses for the origin of the Bill of Rights.[4] These hypotheses are outlined briefly here:

> Hypothesis A: The Bill of Rights was the original product of one or a few minds and was created without precedent in 1789.

> Hypothesis B: The Bill of Rights was an extension of English common law and thus essentially a descendent of such English codifications as Magna Carta (1215) and the English Bill of Rights (1689).

> Hypothesis C: The Bill of Rights was written by James Madison to contain the common proposals for amendments suggested by the state conventions that met to ratify the proposed U.S. Constitution in order to satisfy or placate the Antifederalists.

> Hypothesis D: The U.S. Bill of Rights summarized the American view of fundamental rights that had been developed during the colonial era and codified in the declarations of rights attached to the first state constitutions.

We shall explore each of these hypotheses in turn. The first two can be considered together, since the moment we find any connection with English common law, we can reject Hypothesis A. The highly respected scholar Bernard Schwartz traced only two of the twenty-six rights in the U.S. Bill of Rights back to the English Magna Carta, one to the English Petition of Right (1628), and two to the 1689 English Bill of Rights. This would make a total of five out of twenty-six. I trace four of the twenty-six rather than Schwartz's two to Magna Carta, for a total of seven rights in the U.S. Bill of Rights that can be traced to a major English common-law document.[5] Looking at it from the other direction, only four of the sixty-three provisions of Magna Carta made it into the U.S. Bill of Rights. This lack of overlap is not surprising, since Magna Carta's functions were enormously different from that of the U.S. document. Whereas the former defined the relationship between a king and his barons, the latter placed limits on all branches of government vis-à-vis an entire citizenry. Despite the enormous historical importance of Magna Carta, it is only a distant forerunner of the U.S. Bill of Rights in terms of content, form, and intent. By comparison, seven U.S. rights can be traced to a single American colonial document: the Massachusetts Body of Liberties (1641). Another nine were first protected in other American colonial documents (see Table 1).

Table 1. First Statement of Each Right in the U.S. Bill of Rights

BILL OF RIGHTS GUARANTEE	FIRST DOCUMENT PROTECTING	FIRST AMERICAN GUARANTEE	FIRST CONSTITU-TIONAL GUARANTEE
1. Establishment of religion	Rights of the colonists	Same (Boston)	N.J. Constitution, Art. 19
2. Free exercise of religion	Md. Act Concerning Religion	Same	Va. Declaration of Rights, S. 16
3. Free speech	Mass. Body of Liberties, S. 12	Same	Pa. Declaration of Rights, Art. 12
4. Free press	Address to Inhabitants of Quebec	Same	Va. Declaration of Rights, S. 12
5. Right to assemble	Declaration and Resolves of the Continental Congress	Same	Pa. Declaration of Rights, Art. 16
6. Right to petition	Bill of Rights (England, 1689)	Declaration of Rights and Grievances (1765), S. 13	Pa. Declaration of Rights, Art. 16
7. Right to bear arms	Bill of Rights (England, 1689)	Pa. Declaration of Rights, Art. 12	Same
8. Quartering soldiers	Petition of Right (England), S. 6	N.Y. Charter of Liberties	Del. Declaration of Rights, S. 21
9. Searches	Rights of the Colonists	Same (Boston)	Va. Declaration of Rights, S. 10
10. Seizures	Magna Carta, c. 39	Va. Declaration of Rights, S. 10	Same

Bill of Rights Guarantee	First Document Protecting	First American Guarantee	First Constitutional Guarantee
11. Grand jury	N.Y. Charter of Liberties	Same	N.C. Declaration of Rights, Art. 8
12. Double jeopardy	Mass. Body of Liberties, S. 42	Same	N.H. Bill of Rights, Art. 16
13. Self-incrimination	Va. Declaration of Rights, S. 8	Same	Same
14. Due process	Magna Carta, c. 39	Md. Act for the Liberties of the People	Va. Declaration of Rights, S. 8
15. Just compensation	Mass. Body of Liberties, S. 8	Same	Va. Declaration of Rights, Art. 2
16. Speedy trial	Va. Declaration of Rights, S. 8	Same	Same
17. Jury trial	Magna Carta, c. 39	Mass. Body of Liberties, S. 29	Va. Declaration of Rights, Art. 2
18. Cause and nature of accusation	Va. Declaration of Rights, S. 8	Same	Same
19. Witnesses	Pa. Charter of Privileges, Art. 5	Same	N.J. Constitution, Art. 16
20. Right to counsel	Mass. Body of Liberties, S. 29	Same	N.J. Constitution, Art. 16
21. Jury trial (civil)	Mass. Body of Liberties, S. 29	Same	Va. Declaration of Rights, S. 11
22. Bail	Mass. Body of Liberties, S. 18	Same	Va. Declaration of Rights, S. 9
23. Fines	Magna Carta, Sc. 20–22	Pa. Frame of Government, S. 18	Va. Declaration of Rights, S. 9
24. Punishment	Mass. Body of Liberties, S. 43, 46	Same	Va. Declaration of Rights, S. 9
25. Rights retained by people	Va. Constitution Proposed Amendment 17	Same	Ninth Amendment, U.S. Constitution
26. Reserved powers	Mass. Declaration of Rights, Art. 4	Same	Same

Writers on English common law tell us that Magna Carta had to be continually reconfirmed, at least forty-seven times by one count, because the
document was ignored for long periods of time and its contents were at best
honored in the breach.[6] Despite the written guarantees for certain English
common-law rights contained in major documents of English common law,
at the time of the American Revolution these rights were either not protected at all or were not protected in England to the extent that they were in
America.[7]

Even in those instances where protection of a right in England approached
that in America, there was a fundamental difference in the sense of whose actions were limited. Partly for this reason, James Madison said that there were
too many differences between common law and the U.S. Bill of Rights to
warrant comparison:

> [The] truth is, they [the British] have gone no farther than to raise a
> barrier against the power of the Crown; the power of the Legislature
> is left altogether too indefinite. Although I know whenever the great
> rights, the trial by jury, freedom of the press, or liberty of conscience,
> come into question [in Parliament] the invasion of them is resisted by
> able advocates, yet their Magna Charta does not contain any one pro-
> vision for the security of those rights, respecting which the people of
> America are most alarmed. . . . [T]hose choicest privileges of the peo-
> ple are unguarded in the British Constitution. But although . . . it may
> not be thought necessary to provide limits for the legislative power in
> that country, yet a different opinion prevails in the United States.[8]

Despite Madison's reservations, any investigation of rights in America
would need to begin with Magna Carta (1215), the English Petition of Right
(1628), and the English Bill of Rights (1689). This holds for several reasons.
First, as we see from Table 1, seven of the twenty-six rights listed in the U.S.
Bill of Rights do come explicitly from English common law. Also, it is useful to read these English documents to see how very different they are from
American rights documents due to the presence of an aristocracy and an established church in England. A clear sense of the dissimilarity between the
English and American background helps us to recognize American innovations in rights theory. Finally, the English documents serve as a platform for
understanding the English definition of rights—a definition that was and is
different from ours.

At the very least, any easy attribution of the U.S. Bill of Rights to English common law—including such major documents as Magna Carta—can no longer be accepted. The connection with English common law turns out to be so slight that we can reject Hypothesis B. At the same time, Hypothesis B has enough support for us to reject Hypothesis A. So we must turn instead to documents written on American shores, first considering Hypothesis C.

In support of Hypothesis C, the U.S. Bill of Rights resulted from the Antifederalists' insistence that the U.S. Constitution be amended in certain ways. Seven of the state ratifying conventions passed resolutions suggesting specific amendments; and at a critical point in the ratification process, James Madison promised to lead the fight for a bill of rights if the proposed constitution were ratified. True to his word, early during the first session of the postratification Congress meeting under the now-ratified Constitution on June 8, 1789, Madison introduced nine amendments containing forty-two separate rights. He personally wrestled the proposed amendments through the congressional process. After action by the Senate and further action by the House of Representatives, the states were sent a somewhat reduced package of twenty-six rights, which was approved as our U.S. Bill of Rights. Legal writers often speak as if Madison's proposed amendments were simply the common denominator of rights proposed by the state ratifying conventions. However, as Table 2 shows, this is not the case. The conventions together proposed more than ninety distinct rights, and while Madison needed to address Antifederalist concerns, he was selective in his response. The forty-two distinct rights Madison proposed bear only a modest relationship to those proposed by the state ratifying conventions (see Table 2).

Thirty-five of the amendments proposed by the state ratifying conventions appeared on Madison's list, but sixty-one did not. Seven rights proposed by Madison were not suggested by any convention, nor was there a "dense" connection between Madison's list and the suggestions of the ratifying conventions. The data in Table 2 constitute a matrix that is seven cells wide and ninety-six cells from top to bottom. If we consider only the top forty-two rows of this matrix, the more cells with an X in them, the denser the relationship between Madison's list and the conventions' proposals. Thirty-two percent of the cells are filled (96 out of 294 cells), which does not suggest an especially dense relationship between the ratifying conventions' proposals and Madison's list of rights.[9]

The last conclusion can also be supported by looking at the proposed

Table 2. Amendments Proposed by State Ratifying Conventions Compared with Madison's Original Proposed Amendments

	MA	MD	SC	NH	VA	NY	NC	MADISON
1. Power derived from the people					X		X	X
2. Government exercised for the common good					X		X	X
3. Life, liberty, property, and happiness					X		X	X
4. Right of people to alter or abolish government		X			X		X	X
5. Number of representatives	X			X	X	X	X	X
6. Congressional pay raises					X	X	X	X
7. Religious freedom		X	X	X	X		X	X
8. Right to a free conscience				X	X		X	X
9. Free speech		X			X		X	X
10. Free to write		X			X		X	X
11. Free press		X			X		X	X
12. Assembly					X		X	X
13. Petition and remonstrance					X		X	X
14. Right to bear arms				X	X		X	X
15. Pacifists need not bear arms					X		X	X
16. No quartering of troops in peacetime		X		X	X		X	X
17. No quartering without warrant					X		X	X
18. No double jeopardy		X						X
19. No double punishment								X
20. No self-incrimination					X		X	X
21. Due process of law guaranteed		X			X		X	X
22. Compensate for property taken								X
23. No excessive bail or fines					X		X	X
24. No cruel or unusual punishment					X		X	X

	MA	MD	SC	NH	VA	NY	NC	MADISON
25. No unreasonable search and seizure		X			X		X	X
26. Speedy and public trial					X		X	X
27. Told nature of crime		X			X		X	X
28. Confronted with accusers		X			X		X	X
29. Can call witnesses for own defense					X		X	X
30. Right to counsel		X			X		X	X
31. Rights retained by states or people					X		X	X
32. No implied powers for Congress		X			X		X	X
33. No state violate 8, 9, 11, or 26 above								X
34. Appeal limited by dollar amount								X
35. Jury cannot be bypassed								X
36. Impartial jury from vicinity		X			X		X	X
37. Jury unanimity required								X
38. May challenge any judicial decision								X
39. Grand jury indictment required	X			X				X
40. Jury trial for civil cases	X	X			X		X	X
41. Separation of powers required					X		X	X
42. Powers reserved to the states	X		X	X	X		X	X
43. Limit national taxing power	X	X	X	X	X	X	X	
44. No federal election regulation	X		X	X	X	X	X	
45. Free elections					X		X	
46. No standing army		X		X	X	X	X	
47. State control of militia					X		X	
48. State sovereignty retained						X		
49. Limits on judicial power	X	X			X	X	X	

	MA	MD	SC	NH	VA	NY	NC	MADISON
50. Treaties accord with state law		x						
51. Concurrent jurisdiction for state and national courts		x						
52. No infringing of state constitutions		x				x		
53. State courts to be used as lower federal courts				x		x		
54. Can appeal Supreme Court decisions						x		
55. Defend oneself in court					x		x	
56. Civil control of military					x		x	
57. Trial in state crime orders	x							
58. Judges hold no other office	x							
59. Four-year limit on military service					x		x	
60. Limit on martial law		x			x			
61. No monopolies	x			x		x	x	
62. Reduce jurisdiction of Supreme Court	x			x				
63. No titles of nobility	x			x		x		
64. Keep a congressional record					x	x	x	
65. Publish information on national use of money					x		x	
66. Two-thirds of Senate to ratify commerce treaties					x		x	
67. Two-thirds of both houses to pass commerce bill					x		x	
68. Limit on regulation of D.C.					x	x	x	
69. Presidential term limited to eight years					x		x	
70. President limited to two terms						x		
71. Add state judges to impeachment process						x		

	MA	MD	SC	NH	VA	NY	NC	Madison
72. Senate does not impeach senators					x		x	
73. Limit use of militia out of state		x				x		
74. Judicial salaries not changed					x		x	
75. Add requirements for being president						x		
76. Two-thirds vote of both houses needed to borrow money						x		
77. Two-thirds vote Congress must declare war						x		
78. Habeas corpus						x		
79. Congressional sessions to be open						x		
80. No consecutive terms in Senate						x		
81. State legislature must fill vacant Senate seat						x		
82. Limit on power of lower federal courts						x		
83. Congress may not assign duties to a state							x	
84. Congress may not regulate state paper money							x	
85. No foreign troops to be used							x	
86. State law used on military bases						x		
87. No multiple office holding		x			x	x	x	
88. Limit on bankruptcy laws						x		
89. No presidential pardon for treason						x		
90. President not the commander of the army		x				x		
91. Official form for president's acts						x		
92. No poll tax		x						

	MA	MD	SC	NH	VA	NY	NC	MADISON
93. No suspension of laws by executive					x		x	
94. No separate emoluments					x		x	
95. Judicial system may not be bypassed					x		x	
96. Advisory council for president							x	

Note: The first forty-two rights are arranged in the order used by Madison in his original version sent to the House of Representatives. Going from left to right, the states are arranged in the order in which their ratifying conventions produced a list of recommended amendments, from earliest to latest. When an X under "Madison" is underlined, it means that the proposed right eventually was included in the U.S. Bill of Rights.

Sources: The proposed amendments for each state are taken from Merrill Jensen, John P. Kaminski, Gaspare J. Saladino, et al., eds., *The Documentary History of the Ratification of the Constitution* (Madison, WI: University of Wisconsin Press, 1976). Madison's forty-two proposed rights are based upon an examination of the original documents in the National Archives.

amendments made by the ratifying conventions that most directly addressed the protection of state sovereignty. Numbers 31, 32, and 42 through 53 seem to be the best candidates, yet only three of these fourteen proposals are on Madison's list. One can see in Madison's selection process a clear inclination away from proposed rights that would check the power of the national government by withholding a specific power—such as the power to levy direct taxes, to grant monopolies, or to borrow money. There is also an inclination away from proposals that would alter a national institution so as to weaken it—for instance, by making senators ineligible for consecutive terms, by giving state and national courts concurrent jurisdiction, or by requiring a two-thirds vote in both houses on any bill dealing with navigation or commerce. In contrast, Madison inclined toward a third type of proposal: one suitable for a bill of rights as we now understand it. The rights to speak, write, publish, assemble, and petition government for redress of grievances safeguarded the ability of a people to organize politically. He also included prohibitions on self-incrimination, double punishment, excessive bail, and searches without a warrant—rights that define an impartial legal system. In effect, Madison avoided any proposed amendment that would alter the institutions defined by the Constitution. Largely ignoring specific prohibitions on national power, he opted instead for a list of rights that would clearly connect with the preferences of state governments but would not increase state power vis-à-vis the national government. A discussion about powers was thus subtly shifted to one about rights.

Therefore, the immediate background for the U.S. Bill of Rights was formed by the state declarations of rights attached to the state constitutions written between 1776 and 1787. Madison effectively extracted the common denominator from these state bills of rights, excepting those rights that might reduce the power of the national government. Almost every one of the twenty-six rights in the U.S. Bill of Rights can be found in two or three state documents and most of them can be found in five or more state documents.[10] Thus we must reject Hypothesis C as well.

The state bills of rights typically contained a more extensive listing than what came to be found in the national Bill of Rights. Maryland's 1776 document, for example, listed forty-nine rights in forty-two sections; Massachusetts's 1780 document listed forty-nine rights in thirty sections, and New Hampshire's 1784 one listed fifty rights in thirty-eight sections.[11] Virginia's forty-two rights and Pennsylvania's thirty-five rights, both documents promulgated in 1776, came closest to the size but not to the content of the national Bill of Rights.[12]

Clearly, a strong connection exists between the state bills of rights and Madison's proposed amendments (see Table 3).

If we look at the matrix formed by the forty-two rights on Madison's list and the seven state bills of rights in existence at the time, 50 percent of the cells in the matrix (173 out of 294) are filled compared to the 32 percent density when we correlate Madison's list with the amendments proposed by the state ratifying conventions. Remember, these state bills of rights had been written, adopted, and appended to their respective state constitutions well before the state ratifying conventions made their recommendations. If we construct a matrix using the contents of the state bills of rights and the rights on Madison's list that were eventually ratified as the U.S. Bill of Rights, we find that the percentage of the matrix filled rises to 60 percent. By contrast, only 36 percent of the matrix is filled when we compare the proposals of the state ratifying conventions with the rights actually ratified as part of the national Bill of Rights. A final comparison can be made using Tables 2 and 3. In Table 3, rights 43 through 52 have a very high density (73 percent), and they also happen to be addressed in the body of the U.S. Constitution, as are numbers 55,

Table 3. Madison's List of Proposed Amendments Compared with Provisions in the Existing State Bills of Rights

	VA	PA	DE	MD	NC	MA	NH	MADISON
1. Power derived from the people	x	x	x	x	x	x	x	x
2. Government exercised for the common good	x	x	x	x		x	x	x
3. Life, liberty, property, and happiness	x	x	x	x		x	x	x
4. Right of people to alter or abolish government	x	x		x		x	x	x
5. Number of representatives								x
6. Congressional pay raises								x
7. Religious freedom			x	x	x	x	x	x̲
8. Right to a free conscience	x	x	x	x	x	x	x	x
9. Free speech		x						x̲
10. Free to write								x
11. Free press	x	x	x	x	x	x	x	x̲
12. Assembly	x			x	x			x̲
13. Petition and remonstrance	x	x	x	x	x			x̲
14. Right to bear arms		x			x	x		x̲
15. Pacifists need not bear arms								x
16. No quartering of troops in peacetime			x	x		x	x	x̲
17. No quartering without warrant			x	x		x	x	x̲
18. No double jeopardy							x	x̲
19. No double punishment								x
20. No self-incrimination	x	x	x	x	x	x	x	x̲
21. Due process of law guaranteed	x	x	x	x	x	x	x	x̲
22. Compensate for property taken				x	x	x	x	x̲
23. No excessive bail or fines	x		x	x	x	x		x̲
24. No cruel or unusual punishment	x		x	x	x	x		x̲

	VA	PA	DE	MD	NC	MA	NH	Madison
25. No unreasonable search and seizure	x	x	x	x	x	x	x	x
26. Speedy and public trial	x	x	x	x	x	x	x	x
27. Told nature of crime	x	x	x	x	x	x	x	x
28. Confronted with accusers	x	x	x	x	x	x	x	x
29. Can call witnesses for own defense	x	x	x	x		x	x	x
30. Right to counsel		x	x	x		x	x	x
31. Rights retained by states or people		x	x	x		x	x	x
32. No implied powers for Congress								x
33. No state violate 8, 9, 11, or 26 above								x
34. Appeal limited by dollar amount								x
35. Jury cannot be bypassed								x
36. Impartial jury from vicinity	x	x	x	x				x
37. Jury unanimity required								x
38. May challenge any judicial decision								x
39. Grand jury indictment required					x			x
40. Jury trial for civil cases	x							x
41. Separation of powers required	x			x	x	x	x	x
42. Powers reserved to the states or people						x	x	x
43. No taxation without consent	x	x	x	x	x	x	x	
44. Free elections protected	x	x	x	x	x	x	x	
45. Frequent elections required	x	x	x	x	x	x	x	
46. No standing army permitted	x	x	x	x	x	x	x	
47. Civil control of military	x	x	x	x	x	x	x	

	VA	PA	DE	MD	NC	MA	NH	MADISON
48. No martial law (suspending law)	x		x	x	x	x		
49. No compulsion to bear arms	x	x					x	
50. No ex post facto laws			x	x	x	x	x	
51. No bills of attainder				x		x		
52. Habeas corpus	x	x						
53. Justice not sold			x	x		x	x	
54. Location of trial convenient				x		x	x	
55. Independent judiciary			x	x		x		
56. Recurrence to fundamentals	x	x			x	x		
57. Stake in community to vote	x			x				
58. Equality is supported					x	x		
59. Majority rule is protected	x							
60. Frequent meeting of legislature			x	x		x		
61. Free speech in legislature				x		x		
62. Convenient location of legislature				x				
63. Public office not hereditary	x					x	x	
64. No title of nobility				x				
65. No emoluments or privileges					x			
66. No taxing of paupers				x				
67. No monopolies				x	x			
68. Collective property right					x			
69. No sanguinary laws				x			x	
70. Right to common law				x				
71. Right to migrate	x							
72. No poll tax				x				
73. No infringing of state constitutions	x							
74. No religious test				x				

	VA	PA	DE	MD	NC	MA	NH	MADISON
75. Support of public worship						x	x	
76. Attend religious instruction						x		
77. Uniform support of religion						x	x	
78. Support of public teachers						x		
79. Time to prepare legal defense				x				
80. Rotation in executive office	x							
81. No multiple office holding	x							
82. Proportional punishment							x	
83. Qualified jurors							x	

Note: The first forty-two rights are those Madison compiled and sent to the House of Representatives; the order is the one used in his list. The rest of the rights are those found in the state bills of rights but not in Madison's proposed amendments. When an X under "Madison" is underlined, it means that the proposed right eventually was included in the U.S. Bill of Rights.

Sources: Madison's list is taken from the original documents in the National Archives; the rights in the state bills of rights are based on the documents collected in Francis N. Thorpe, ed., *The Federal and State Constitutions, Colonial Charters, and Other Organic Laws of the United States*, 7 vols. (Washington, DC: Government Printing Office, 1907).

60 through 65, and 81. In other words, seventeen provisions commonly found in state bills of rights had already been guaranteed by the U.S. Constitution and thus did not need to be included in a formal national bill of rights. Finally, few of the state bills of rights provisions are directly contradicted by anything in the U.S. Constitution. On the other hand, only eight of the provisions proposed by the state ratifying conventions had been covered in the proposed U.S. Constitution, whereas the Constitution directly contradicted twenty-three of the remaining provisions suggested by the state ratifying conventions.

These simple empirical tests support Hypothesis D, stating that the U.S. Bill of Rights summarized the American view of fundamental rights that had developed during the colonial era and been codified in the declarations of rights attached to the first state constitutions. The same tests allow us to reject the other hypotheses. When we ask where the basic American rights come from, we can answer that, if we define these rights as the ones contained in the

U.S. Bill of Rights, our basic rights come from state bills of rights and constitutions; these in turn are codifications of their respective colonial common-law developments. Still, the colonists were mostly Englishmen and they came to America with the English common-law rights that in turn emerged over time through political struggles in England. The point to emphasize is that U.S. rights did not result from Madison having sat down one day to write up a list of rights. Instead, U.S. rights are deeply rooted in a political process that began long ago in England, continued through the colonial era, and continues to this day. *In sum, American rights were emergent from political processes and contingent upon the issues that arose during those processes.*

Let us step back and consider the emergent and contingent nature of rights at greater length. In English common law, a right was originally more a privilege, since it denoted some exception to the law. For example, say that there was a law precluding monopolies but the king nevertheless grants Oxford University a monopoly in the delivery of higher education in its shire. This exception would be both a privilege and a right. Or perhaps there is a sumptuary law that prohibits anyone from wearing ermine who is not at least an earl in the aristocratic hierarchy; but the king grants the privilege of wearing ermine collars to clerics with an advanced degree from Cambridge as long as the ermine collar is worn only when conducting official church services and not otherwise worn in public. These clerics can then claim a right.

More broadly, since the law is always the will of the monarch, granting jury trials to those accused of crimes places the accused temporarily beyond the will of the local aristocrat sitting as judge and representing the crown. Put another way, the law (or will of the crown) establishes various dukes, for example, as serving in place of the king in courts scattered across the realm. Trial by a jury of peers was a way for the commoners to escape temporarily any possible tyranny by the aristocracy. The right to appeal legal decisions to the crown and the right to petition the king on nonlegal matters were other rights commoners had that allowed them to bypass local aristocrats. Over time, one king or another would oppress the people in some way that led to a reaction by those aristocrats or commoners who were affected. This reaction might well have led to the king's agreeing never to use such cruel and unusual punishment again, or never again to imprison someone without a writ of *habeas corpus.* A new right or privilege would then enter English common law. Gradually, a stable and generally recognized set of general rights emerged from this complicated political process and the precise list of rights that *emerged* was *contingent* upon the particular controversies that had arisen. Another set of controversies in England would have produced a different set of rights.

When Englishmen came to America, they brought the rights that had emerged to that point. The *emergent* process continued in England and in American common law during the colonial era. That is, just as additional rights continued to emerge in English common law, political controversies led to rights emerging in the colonies as well—although these rights were different and more numerous. Typically, colonial political processes introduced biblical considerations in a way not found in England. Nathaniel Ward, for example, who compiled and set the Massachusetts Body of Liberties (1641) down on paper, was both a lawyer trained in English common law and a congregational minister versed in covenant theology. The Massachusetts Body of Liberties was a code of law that brought together all the rights and liberties that had emerged in Massachusetts law to that point. This code of law would provide the first statement of seven of the twenty-six rights that were later found in the U.S. Bill of Rights.

The influence of covenant theology, at least in the colonies, seems to have had a positive effect on rights rather than a negative one. It helped create a broader definition of rights, drastically reduced the list of capital crimes, prohibited cruel and unusual punishment, and introduced a strong element of equality. The other colonies also developed early codes of law like the Massachusetts document, and all the colonies periodically revised and updated their respective codes of law as new rights emerged. By 1776, these various colonial legal codes came to look very much like one another, at least in part because they borrowed and copied from each other. For example, when William Penn wrote his list of fundamental liberties for Pennsylvania in the 1690s, he first consulted the rights documents of New York and Virginia. It may also be that similar colonial environments produced similar political controversies, which served as the seedbeds for similar rights. Regardless, the Virginia Declaration of Rights (1776), the Pennsylvania Declaration of Rights (1776), and the Massachusetts Declaration of Rights (1780) are so similar in content that entire sections are identical. Their similarities imply the emergence of a common national citizenship (a single people) defined by a common set of rights.

The opening sentence of the Declaration of Independence declares that the American people are a separate people from the English people—at least they were by 1776. The long list of grievances that compose the last two-thirds of the Declaration elaborates a set of rights assumed by the American people as a people;

and that set is distinct from the list of rights assumed by the English people. As Eric Voegelin has shown, a people is defined by a set of shared symbols that are articulated in its earliest political documents. Over time, these symbols are "differentiated" or unfolded in later documents. American political history presents an excellent example of Voegelin's theory: examination of early American political documents shows the political symbols in embryonic form. We watch these symbols unfold during the colonial era and then assume a more or less complete articulation in the Declaration of Independence and the declarations of rights attached to the early state constitutions. These basic shared rights were then collected in final form in the U.S. Constitution and its Bill of Rights.[13]

The history of rights formation not only supports Voegelin's theory; it also casts light on the question George Carey asked us long ago, "Is the U.S. Constitution an organic act by the American people or a compact among the states?" From the evidence of basic rights found in the body of the Constitution and its first ten amendments, the answer would appear to be *both*.

Let us take a moment to consider this answer. Congress, as representing the people of the United States, adopted the U.S. Bill of Rights. It was then approved by thirteen state conventions representing thirteen peoples as organized into thirteen separate states. The content of the Bill of Rights was the common denominator of the then-existing state declarations of rights. Each state had worked out its respective list during the colonial era, but by 1789 there was a common set of rights that belonged to the American people as citizens of the U.S. These rights happened to be essentially the same rights that citizens of the various states also possessed. Therefore, in terms both of content and of the method of adoption, the U.S. Bill of Rights expressed simultaneously the will of the people of the U.S. and the will of the peoples of the thirteen states. The twenty-six rights in the U.S. Bill of Rights have the same roots and the same status as the eighteen or so rights found in the body of the U.S. Constitution. These eighteen rights, also found in most state declarations of rights, were adopted by both national and state conventions. A broader look at the U.S. Constitution shows that it, too, comprises something that looks like the common denominator of the state constitutions in effect in 1787.[14] In sum, the roots of American rights can be traced back from the U.S. Bill of Rights to the state declarations of rights attached to the first state constitutions adopted during the 1770s and then back to the colonial documents that led to each state declaration of rights. I lay out this somewhat complicated development in *The Origins of American Constitutionalism* (1988), and the argument I make there essentially follows the one made by George Carey and Willmore Kendall in *The Basic Symbols of the American Political Tradition.*

To be fair, I need to report what Carey's voice now says in my head. "Fair enough, Lutz. I like the words *emergent* and *contingent,* but only up to a point. Certainly I have said many times that we need to rely on the American political process rather than on some rationalistic solution, whether buttressed by mathematics or ideology. For example, as an interpreter or reviser of the meaning of the U.S. Constitution, the U.S. Supreme Court is inferior to the formal amendment process or even the thorough political airing that congressional resolution provides. However, as much as I like Oakeshott's use of emergent and contingent, please do not turn me into a historicist. I believe that there are truths that transcend history and culture. Basic American rights are among these truths, as our founders believed, and they fought a revolution because they believed this. At the same time, the story you have told about the historical emergence of American rights in English and American colonial common law simply illustrates how normal political processes are the best and perhaps the only way to discover these rights."

And so I continue to argue with George Carey forty-five years later, or at least continue to chew on the problems he set before us. My hope is that this book will both honor George Carey adequately and help project into the indefinite, distant future the fruitful impact of this most remarkable teacher and scholar.

Federalists, Antifederalists, and the Philadelphia Constitution

GORDON LLOYD

Professor George Carey's most provocative and essential contribution to our understanding of constitutional republicanism is his diagnosis of the meaning and health of the Philadelphia Constitution of 1787. Here I build on Professor Carey's enduring concern about the nature and well-being of the Philadelphia Constitution. While I do pay attention to the important differences and fundamental agreements between the Federalists and the Antifederalists, I do not provide a checklist of Federalist/Antifederalist agreements and disagreements. Nor do I provide a blow-by-blow account of the ratification struggle. My purpose here is to revisit two central "Carey questions." First, is the Philadelphia Constitution a "crossroads" Constitution? And second, is the Philadelphia Constitution a dead Constitution?

In 1965, Carey and Willmoore Kendall portrayed the Philadelphia Constitution—the one that left the hands of the framers in September 1787 when a bill of rights was not even a twinkle in anyone's eyes—in a highly uncharacteristic way. They called it actually "many constitutions: a crossroads from which, once having situated itself there, the people of America might have moved in any of several directions." Kendall and Carey portray the Philadelphia Constitution as "potentiality," as a constitution capable of generating either plebiscitary democracy or constitutional republicanism, capable of moving in the direction of either a full-blown nation-state or a loose confederation of independent states.

Fortunately, Kendall and Carey argue, along came *The Federalist Papers.* The authors are not only relieved that they appeared, but downright pleased. Where they would have feared for the Philadelphia Constitution alone, they are optimistic about the enduring potential of the Philadelphia-Publius Constitution to fight off liberal predators. Publius, they argue, not only provided an authoritative teaching on constitutional republicanism—and especially on the kind of constitutional morality needed to secure self-government—but the Philadelphia-Publius Constitution is alive and kicking. It is winning the political wars, despite all the efforts to destroy *the* principle that defines it: namely, "the deliberate sense of the community." Publius did not simply *faithfully report* the meaning of the Constitution as delivered by the Convention, then; he bequeathed a special understanding of it, and one that is coherent and relevant.[1]

In 2001 and without Kendall, Carey published the provocative piece, "Who or What Killed the Philadelphia Constitution?"[2] In this article he portrays the original Philadelphia Constitution as possessing a clear and discoverable meaning. It is not a document of sheer potentiality onto which several competing theories of democracy can be grafted but rather has a coherent meaning that was *faithfully reported* by Publius. Publius reminds us of the Philadelphia Constitution's central features. First, in *Federalist* 39 and 45, Publius explains that the federal government is limited to enumerated powers and that the states are sovereign with respect to the remainder.[3] Second, in *Federalist* 47 through 51, in the institutional arrangement of those powers, Congress will prevail over the president and the Court. And third, in *Federalist* 10, the acquisitive side of human nature must be accommodated rather than abolished. But there is a pessimistic ending to Carey's 2001 account: "the structural integrity of the Philadelphia Constitution has been damaged beyond repair." The Philadelphia Constitution is not only irrelevant; it is dead.

Carey offers three possible explanations for this irreversible structural damage. Perhaps, as a first, the "framers were not prescient enough; they could not anticipate changes in the political landscape?" I would agree with Carey that this explanation is insufficient. Like Carey, I think that the framers institutionalized a "constitutional morality" so that Americans of each generation could govern themselves. The framers' point is that each and every generation should be "prescient enough" to govern itself.[4] As a second possibility: perhaps the Seventeenth Amendment is the culprit? This amendment replaces the election of United States senators by each state legislature with their popular election. Carey asks: "Did the Seventeenth Amendment kill federalism?" He answers, "No." I agree that this "election test" of the health of federalism deals with the symptoms and not the cause. The framers thought that the health of federalism should be determined by attention to concerns of structure and powers and not by an "election test"—one that three-quarters of the state legislatures willingly abandoned in the early twentieth century![5] Third, perhaps the death of the Philadelphia Constitution has been the result of the Supreme Court's expansive reading of the interstate-commerce and general-welfare clauses over several generations? "No," says Carey: this emphasis on the Supreme Court misses the seriousness of the problem. Carey rejects these explanations because they fail to capture the "underlying ideological sea change" caused by Herbert Croly and the progressives, parties that Carey claims have hijacked and killed the Philadelphia Constitution. Thanks to their unrelenting efforts, he argues, there has been an enormous centralization of power; a derangement of the functions of the three branches away from Congress and toward the executive bureaucracy and the judiciary; and a flirtation with the notion that human nature can be transformed. The progressives killed the Philadelphia Constitution.

Well, I suggest, not quite. The Marshall Court played a large role in undoing the "accommodation" of national and federal features and the culprit clause has been the necessary and proper clause. In my view, the Marshall Court endangered the life of the Constitution long before the progressives appeared on the scene. The secessionist and Reconstruction movements also seemed determined to lay the Philadelphia Constitution to rest. No doubt, the progressives were responsible for the further movement toward administrative centralization and judicial domination. The Constitution was further tested by the Great Society programs. And yet at the last sighting, it seems still to be gasping away.

I am hopeful that the Philadelphia Constitution—the crucial components of which are the partly national and partly federal concept and the necessary and proper clause—is still alive, although it is in poor health. If dead, it certainly refuses to lie down. But how might we restore the health of the Philadelphia Constitution? In answering this question, we must recur to the debates that took place at the Constitutional Convention of 1787 and recapture the concept of the deliberate sense of the community. For without this concept, the Philadelphia Constitution is indeed a lifeless parchment.

RESPONDING TO THE TWOFOLD CAREY CHALLENGE

Two issues have been neglected in the scholarly literature; namely, the origin of the partly federal–partly national concept and the origin of the necessary and proper clause. My thesis is the following: first, both the concept and the clause are endowed with a "potentiality" to go in either centripetal or centrifugal directions. Second, both the concept and the clause contain the further potentiality completely to destroy either the sovereignty of the nation or the sovereignty of the states. Third, the Philadelphia Constitution contains an inherent potentiality to be destroyed, if the federal-national agreement is viewed as a "mere accommodation" that can be broken by the right kind of person—by one who winks and nods us all the way to being wholly national or wholly federal. And fourth, the Constitution could be destroyed if the necessary and proper clause is interpreted as having either a "sweeping" elasticity making the Constitution whatever we want it to be or a fixed meaning making self-government impossible.

Both the necessary and proper clause and the partly national–partly federal concept were absent from the American landscape prior to the Philadelphia Convention. As creations of that Convention, the two elements left the framers' hands in a condition of "potentiality." The Philadelphia Convention shows that, even after "the fullest and most mature deliberation," the meaning of both the national-federal concept and the necessary and proper clause were unclear when the delegates signed the document on September 17, 1787. Following Madison, their meaning was to be "liquidated" over time. The health of the Philadelphia Constitution, therefore, depends on the ability of each generation to "liquidate" the meaning of the concept and clause in a way that fulfills the idea of deliberative self-government. The Philadelphia Constitution is alive and well only so long as the constitutional morality of "deliberate liquidation" is also alive and well.[6]

ON THE ROAD TO PHILADELPHIA

Although the phrase "partly federal, partly national" does not expressly appear in the Philadelphia Constitution, it is implicit in virtually every one of its seven articles. The framers agreed to have the House both elected by the people and for it to represent them, whereas the Senate would be elected by the state legislatures and would represent each state equally. An Electoral College also follows this model for election of the president. Article III recognizes the distinction between state and general courts, while Article IV indicates the obligations of one state to another state. The amending process is also a mixture of both national and federal principles, as is the method adopted for ratification of the Philadelphia Constitution in Article VII.

If we turn to the structural and power components of the arrangements that had prevailed in the 1780s—namely, to the Articles of Confederation and the various state constitutions—we get a different story. In the Articles of Confederation, each state is equally represented in a single chamber, and amendments require the unanimous consent of state legislatures. Article II declares that "each state retains its sovereignty, freedom, and independence, and every Power, Jurisdiction and right, which is not by this confederation expressly delegated to the Unites States, in Congress assembled." Article IX outlines the power and authority of Congress in express detail. There is no necessary and proper clause. The Articles of Confederation does not establish a government over individuals; it is a wholly federal arrangement with "governments" existing at the level of the state constitutions. I have scoured the state constitutions created between 1776 and 1780 and have come up completely empty on precursors of the necessary and proper clause. State constitutions shied away from enumerating a list of assembly powers, preferring instead to list in the form of a bill of rights what the assembly shall not do. Not one constitution ends the section on legislative powers with an appeal to a necessary and proper clause—Virginia, Massachusetts, and Pennsylvania are good examples. But each constitution does have a prefatory bill of rights. These prefatory declarations detail in unambiguous language why government is necessary and what the government should *not* do.

Put differently, the partly national–partly federal concept and the necessary and proper clause have no history prior to the Philadelphia Convention. Thus, we must turn to the deliberations of that convention to discover the birth of these two vital components of the Philadelphia Constitution.

THE PHILADELPHIA CONVENTION:
PARTLY FEDERAL AND PARTLY NATIONAL

Let us begin with James Madison's famous five tests in *Federalist* 39:

> The proposed Constitution, therefore, even when tested by the rules
> laid down by its antagonists, is, in strictness, neither a national nor a

federal Constitution, but a composition of both. (1) In its foundation it is federal, not national; (2) in the sources from which the ordinary powers of the government are drawn, it is partly federal and partly national; (3) in the operation of these powers, it is national, not federal; (4) in the extent of them, again, it is federal, not national; and finally (5) in the authoritative mode of introducing amendments, it is neither wholly federal nor wholly national.[7] (numbers added)

The Convention adopted the sources or structure test (2) after six weeks of debate. Madison's admission that the Constitution is national (3) in its operation validated "the cry" of the Antifederalists for a Bill of Rights. His claim that the Constitution is federal because its powers are enumerated (4) begs the question: what is a necessary and proper reading of the enumeration? Tests (1) and (5) became more important in the early-nineteenth-century debates and are not central to the meaning and health of the Philadelphia Constitution.[8]

The Virginia Plan introduced at the beginning of the Philadelphia Convention was "wholly national." Of particular importance was its lack of any structural representation for the states. According to Resolutions 3, 4, and 5, the general government was to have a bicameral legislative structure with neither branch elected by the states and neither branch representing the states. According to Resolution 6, Congress would be granted the power to "(1) legislate in all cases to which the separate States are incompetent" and to "(2) negative all laws passed by the several States, contravening in the opinion of the National Legislature the articles of Union." In terms of powers, the Virginia Plan was "wholly national" as well.[9] There was also no necessary and proper clause, no bill of rights, and no provision for an expressly delegated powers clause; nor was there a supremacy clause, general welfare clause, or common defense clause. We move here in "wholly national" waters in terms of both structure and power.

Although a day-by-day account of what occurred from the introduction of the Virginia Plan to the passage of the Connecticut Compromise is beyond the scope of this essay, it might be helpful to highlight ten turning points between May 29 and July 16.

1) On May 31, the delegates rejected the resolution that the second house be elected by the first house. Madison's disappointment deserves citation: "a chasm (was) left in this part of the plan."[10]

2) On June 7, the state delegations unanimously agreed to election of the second house by the state legislatures. Madison's "chasm" was filled and the states were now structurally represented in the general government.[11]

3) On June 11, the delegates overwhelmingly agreed that representation in the lower house should be based on population as well as be elected by the people. By a 6–5 vote, the delegates rejected a proposal made by Roger Sherman and Oliver Ellsworth that each state be equally represented in the Senate. Put differently, the Connecticut delegation proposed the "Connecticut Compromise" on June 11—popular representation in the lower house and equal representation for the states in the upper branch. This compromise failed to pass by the slimmest of margins.[12]

4) On June 15, William Paterson submitted the New Jersey Plan, one that enhanced the enumeration of powers granted to Congress by the Articles of Confederation. The plan included the powers to tax and to regulate interstate commerce, but scrapped all the popular representation provisions of the Virginia Plan. The New Jersey Plan was introduced, according to John Dickinson, because James Madison "went too far" in completely excluding representation of the states.[13]

5) On June 19, the New Jersey Plan was defeated 7–3–1. This did not mean that Madison was victorious and that it would be smooth sailing for the Virginia Plan. For the remainder of June, the delegates returned repeatedly to the compromise proposed on June 11.[14] The opposition argued that the Virginia Plan both violated the congressional mandate to "revise" the Articles and that it would never be adopted by the electorate.

6) On June 29, Ellsworth reintroduced the motion of June 11: equal representation for the states in the upper house with proportional representation in the lower house.[15]

The ensuing discussion is vital. Ellsworth accepted the principle of proportional representation in the lower house and "hoped it would become a ground of compromise to the 2d branch." And for the first time, the case for representation of the states was elevated from one of convenience to one of principle. Ellsworth declared, "We were partly national; partly federal." He trusted "that on this middle ground a compromise would take place."[16]

7) On June 30, Ellsworth again appealed to "the plighted faith" of the American tradition according to which every state had equal representation. Madison argued, unsuccessfully, that the equal-representation issue was contrary to the principles of justice. Then out of the blue, the youngest delegate, Jonathan Davie of North Carolina—until then a pretty staunch nationalist—spoke for the first time: "We were partly federal, partly national in our Union," he declared. "And he did not see why the Govt. might [not] in some respects operate on the States, in others on the people." Moreover, "the system on the table [The Virginia Plan] is a novelty, an amphibious monster; and he was persuaded that it never would be recd. by the people." Mr. Franklin lent his considerable weight in support of Davie's observation.[17]

8) On July 2, the Ellsworth proposal was defeated on a tie vote: 5–5–1. Nevertheless, a committee of eleven—one delegate from each state— was created to seek a compromise on the representation question. The composition of the committee reveals that Madison's attempt to exclude the states from the structure of the general government had been halted in its tracks. Gerry was chosen over King from Massachusetts, Yates over Hamilton from New York, Franklin over Wilson from Pennsylvania, Davie over Williamson from North Carolina, Rutledge over Pinckney from South Carolina, and Mason over Madison from Virginia.[18]

9) From July 5 to 7, the Gerry Committee defended both equal representation for the states in the Senate and popular representation in the House. We must put theoretical niceties to one side, Gerry said, and think about "accommodation." "We were . . . in a peculiar situation. We were neither the same Nation nor different Nations. If no compromise should take place what will be the consequence." Mason concurred: "There must be some accommodation." Paterson, also on the committee, urged adoption of the report, for "there was no other ground of accommodation."[19]

10) On July 16, the delegates agreed (5–4–1) to the Gerry Committee Report, also known as the Connecticut Compromise. The losing delegates—Madison, Wilson, G. Morris, Pinckney, and King—decided not to challenge the outcome.[20]

The Convention decided that the Philadelphia Constitution would be a mixture of federal and national principles.[21] While the delegates had moved away from the wholly federal Articles of Confederation, the Virginia Plan was dead in the water. Over this six-week period, the wholly national Virginia Plan received two serious structural defeats: not only were the state legislatures chosen to elect senators but each state was to be represented equally in the Senate. On July 16, a majority of the delegations concurred that the Philadelphia Constitution should be partly national and partly federal in structure and they pushed this compromise on an unwilling Madison. The core outcome of the debate, therefore, was its discovery that we were partly national and partly federal.[22]

This structural compromise—the decision that Congress would be partly federal and partly national—became the deliberate sense of the community by the end of the Convention. The delegates returned to this model for resolution of the most durable of issues: election of the president. The Brearley Committee—composed of Gilman, King, Sherman, Brearley, G. Morris, Dickinson, Carroll, Madison, Williamson, Butler, and Baldwin—was a veritable cross-section of the delegates; and it proposed the adoption of an Electoral College in which both the people and the states are represented in the election of the president.[23] This resolution of the difficult matter of presidential election clearly meant that the partly national–partly federal model had become the deliberate sense of the Convention.

THE PHILADELPHIA CONVENTION:
THE NECESSARY AND PROPER CLAUSE

Article I, Section 8 of the Philadelphia Constitution enumerates the powers of Congress. The eighteenth and final entry states: "To make all Laws which shall be necessary and proper for carrying into Execution the foregoing Powers vested by this Constitution in the Government of the United States, or in any Department or Officer thereof." When and how did this phrase make its appearance in the convention deliberations? What is the original understanding of the necessary and proper clause? Was this clause well-known for lending what we shall call an "obvious elasticity" to the enumerated list? If so, how far could one bend the clause without breaking it?

Despite the arguments of *The Federalist Papers* that there is an "obviousness" to the necessary and proper clause, the clause did not even exist before the Philadelphia Convention. Furthermore, it left the Convention in ambiguity. Despite its "obviousness," *The Federalist Papers* provide two separate explanations of the clause: the first comes from Hamilton in his analysis of federalism, and the second is offered by Madison in his defense of the republicanism of the Philadelphia Constitution. The Antifederalists had warned that the clause contained the potential for much mischief.[24] They argued that "the sweeping clause" contained the potentiality to shift authority away not only from the states to the nation but from Congress to the president and the courts.

The Antifederalists contributed to discussion of the powers question by reminding us that the necessary and proper clause is also a constitutional compromise. This time we witness not a structural compromise but the emergence of a third sense: one somewhere between the Federalist disposition not to enumerate any congressional powers at all—a vital part of a wholly national arrangement—and the Antifederalist concern to limit the reach of Congress to those items expressly itemized. In fact, Hamilton admits the accuracy of the Antifederalist claim that the "necessity and propriety" of "the sweeping clause" is to be determined by the "national government." And despite Madison's portrayal of the Antifederalist objections to this clause—"few parts of the Constitution have been assailed with more intemperance than this"—he too admits, "without the *substance* of this power, the whole Constitution would be a dead letter."[25]

Again, it is helpful to highlight ten turning points between July 17 and the end of the Convention in order to show that, by September 17, the delegates were unclear concerning what the enumeration of powers in general and the necessary and proper clause in particular included or excluded.[26] They had moved to that position as a result of deliberation and choice, but the very lack of clarity was what encouraged George Mason, Edmund Randolph, and Elbridge Gerry first to call for the addition of a bill of rights and then to withhold their signatures.

Recall that the Virginia Plan, written by Madison, was wholly national. Of particular importance was the absence of two ingredients: first, of any enumeration of congressional powers empowering Congress to legislate in all areas where the states were "incompetent"; and second, of a bill of rights on behalf of either the states or the people. Yet the heart of the discussion of the final two months of the Convention concerned the enumeration of congressional powers. Although delegates moved away from the strict enumeration model of the Articles, in the end they did not endorse the nonenumeration of powers of the Virginia model, either.[27]

1) On July 17, the delegates discussed a possible enumeration of congressional powers and debated the provision of the Virginia Plan, establishing a congressional negative veto over state laws. Exchange on the latter dominated the discussion:

> Gouvernor [sic] Morris [opposed the negative veto because it was] not *necessary*, if sufficient Legislative authority should be given to the Genl. Government.
>
> Mr. Sherman thought it *unnecessary* . . .
>
> Mr. L. Martin considered the power as *improper* & inadmissible. Shall all the laws of the States be sent up to the General Legislature before they shall be permitted to operate?
>
> Mr. Madison considered the negative on the laws of the States as essential to the efficacy & security of the General. Govt. . . . A power of negativing the *improper* laws of the States is at once the most mild & certain means of preserving the harmony of the system.
>
> On the question for agreeing to the power of negativing laws of States &c, [It passed in the negative . . . 3–7.][28]

This was Madison's third defeat in his attempt to establish a wholly national plan. The vote was not close. Incidentally, this was the first time that the necessary and proper language was used at the Convention.

Right after the vote on the negative veto, Luther Martin proposed the following resolution: "that the Legislative acts of the U.S. made by virtue & in pursuance of the articles of Union, and all treaties made & ratified under the authority of the U.S. shall be the supreme law of the respective States."[29] The resolution passed.

It seems odd that Martin, a warm supporter of state sovereignty, should introduce the supremacy clause. But there is a plausible explanation. The supremacy clause, far from pointing the national-federal accommodation in a wholly national direction, was intended by the delegates to confirm that the system is partly federal and partly national. Instead of accepting the congressional veto—Madison's wholly national solution—delegates overwhelmingly adopted an oath acknowledging the supremacy, where appropriate, of U.S. laws as a substitute. No one at the Convention envisioned that one day "wholly national" advocates would use the clause to undermine the partly federal–partly national principle.[30]

2) Also on July 17, the delegates agreed (6–4) to adhere to the provision of the Virginia Plan vesting in Congress the power "to legislate in all cases to which the separate States are incompetent." Now this too seems a bit odd, given how far the Convention had embraced the national-federal accommodation. This vote, however, should not be interpreted as a Madisonian victory but as a prelude to his fourth serious defeat on the federal-national issue. Prior to July 17, the "incompetent" clause had sailed through without more than a murmur of opposition. Now it was on its last gasp.[31]

3) On July 24, the Convention chose Rutledge, Randolph, Gorham, Ellsworth, and Wilson to form a Committee of Detail.[32] This committee moved the convention completely away from a wholly national understanding of the powers of Congress.

4) On August 6, the Committee of Detail presented the first draft of the Constitution. The next day, the delegates began their deliberations of the twenty-three articles.[33] Significant about the report is that, in it, the powers of Congress are enumerated for the first time.

5) On August 16, the delegates began discussing the enumeration of congressional powers.[34] Significantly, no one said: "Why are we writing down the powers of Congress? Have not we agreed over the last two months that Congress should do everything the states are 'incompetent' to do?" In short, the case in favor of nonenumeration had evaporated. This was the fourth defeat for Madison. It confirmed, for the fourth time, that the Philadelphia Constitution was intended to be partly federal and partly national—initially in terms of structure and now in terms of powers.

6) On August 20, the delegates turned to the final enumerated power that had never before been part of the constitutional conversation: "And to make all laws that shall be necessary and proper for carrying into execution the foregoing powers and all other powers vested, by this Constitution, in the government of the United States, or in any department or officer thereof."[35]

According to Madison's notes, the clause was read on August 20 and then "Mr. Madison and Mr. Pinckney moved to insert between 'laws' and 'necessary' 'and establish all offices,' it appearing to them liable to cavil that the latter was not included in the former." [36] We witness here Madison's frequent warning that once you start listing powers—and the same goes for listing rights—you risk leaving one power or one right out. In addition, to avoid the temptation to "cavil," it is prudent to be as clear as possible when designing a constitution that is to "endure for ages."[37] It is unclear what future "cavil" Madison and Pinckney hoped to avoid, but they clearly thought that the clause, as it stood, had the "potentiality" to undermine the nation's ability to take care of itself. It is instructive to read the exchange that followed:

> Mr. Govr. Morris, Mr. Wilson, Mr. Rutledge and Mr. Elseworth urged that the amendment could not be *necessary.*
> On the motion for inserting "and establish all offices" N.H. no. Mass, ay. Ct. no. Pa. no. Del. no. Md. ay. Va. no. N-C no. S.C. no. Geo. no.
> The clause as reported was then agreed to *nem.con.*[38]

We are not told why three members of the Committee of Detail thought it unnecessary to adopt the Madison-Pinckney amendment. Was it unnecessary because they thought the addition would be redundant? Was a congressional power to "establish all offices" obviously implied in the clause itself? What *is* clear is that Madison and Pinckney failed to persuade their own delegations and that the delegates were perfectly happy with the necessary and proper clause as it stood.[39]

7) From August 18 to 20, the delegates discussed additions to the list of enumerated powers.[40] The Convention agreed to enhance congressional authority over the military. Mason proposed that Congress be given authority to enact sumptuary laws and the delegates debated whether or not Congress should control the slave trade. In the process,

the delegates added that Congress could incur debts "for the common defense and general welfare." Unlike the necessary and proper clause, this inclusion did not generate any interpretational disputes—if for no other reason than that these two clauses had already been part of the constitutional conversation under the Articles.

8) By September 10, Randolph and Gerry were convinced that Congress now possessed sufficient powers to turn the Philadelphia Constitution into a wholly national document. They decided to withhold their signatures.[41] Randolph listed "the general clause concerning necessary and proper laws" as a major source of future tyranny. Gerry concurred: "the rights of the citizens were . . . rendered insecure . . . by the general power of the Legislature to make what laws they may please to call necessary and proper."[42]

9) On September 15, Mason also criticized the presence of the necessary and proper clause in the Constitution:

> Under their own construction of the general clause, at the end of the enumerated powers, the Congress may grant monopolies in trade and commerce, constitute new crimes, inflict unusual and severe punishments, and extend their powers as far as they think proper; so that the State legislatures have no security for the powers not presumed to remain to them, or the people for their rights.[43]

Mason proposed that a general bill of rights be adopted because the necessary and proper clause endows the Constitution with the "potentiality" to violate the partly federal–partly national accommodation. The Convention, however, was in no mood to act on Mason's proposal.

10) From September 12 to 17, the report produced by the Committee of Style—the final draft of the Constitution—was debated.[44] No one was concerned about the interstate commerce, general welfare, common defense, and supremacy clauses. This was not true of the necessary and proper clause. In fact, one gains the impression that the framers were engaged in an initial "liquidation" of the meaning of the clause.

The following two exchanges occurring on September 14 illustrate the crossroads the delegates had come to on the meaning of the necessary and proper clause. Here is the first:

> Docr Franklin moved to add after the words "post roads" [Art 1 Sect. 8.]
>
> > "A power to provide for cutting canals where deemed *necessary*."
> >
> > Mr. Wilson seconded the motion.
> >
> > Mr. Sherman objected. The expence in such cases will fall on the U—States, and the benefit will accrue to the places where the canals may be cut.
> >
> > Mr. Wilson. Instead of being an expence to the U.S. they may be a source of revenue.
> >
> > Mr. Madison suggested an enlargement of the motion into a power "to grant charters of incorporation where the interest of the U.S. might require & the legislative provisions of individual states may be *incompetent*."
> >
> > Mr. King thought the power *unnecessary*.
> >
> > Mr. Wilson. It [Franklin's motion] is *necessary* to prevent a *State* from obstructing the *general* welfare. [Madison's amendment on mercantile monopolies is *unnecessary*] because they are already included in the power to regulate trade.
> >
> > Col. Mason was for limiting the power to the single case of Canals. He was afraid of monopolies of every sort, which he did not think were by any means already implied by the Constitution as supposed by Mr. Wilson.
> >
> > The motion being so modified as to admit a distinct question specifying & limited to the case of canals.
> >
> > Ayes 3, Noes 7.
> >
> > The other part fell of course, as including the power rejected.[46]

What have the framers agreed to in this exchange other than to beat back Madison's last-minute effort to reestablish the once unassailable incompetency clause? What is in and what is out?[47] The second exchange:

> Mr. Madison and Mr. Pinckney then moved to insert in the list of powers vested in Congress a power—"to establish an University, in which no preferences or distinctions should be allowed on account of religion."

> Mr. Wilson supported the motion.
>
> Mr. Govr Morris. It was not *necessary*. The exclusive power at the Seat of Government will reach the object.
>
> On the question, it was defeated Ayes 4, Noes 6, divided 1.[48]

Have they agreed that the Congress can create a university even though it is not expressly listed? In the First Congress, several of the original framers continued their discussion of the meaning of the necessary and proper clause. Representative Roger Sherman, on May 3, 1790, noted "that a proposition to vest Congress with power to establish a National University was made in the General Convention; but it was negatived. It was thought sufficient that this power should be exercised by the States in their separate capacity." If we take Sherman's remark as authoritative, then the framers had intended their silence to mean the absence rather than presence of the authority to create a university.[49]

ON THE ROAD FROM PHILADELPHIA

Hamilton, certainly, thought that the framers intended the Constitution to be as wholly national as possible—but he was absent from the critical Convention deliberations. Thirty years later, John Marshall stated that the necessary and proper clause of the Philadelphia Constitution meant that we are in effect wholly national—but he failed to cite the framers or the original records in support of his opinion. More important for our understanding of the Philadelphia Constitution, therefore, is what accommodationist delegates like Sherman, Ellsworth, and Dickinson thought of both the federal-national compromise and the necessary and proper clause.

Sherman, Ellsworth, and Dickinson understood "the accommodation" to be more than "a mere compromise." On September 26, 1787, Sherman and Ellsworth recommended that Connecticut ratify the Constitution. They emphasized that "equal representation of the states in the Senate" would secure the equal rights of the states.[50] Sherman, in the second of his *Citizen of New Haven Letters*, takes the partly federal–partly national settlement seriously: "the rights of the people will be secured by a representation in proportion to their numbers in one branch of the legislature, and the rights of the particular states by their equal representation in the other branch."[51] Dickinson clearly defends the partly federal–partly national accommodation on grounds of principle:

"It has been said that this representation was a mere compromise. It was not a mere compromise. The equal representation of each state in one branch of the legislature, was an original substantive proposition, made in convention, very soon after the draft offered by Virginia. . . . The proposition was expressly made upon . . . principle."[52] Again: "Where was there ever a confederacy," writes Dickinson in his *Fabius Essay VIII*, "in which, each state was equally represented in one legislative body, the people of each state equally represented in another, and the sovereignties and people of all the states conjointly represented, possessed such a qualified and tempering authority in making laws?"[53] For his part, Ellsworth claims that the powers of Congress "extend only to matters respecting the common interests of the union, and are specially defined, so that the particular states retain their sovereignty in all other respects."[54] Similarly, Sherman argues that "the powers vested in the federal government are clearly defined, so that each state still retain its sovereignty in what concerns its own internal government, and a right to exercise every power of a sovereign state not particularly delegated to the government of the United States." Put differently, the subsequent passage of the Tenth Amendment was intended to avoid a "cavil" created by wholly national advocates intent on twisting the necessary and proper clause to serve a wholly national political agenda.

Throughout the nine-month ratification campaign, proponents of the Constitution defended its lack of a bill of rights. James Wilson's statehouse speech articulated the Federalist position that a bill of rights is unnecessary and improper. He argued that a bill of rights is necessary and proper at the *state* level because "everything which is not reserved, is given." But such a bill would be "superfluous and absurd" at the federal level because "everything which is not given, is reserved."[55] This argument is ingenious at best, since it suggests that the Philadelphia Constitution is identical to the wholly federal Articles of Confederation. Wilson's argument that the Philadelphia Constitution is wholly federal brought a cry of protest from the Antifederalists. They pressed their claims for a bill of rights on the accurate observation that the Constitution, by Madison's five tests, was at least partly national; and by misconstruction of the necessary and proper clause, it could become wholly national.

On November 28, Antifederalist Robert Whitehill made the following observation at the Pennsylvania ratifying convention: "We find in this Constitution [Article I, section 8] an authority is given to make all laws that are necessary to carry it effectually into operation, and what laws are necessary is a consideration left for Congress to decide." John Smilie made a similar remark, prompting Wilson to respond on December 1:

> [John Smilie] strongly insists that the general clause at the end of the eighth section gives to Congress a power of legislating generally; but I cannot conceive by what means he will render the words susceptible of that expansion. Can the words "the Congress shall have power to make all laws, which shall be necessary and proper to carry into execution the foregoing powers" be capable of giving them general legislative power? . . . I trust it is meant that they shall have the power of carrying into effect the laws, which they make under the powers vested in them by this Constitution.[56]

So during ratification, Federalists—including Wilson, author of the necessary and proper clause—argued that, in both structure and powers, the Philadelphia Constitution differs from the Articles of Confederation in degree rather than kind. Accordingly, we are left wondering what the fuss about radically changing the structure and adding powers was all about. On the other hand, Antifederalists were willing to accept a partly national arrangement, but warned that the necessary and proper clause contains the potentiality to turn the Philadelphia Constitution into the Virginia Plan.

IF DEAD, IT WON'T LIE DOWN

According to Kendall and Carey, despite repeated onslaughts—and particularly the onslaught of modern liberalism against the deliberative process—the Philadelphia Constitution was still in good health in the 1960s. Yet Professor Carey has recently announced the death of the Philadelphia Constitution at the hands of the progressives.

I agree that the American regime is not in as good health now as it was prior to the 1960s. I also agree that this has been in no small part due to the ascendancy of the federal judiciary, operating in alliance with the administrative state at the general level and the extensive use of referenda and propositions at the state and local levels. I also agree with the implications of Carey's thesis: that our representatives indeed seem keener to logroll than to deliberate and our executives are even bolder than they in ignoring the language and spirit of the Constitution. And nothing could possibly be more fatal to the

Philadelphia Constitution than the doctrine holding that the Constitution is whatever the Supreme Court says it is. Thus, I do think that the Philadelphia Constitution is in poor health. But from the very beginning, the Philadelphia Constitution had the potential for good or bad health.

Did the progressives hijack and kill the Philadelphia Constitution? No. I think we have been seduced by the empowering potential of the Constitution and inattentive to the Constitution as a document about limits and ambiguities. I do not believe that the Philadelphia Constitution precludes shifting the line of partition between the nation and the states; nor does it preclude altering the relationship of national and federal sovereignty. Nor does it fix once and for all what is necessary and what is proper. It does require that these changes be made by "the deliberate sense of the community" or by "deliberate liquidation," whereby the "meaning be liquidated and ascertained by a series of particular discussions and adjudication."[57] What the Philadelphia Constitution certainly did not need were the heavy-handed decisions of Justice John Marshall and the secessionist writings of John C. Calhoun. Moving in opposite directions, these two men undid the two compromises concerning the federal-national concept and the necessary and proper clause that had been made at the Philadelphia Convention.[58]

Currently, we the people lack *gravitas* in our understanding of the Philadelphia Constitution. We also lack an understanding of the importance the framers attached to the notion that the deliberate sense of the majority should prevail in every generation. The preservation of free government requires a commitment to reason and prudence as well as a decent respect for the tradition of constitutional morality. It all begins with a recurrence to fundamental principles. It continues with a rejuvenated Congress and state assemblies reestablishing the deliberate sense of the community over and against the administrative and judicial branches of government. It ends when we the people provide a sterner answer to the question, "What is it necessary and proper of government at any level to do?" and when we realize that we live under a Constitution, and that the Constitution means what two-thirds of the Congress and three-quarters of the state legislatures say it means. Perhaps then we will find ourselves at another crossroads rather than in a funeral parlor.

James Madison and the Extended Republic

QUENTIN TAYLOR

If asked to identify the chief safeguards of American liberty, few respondents —whether ordinary citizens, textbook authors, or constitutional scholars —would likely place an "extended republic" at the top of their list. In fact, few could be expected to list it at all. The "Bill of Rights" would undoubtedly chart first, followed by "separation of powers," "checks and balances," and "limited government," with perhaps some references to "federalism" and "judicial review." As for the general citizenry, many of whom have never heard of the concept, the failure to identify an "extended republic" as a palladium of liberty is not surprising insofar as "liberty" has become synonymous with "rights," which in turn are almost exclusively linked to the amended Constitution. That scholars—historians, jurists, political scientists—tend to recapitulate the popular wisdom underscores the *consensus omnium* regarding the pillars of American liberty.

While this consensus rests on several decades of constitutional construction (in the courts, in the press, and in classrooms), it does not reflect the consensus reached by the framers of the Constitution or its most incisive and authoritative expositors, viz., the authors of *The Federalist Papers*. The terms "separation of powers," "checks and balances," "limited government," "federalism," and "judicial review" do not appear in the Constitution, although they are all (to one degree or another) provided for or implied. Nor did the original Constitution contain a bill of rights, which was rejected by the framers as a superfluous (and potentially dangerous) addition to a document that explicitly limited the national government to certain enumerated powers. In *The Federalist Papers*,

Publius did speak to those unstated provisions in the Constitution designed to protect freedom and self-government, but in a manner considerably removed from our current understanding. Moreover, he defended the absence of a bill of rights, maintaining (like the framers) that "the Constitution is itself . . . A BILL OF RIGHTS" (*Federalist* 84).[1] And while a statement of rights would be added to the Constitution two years after its ratification, it was clearly not considered essential to the preservation of liberty by the framers or by those who voted for adoption in the state ratifying conventions.[2] Nor did Publius believe that mere "parchment barriers" between state and federal authority or between the departments of the central government were sufficient to prevent abuses of power or encroachments on liberty. The same may be said of our much-vaunted "checks and balances," which are mentioned only once by name in *Federalist* 9.

These "revelations" raise an obvious if awkward question for the purveyors of the conventional constitutional wisdom: How did the framers believe the political order established by the Constitution *would* protect the rights and liberties associated with a free, self-governing people? Admittedly, they placed a due measure of faith in (1) the formal division of power between the state and national governments; (2) provisions for separate and independent branches of the central authority; (3) a series of internal checks among these branches, and; (4) a fundamental law that limited the scope of government to specific delegated powers. Yet they recognized that the horizontal and vertical structures that divided, limited, and checked power were inadequate to sustain a free republic. It was left to Publius to expand on these "auxiliary precautions" and explain how such "inventions of prudence" would operate upon the perennial and peculiar elements of the American polity to render a viable formula for preserving liberty.

The chief perennial element he relied on was *human nature*, primarily in its political dimension. Americans, Publius observed, had exhibited a "genius" for self-government, but they were hardly immune from the vices and foibles that marked other peoples. Accordingly, a realistic (and essentially static) view of human nature—a composite of passion and reason, virtue and vice—served as a constant variable in his political calculations. Another perennial variable was *power*, which was seen to have a natural tendency to expand, encroach, and corrupt. Yet power per se was as necessary for a republic as for a monarchy, and the *lack* of "energy" in government (as the experience under the Articles of Confederation had shown) was no less a threat to the public good than was its abuse. For Publius, the relevant question in establishing a viable republic was not so much the *amount* of power bestowed on the government, but rather its *proper* and *adequate* use.

Among the *peculiar* features of the American scene were a heritage of liberty and a republican *ethos*. Since the early colonial period, Americans had nurtured an independence of spirit and displayed a remarkable capacity for self-rule. For generations they had looked upon themselves as a free people who had made a distinct break with the old (and corrupt) world of Europe. By the 1760s, when authorities in England began to "tighten the screws" on the colonists, the response was immediate and decisive. From that time forward, American rebels and revolutionaries marched toward their republican destiny. By the time independence was achieved, most Americans had firmly embraced the republican faith and confidently looked to a republican future. The difficulties, disappointments, and frustrations that marked "the critical period" which followed may have dimmed the hopes of some, but it did not shake Americans' fundamental belief in republican values or self-government. Such developments did, however, convince many (including the most prescient) that the present system was incapable of preserving their cherished values and institutions. The fears evoked by Shays' rebellion in the winter of 1786–87 only reinforced the growing conviction that if republicanism was to survive, Americans would have to substantially re-edify their frame of government.

The men who met in Philadelphia in mid-1787 shared a basic understanding of the national landscape and a common approach to the problems of political architecture as they labored to "save the Revolution" from the very forces it had unleashed. In doing so there was much they could take for granted, including the perennial and particular variables noted above. This *donnée* would prove a great advantage, but it did not provide a positive guide to the formidable task before them. That task (as Publius recounted) was "[t]o secure the public good and private rights . . . and at the same time preserve the spirit and form of popular government . . ." (*Federalist* 10). The very formulation implied a possible conflict between order and stability on one hand and consent and self-rule on the other. It was the determination to reconcile the two that drove the proceedings in Philadelphia and shaped the document that emerged. And while the provisions therein gave every hope of securing the ends of "a more perfect union," the signers understood that the long-term success of their undertaking rested as much on intangible qualities such as national character as on the intricacies of constitutional mechanics. The influence of *extra*-constitutional factors was certainly a common concern, but only one framer singled out a particular feature of the American scene that promised to provide "a republican remedy for the diseases most incident to republican government." The diseases in question were *factions*; the remedy prescribed was an "extended republic"; the attending physician was James Madison.

The notion that "factions" were the bane of the body politic was as old as Aristotle, and history was replete with examples of commonwealths torn asunder and brought to ruin by one group of citizens chasing its interests at the expense of another. The experience under the Articles had convinced Madison and others that short of significant and timely reforms, the American experiment in republican government—indeed the cause of republicanism itself —was doomed to share a similar fate. And since factions, particularly *majority* factions, were viewed as the particular curse of *republics*, it was a desideratum of statecraft to confront this threat in designing a regime that would vindicate the republican creed. Madison, more than any of his colleagues, was familiar with the turbulent histories of republics and confederacies, and drew sharp analogies between the causes of their troubles and the sources of America's woes. He was also well-versed in modern political theory, from which he drew principles deemed relevant to the task of reform. Combined with a vast knowledge of public affairs gained through years of experience in Congress and the Virginia legislature, Madison was arguably the best-informed man in the nation. When he joined his fellow delegates in the Philadelphia State House in May 1787 he was also the best prepared.

On the basis of what transpired that summer, Madison became known to posterity as "the father of the Constitution." While he rightly denied it was "the offspring of a single brain," his overall contribution to framing, explaining, ratifying, and amending that document merits the palm of distinction. Students of the Convention are fond of pointing out the discrepancies between many of Madison's proposals and the finished product, yet none gainsay his formidable influence and weighty contributions to the process.[3] This said, it is not Madison the framer, but Madison the *theorist* of the Constitution who has captured the imagination of modern scholars and framed the debate over the intent of the founders and the nature of the political system they devised.

Madison's status as the key to unlocking the "secrets of the system" rests almost entirely with his contributions to *The Federalist Papers*. It is a reputation full of ironies.[4] The idea of writing a series of essays defending the Constitution and supporting its ratification did not originate with Madison, nor was he selected as Hamilton's main collaborator. The illness of John Jay allowed Madison to join the project, but he penned less than half the number of essays Hamilton contributed. As the decades rolled by after ratification, the Supreme Court made occasional use of *The Federalist Papers*, while prominent jurists, statesmen, and scholars contributed to its canonization as the leading commentary on the Constitution.[5] It was only with the appearance of Charles Beard's *An Economic Interpretation of the Constitution* in 1913, however, that Madison was identified as *the* mind behind the machine. Beard was first to single out Madison's *Federalist* 10 as the Rosetta stone of the framers' intentions. Given the timing of his explosive charges (the high-water mark of progressivism), Beard's neo-Marxist analysis of No. 10 was enormously influential on a generation of scholars, who in turn popularized it among a generation of students. While Beard's more extravagant claims were clipped by subsequent research, his notion that Madison's discussion of factions in No. 10 held the key to the motives behind the Constitution not only survived but remains the prevailing orthodoxy. Whether consciously or not it informs virtually every analysis of the American political system, not to mention accounts of the framing and ratification of the Constitution. Entire theories of politics (economic, pluralist, behaviorist) have either been inspired or influenced by Madison's No. 10, which—along with its companion piece No. 51—invariably appears alongside the Declaration of Independence and the Constitution as appendices to U.S. government textbooks.[6]

The searing focus on Madison as the mastermind behind the Constitution has resulted in one final irony. Not only has his performance as Publius largely overshadowed his subsequent (and highly notable) contributions as congressional leader, party organizer, secretary of state, and president, but this very performance has been used by modern scholars to critically question the achievement of the framers, and especially Madison, as architects of the American system. Of course, criticism of the framers (and Publius) can be traced back to the Antifederalists during the ratification debates.[7] Opposition was largely blunted by the adoption of the Constitution, the addition of a bill of rights, and the notable improvement in conditions which followed, but many of the fears raised during ratification kindled into controversies, and Publius was never without an influential detractor or two. The sectional crisis of the 1850s and the Civil War which followed signaled a collapse in the theory and practice of the "compound republic," rendering the solicitations of

Publius on the system's ability "to break and control the violence of faction" temporarily obsolete. Only after Reconstruction—another era of constitutional aberration—was it possible to reapply the Madisonian model *in toto*, albeit to a landscape significantly altered by the Fourteenth Amendment and westward expansion.

If these developments appeared to diminish the relevance of the political and constitutional musings of the framers, the emergence of "modern America" in the late nineteenth and early twentieth centuries only accentuated the distance between past and present. Ironically, it was precisely at this time, when industry and technology were transforming the face of America, that the framers and *The Federalist Papers* reemerged in the intellectual life of the nation.[8] New and improved editions of the papers appeared and the Supreme Court would cite Publius in some of its most important cases.[9] Moreover, historians and political scientists began to examine the American founding from a fresh perspective, a development stimulated by the conjunction of two events: the rise of "professional" academia and turn-of-the-century reform movements. The confluence of the "new" methods and the "new" politics was duly reflected in the ideological approach and revisionist findings of the "new" scholarship.

James Allen Smith's *The Spirit of American Government* (1907) is typically identified as the first work to substantially revise the traditional account of the framers. Smith emphasized the undemocratic, class-based outlook of the men who gathered in Philadelphia and the reactionary nature of their handiwork. Charles Beard's more famous polemic of 1913 went a step further by providing detailed "evidence" to support the charge that the framers were primarily motivated by personal economic interests. As noted above, Beard turned to the tenth *Federalist* to illustrate the economic foundations of the Constitution, which he found in Madison's theory of factions. The Beardian thesis, including the focus on No. 10, revolutionized the study of the founding and *The Federalist Papers*. Prominent progressive and liberal historians, such as Vernon Parrington and Richard Hofstadter, embraced the revisionist reading and heartily took sides with the "opposing" American tradition (agrarian, populist, democratic) sadly bypassed by the hard-boiled Federalists.[10]

Having been seized upon as the "Marx of the ruling class" and chief architect of the American Thermidor, a number of influential political scientists descended on the battered Madison like vultures on a carcass. E. E. Shattschneider, Robert Dahl, and James MacGregor Burns, all presidents of the

American Political Science Association, trained their analytical lens on *Federalist* 10 and 51 and found their author guilty of constructing a system deficient in logic, undemocratic in spirit, and self-defeating in practice.[11] It was Dahl's *Preface to Democratic Theory* (1956), however, that had the largest impact among the profession, similar to Beard's influence among historians. This is not to say that the revisionist reading of Madison and the framers ever held the field uncontested or even gained the loyalty of a majority of scholars in its more extreme form. It has nonetheless profoundly shaped current thinking about the founding and has given rise to an enormous and remarkably diverse literature on the sources and meaning of early American political thought. Beginning in the 1970s, the focus of many scholars shifted to elucidating the various strands of Revolutionary-era thought and the evolution of republican doctrine.

While not as overtly ideological or sophistic as Beard or Dahl, historians such as Bernard Bailyn, Gordon Wood, and John Pocock inspired a new "school" of interpretation that associated *The Federalist Papers* with "the end of classical politics" and the triumph of modern, individualistic liberalism.[12] Conversely, many looked back (à la Beard, Parrington, and Hofstadter) with wistful nostalgia on the "road not taken" as embodied in the egalitarian, participatory, and democratic vision of Jefferson and the Antifederalists. Naturally, others took exception to such attempts to construct a serviceable history for reviving communitarian politics, but the resulting body of scholarship did serve to place early American political thought at the forefront of the discipline.[13]

Still others, including political scientists and academic lawyers, continued to hammer away at the Constitution itself. Throughout the 1980s and 1990s titles such as *The Case Against the Constitution, The Constitution and the Pride of Reason, The Rise and Fall of Democracy in Early America*, and *The Frozen Republic: How the Constitution is Paralyzing Democracy* fell from the presses. In 2001, forty-five years after his "devastating" critique of Madison, Robert Dahl again asked *How Democratic Is the American Constitution?* (His answer had not changed.) In each case, the framers, and particularly Publius, were singled out as reactionaries, bunglers, or obstructionists whose handiwork and rationalizing gloss stands in need of revision.[14]

The contrarian view still represents a "minority report" on the founding, but it does serve the purpose of challenging the hagiography that sometimes surrounds the framers and their "most wonderful work."[15] As such, each generation is stirred to attack, defend, revise, and reexamine the men and ideas of

America's seminal epoch. Yet any student of the founding can easily find himself overwhelmed by the welter of contrasting and conflicting opinion over what the framers *really* meant or intended, not to mention the significance of their achievement. And as citizens of the United States continue to live under the (amended) Constitution, it is not altogether idle to seek clarity on such questions in this clouded atmosphere. I say "clarity" advisedly, since questions of intent, meaning, and significance are rarely subject to definitive explanation, and this certainly applies in the present case. It is virtually impossible to discern precisely what the thirty-nine men who signed the Constitution meant by all of its provisions, much less how they envisioned the new system would operate in practice. If this is true of the framers it is even more so in the case of the hundreds of delegates who voted for adoption in the state ratifying conventions, where the Constitution was often debated at length. The records of the conventions, federal and state, allow one to trace the process by which the Constitution was framed and contested, but like reading the transcript of a trial, we are left with a great deal of argument but little understanding.[16]

For these reasons it has been customary since the time of the Constitution's ratification to consult what by near-universal acclaim is the single best treatment of the contents and projected workings of that document: *The Federalist Papers*. This is not the place to catalogue the many encomia to the genius of "Publius," but his eighty-five essays written between September 1787 and May 1788 uniquely capture the thinking that resulted in the Constitution. *The Federalist Papers* are the most signal source for understanding not only the original Constitution, but the foundations of the polity for which it furnished a government. For anyone interested in uncovering the roots of the American political order, *The Federalist Papers* remain the place to start, even if they do not always provide the final word.

As suggested above, interpretations of the meaning and significance of *The Federalist Papers* vary considerably, and the number of divergent readings of No. 10 alone is enough to "jade the brains of any poor sinner."[17] While hoping to avoid further confusion, the remainder of this essay will explore what is typically regarded as at once the most original and enigmatic teaching in *The Federalist Papers*: Madison's theory of the "extended republic." What would appear to distinguish this feature of his political thinking is (1) its non-institutional or extra-constitutional nature; and (2) its alleged capacity to supply "a republican remedy for the diseases most incident to republican government" (No. 10). More accurately, it was the quality of extensiveness *in conjunc-*

tion with the "proper structure of the Union" that he lauded for its "tendency to break and control the violence of faction." It will be recalled that Madison identified "factions" as the greatest threat to the rights of person and property in republics and the principal cause of their chronic instability. Hence to have discovered a "cure" for factions consistent with republican principles at a time when many had come to doubt the future of popular government in America appeared like a stroke of providential genius to its troubled supporters.

What made this "discovery" all the more remarkable was that it appeared to reverse the prevailing orthodoxy on the relation between size of territory and form of government. Montesquieu, perhaps the most widely read and respected political author in America, had argued that a republic could only be maintained in a relatively small area, while a monarchy was necessary to govern a large one.[18] Yet it was not Madison but Hamilton (in *Federalist* 9) who first publicly confronted the conventional wisdom (a mainstay of Antifederalist critics) and found in Montesquieu's treatment of the "confederate republic" a compelling support for the proposed Union. Similarly, it was Hamilton who first underscored the fatal dangers of "domestic faction" in republics and identified an extensive republic among the advances in the "science of politics" that "will be of the utmost moment to the peace and liberty of the States. . . ." He specifically refers to "the ENLARGEMENT of the ORBIT within which such systems are to revolve" as contributing to a capacity "to suppress faction and to guard the internal tranquility of States . . ." Far from precluding the union of liberty and security, a confederation over an extended territory has (in the words of Montesquieu) "all the internal force of a republican, together with the external advantages of a monarchical, government."[19]

If Hamilton cleared the deck for Madison to focus on these "advantages" in No. 10, it is the latter who deserves credit for first developing the theory, applying it to the concept of representation and elevating it to an article of republican faith. The theory itself was (as Hamilton noted) "not a new idea"—it was adumbrated by the author of *L'esprit des lois* and developed in some detail by David Hume in his political essays. Based on close parallels in conception and wording, historian Douglas Adair identified Hume as the main source behind Madison's focus on the problem of factions and his solution of the extended republic.[20] The notion that Hume, and the Scottish Enlightenment more generally, exercised a profound influence on the American founding was subsequently popularized by Garry Wills, whose "Publius" spoke with a marked Scottish accent.[21]

If Madison borrowed heavily from Hume (and it appears he did) he left little if any direct evidence of it. Nowhere in his writings on the extended republic (whether in his pre-Convention papers, Convention speeches, or post-Convention papers) does he cite Hume by name or direct quotation. Of course, then as now, authors are often loath to acknowledge their sources, and there were good ideological grounds for not citing a confirmed Tory such as Hume.[22] The point here is that Madison identified the problem of faction and highlighted its relevance well before his contributions to *The Federalist Papers*: his "remedy" was not a hastily contrived response to Antifederalist attacks.[23]

Yet for all the attention lavished on the "extended republic," few scholars have gone beyond its classic statement in Nos. 10 and 51 to explore its pre–*Federalist Papers* origins or postratification history in Madison's thought. To do so would not only clarify the *idea* in its various relations, but assist in gauging its *significance* against the balance of his political and constitutional views. Yet even this would fail to provide a full and comprehensive account of the "extended republic" in the founding era. In addition to tracing its development in Madison, it would be necessary to consider its place in the thought of others; viz., (1) his colleagues at the Philadelphia Convention; (2) Hamilton and Jay in *The Federalist Papers*; (3) the Antifederalists; and (4) postratification observers. Such an undertaking is well beyond the present scope, but it does suggest a more fruitful approach than an exclusive focus on Publius. A few examples will illustrate how this approach not only promises to expand our understanding of this key and elusive concept, but also how it points to a reassessment of its status in Madison's thought and American constitutional theory.

Students of Madison often note that the polished arguments of *Federalist* 10 and 51 are substantially prefigured in his pre-Convention notes and Convention speeches.[24] Some trace his concern with majority factions to his opposition to a proposed tax to support religion in his native Virginia. In his influential (albeit anonymous) "Memorial and Remonstrance" (1785), he recognized that "the will of the majority" was the only existing rule "by which any question which may divide a Society, can be ultimately determined," but he also noted "that the majority may trespass on the rights of the minority."[25] Here Madison provides the first clear formulation of the chief paradox of popular rule. Resolving this paradox—reconciling a canon of republicanism (majority rule) with a principle of justice (minority rights)—became a focus of his thought in the months prior to the Convention. The result was "Vices of the Political System of the United States" (1787), which took aim less at the defects of the Articles of Confederation (well known to Madison from his years in Congress) than at the derelictions of the state governments.[26]

The problem of majority faction emerges from Madison's indictment of the "multiplicity," "mutability," and "injustice" of state laws.[27] This problem is "all the more alarming . . . because it brings more into question the fundamental principle of republican Government, that the majority who rule in such Governments, are the safest Guardians both of public Good and of private rights." In order to redeem this principle—Madison's task—it was necessary to first identify the "causes" of the "evil" and then provide a "remedy." The causes are two: "a majority in the legislative Councils" with interests contrary to the public good, and "still more fatal . . . the people themselves." After rejecting the customary restraints on human conduct, and noting the "notorious factions & oppressions which take place in corporate towns . . . and in little republics," Madison introduces "an enlargement of the sphere" as a solution for *popular* tyranny. On one hand, it is less likely that a "common impulse or passion" will be perceived *as such*, should it occur in a majority; and *should* it suffer to occur, the extent of territory will impede the formation of "requisite [majority] combinations." On the other hand, the various interests in society are "broken" (i.e., dispersed) in a large country, serve to "check each other," and "have less opportunity of communication and concert."

The solution to a tyrannical majority is not directly addressed, but Madison does adumbrate the other crucial function of an extended republic: "a process of elections as will most certainly extract from the mass of the Society the purest and noblest characters which it contains. . . ." Nor does he enter into the somewhat disingenuous distinction between a democracy and a republic that marks *Federalist* 10, although his reference to "corporate towns" and "little republics" hints at it. Here the *representative* principle, which in No. 10 serves "to refine and enlarge the public views," is simply taken for granted. He does, however, underscore the need for a government that is "sufficiently neutral" to adjust disparate interests and adjudicate partisan disputes while remaining faithful to the public good. This is the second paradox Madison confronted in his effort to "redeem the honor of the republican name."[28] In "Vices" he looks to "a modification of the Sovereignty" as the means of establishing a neutral power, but he rejects as defective the methods of "absolute Monarchies" and "small Republics." The "evils" peculiar to each, Madison suggests, cannot be fully excised, but by limiting the one and extending the other they can be reduced. "As a limited monarchy tempers the evils of an absolute one; so an extensive Republic meliorates the administration of a small Republic." This is a further dimension of the *positive* or *constructive* side of an extended republic: it not only obstructs untoward combinations of citizens, but enhances the neutrality of the government itself, presumably through the electoral process.

That Madison had not satisfactorily solved the problem of neutrality in "Vices" is clear from a letter to George Washington written around the same time. Once more "some disinterested & dispassionate umpire" is identified as the "great desideratum" of republican government, but instead of offering an "enlargement of the sphere" as a solution, he cites a "negative" or veto over the laws of the states.[29] This striking shift is evident in the absence of "small Republics" from the neutrality equation, and the focus on "Kingly prerogative" as the "absolutely necessary" means for checking the vices of the states. Madison cautiously projects that the national authority will show itself "sufficiently disinterested" and "sufficiently restrained" to exercise the negative with sufficient neutrality. The projection itself would appear to rest on the "extractive" function of the extended republic. Yet in pointing to the Confederation Congress as an example (whose members were appointed by the very state legislatures he condemned) the inference is defeated.

The discrepancy between "Vices" and the letter to Washington raises the question of whether Madison, on the eve of the Convention, changed his mind about the "great desideratum" of republican government? A review of the Convention records suggests that the discrepancy was more apparent than real. In all probability Madison expected the national veto and the extended republic to work in tandem to combat disorders in the states and promote neutrality in the government.[30] In the letter to Washington he called for "a negative *in all cases whatsoever*," a provision which (in milder form) reappeared in article six of the Virginia Plan. On May 31, just two days after it was introduced, the veto power was adopted unanimously without debate.[31] The capstone of the Madisonian edifice merely awaited the raising of the foundation.

By an interesting coincidence, the first reference to the "extent" of the country occurred on the next day. It was not James Madison, however, but James Wilson who first observed that the "great" size of the country (along with its republican "manners") dictated "nothing but a great confederated Republic" for America. If Madison spoke on the matter that day it is not recorded in his notes, yet Hamilton's contain the following entry next to Madison's name: "The way to prevent a majority from having an interest to

oppress the minority is to enlarge the sphere." Perhaps this thought was communicated privately, but it serves as a link between "Vices" and Madison's
speech of June 6. In that speech, the problem of majority faction, with its roots
in divergent economic interests, is once more cited as the bane of republics,
and "enlarg[ing] the sphere" is again embraced as "the only defence agst. the
inconveniences of democracy consistent with the democratic form of Govt."

For Madison, the "democratic form" required that at least one of the two
branches of the national legislature be directly elected by the people. In addition to avoiding an undue influence by the state governments, this method had
the advantage of "securing better representatives," presumably through large
electoral districts. Yet the connection between *size* of territory and *quality* of
representatives is never made—at least not in Madison's notes. We find neither
the "process of elections" in "Vices" nor the "proportion of fit characters" in
Federalist 10. Instead, the injunction to "enlarge the sphere" is advanced for its
negative function of preventing the formation of oppressive majorities.

Only in the notes of Rufus King and Hamilton is the missing ("positive")
element supplied. King credits Madison with asserting that "[t]he election
may safely be made by the People if you enlarge the Sphere of Election—Experience proves it—if bad elections have taken place from the people, it will
generally be found to have happened in small Districts." Hamilton's remarks
are even more revealing. After listing the twofold advantage of an enlarged
sphere, he writes: "There is truth in both these principles but they do not
conclude so strongly as he supposes. . . ." Even a process "calculated to refine" representation cannot remove "all the passions of popular assemblies"
or prevent the rise of an "influential demagogue." Hamilton appears to have
kept these shrewd doubts to himself for the time, but his survey of the general
situation in his five-hour speech of June 18 "almost led him to despair that a
Republican Govt. could be established over so great an extent." All this from
the man who (*qua* Publius) would champion "the ENLARGEMENT of the
ORBIT" for its ability "to suppress faction and to guard the internal tranquility of the States. . . ."

Given the vital role of the "extended republic" in *The Federalist Papers*,
its minor and equivocal appearance in the Convention suggests that Madison, like Hamilton, elevated its value for producing "fit characters" beyond
his considered view. It will be recalled that the Virginia Plan called for the
popular election of the lower house of the legislature, and the election of the
upper chamber by members of the first from a list of candidates supplied by

the state legislatures. Accordingly, only the lower chamber would result from "a process of elections" based on the principle of extension; candidates for the upper house might be drawn from a narrow clique. Moreover, Madison believed it was the popular branch of the legislature that was most prone to dissension and instability and that stood in need of a "salutary check" in the upper, "the great anchor of the Government."[32] Bicameralism was certainly a useful device for countering the defects of a unitary legislature, but Madison's characterization of the House of Representatives and Senate runs counter to the principle of extension; indeed, it turns it on its head. If the people can be trusted to make a "fit choice" in selecting members of the House, why not in the case of the Senate? Yet it is the Senate which he would assign the task of moderating the actions of the very body that elected it!

The Senate's superiority as outlined by Madison in *Federalist* 62 and 63 has nothing to do with its mode of selection but rather is ascribed to its smaller size on one hand, and the longer tenure, greater dignity, and expansive views of its members on the other. In the Convention, his principal concern was, first, to establish proportional representation in the upper house, and second, to prevent placing selection of its members in the hands of the state legislatures. He failed on both counts. At the time he considered equality in the Senate and election by the states *fatal* defects: the one "must infuse mortality into a Constitution we wished to last forever," the other would replicate "only another edition of [the existing] Cong[ress]. . . ."[33]

Once the Great Compromise was effected on July 16, Madison might have sought to apply the principle of extension to the Senate by reopening the question of its mode of selection. During the first debate on this issue (June 7), he opposed creating too large a number as well as vesting the selection with the state legislatures, but he did not advocate popular election. (Apparently he was holding fast to the method proposed in the Virginia Plan.) It was James Wilson who made the "Madisonian" argument for enlarging the sphere in selecting the Senate. "He was for an election by the people in large districts which wd. be most likely to obtain men of intelligence & uprightness." Madison, who spoke next, considered the possibility of popular election, but did not endorse it or even allude to the argument he had advanced in "Vices" and would advance as Publius. Conversely, others argued that "refinement" of representation, the selection of "fit men," and a "permanent & independent" upper house were best secured through appointment by the state legislatures. The vote to do so carried 9 to 2.

Madison did recognize the need "to fill all offices with the fittest characters, & draw the wisest & most worthy citizens into the Legislative service" and frequently underscored the danger of majority factions, but he did not identify an extended republic as a factor in securing the former and thwarting the latter. His call for "the fittest characters," for example, followed his motion to allow members of Congress to hold other federal offices. According to the notes of Robert Yates, he rejected the idea that "patriotism" alone would attract men of talent without the prospect of adequate remuneration. "If we expect to call forth useful characters, we must hold out allurements." As in *Federalist* 51, Madison adopts the "policy of supplying . . . the defect of better motives," but not through the "auxiliary precautions" of separation of powers, checks and balances, and federalism. Rather, he enlists the "Hamiltonian" strategy of redirecting "ambition" and "interest" "in order to make them subservient to the public good."

Madison would go on to emphasize the need to "divide" and "check" power as the principal means of achieving the chief end of government: "to protect the people agst. their rulers" and "to protect [the people] agst. . . . . themselves." The emphasis, however, is typically directed at the lower house and its electors, the people. Because both are "liable to temporary errors," owing to a want of "competent knowledge" and "from fickleness and passion," they may be "tempted to commit injustice on the minority." Hence the need for a second house, "sufficiently respectable for its wisdom & virtue" to withstand the "vortex" of the popular will. Again, the one institution directly drawn from the country's "extensiveness" is identified as the *most likely source* of oppression and injustice, and the one that stood in greatest need of restraint. As for the prospect of the legislature as a whole becoming a menacing "vortex" of power, Madison turned to checks and balances, "the necessity of giving every defensive authority to the other departments," neither of which partook of extensiveness.

A final example drawn from the Convention further supports the suspicion that the principle of extension—as a condition for selecting representatives —was conspicuously absent from Madison's reasoning. In *Federalist* 10, he argued that "extensive republics are more favorable to the election of proper guardians of the public weal" for two reasons. First, an extensive republic will contain a greater "proportion of fit characters" to choose from due to its larger population. Second, the large number of electors for each representative will hinder "unworthy candidates" from successfully plying "the vicious arts" of electioneering, and "will be more likely to . . . [select] men who possess the most attractive merit and the most diffusive and established characters." Clearly, Madison's argument for "a greater probability of a fit choice" in the large electoral districts of an extensive republic rests on certain (uncritical) assumptions that he chose to ignore. This aside, a "fit choice" is also predicated on a proper ratio of electors to representatives. If the ratio is too great the representative will be "too little acquainted" with local conditions and interests, but if too small, he will be "unduly attached" to these and unable to encompass objects of national interest. In *Federalist* 55, Madison defended the ratio for the lower house (1:30,000) established by the Convention. Some opponents of the Constitution had argued that the sixty-five members who would compose the first House of Representatives were too few to adequately (or safely) represent the people of America. In response, Publius did not meet all the Antifederalist objections and ultimately relied upon the "genius" of the American people, the "spirit" of the state legislatures, and the "principles" of the citizenry to thwart any attack on popular liberties or a betrayal of the national interest from this quarter.

In the Convention, Madison assumed quite a different posture. After the committee assigned to establish the number of representatives in the lower house for each state issued its report, he "moved that the number allowed to each state be doubled." That number stood at sixty-five, which he deemed "too small a number to represent the whole inhabitants of the U. States; they would not possess enough of the confidence of the people, and wd. be too sparsely taken from the people, to bring with them all the local information which would be frequently wanted. Double the number will not be too great even with the future additions from New States." Here Madison sounds more like an earnest opponent of the Constitution than its chief defender. In *Federalist* 10, he argued that "there is a mean" in the ratio of electors to representatives, and he implied (No. 55) that the ratio rendering just sixty-five members for the lower house was within the mean. In fairness, he does emphasize that the number will grow rapidly and within twenty-five years rise to some two hundred members. Yet because the ratio would remain the same (indeed increase once an optimal number had been reached), Madison's initial misgivings speak to the limits of his faith in extensiveness as a condition for procuring "fit characters." In conjunction with his admission that at some point extensiveness per se loses its capacity to perform its dual function of checking faction and refining public opinion, these doubts present a curious contrast to the confident predictions of Publius.

Adopting proportional representation, augmenting the powers of the central government, and authorizing it to act directly on the people were all desiderata of Madison's plan of reform, but without the negative on state laws he doubted the work of the Convention could achieve its ends. In a letter to Jefferson written shortly before the Convention adjourned, he predicted that if adopted, the plan "will neither effectually *answer* its *national object* nor prevent the local *mischiefs* which every where *excite disgusts agst state governments*."[34] Two weeks later, in a missive to Edmund Pendleton, he took a neutral stance toward the document to which he had affixed his name just three days earlier.[35] Indeed, his correspondence of this time is bereft of an unequivocal statement of support for its adoption, although he does take note of the emerging configuration of forces, pro and con.

Madison's pledge to supply Jefferson with the "grounds" of his opinion that the plan was defective was fulfilled in his famous letter of October 24. Noting the Convention's rejection of the negative on state laws, he reasserted his conviction that such a check was "necessary" and that without it "our system involves the evil of *imperia in imperio*."[36] That he viewed this "evil" as fatal is reinforced by his characterization of the Constitution as creating "a feudal system of republics." The hallmark of this system was "a continual struggle between the head and the inferior members" until one side had overcome the other. In this sense the "system" proposed was even *worse*, for while the feudal sovereign was independent of the member republics, "[i]n the American Constitution the general authority will be derived entirely from the subordinate authorities." Such an arrangement was well-calculated to prevent encroachments on the states, but, "continually sensible of the abridgment of their power," the states will be "stimulated by ambition to resume the surrendered portion of it" by encroachments on the general government. Madison does entertain the prospect that the "[j]udicial authority . . . will keep the States within their proper limits, and supply the place of a negative on their laws"; yet "it is more convenient to prevent the passage of a law, than to declare it void after it has passed," particularly insofar as noncompliance would necessitate a "recurrence to force."

Madison also considered the negative essential "to secure individuals agst. encroachments on their rights." Had not alarm at violations of rights by the states been a greater impetus for the movement that resulted in the Convention than the palpable inadequacies of the Confederation itself? "A reform therefore which does not make provision for private rights, must be materially defective." The prohibitions on states printing money, violating contracts, and so on, are deemed inadequate to prevent willful majorities from acts of injustice. Once more Madison was faced with the perennial paradox of popular government: how to reconcile majority rule with minority rights. If the general and the state governments are structured much the same and operate on the same principles, how will private rights be more secure under the former?

Had Madison not already formulated an answer in his pre-Convention studies, his bleak post-Convention forecast would seem to require a confession of defeat. Yet just as he had found a silver lining at the failed Annapolis conference, Madison repaired to the extended republic in order to rescue the Constitution from "the political monster of *imperium in imperio*."[37] Since the Constitution was "materially defective," it was necessary to step outside its framework to discover a remedy. In the principle of extensiveness, he not only found *a* solution to the problem of majority faction, but the *only* one consistent with the "true principles of Republican Government."[38] He also found a solution to the related problem of "neutrality" in the form of the general government, although he does not say how this neutrality will come about.

Yet for all its anticipations of the tenth *Federalist*, Madison's account relies exclusively on the negative or defensive function of extensiveness to restrain unjust combinations. "*Divide et impera*, the reprobated axiom of tyranny, is under certain qualifications, the only policy, by which a republic can be administered on just principles."[39] As Publius, he would avoid such stark and paradoxical language, and conjoin the atomizing function of an extended territory with the positive quality of refining and enlarging the public councils. He would also have to acknowledge that even in an extended republic, the national legislature could not be expected to exercise a stoic neutrality, since its members were necessarily both "parties" and "judges" (*Federalist* 10).

Whatever his ultimate faith in the efficacy of extensiveness as a regulative principle, the letter to Jefferson signals the conversion of Madison the skeptic to the cause of ratification.[40] If he continued to nurse reservations about the defects of the Constitution, he kept them under his *chapeau bras*, and within a month of denouncing the "feudal system of republics" it created, he was proclaiming "a republican remedy for the diseases most incident to republican government."[41] Again, it was not merely the "extent" of the Union, but also its "proper structure" that promised the cure, a fact sometimes forgotten or obscured in discussions of the extended republic. This is why *Federalist* 10 and

51 are best read as companion pieces, the first providing the extra-constitutional, horizontal principle of republicanism, and the second superimposing a
series of formal, vertical provisions for securing the responsible use of power.
The fourteenth paper, which is often overlooked, serves as an intermediate
stone in the edifice. Here the case for an extended republic is reinforced with
arguments ranging from the limited jurisdiction of the general government to
"new improvements" in transportation.

That Madison found argument alone insufficient in "selling" the idea of
an extended republic is clear from the final paragraph of No. 14. *The Federalist Papers* are filled with exhortations aimed at stirring the reader's sense of
honor, candor, and patriotism. Nowhere else does Publius soar to such sustained heights of impassioned eloquence. He implores his "fellow citizens"
to "[h]earken not" to those who condemn an extended federal republic as
"a political novelty in the world," a form of government never recognized
"in the theories of the wildest projector," a system which "rashly attempts
what . . . is impossible to accomplish." For Publius such rhetoric was not
merely *de trop*, but "unhallowed," and "poison" to the "mingled blood" shed
by Americans to secure their "sacred rights" and "consecrate their Union." An
extended republic may indeed be a novelty, but even more "novel," "wild,"
and "rash" is attempting to preserve those rights without a firm union. The
American Revolution was itself a novelty, as are the "fabrics of [state] governments which have no model on the face of the globe." Why, then, "is the
experiment of an extended republic to be rejected, merely because it may
comprise what is new?"

Having moved from *argumentum* (No. 10) to *hortatio* (No. 14) in extolling
the virtues of extensiveness, Madison felt compelled to return to the subject
with one last tour de force. As such, *Federalist* 51 represents the culmination of
his thoughts on the extended republic and the capstone of his political theory.
If No. 10 establishes the tendency of an extensive territory to prevent the
combination of factious majorities on one hand and produce capable leaders
on the other, No. 51 superimposes the constitutional mechanisms that will
"oblige [government] to control itself": separation of powers, bicameralism,
checks and balances.[42] These are the "auxiliary precautions" which will serve
to prevent usurpations of public authority when "better motives" are lacking.
In contradistinction to the pluralist school, such "inventions of prudence"
were not viewed by Madison as substitutes for responsible, informed leadership, but as essential barriers against prospective abuses and dereliction. Nor

did he understand the "public good" as the product of a "clash of interests" or the common denominator of coalition politics, but as an objective if at times elusive entity that he identifies with "the permanent and aggregate interests of the community."

Upon asserting that the federal constitution is in greater conformity with the principle of separation of powers than the constitutions of the states, Madison points to two additional principles recommending the plan. The first is *federalism*, the division of political power between state and national authority. Along with a separation of powers at both levels, a "compound republic" provides a "double security . . . to the rights of the people," with each government controlling the other while simultaneously controlling itself. With the second point, Madison reintroduces the argument of No. 10, the tendency of extensiveness to break society "into so many parts, interests and classes of citizens, that the rights of individuals, or of the minority, will be in little danger from interested combinations of the majority." There is, however, an apparent anomaly here. First, he only mentions the *atomizing* aspect of extensiveness and omits the positive function of enhancing the "probability of a fit choice." Recall that it was just this feature that gave an *extended* republic such an advantage over democracies and small republics in selecting representatives "whose wisdom may best discern the true interest of their country, and whose patriotism and love of justice will be least likely to sacrifice it to temporary or partial considerations." If, as Madison claims, "[j]ustice is the end of government," that end will best be attained through a choice of representatives of "enlightened views and virtuous sentiments." Yet this component is missing from the restatement in *Federalist* 51. (It is Hamilton who in No. 27 argues that senators will possess "greater knowledge and more comprehensive information in the national councils, *on account of the extent of the country* . . . [emphasis added].") Rather, the reader is told that extensiveness will not only block "oppressive combinations" of the majority, but also that when a majority of the whole *does* occur, it "could seldom take place upon any other principles than those of justice and the general good." Such a claim was perhaps implicit in No. 10, but by directly linking "justice and the general good" with the "negative" function of extensiveness, Madison manages to square the circle, placing the final stone in the republican edifice.

In placing such faith in extensiveness, a noninstitutional feature of the proposed system, Publius had traveled a considerable distance from the man who found that system "materially defective" just months before. It is interesting, however, that he made such little use of the argument in the Virginia ratifying convention, where he emerged as the Constitution's principal defender.[43] He did underscore the perennial problem of majority factions, and how religious pluralism in America had preserved religious freedom, but he did not link either to extensiveness or the principle of representation. In fairness, Madison was primarily occupied with responding to attacks on the Constitution as opposed to expounding its virtues. And yet he did provide an answer to what some observers have identified as a principal oversight in his theory of the extended republic: the assumption that the people will likely select "fit characters" for office. In response to the assertion that it is foolish to place too much confidence in the people's representatives owing to the possibility of an unfit choice, Madison provides the missing piece:

> But I go on this great republican principle, that the people will have virtue and intelligence enough to select men of virtue and wisdom. Is there no virtue among us? If there be not, we are in a wretched situation. No theoretical checks—no form of government can render us secure. To suppose that any form of government will secure liberty or happiness without any virtue in the people, is a chimerical idea. If there be sufficient virtue and intelligence in the community, it will be exercised in the selection of these men.[44]

In *The Federalist Papers* and elsewhere Madison had frequently pointed to the inadequacy of "parchment barriers" to prevent abuses of power, yet never before had he so frankly admitted that no amount of contrivance could secure a popular government without "sufficient virtue and intelligence" among the people. This is the great (and largely veiled) desideratum of his political teaching; it is the wager made on behalf of republicanism, for "[r]epublican government presupposes the existence of these qualities in a higher degree than any other form" (No. 55). Without this article of faith—a faith Madison found reasonable in light of American experience—not even the wisest political architect could design a system for posterity. And so while even a society of many Socrates may require "auxiliary precautions" to prevent depredations by the *demos*, such "inventions of prudence," including the extended republic, will be of little avail if the citizens do not themselves exhibit a degree of Socratic virtue. Here one finds the golden thread that links the ancients and the moderns, Aristotle and Madison.

The Virtue of Education: The Founders' Vision

JEFFRY MORRISON

Second only to religion, the American founders believed in the importance of education to the success of their experiment in self-government.[1] Of course, to men of that era religion and education went hand-in-glove, and we need look no further than the Northwest Ordinance of 1787 for proof of that. Article III of the ordinance (the third of our organic laws) reads: "Religion, morality, and knowledge, being necessary to good government and the happiness of mankind, schools and the means of education shall forever be encouraged." Thus, the founders—those who sat in the Confederation Congress and wrote and passed the Northwest Ordinance, and those in the First U.S. Congress who reaffirmed it—collectively viewed religion and education as the two legs that would support the formal institutions of the government. They may not all have been as dewy-eyed as Thomas Jefferson ("Enlighten the people generally, and tyranny and oppressions of body and mind will vanish like evil spirits at the dawn of day"),[2] but the founders believed that education was important, even vitally important.

Religion and education, so the logic ran, formed American souls and minds; they generated the habits of thinking and acting that were required of good republican citizens. The founders took it for granted, as the Northwest Ordinance demonstrates, that churches and schools would work together; and private tutors (like those of Jefferson and James Madison) as well as the presidents of academies and colleges were almost always clergymen. Once they had improved the mechanisms of government and created a "more perfect union," the framers of the Constitution were counting on churches and schools to produce people who could be governed—and govern themselves—in a climate of ordered liberty. In short, they were relying on that much-used eighteenth-century prop of republicanism: on "virtue" in the people. Moreover, they believed that there is a difference between a constitution and constitutionalism: between the form of a limited government and the morality of the people that make it up. That morality was to include not only the traditional moral, intellectual, and even theological virtues, but also what we might call political virtues, or even republican virtues—ways of thinking and acting properly in a republic.

These are distinctions which George Carey has always made in the body of his written work. He has written, for instance, of a new (but not improved) "constitutional morality" that has supplanted the constitutional morality held by the framers and expounded in *The Federalist Papers*.[3] Like his late colleague Willmoore Kendall, he has always been alive to the importance of religion and education in shoring up the American constitutional edifice, today and especially in the eighteenth century. This essay seeks to flesh out these emphases in Carey's work by examining the founders—and one in particular—on the virtue of education.

In addition to the Northwest Ordinance, the founders' collective trust in education was revealed in a proposal at the Constitutional Convention to "establish and provide for a national University at the Seat of the Government of the United States."[4] Individual founders such as George Washington, Benjamin Rush, and that forgotten founder, John Witherspoon of New Jersey, made efforts to establish such a university. We associate Washington more with actions than with thought, yet he spent considerable energy in the last decade of his life advocating the creation of a national university. In his final annual message to Congress (1796), in letters to Jefferson (1795) and Hamilton (1796), and finally in his will (1799), Washington suggested erecting a university on the Potomac where students could learn the moral and intellectual virtues necessary for a republic. This they would do by reading books and by observing public officials transact the business of the federal government.[5] In short, Washington wanted a distinctly American university where future statesmen could obtain "political education in the principles and practice of self-government: the same kind of education he had given himself."[6]

Benjamin Rush, another booster of the national university (and of Witherspoon), suggested a curriculum for such an institution.

> We have changed our forms of government, but it remains yet to effect
> a revolution in our principles, opinions, and manners so as to accom-
> modate them to the forms of government we have adopted. This is
> the most difficult part of the business of patriots and legislators of our
> country. . . . Call upon the rulers of our country to lay the foundations
> of their empire in *knowledge* as well as virtue. . . . Let us have colleges
> in each of the states, and one federal university under the patronage
> of Congress, where the youth of all the states may be melted (as it
> were) together into one mass of citizens after they have acquired the
> first principles of knowledge in the colleges of their respective states.
> Let the law of nature and nations, the common law of our country,
> the different systems of government, history, and everything else con-
> nected with the advancement of republican knowledge and principles,
> be taught by able professors in this university. This plan of general
> education alone will render the American Revolution a blessing to
> mankind.[7]

Of course there never has been a de jure national university; there was (and
is) too much diversity in America for that. Nevertheless, there was a de facto
national university during the founding: the College of New Jersey under the
presidency of John Witherspoon, the focus of this essay.

Witherspoon (1723–94) was a Scottish Presbyterian divine who had been
coaxed to America by Rush, the trustees of the College of New Jersey, and the
Anglican revivalist George Whitefield. He would become the sixth president
of what is now Princeton University, where he remained until his death at
age seventy-one. (Prior presidents, like Jonathan Edwards, had had an unfor-
tunate habit of dying young.) Witherspoon was a unique figure who stood at
the crossroads of politics, religion, and education in founding-era America.
He was an active Continental Congressman from 1776 to 1782 and the only
clergyman and college president to sign the Declaration of Independence.
John Adams, who generally mistrusted preachers, called him "as high a Son of
Liberty as any Man in America."[8] Witherspoon argued down conservatives in
the Second Continental Congress around the first of July 1776 and helped tip
the scales toward declaring independence. Between signing the Declaration
and Articles of Confederation and then ratifying the Constitution in late 1787,
he helped pass three of the four organic laws of the United States. He also produced the most remarkable leadership cohort in American collegiate history.

The early trustees of the College of New Jersey expressed their desire that "[t]hough our great intention was to erect a seminary for educating ministers of the Gospel, yet we hope it will be a means of raising up men that will be useful in other learned professions—ornaments of the State as well as the Church. Therefore we propose to make the plan of education as extensive as our circumstances will admit."[9] Princeton was ideally situated to realize such a desire: midway between the northern and southern colonies, the College of New Jersey was not easily identifiable with either the Puritan religious zeal of New England or with the genteel Anglicanism and secular philanthropy that characterized the origins of Virginia and Georgia, for example. New Jersey had never had an established religion; and the founders of the college incorporated the principle of nonestablishment, citing the New Jersey charter of 1664, in their own charter of 1746. Since "no Freeman within the said Province of New Jersey, should at any Time be molested, punished, disquieted, or Called in Question for any difference in opinion or practice in matters of Religious Concernment, who do not actually disturb the civil Peace of the said Province," the college founders "have also expressed their earnest Desire that those of every Religious Denomination may have free and Equal Liberty and Advantage of Education in the Said College."[10] Witherspoon emphasized the nonsectarian nature of the college in his "Address to the Inhabitants of Jamaica, and Other West-India Islands in Behalf of the College of New-Jersey" (1772): "[t]his college was founded, and hath been conducted upon the most catholic principles. . . . Accordingly there are now, and have been from the beginning, scholars of various denominations from the most distant colonies," some of whose religious affiliations Witherspoon did not even know or care to know.[11] Under his leadership, Princeton, as the college was casually known by 1756 and as it was formally renamed in 1896, became the most nationally minded of the nine colleges in existence by 1776.

Witherspoon made the most of Princeton's fortunate location and circumstances, so that at the end of the Revolution he was able to realize the hopes of the early trustees. By 1783, toasts were being offered to "Nassau Hall. May she again flourish and continue the nursery of statesmen, as she has been of warriors."[12] Reflecting on Princeton's record in 1896, Woodrow Wilson, himself a president of the institution, concluded that the college seemed "a seminary of statesmen rather than a quiet seat of academic learning" during the founding.[13] In fact, it is safe to say that no single educator in early America matched Witherspoon's record of making politicians and patriots.

The list of his Princeton graduates is a roll call of early American notables. Among these were twelve members of the Continental Congress; five delegates to the Constitutional Convention; one U.S. president (James Madison); a vice president (Aaron Burr); forty-nine U.S. representatives; twenty-eight U.S. senators; three Supreme Court justices; eight U.S. district judges; one secretary of state; three attorneys general; and two foreign ministers. In addition to these national officeholders, twenty-six of Witherspoon's graduates were state judges, seventeen were members of their state constitutional conventions, and fourteen were delegates to the state conventions that ratified the Constitution. Chief among Witherspoon's graduates was of course Madison, "Father of the Constitution" and reluctant architect of the Bill of Rights. Madison stayed on an extra term following graduation to study Hebrew and law under the "old Doctor's" direction. He then proceeded to carry certain elements of Witherspoon's political creed into his own public career, culminating in his two stormy terms as president from 1809 to 1817. Garry Wills has accordingly tagged Witherspoon "probably the most influential teacher in the entire history of American education."[14]

Witherspoon fed his developing politicians a curriculum flavored with republican theory, and he also led by example—precisely the combination Washington had suggested for a national university. Witherspoon insisted that "[e]xample is itself the most powerful and successful instruction; and example is necessary to give meaning and influence to all other instruction."[15] Yet throughout his years of public service, Witherspoon always reserved a good part of his considerable energies for teaching and college administration. We would know that he shared the founders' lofty view of the importance of education for future statesmen even if he had not said so in plain language: his entire life in America, twenty-six years in all, was spent as president of the College of New Jersey (although in later years, as his health declined, he had half of his salary paid to Samuel Stanhope Smith, who was in effect a co-president with Witherspoon). In his "Address to the Inhabitants of Jamaica," Witherspoon appealed to their sense of public duty: "[Higher education] is also of acknowledged necessity to those who do not wish to live for themselves alone, but would apply their talents to the service of the Public and the good of mankind. Education is therefore of equal importance, in order either to enjoy life with dignity and elegance, or employ it to the benefit of society in offices of power or trust."[16] Even while sitting in the Continental Congress during the Revolutionary War years, Witherspoon continued to direct the college. Never missing a board of trustees meeting, he presided over every commencement and returned to Princeton at every opportunity. Perhaps his most permanent and wide-reaching contribution as president of the College of New Jersey were his *Lectures on Moral Philosophy* (published posthumously). The influence of these lectures on early American political thought (and practice) is difficult to overestimate.

The *Lectures on Moral Philosophy* are arranged as sixteen numbered lectures and one "Recapitulation," which concludes with a bibliographical essay on various writers, including some of "the chief writers upon government and politics."[17] The subject matter of the *Lectures* moves from analyses of what might be called prepolitical or subpolitical structures to more formal political arrangements. Lecture I introduces the student to moral philosophy, "that branch of Science which treats of the principles and laws of Duty or Morals. It is called *Philosophy*, because it is an inquiry into the nature and grounds of moral obligation by reason, as distinct from revelation" and is "nothing else but the knowledge of human nature."[18] In other words, this was not to be a course on systematic theology—there were his *Lectures on Divinity* for that. Still, the pious student need not be alarmed: "If the Scripture is true, the discoveries of reason cannot be contrary to it; and therefore, it has nothing to fear from that quarter. And as we are certain it can do no evil, so there is a probability that it may do much good." After the introduction, Witherspoon divided the remaining lectures between "Ethics and Politics," the "two great branches" of moral philosophy.[19] Lectures II through V deal with human nature and the relation of virtue to government; Lectures VI through IX deal with ethics; Lectures X through XIII consider politics (individual lectures are titled "Of Politics," "Of Civil Society," and "Of the Law of Nature and Nations"). Lectures XIV through XVI are devoted to jurisprudence ("Jurisprudence" and "Of Oaths and Vows"). The seventeenth lecture is a "Recapitulation" and abbreviated bibliography. Jack Scott, the editor of the best edition of the *Lectures,* has conclusively demonstrated Witherspoon's indebtedness to Francis Hutcheson's *System of Moral Philosophy* (1755) in both structure and content, while noting that Witherspoon did not copy it "slavishly."[20] Of course, the danger in tracing the sources of such intellectual rivers is that the headwaters are almost impossible to find. In the case of Hutcheson's *System,* for example, its own outline is nearly identical to Samuel Pufendorf's *On the Law of Nature and Nations* (1672),[21] and one imagines that Pufendorf did not conjure his own moral philosophy out of nothing, either. More important for our purposes than tracing precisely who got what philosophical tidbit from whom is to note the harmonies between the Scottish and American moral philosophies, as well as Witherspoon's central role in producing what Jefferson called the "harmonizing sentiments of the day" during America's founding.

Some of the most important sentiments of that day were a belief in a "moral sense," a qualified optimism about the new methods of science, a bias toward pragmatism, and a predilection for republican self-government. All of these sentiments were driven home in Witherspoon's *Lectures on Moral Philosophy*. In fact, Benjamin Rush likely had his friend's *Lectures* in mind when he suggested that his national curriculum should include "the law of nature and nations, the common law of our country, the different systems of government, history, and everything else connected with the advancement of republican knowledge and principles." And well he might have: not only were Witherspoon's *Lectures* the first presidential lectures of their kind in the colonies, but more importantly, through them Witherspoon almost single-handedly gave a philosophy to the embryonic nation and helped transform a generation of young idealists into hardheaded politicians of the first rank.

The Scottish Enlightenment philosophy Witherspoon brought with him to America and passed to his students is best typified by Thomas Reid's phrase (nearly ubiquitous in the late eighteenth century) "common sense." The locution enjoyed wide circulation during the founding; and it was put to use by thinkers with the most opposite opinions, particularly concerning religion. That the same words could appear, for instance, in the titles of the freethinking Thomas Paine's *Common Sense* (1776) and the devout James Oswald's *Appeal to Common Sense in Behalf of Religion* (1766–72) is testimony to both the plasticity and the rhetorical power of the phrase. Nor was Paine the only political pamphleteer to employ it. *The Federalist Papers* contain nine references to "common sense"—eight from the pen of the half-Scot Hamilton. All references align the dictates of common sense on the side of the newly proposed Constitution.[22]

The upshot of Scottish moral-sense and common-sense thinking was that the deliverances of the human faculties were reliable, and that experience was a key to understanding in the physical and moral worlds. If the metaphysical speculations of an irreligious philosopher like David Hume—or a pious one like Jonathan Edwards—led us to doubt the obvious conclusions drawn from our common experiences of the world; if they led us to doubt the existence of a mind-independent material universe as Edwards had or to undermine belief in cause and effect as Hume had; then so much the worse for those speculations. They were to be rejected as patently absurd. To Reid, Witherspoon, and the other common-sense philosophers, such conclusions were the inevitable result of too much "metaphysical" speculation; not enough attention had been paid to the dictates of what Witherspoon praised as "plain common sense."[23] The word "metaphysical" almost invariably carried a pejorative meaning in Witherspoon's *Lectures on Moral Philosophy*. Hume's efforts to shake our common-sense belief in cause and effect were dismissed as "metaphysical subtleties" and the immaterial system shared by Bishop George Berkeley and Edwards was labeled a "wild and ridiculous attempt to unsettle the principles of common sense by metaphysical reasoning."[24] Absurd conclusions like these came from brains addled by too much "theory"—long on armchair metaphysics, they were woefully short on empirical science.

The Scottish common-sense approach led to conclusions that fit seamlessly with the thinking of Witherspoon's colleagues in the New Jersey legislature and the Continental Congress. For example: despite deep differences over theological questions such as the inspiration of the Bible, the similarities between Witherspoon, a product of the Scottish Enlightenment, and Jefferson, a product of the American Enlightenment, are striking. Jefferson and Witherspoon held to precisely the same definition of the moral sense; in fact, entire sections of Witherspoon's *Lectures on Moral Philosophy* could be replaced with passages from Jefferson's correspondence without disrupting at all the sense of the *Lectures*. Jefferson wrote:

> Man was destined for society. His morality therefore was to be formed to this object. He was endowed [by his Maker] with a sense of right and wrong merely relative to this. This sense is as much a part of his nature as the sense of hearing, seeing, feeling; it is the true foundation of morality. . . . The moral sense, or conscience, is as much a part of man as his leg or arm. It is given to all human beings in a stronger or weaker degree, as force of members is given them in a greater or less degree. It may be strengthened by exercise, as may any particular limb of the body. This sense is submitted indeed in some degree to the guidance of reason; but it is a small stock which is required for this: even a less one than what we call Common sense. State a moral case to a ploughman and a professor. The former will decide it as well, and often better than the latter, because he has not been led astray by artificial rules.[25]

Jefferson continued to hold to this definition of the moral sense until at least 1814, as evidenced by a letter he wrote to Thomas Law:

> [H]ow necessary was the care of the Creator in making the moral principle so much a part of our constitution as that no errors of reasoning or of speculation might lead us astray from its observance in practice. . . . The Creator would indeed have been a bungling artist, had he intended man for a social animal, without planting in him social dispositions. It is true that they are not planted in every man, because there is no rule without exceptions; but it is false reasoning which converts exceptions into the general rule. Some men are born without the organs of sight, or of hearing, or without hands. Yet it would be wrong to say that man is born without these faculties, and sight, hearing, and hands may with truth enter into the general definition of man.[26]

These words could just as well have been Witherspoon's. "This moral sense," Witherspoon said, "is precisely the same thing with what, in scripture and common language, we call conscience. It is the law which our Maker has written upon our hearts, and both intimates and enforces duty, previous to all reasoning."[27] Furthermore, "we ought to take the rule of duty from conscience enlightened by reason, experience, and every way by which we can be supposed to learn the will of our Maker, and his intention in creating us such as we are. And we ought to believe that it is as deeply founded as the nature of God himself, being a transcript of his moral excellence, and that it is productive of the greatest good."[28] Thus, when it came time to sign the Declaration of 1776, with its reference to truths that were "self-evident" and confirmed by "all Experience," Witherspoon could subscribe without hesitation.[29] After all, Jefferson and Witherspoon spoke the same moral language and shared a common moral epistemology.

Such close agreement between Witherspoon and Jefferson can be explained by their common debt to Scottish philosophy. Jefferson found Reid's protégé Dugald Stewart "a great man, and among the most honest living. . . . I consider him and [Destutt de] Tracy as the ablest metaphysicians living; by which I mean investigators of the thinking faculty of man. Stewart seems to have given its natural history from facts and observations; Tracy its modes of action and deduction, which he calls Logic and Ideology." Jefferson had met Stewart in Paris and "became immediately intimate" with him there; they called "mutually on each other and almost daily, during [his] stay at Paris, which was of some months."[30]

Because they shared a moral epistemology that emphasized experience and a common moral faculty, Witherspoon and Jefferson also agreed that ordinary people were trustworthy enough for self-government. Although Witherspoon was essentially a Federalist, whereas Jefferson had Antifederalist leanings, both had sufficient faith in the ability of common people to reason aright on moral and political questions and therefore to govern themselves. Jefferson's "ploughmen" (Thomas Reid used the same illustration)[31] were Witherspoon's more cumbersome "persons of the middle degrees of capacity." Such persons, Witherspoon said, "perhaps generally fill the most useful and important stations in life."[32] Moreover, in a newspaper article defending Thomas Paine's *Common Sense,* he came down squarely on the side of the political instincts of the common American people, who were behind independence. Paine's arguments for American self-government were, to Witherspoon's mind, irrefutable. *Common Sense* may have "wanted polish" in places, he observed, and "sometimes failed in grammar, but never in perspicuity."[33]

Having rehearsed the major tenets of Witherspoon's Scottish philosophy and seen how that philosophy dovetailed with the positions of other founders, chiefly of Jefferson, we are now in a position to see a concrete example of one of those tenets in action. Confidence in the "heart," as Witherspoon expressed it, and in the common sense of the average sturdy American, helped provide answers to the grave questions that were being asked at the time of the American Revolution. For one: how were persons of "integrity" (Witherspoon's word) such as the Americans to know whether they had a natural right to separate themselves from an oppressive mother country? Or another: how, in the words of the Declaration, might one people determine whether the time had come to "dissolve the political bands which [had] connected them with another"? The answer of Witherspoon's Scottish philosophy was, in essence, to consult the self-evident truths written on the hearts of the people by their Creator, rather than arcane theories. "The chief use of books and systems," he said, was "to apply the principle to particular cases and suppositions differently classed, and to point out the practice of nations in several minute and special particulars, which unless ascertained by practice, would be very uncertain and ambiguous."[34] Here is Alexander Hamilton's answer to the same question: "The sacred rights of mankind are not to be rummaged for among old parchments or musty records. They are written, as with a sunbeam, in the whole volume of human nature, by the hand of Divinity itself, and can never be erased or obscured by mortal power."[35] The logic of the American Revolution, as expressed by Hamilton, and supremely in the Declaration of Independence, presumes the moral epistemology of Witherspoon and his Scottish philosophy and thus provides us with an example of its practical application in founding politics.[36] As Michael Novak has recently written in a similar context, there are *political corollaries* to metaphysical premises.[37]

By common consent, Witherspoon was a principal carrier of the Scottish philosophy in early America, and the importance of that role should not be minimized. For one thing, through Witherspoon that Scottish philosophy inoculated Americans of the Revolutionary era against the kind of utopian excesses (to say nothing of the terror) that infected the French during their own Revolution. To be sure, historians of colonial philosophy have always acknowledged Witherspoon's role in transmitting the Scottish philosophy to the colonies, but the more influential among them—I. Woodbridge Riley and Herbert Schneider, for example—have not thought too highly of either Witherspoon or the Scottish philosophy, especially the philosophy of common sense associated with Thomas Reid and Dugald Stewart.[38] And yet Schneider himself admits that "the Scottish Enlightenment was probably the most potent single tradition in the American Enlightenment,"[39] and no one did more to see that tradition established in America than John Witherspoon. The merits of the Scottish philosophy may be open to debate, but the fact remains that it was (if we extend Scottish realism into the pragmatism of the late nineteenth and early twentieth centuries) the dominant philosophical school in America for nearly a century and a half after Witherspoon established it at Princeton. For such reasons, some historians of philosophy have instead given Witherspoon higher marks as a moral philosopher. One insists that "Witherspoon must be included among the early American philosophic thinkers."[40] Another, writing in the *William and Mary Quarterly,* names only four "colonial philosophers who deserve the title in its full meaning: Jonathan Edwards, Samuel Johnson, Cadwallader Colden, and John Witherspoon."[41]

Others have viewed the influence of Scottish philosophy on American thought in a more positive light. The political philosopher Eric Voegelin, for one, felt the power of the Scottish common-sense legacy in America. After seeing the connection between Thomas Reid and Sir William Hamilton and American thought, Voegelin "began to sense that American society had a philosophical background far superior in range and existential substance, though not always in articulation, to anything that I found represented in the methodological environment [in Austria] in which I had grown up."[42] Douglass Adair, for another, saw the mark of the Scottish philosophy on the American founding, particularly in the influence of David Hume on *Federalist* 10.[43] And Frank Balog has noted that "[Adam] Smith's influence on [John] Adams's work was extensive."[44]

A further philosophical legacy of John Witherspoon is the ultimate triumph of Scottish realism over idealism in the colonies. One of the seminal debates in early American philosophy was between the idealism of Jonathan Edwards, who was elected president of the College of New Jersey in 1758, and the realism of Witherspoon, who became president ten years later. Witherspoon even claimed that before he went to America he had anticipated in print the arguments of Reid, James Beatty, and others against George Berkeley's idealism. Ashbel Green heard Witherspoon claim "that before Reid and Beatty, or any other author of their views, had published any thing on the ideal system, he wrote against it, and suggested the same train of thought which they adopted, and that he published his essay in a Scotch Magazine."[45]

When Witherspoon arrived in Princeton he found to his consternation that the college was overrun with what Green called the "Berklean [sic] system of Metaphysics."[46] (In point of fact, Princeton's idealism probably owed more to Jonathan Edwards and Samuel Johnson, Edwards's tutor at Yale, than to Bishop Berkeley.) The idealists held, in brief, that the universe consists solely of minds and ideas, and that there is no such thing as mind-independent matter. At the time Witherspoon became president, nearly all of the Princeton tutors (especially Jonathan Edwards Jr.) held to the ideal system, and Witherspoon, who was no friend to it, quickly laid the ax at the root of the idealist teaching at the college. Indeed, except for agreement on the basic theological tenets of Calvinism, Witherspoon was opposed to Edwards on almost every front. Edwards was a New Light Congregationalist revivalist, Witherspoon a Presbyterian who apparently had doubts about the religious enthusiasm that swept the Princeton campus in the early 1770s; Edwards was a philosophical idealist while Witherspoon was an uncompromising realist; Edwards found it necessary to attack the moral-sense epistemology of Francis Hutcheson while Witherspoon always remained a firm believer in the moral sense.

By the end of 1769, Witherspoon's first full year at the helm of the college, all of the idealist tutors, including Edwards Jr., had been replaced with common-sense realists. By his own example at Princeton; through his graduates, many of whom later founded academies and colleges; and with the influence of his *Lectures on Moral Philosophy,* Witherspoon and Scottish realism prevailed over Edwards's idealism, thereby helping to set the course of American philosophy for the next century and a half. The victory of realism over idealism had far-reaching implications for the life of the mind in America, for it allowed realism to act as "a bridge between the Enlightenment and the pragmatists."[47] This in itself seems reason enough to count Witherspoon among the handful of moral philosophers in colonial America.

A second conflict between the philosophies of Edwards and Witherspoon concerned Hutcheson's moral-sense epistemology. In 1755, the year that Francis Hutcheson's *System of Moral Philosophy* was published, Edwards wrote out his own moral philosophy in a brief treatise titled *The Nature of True Virtue.* In the treatise, which was not published until ten years later, Edwards located virtue in the will rather than in a separate moral sense as had Hutcheson. Thus, Edwards was compelled by the logic of his theory of virtue to argue against Hutcheson, whose views he had actually accepted while a teenager at Yale. Arguing that true virtue was a benevolence rooted in the will toward "Being in general," not toward particulars or individuals, Edwards parted company with Hutcheson and the moral-sense philosophers, who thought benevolence to individuals was indeed true virtue.[48] Edwards's assault on moral-sense epistemology simply gave Witherspoon another reason to root out the Edwardsean philosophy at Princeton. Once again, by siding with Hutcheson against Edwards in favor of the moral sense, Witherspoon supported a moral epistemology that ended up dominating American thinking.

Witherspoon was therefore a bona fide moral philosopher of considerable influence in early American thought. Few intellectual historians, however, have seen him in this light. Many have instead trivialized Witherspoon's contribution and his intellectual abilities because his moral philosophy was unoriginal, eclectic, and occasionally naïve. Compared to several other supposedly more sophisticated founders, Witherspoon is thought to be second-rank. Although Witherspoon was not the first to introduce Hutcheson's moral-sense epistemology into the colonies, and many other Americans (Jefferson, John Adams, and James Wilson among them) accepted the moral sense, by arguing for the moral sense in his *Lectures on Moral Philosophy* Witherspoon did a great deal to disseminate that view in the colonies. By contrast, Thomas Jefferson, for all his infatuation with theory, never wrote anything approaching a treatise on a philosophical subject, and he thought that moral philosophy as a discipline was worthless. Writing to the young Peter Carr concerning his studies at Williamsburg, Jefferson recommended avoiding "Moral philosophy. I think it lost time to attend lectures in this branch. He who made us would have been a pitiful bungler if he had made the rules of our moral conduct a matter of science."[49] Jefferson also wrote to Witherspoon at Princeton, suggesting that an acquaintance who was studying under Witherspoon be exempted from the study of moral philosophy. "As he [Bennet Taylor of Virginia] has no time to spare, I have mentioned to him that I thought he might undertake the subject of Moral philosophy in his chamber, at leisure hours, and from books, without attending lectures or exercises in that branch."[50] We can assume that in the event, Jefferson's young friend found little or no leisure for such study. Witherspoon, by contrast, insisted in his *Lectures on Moral Philosophy* that "[t]he languages, and even mathematical and natural knowledge, are but hand-maids to this superior science [moral philosophy]."[51]

Nor does the fact that Witherspoon borrowed widely from Hutcheson and others negate his importance as a moral philosopher in America. Jefferson himself was a borrower of legendary proportion. So, for that matter, were all the founders. There was not a man among them—not Jefferson, not Franklin, not Washington, not even the cerebral Madison—who was an original thinker or profound philosopher in his own right. The Sage of Monticello contributed nothing original to formal philosophy in America and in fact was accused of outright plagiarism of John Locke in the Declaration. Jefferson later defended himself by essentially admitting to a lack of originality and denying that the Declaration was ever meant to be original. The object of that document, Jefferson said, was precisely to be *un*original and eclectic.

> Neither aiming at originality of principle or sentiment, nor yet copied from any particular and previous writing, it was intended to be an expression of the American mind, and to give to that expression the proper tone and spirit called for by the occasion. All its authority rests then on the harmonizing sentiments of the day, whether expressed in conversation, in letters, printed essays, or in the elementary books of public right, as Aristotle, Cicero, Locke, Sidney, etc.[52]

Jefferson was representative of the whole revolutionary generation in this respect. According to Morton White, "we may repeat what scholars have always known, and what the most candid rebels always admitted, namely, that they did not invent a single idea that may be called philosophical in the philosopher's sense of the word."[53]

We should not, therefore, be shocked to find that Witherspoon borrowed heavily from other thinkers. In this respect he was a typical American founder. Nor should we think less of him just because he was a philosophical borrower. If we do, then consistency demands that we think less of famous founders like Jefferson as well. And in at least one respect Witherspoon seems to have been more philosophically original, or at least more innovative, than many colonial American thinkers. Frederick Mayer notes that "[i]n colonial times the progress of philosophy was hindered by the ecclesiastical tradition. . . . There were two ways of thinking: one severely orthodox, usually Calvinistic; the other scientific and Newtonian and usually exposed to the antagonism of the clergy."[54] If this characterization is accurate, then Witherspoon was a happy exception to the rule. By synthesizing Calvinism and Enlightenment science, Witherspoon was arguably more original than most orthodox thinkers of his day.

Similarly, the charge that Witherspoon's moral philosophy lacked the depth and consistency to make him a genuine philosopher seems rather selective when Witherspoon is compared to the more revered founders. True enough, Witherspoon was no great philosopher in the technical sense of that word: he seems not to have understood some of Hume's arguments very well, and there are instances in his *Lectures* where he has gotten Hume and Berkeley confused. Certainly when weighed against such contemporaries as Adam Smith and Immanuel Kant, Witherspoon fares poorly. But once again, Jefferson could be just as inconsistent—if that is the correct word for it. For example, it has frequently been remarked that Jefferson's philosophy was thoroughly Lockean, and indeed he did rank Locke as one of "the three greatest men that have ever lived, without any exception."[55] But we must recall that this same Jefferson also called Reid's disciple Dugald Stewart one of the two greatest philosophers of the age, even though Stewart made a career of attacking Locke for his theory of ideas. So it seems that Thomas Jefferson, at least in several instances, was manifestly unoriginal, eclectic, and inconsistent as a moral philosopher.

Although he may not have been a great moral philosopher in the European mold, Witherspoon was a legitimate *American* moral philosopher. This may be rather faint praise considering how few philosophers there were in colonial America, but it does place Witherspoon above Franklin, Jefferson and other founders more renowned for their so-called philosophical abilities. For example, there were very few pure or formal philosophers among the early members of the American Philosophical Society, America's first learned society, for the simple reason that America had few pure philosophers anywhere at all. Neither Franklin (the founder of the society) nor David Rittenhouse or Jefferson (both early officers in the society) ever wrote anything approaching Witherspoon's *Lectures on Moral Philosophy*. Franklin, considered by many a sort of American Socrates, made only one detour into metaphysics as a young man, his "Dissertation on Liberty and Necessity, Pleasure and Pain" (1725), and then spent the rest of his life dismissing it as a youthful indiscretion.

In fact, early Americans were remarkably uninterested in formal philosophy, as Tocqueville was quick to notice. "Less attention, I suppose, is paid to philosophy in the United States than in any other country of the civilized world. The Americans have no school of philosophy peculiar to themselves, and they pay very little attention to the rival European schools. Indeed they hardly know their names." Tocqueville concluded that "of all countries in the world, America is the one in which the precepts of Descartes are least studied and best followed,"[56] by which he meant that Americans preferred to make themselves and their own *experiences* the starting points of their thinking, as Descartes had, rather than the theories of others. Surely Tocqueville was correct in his observation: Americans generally have been, and eighteenth-century American politicians certainly were, rather skeptical of formal philosophy. Americans like John Adams were more likely to see philosophers as "mad" than as trustworthy guides to truth. (Adams once wrote Jefferson that "[p]hilosophers antient and modern appear to me as Mad as Hindoos, Mahomitans and Christians.")[57] Even the theoretical Jefferson saw little profit to studying moral philosophy because most people could judge for themselves and would only be led astray by "artificial rules" invented by "professors."[58] Jefferson, Witherspoon, and their colleagues were more inclined to rely on what "all experience" could teach them, as they wrote in the Declaration of Independence, than on theories found in dusty books.

Witherspoon's training in Scottish philosophy, and in moral-sense and especially in common-sense epistemology, could hardly have been better preparation for his distinguished career in American politics. When he arrived in 1768, just as trouble with England was beginning to boil over in the colonies, Witherspoon brought along a mind naturally inclined toward the pragmatic and stocked with concepts and language—"experience, moral sense, common sense, self-evidence"—that enjoyed the widest currency among his American colleagues. In short, he and the other founders spoke the same language of moral discourse.

His mind was cast in essentially the same mold as theirs: pragmatic, willing to use formal philosophy but at root skeptical of too much "metaphysical" theorizing. Witherspoon was intimately acquainted with the common-sense philosophy of Reid, whom the Supreme Court Justice James Wilson quoted verbatim in *Chisholm v. Georgia* (1793), and with Reid's pupil Dugald Stewart, later Jefferson's friend and philosophical hero. He was also conversant, though to a lesser extent, with David Hume, whose language on experience Hamilton used to close out *The Federalist Papers*. The formal philosophers Witherspoon knew and borrowed from were the least metaphysical and the most empirical and pragmatic; they were the most—if it can be put this way—*un*philosophical of philosophers. And they were the only philosophers whom pragmatic Americans were likely to heed. By teaching him to hold high the lamp of experience, the Scottish philosophy ideally prepared Witherspoon for his highly successful political career in America.

As a moral philosopher, and as a formal philosopher more generally, Witherspoon must rank among the few true philosophers in early America. Although his mind was more synthetic than original, this charge does not seem terribly damaging when we reflect that it can be leveled against practically any thinker, including an undisputed philosopher like John Locke. For example, it has been said that "[i]t is doubtless true that Locke himself brought to articulate expression an already existing movement of thought; but this articulate expression was itself a powerful influence in the consolidation and dissemination of the movement of thought and drift of political life which it expressed."[59] Even less were the American founders creative moral philosophers.

The importance of Witherspoon's contribution to American moral philosophy, political thought, and education lies in his promotion of Scottish realism over idealism, and in his articulation of Scottish moral-sense epistemology in his *Lectures on Moral Philosophy,* through which these ideas were passed at Princeton to Madison and a host of other future prominent politicians, clergy, and educators. Certainly Witherspoon was a more influential and sophisticated moral philosopher than either Jefferson or Franklin, who wrote exactly one philosophical treatise between them. In fact, the founding generation was almost entirely devoid of men who could be considered formal philosophers—a point that George Carey has been making for decades. Witherspoon thus stands out as a founder who made a genuine contribution to moral philosophy in America and to American political culture. His *Lectures on Moral Philosophy,* and indeed his educational and political careers, are perhaps the clearest proof in American history of Tocqueville's observation that "[t]here is no country in the world in which the boldest political theories of the eighteenth-century philosophers are put so effectively into practice as in America."[60]

No Presidential Republic:
Representation, Deliberation, and Executive Power in The Federalist Papers

GARY L. GREGG II

The achievement of ordered liberty has never been automatic and should never be taken for granted. Of course, the cultural and educational necessities leading to the order of spirit are the essential starting ground for an ordered community. But achievement of ordered liberty also depends upon creating community powers (government) that have power enough to control the governed and yet also the predisposition to control themselves. Only under the power of government can we have liberty. Only under a government controlling itself can we have order. This was one of the great insights the authors of *The Federalist Papers* gathered from experience and from previous writers like Baron de Montesquieu.

As explicated in *The Federalist Papers*, the American Founding Fathers created a balanced constitutional system whereby enough power was invested in the federal government to enable it to control those elements of life properly falling within its sphere. And yet the federal government was properly limited to that sphere; it was hemmed in by a written Constitution of delegated powers, by state governments jealously guarding against encroachments, and by a division of powers and men within the federal government itself. This essay explores this last security for ordered liberty: representative government funneled through a system of rival power centers established, in part, to keep one another in check and promote good government.

To the degree that any of the various institutions—or men filling the positions composing those institutions, we would more appropriately say—fail to adhere to their designated roles, the balance of order and liberty may become unhinged and tyranny may be encouraged. This unbalancing of the system could happen because one group is particularly good at fulfilling its ambitions for power; but it could also just as regularly come from institutions demonstrating a lack of resolve and ambitions of their own.

Since the founding, the proper balance of the institutions of the American republic has been a perennial question for those concerned with ordered liberty.[1] This essay explores Publius's understanding of the importance of the separation of powers in the American political system and offers some thoughts upon the current state of its health.[2]

INSTITUTIONAL SEPARATION: TOWARD A COMPOUND THEORY OF REPRESENTATIVE GOVERNMENT

Traditionally, it was held that members of the legislative branch of government were the only officials capable of serving as political representatives. In particular, some Antifederalists maintained that no body could be representative unless it was numerous and close to the people. For some, in fact, even the Senate was not considered a representative institution. Rather, as one Antifederalist put it, "This body [the House] is the true representative of the democratic part of the system; the shield and defence of the people."[3] But even the House wasn't representative enough for some Antifederalists. Richard Henry Lee, for instance, maintained that: "The only check to be found in favor of the democratic principle in this system is, the house of representatives; which I believe may justly be called a mere shred or rag of representation."[4]

Such sentiment, however, is derived from a view that regards representatives as the instructed delegates or "mirrors" of their constituencies—a view Publius did not share. Publius's general theory of representation need not be limited to the House of Representatives or even to the legislature as a whole. Rather, all branches of government were to be representative in the American system of free government. In the Constitution, he explains, "the whole power . . . is lodged in the hands of the people, or their representatives and delegates" (8:34).[5] Publius defines republic in *Federalist* 10 as "a government in which the scheme of representation takes place" (10:46). In *Federalist* 39 he defines republic as "a government which derives all its powers directly or indirectly from the great body of the people, and is administered by persons holding their offices during pleasure for a limited period, or during good behavior" (39:194). Because all powers were derived from and to be exercised according to the dictates of republicanism, each institution of the new government was to be considered a place of political representation.

Conceiving each political institution created by the Constitution as a representative one demands a certain view of political representation and what it requires. First, we must be sure as to what clearly is not necessary for representation to exist. The representative need not be "representative" in the sense of being an average citizen who could simply reflect constituents' opinions and beliefs in government. Neither would the representative be beholden to the mandates of his fellow citizens. Indeed, Publius is concerned that these not be the characteristics of representatives. As I have argued elsewhere, Publius was concerned to establish a constitutional distance between the government and the citizenry—a distance that would allow representatives the freedom and independence necessary for the deliberative process.[6] A constitutional space of this kind was to be enabled primarily by the extended republic, by indirect elections for senators and the president, and by relatively lengthy terms with re-eligibility.

But would independence from the people render the new government by definition unrepublican and dangerous to liberty, as the Constitution's opponents claimed? Publius believed that it would not, because the scheme of representation established also provided for the needs of republican safety. Such needs were met at the most basic level by the fact that all governmental power was recognized as originating from the people themselves. The Constitution delegated power to those temporarily empowered within the institutional scheme, which itself provided the system of checks and balances. Further safeguards to republican liberty could be found in the election of the House and Senate as well as of the president for limited terms by the people or people's servants; and, should it prove necessary, all representatives were subject to a process of removal from office.

Perhaps most fundamental to Publius's concept of representation is its distinction between responsiveness and responsibility. While some opponents of the Constitution argued that a representative must be kept responsive to the public's wishes, Publius held responsibility to be the more necessary element. The former would require compliant delegates acting according to the people's wishes, the latter that representatives be returned periodically to the judgment of the people or their servants. Even if retroactively, the people's voice was to be heard the loudest and filtered the least. The people were to render judgment on the *effects* of governmental actions, not on the appropriateness or inappropriateness of the proposed measures themselves. Representatives would be held responsible to the people through the electoral process—an element found in each institution.[7] Indeed, as will be shown below: on this essential point Publius argued that the unitary office of the presidency was actually more representative than the other institutions, as it offered a more intense focus of responsibility on one man than was possible in a numerous body.

The Senate, presidency, and House of Representatives were designed to be representative institutions. They were not, however, designed to be uniformly representative or to bring the same basic elements to government. As Publius tells us, "the several members of government [stand] on as different foundation as republican principles will well admit" (55:290).[8] Equipped with this understanding of Publius's concept of representation, we can see in *The Federalist Papers* "levels" or "tiers" of representation that correspond to these constitutional institutions. Each of these levels, including the presidency, contributes in its unique way to the deliberative republic. Before exploring the representational aspects of the presidency, it is necessary briefly to explore the other major institutions of the deliberative republic. Such exploration is required by Publius's own logic of a deliberative republic comprising separate and equally legitimate representative institutions.

THE HOUSE OF REPRESENTATIVES

Clearly, the institution established by the Constitution of 1787 that was to be the closest to the people themselves was the House of Representatives. Members of the House were to be the only members of the new government that would be directly elected by the people; and members would be elected from the smallest constituency and for the shortest term of any member of the federal government. They were to be "the immediate representatives of the people" (58:303). But what does Publius have in mind with the phrase "immediate representatives"?

In refuting the Antifederalists' charges that the Constitution would serve "the elevation of the few on the ruin of the many," Publius returns to the argument he had made in *Federalist* 10. In *Federalist* 57, he assures us that extending the size of the constituency of each representative would help ensure the requisite "fit characters." "Reason assures us that as in so great a number a fit representative would be most likely to be found" (57:298). And why will the people elect the man of fit character? Because the "object of popular choice" will be "every citizen whose merit may recommend him to the esteem and confidence of his country" (57:296). Publius appeals to his understanding of human nature and experience in refuting the Antifederalist position "that a diffusive mode of choosing representatives of the people tends to elevate traitors and to undermine public liberty" (57:300). Contrary to those who find an uncompromisingly Hobbesian view of man in *The Federalist Papers*, the public is seen here to have at least enough virtue to see and elect men of upright character and to render mature judgments on the effects of governmental actions.[9]

Composed of members directly elected by the people every two years, the House has a structure that provides most directly for the expression of republican jealousy. The people directly control the House—or at least they control the makeup of the House and can change that composition biennially. But the extended republic helps distance the members from their constituents' opinions and interests, thereby limiting the people's control of the operations of the House. Such independence is essential to the deliberative process.

While not beholden to constituency opinion, the House does make a special contribution that involves parochial interests.[10] Representatives are to bring not only their uncommon virtue and good judgment to the deliberative process but also a knowledge of the conditions and interests of their local constituency. Publius informs us that the "representative ought to be acquainted with the interests and circumstances of his constituents" (56:291). Such knowledge, when brought to the deliberative process and reported to the other representatives, enhances the quality of the discussion and the legislative product resulting from it.[11] Through the deliberative process, the members collectively "will provide a picture of the whole so that, unlike an ordinary constituent, the representative can weigh and measure with greater knowledge and certainty the impact of particular policies upon the whole country, not just one section or district."[12]

THE SENATE

Further insulated from the passions that may from time to time sweep through the people, the Senate stands as a stabilizing force against legislation emanating from passions and temporary interests. Any popular influence on the Senate must first pass through the state legislatures, themselves a chosen body of citizens. The mode of election for senators also contributes to the upright character of the institution's occupants. Election by the state legislatures rather than by the people at large would favor a deliberate choice encouraging "a select appointment" (62:320).

As Publius argues about the Electoral College method of electing the president, the state legislatures "will in general be composed of the most enlightened and respectable body of citizens." State representatives will accordingly turn their attention and votes "to men only who have become the most distinguished by their abilities and virtue, and in whom the people perceive just grounds of confidence" (64:333). The result would be the election of men who "will always be of the number of those who best understand our national interests, whether considered in relation to the several states or to foreign nations, who are best able to promote those interests, and whose reputations for integrity inspires and merits confidence" (64:333).

The Senate will provide a "due sense of national character" to the system that will help protect the Republic from "unenlightened and variable policy" (63:325). Essentially, the senators bring three primary elements to the policy-making process: their enlightened characters, their knowledge of national and international affairs (derived from both their enlightened characters and their extended time in office), and stability. These elements are beneficial because there are times when the people "may call for measures which they themselves will afterwards be the most ready to lament and condemn" (63:327). In such times, when the public is "stimulated by some irregular passion," Publius tells us, "such an institution may be sometimes necessary as a defense to the people against their own temporary errors and delusions" (63:327).

The Senate's special sense of national character is a stabilizing element in government, providing a check on the mutable and sometimes unenlightened legislation that may from time to time emanate from the lower house. Publius concedes that, on occasion, those representatives who are closest to the people could bow to their temporary delusions, mislead them through demagogic appeals, or sacrifice the public interest to more parochial ones. Exercising independent reason through deliberation, senators could step in and delay such legislation until time allows the cool and deliberate sense of the community to return to the public councils. All legislation, after all, must be considered by the institution embodying this "national character" before becoming law. The

Senate's representatives, drawn from the individual states, introduce order and stability to the immediate popular majorities of the House.

THE PRESIDENCY

In explaining and defending aspects of the Constitution relating to the presidency, Publius realizes that his chief task will be to undermine the republican jealousy manifested in the criticisms that find an embryonic monarchy in the office. To that end he dedicates *Federalist* 69 in particular. Running through this essay is the concern to develop an understanding of a middle ground between a monarchical institution on the one hand and a weak, compliant, and perhaps even fragmented executive authority on the other. By comparing the characteristics and powers of Great Britain's monarchy, New York's governor, and the presidency, he shows that middle ground to be occupied by the American presidency. Publius lays here the foundation for the concept of a representative executive authority.

The officer most removed from the people was to be the chief magistrate of the Republic. Governing over one extended land and elected by electors drawn from every state, he alone among elected officials would have an entirely national origin. Despite the president's distance from the people and what critics termed his despotic nature, in the republican vision of Publius the president was considered to be a representative. As with the House but to a greater extent, the extended republic would tend to distance the president from parochial interests. Furthermore, the diversity of interests within the Union would encourage his independence from any particular interest or combination of interests. He would occupy constitutional and political ground different from that of both legislative houses; this would afford a different perspective on governmental measures and the needs of the nation. Despite the differences between the presidential office and the legislative bodies, however, the president's origin and powers as well as the nature of his responsibilities make him a central representative in the American political system.

The Electoral College mode of electing the president was particularly capable of yielding an enlightened and upright citizen possessing those virtues and qualities which Publius was so concerned to see in office. Besides the personal characteristics the president was to bring, perhaps his most important contribution to Publius's republicanism would be his energizing of the political system. Publius acknowledges the traditional belief holding "that a vigorous executive is inconsistent with the genius of republican government," but he goes on to argue that, in actuality, such an institution is absolutely essential to the survival and flourishing of that same republican form of government: "Energy in the executive is a leading character in the definition of good government" (70:362). Whereas the legislature represents the people and their collective good through "the jarring of parties" that often promotes "deliberation and circumspection," the executive represents the capacity of the people to act with firmness and vigor when this is necessitated by the changing tides of human affairs (70:365). Such times would obviously include times of war, when an energetic executive would be needed to protect the community from foreign powers. An energetic executive would also be necessary in dealing with other nations, including negotiating treaties. Justice may also demand that an energetic executive invoke his authority "to grant reprieves and pardons" when "good policy" as well as "humanity" would dictate such actions. Here the president, as the "dispenser of mercy," acts as the representative of the people's sense of a justice higher than the written laws of the country could fully contain.

Energy and dispatch would be essential to "the steady administration of the laws" (70:362). Indeed, in defending the president's capacity as administrative head of the government, Publius seems specifically to attack the "theory" that an energetic executive is inconsistent with representative government. "A feeble executive implies a feeble execution of the government. A feeble execution is but another phrase for a bad execution; and a government ill executed, *whatever it may be in theory, must be, in practice, a bad government*" (70:362) (emphasis added).

Not only is this characteristic of the presidency necessary for the execution of the laws and its holder's responsibility as commander-in-chief, but energy also contributes to the deliberative process of government. An energetic executive is needed as a protection against "irregular and high-handed combinations" that would act unjustly, and it is necessary "to the security of liberty against the enterprises and assaults of ambition, of faction and of anarchy" (70:362). Though Congress in particular is formed so as to encourage deliberation, the president occupies a central place in the deliberative republic—that of checking, or at least slowing, the progress of legislation of the wrong character. On this front, the president's energy will allow him to act with dispatch and quickness when times demand it; but this same characteristic allows the president to slow the government, cool the passions, and thereby improve the deliberative process.

The legislative power delegated by the people to their representatives is complex and fragmented in American constitutional democracy. In keeping with the character of the legislature, the presidency was not meant to be an office simply for administration and the neutral execution of the laws. Rather, the president was given an important role to play in the tricameral division of legislative powers: the presidency was invested with the responsibility of being an institution of legislative representation. As a general rule, the House, the Senate, and the president must all agree in order to enact legislation. If they do not agree among themselves, they must at least interact and thereby influence one another before changes can occur in law. The president combines his energy and independence with legislative powers in the veto to become part of the deliberative process for promoting the common good. He is given a qualified negative, not an absolute one. This serves both to keep his power within republican limits as well as to put the presidency at the heart of a legislative process that is designed always to foster circumspection and debate rather than either to facilitate immediate action or to check activity completely.

For example, if the president were given no veto power at all, improper legislation could more easily navigate the process and become law. Or if given an absolute veto, the president would have the power completely to hinder any legislative activity with which he would disagree. As it is, the qualified presidential power of "returning all bills *with objections*"[13] forces the legislature to deliberate further in light of those objections and thus to reconsider what it might have failed to consider adequately the first time around. As Publius notes, "The oftener the measure is brought under examination, the greater the diversity in the situation of those who are to examine it, the less must be the danger of those errors which flow from want of due deliberation, or of those missteps which proceed from the contagion of some common passion or interest" (73:381).

Publius understands that the legislature, although designed to ensure the enactment of proper legislation, cannot always be counted on to act wisely or from the right motives. The qualified veto "establishes a salutary check upon the legislative body, calculated to guard the community against the effects of faction, precipitancy, or of any impulse unfriendly to the public good, which may happen to influence a majority of that body" (73:381). If he is to wield his veto properly, the president must act energetically and with independence from both the legislature and any popular majority existing at the moment. But what of the challenge that such power invested in the president may work to "clog" the system and inhibit the passage of needed legislation? Publius's natural conservatism makes him unconcerned about this question. Those who see the danger of mutability in legislation will be able to understand that

> every institution calculated to restrain the excess of lawmaking, and to keep things in the same state in which they happen to be at any given period is much more likely to do good than harm; because it is favorable to greater stability in the system of legislation. The injury which may possibly be done by defeating a few good laws will be amply compensated by the advantage of preventing a number of bad ones. (73:381–82)

More specifically, to what end is the president firmly to enact this important representative role? Publius is clear on this front. He outlines two interrelated representational functions of the president's veto power. First, consistent with the more limited and democratic interpretation of the checks-and-balances system, he is to wield the veto in self-defense against a legislature—whether backed by a popular majority or not—that is bent on intruding on the rights of the other constitutional officers and absorbing their powers. In this respect the president is to function as the representative of the people of the Constitution. That constitutional people agreed to constrain both its own sovereign power and that of its most popular branch, as well as to subordinate both to the needs of a constitutional republic. With Tocqueville, Publius understood that a democratic people will often fail to understand the necessity of political forms and thereby will readily and imprudently attempt to rid itself of such constraints.[14] The president was intended to defend the *forms* of constitutional government through his use of the qualified veto.[15] In other words, he was to be a representative not of any current majority but of an American people enshrined in the Constitution and having a constant interest in the maintenance of constitutionally limited democracy.

Publius makes it clear, however, that use of the veto was not to be limited to self-protection of the presidency and defense of the constitutional forms. Rather, further use of the veto is to furnish "an additional security against the inaction of improper laws" (73:381). Here the president serves as the representative of the national good and of a longer-term and more reasonable public than might seem to be represented from time to time in the legislature. In this representative function, the president's most important role is to stave off legislation that might be improved or set aside upon more mature and sedate reflection. He thereby not only encourages further deliberation in the legislature but may even qualitatively improve such deliberation due to the change engendered by his veto action and the objections he has communicated to Congress. In this way, the president as representative is an *ameliorator* of the product of government as well as an executor.

It is a mainstay of contemporary politics that presidents routinely attempt, validly or not, to claim "mandates" from the people following electoral victories. Is there room in Publius's representative democracy for any such popular mandate? Publius does seem to acknowledge the potential for some level of popular mandate for the executive, albeit a limited one. The popular mandate acknowledged in *The Federalist Papers* is essentially negative—one rendered in response to the current situation and past actions rather than a forward-looking one of a more positive nature. In discussing administrative changes that occur after a change of personnel at the top, Publius writes, "where the alteration has been the result of public choice [elections], the person substituted is warranted in supposing that the dismission of his predecessor has proceeded from a dislike to his measures; and that the less he resembles him, the more he will recommend himself to the favor of his constituents" (72:375).

But, as should be clear from what we have seen, *popular* mandates are not the only ones available to the chief executive in the American republic. Nor would they be the most important. As a representative of the transcendent people of our fundamental compact, the president also has a *constitutional* mandate to defend the forms of our fundamental law and to do his part to ensure that good law emerges from the legislative process. To these we might add the more specific mandates that are attached to his particular *constitutional* powers. If he is properly to live up to these mandates, Publius realized, there will be times when he cannot also represent the existing popular majority. Publius's representational morality affords the necessary room in which constitutional officers might represent without being responsive.

CONCLUSION

Publius was concerned to acquire *virtuous* representatives who would come to the halls of government and *deliberate* on the means to promote the common good of society. Such representatives require a high degree of independence from their respective constituencies and parochial interests. Though each institution of government is to be made up of independent trustees elevated from the great body of the people, members of the various institutions are not unidimensionally independent. The public good is promoted not simply because representatives are more virtuous, experienced, and knowledgeable than the people at large, but also because "they operate in an environment that fosters collective reasoning about common concerns."[16] The diversity of the institutions is an essential ingredient to the existence of this environment.[17]

The degrees of independence found in each institution contribute to the ability of the deliberative process to formulate just laws and the promotion of the commonwealth. But as Willmoore Kendall has reminded us, there is room in such a system for at least one essential mandate: to "produce *just* policy decisions in a certain manner."[18] That certain manner is the constitutional system of deliberation I have outlined. A presidency consistent with the needs of representative government is particularly important to this deliberative process.

The office is established in order to encourage independent judgment in the executive; the president's virtue and knowledge make it likely that he will recognize legislation that is not in the public interest, and his energy and constitutional powers allow him to act upon his judgment to slow and improve the deliberative process. For "servile pliancy of the executive to a prevailing current, either in the community or in the legislature" is a crude and ignorant notion "of the true means by which the public happiness may be promoted" (71:370). The president as representative is an ameliorator of the product of government as well as its executor. The president is representative of, and not merely responsive to, popular will. Acting as the representative of the people of the Constitution, he also is to act in defense of the forms of the Constitution, which properly limit the people's power immediately to enact its will. Thus, he is a guardian of the process of free government as well as an active ameliorator of its product.

The president, then, as a single constitutional officer, is every bit as legitimate a representative as those in the legislative body. His legitimacy is the result of the necessary ingredients he brings to the process of government, his share in the legislative powers delegated by the people, and the republican safety institutionalized in the office. Indeed, one of the great accomplishments of both *The Federalist Papers* and the Constitution they explain has been to show that an energetic executive is necessary to free government and that this traditionally nonrepublican institution could be made consistent with the jealousies and needs of representation.

But that strong balance of ambitions and institutions which was crafted into our constitutional order and explicated by Publius has lately become undone. The modern polity has ushered in a centralized government of powers undreamt of by even the most statist of our Founding Fathers. At the center of that empowered central government stands the American president, supreme both in power and in claims of democratic legitimacy. In contrast to Publius's insistence on an office insulated from the swells of popular opinion, modern presidents have embraced polling and pollsters. Rather than representing the transcendent people of the constitutional order, our presidents have too often seemed more than ready to embrace the popular demands of the time. Under the assertion of having received a "mandate" to govern, modern presidents have attempted to undermine the deliberative and slow processes of legislation by forcing their will upon legislators or circumventing the legislative process entirely through unilateral executive action. Through such unilateralism, presidents have taken the nation on military excursions around the world, have regulated and deregulated American industry, have taken large tracts of land from public use, and have established a regulatory regime that reaches almost every aspect of American life.

Such developments were once the stuff that moved constitutionalists and conservative intellectuals. Yet the voices of James Burnham and Wilmoore Kendall have now grown distant and largely unrecognizable to contemporary conservatives. Where once we celebrated Calhoun, Clay, and Webster for having fought off the executive encroachments of "King Jackson," now we have become preoccupied by other issues and have become intoxicated by the potent elixir of power politics.

And what about Congress, Publius's hope as the core of the deliberative republic? Where Publius would have predicted that congressional ambition would have been piqued by such encroachments, more often than not Congress has been complicit in the growth of executive dominance. By establishing a large regulatory state requiring a massive bureaucracy, by acquiescing in military campaigns embarked on by the executive, and by passing vague laws that allow the executive great latitude in making the central decisions that affect the quality of life of American citizens, Congress has abandoned its responsibility to Publius's deliberative republic and has gone far in helping to replace it with a presidential republic.

A regular recurrence to *The Federalist Papers* is necessary if we are not to abandon completely the vision of the founding generation and the constitutional balance that vision provided to us. In our age no one has done more to remind us of this than George Wescott Carey. That a remnant still holds to the truths of the founding is a testament to his scholarship and his vision.

Rights in a Federalist System

FRANCIS CANAVAN

The major problem in writing on this topic in a volume in honor of George W. Carey is that Professor Carey has already said about all there is to say. I agree with him in holding that the U.S. Supreme Court has brought about a change of the American constitutional regime: it has asserted its power not only to override the laws and acts of the state governments and national Congress when these conflict with the Constitution, but also to find grounds for doing so that are not in the text of the Constitution. The justices perceive these grounds in the light of suppositions that they bring to the text. Carey explains this at length in several of his writings, including, for example, "Judicial Activism and Regime Change."[1]

In that essay he quotes one of the many defenders of judicial activism as saying: "At every turn they [the framers] buffered majority will, insulated representatives from direct influence of majority factions and provided checks on majority decision making."[2] Carey comments, "The Framers' goal, according to this line of reasoning, was to protect liberty, understood in terms of individual rights."[3] The writer on whom he comments confirms this interpretation of her meaning, stating that such constitutional principles as "separation of powers, checks and balances, and federalism—all . . . are more comfortably accepted as devices for protecting individual rights."[4]

Toward the end of his essay, Carey mentions a line of thought that he does not develop: "All the efforts to advance judicial activism presuppose a political philosophy that is never articulated."[5] Here, I will try to go at least some distance in articulating that political philosophy. But first we must see what the framers themselves thought they were doing in the Constitutional Convention of 1787 and then look at constitutional developments. It is true that the framers believed in limited constitutional government; they therefore conferred limited powers on the federal government and imposed some limitations on the powers of the states. But there is little reason to think that their only or even primary purpose was to protect individual rights. I shall base my presentation of their purpose on the notes that James Madison took during the Convention, as found in Charles C. Tansill's *Documents Illustrative of the Formation of the Union of the American States*.[6]

The main business of the Constitutional Convention began on May 29, with a series of motions introduced by Edmund Randolph of the Virginia delegation. These resolutions were thereafter referred to as the Virginia Plan, in contrast to the New Jersey Plan that was later introduced and rejected. The final Constitution of the United States grew out of long and serious debates on the Virginia Plan.

In his speech introducing the plan, Randolph began by stating that in revising "the federal system [of the Articles of Confederation] we ought to inquire 1) into the properties, which such a government ought to possess. . . ." He continued:

> The character of such a government ought to secure 1) against foreign invasion: 2) against dissentions between the members of the Union, or seditions in particular states: 3) to procure to the several States, various blessings, of which an isolated situation was incapable: 4) to be able to defend itself against encroachment: and 5) to be paramount to the state constitutions.[7]

Personal liberty is nowhere mentioned in this list of the goals of the new Constitution to be framed, although it may be included in the "various blessings" of number four. But it clearly was not a major purpose of the Constitution. A main goal, and probably the most pressing one, was to bring the several states under the authority of the national government in a system based on the principle of divided sovereignty, with the nation and the states holding sovereignty within their respective spheres. This purpose occupied a large part of the Convention's time—but not for the sake of protecting individual rights against oppressive state governments.

The device that the Virginia Plan proposed for making the states obey the Constitution was to give Congress the power "to negative all laws passed by the several States, contravening in the opinion of the National Legislature the articles of Union; and to call forth the force of the Union against any member of the Union failing to fulfill its duties under the articles thereof."[8] This proposition was later adopted by the Convention, but was finally dropped as impracticable and possibly dangerous. In its place, on July 17, Luther Martin of Maryland made a motion[9] that was later accepted by the Convention. After modifications in committee, that motion became Article VI of the Constitution as we now have it. In its present words, it reads:

> This Constitution, and the Laws of the United States which shall be made in Pursuance thereof; and all Treaties made, or which shall be made under the Authority of the United States, shall be the supreme Law of the Land; and the Judges in every State shall be bound thereby, any Thing in the Constitution or Laws of any State to the Contrary notwithstanding.

Notably, this article mentions only state judges as being bound by the Constitution and the laws and treaties of the United States; it does not mention federal judges—but not because they are not likewise bound. The purpose of the clause is to ensure that the states will be subordinate to the federal government when acting within its constitutional bounds. Article VI is the method of achieving that. There is no general purpose of guaranteeing personal rights and liberty, these being matters for the most part left to the states and their "police power."

"Police" has been described as "[t]he function of that branch of the administrative machinery of government which is charged with the preservation of public order and tranquility, the promotion of the public health, safety, and morals, and the prevention, detection, and punishment of crime." The "police power" is "[t]he power vested in the legislature to make, ordain, and establish all manner of wholesome and reasonable laws, statutes and ordinances . . . not repugnant to the constitution, as they shall judge for the good and welfare of the commonwealth and of the subjects of the same."[10] Let us not forget that the U.S. Constitution is the basic law of a *federal* system; it did not transfer the police power of the states to the national government, nor would the people of the several states have ratified the Constitution if it had attempted to do that.

The preamble of the Constitution, which was accepted without debate by the Convention on August 7 and later rewritten by the Convention's Committee on Style,[11] now appears in the Constitution in these words:

> We the People of the United States, in Order to form a more perfect
> Union, establish Justice, insure domestic Tranquility, provide for the
> common defense, promote the general Welfare, and secure the Bless-
> ings of Liberty to ourselves and Posterity, do ordain and establish this
> Constitution for the United States of America.

Again, these goals cannot be reduced to the blessings of liberty, nor can the blessings refer only to the protection of individual rights. They may very well include the rights of institutions that are formed by individuals but establish obligations binding individuals to a common good of the family, the community, or the nation. For there are human goods that can be enjoyed only by participating in them, not by enjoying them as solitary individuals. A conversation, for example, is something more than a series of monologues, and the constitution of a civil society is more than a mutual nonaggression pact among individuals.

In the first session of the First Congress of the United States, James Madison introduced a list of proposed amendments to the Constitution in the House of Representatives. Out of these grew the so-called Bill of Rights, consisting of the first eight amendments, plus the ninth and tenth, which explain what the first eight do and do not mean. Constitutional rights are restraints on the powers of the federal government, telling it what it may and may not do; thus, the Ninth Amendment explains that the enumeration of certain rights in the Constitution (in the Bill of Rights in particular) does not mean that these are the only restraints on the powers of the federal government. The Tenth Amendment clarifies that provision by stating that federal powers are only those delegated in the Constitution; the rest are reserved to the states (by whose ratification the federal government exists) or to the people.

One might—and should—ask whether the rights reserved to the people should be understood simply as individual rights. For example, do First Amendment rights merely guarantee the freedom of individuals to believe and preach what they will, to say and publish what they wish, and to assemble for whatever purposes they choose? Or do they aim primarily at taking government out of the dangerous business of settling the kind of doctrinal disputes that had led to wars of religion, and at establishing the necessary preconditions of representative government? Do First Amendment rights thereby intend not only to protect individual rights but also to provide for the common good of a free, orderly, and humane society?

The groundwork of a marked shift in the Supreme Court's interpretation of constitutional rights was laid in the aftermath of the Civil War. The Thirteenth Amendment abolished slavery in 1865; the Southern states replied with Black Codes denying the freed slaves the full civil rights of citizens; and Congress responded with the Civil Rights Act of 1866. The constitutionality of this act was dubious, however, since no clause of the Constitution gave Congress the power to enact it. Section 1 of the Fourteenth Amendment therefore declared: "All persons born or naturalized in the United States and subject to the jurisdiction thereof, are citizens of the United States and the State wherein they reside." This left no ground for denying the citizenship of American-born black persons.

When Congressman John A. Bingham (R-OH) first introduced what would later become Section 1, he stated it in these words:

> The Congress shall have power to make all laws which shall be necessary and proper to secure to the citizens of each State all privileges and immunities of citizens in the several States, and to all persons in the several States equal protection in the rights of life, liberty and property.[12]

Bingham clearly intended his amendment to be a grant of power to Congress to enact civil-rights laws that would override state laws hostile to the recently emancipated slaves.

Bingham's amendment did not meet with favor in the House of Representatives and was tabled. It came back, however, as part of another amendment proposed by the Committee on Reconstruction (of which Bingham was a member), with a Section 1 written by Bingham (except for the citizenship clause, which was later added in the Senate). As finally adopted, the amendment begins with the citizenship clause and continues:

> No State shall make or enforce any law which shall abridge the privileges or immunities of citizens of the United States nor shall any State deprive any person of life, liberty or property, without due process of law; nor deny to any person within its jurisdiction the equal protection of the laws.

It is highly significant that, in its final form, Section 1 of the Fourteenth Amendment does not include an enacting clause. Since the Committee on Reconstruction included three other amendments along with Bingham's—

none of importance today—the enacting clause was shifted to Section 5 of the Fourteenth Amendment: "The Congress shall have power to enforce, by appropriate legislation, the provisions of this article." But that leaves Section 1 a freestanding part of the Constitution: one to which litigants can appeal directly for adjudication without intervening congressional legislation.

Bingham and the other Republican leaders in Congress were not unaware of judicial review as a means of protecting civil rights; but it is difficult to imagine them relying for that purpose on the Supreme Court, which only nine years earlier had handed down the *Dred Scott* decision. In the House of Representatives, Bingham stated emphatically, "[t]he necessity for the first section of this amendment is a want . . . in the constitution of our country, which the proposed amendment will supply." Later in the same speech he explained "[t]hat great want of the citizen and the stranger, protection by national law from unconstitutional State enactments, is supplied by the first section of the amendment. That is the extent it hath, no more."[13] Other supporters of the amendment in the House said the same. Senator Jacob M. Howard of Michigan (R) presented the same case when he opened the debate on the amendment in the Senate: there are rights guaranteed in the Constitution, but Congress does not have the power to enforce them against the states; "therefore if they are to [be] effectuated and enforced . . . that additional power should be given to Congress [to] that end. This is done by the fifth section of this amendment."[14]

The Republicans who framed and passed the Fourteenth Amendment seem almost to have overlooked the fact that, by detaching sections 1 and 5 from each other, they made Section 1 a grant of power directly to the Supreme Court. It must be acknowledged that, for three decades after the Fourteenth Amendment was written, the Court gave Section 1 a narrow interpretation, rendering the privileges-and-immunities clause almost a nullity and giving the due-process clause an interpretation that confined the Court to deciding whether certain state procedures conformed to constitutional procedural requirements.

In the first case it decided under Section 1, the Court said that acceptance of the broad construction of those clauses which the plaintiffs in the case argued for "would constitute this a perpetual censor upon all legislation of the states, on the civil rights of their own citizens."[15] These words, as it turned out, were prophetic.

The future vast expansion of the jurisdiction of the federal courts, and especially of the Supreme Court, lay in what is called substantive due process.

That is to say, a law may be held unconstitutional, not as denying a party to a case his right to proper procedures, but as impairing or denying a substantive right found under one of the headings of life, liberty, or property, or as implicit in the equality guaranteed by the equal protection of the laws. The substance of those terms is to be determined by the Court. As Charles Evans Hughes remarked between his two terms on the Supreme Court: we are under a Constitution, but the meaning of the Constitution is "what the Supreme Court says it is."[16] Although the Court had made some cautious moves in that direction, it was not until 1897 that it interpreted the due-process clause as protecting not only procedural rights but the substantive rights of the citizen "to be free in the enjoyment of all his faculties," including specifically the right "to live and work where he will; to earn his livelihood in any lawful calling; to pursue any livelihood or vocation, and for that purpose to enter into all contracts which may be proper, necessary and essential to carrying out to a successful conclusion the purposes mentioned."[17]

The newfound constitutional right to freedom of contract had a forty-year run, during which the Court struck down a number of state laws regarding wages and hours of labor, thus protecting the right of employers to pay low wages for long hours of work in the name of protecting employees' freedom to contract. The run came to an end during the New Deal, when the Court recognized that

> [t]he Constitution does not speak of freedom of contract. It speaks of liberty and prohibits the deprivation of liberty without due process of law. . . . But the liberty safeguarded is liberty in a social organization which requires the protection of law against the evils which menace the health, safety, morals, and welfare of the people . . . and regulation which is reasonable in relation to its subject and is adopted in the interests of the community is due process.[18]

With these words the Court upheld a law of the state of Washington that regulated the wages of women and minors and effectively put an end to "freedom to contract" as a constitutional right that prevented wages-and-hours legislation.

The Court, however, had earlier begun a process of "incorporating" the federal Bill of Rights into the due-process clause of the Fourteenth Amendment, making these rights binding on the states. It began with *Gitlow v. New York* in 1925, which guaranteed the First Amendment's freedom of speech or of the press clause against abridgment by the states.[19] The process of incorporation has been gradual, and not every clause in the Bill of Rights has been incorporated. But in 1965, the Court faced a case that could not be decided by appealing to any clause in the Bill of Rights or in any other part of the Constitution.[20]

The state of Connecticut had a law that forbade the use of contraceptives and a general statute that forbade aiding and abetting this or any other legal offense. Under these statutes the executive and medical directors of the Planned Parenthood Center in New Haven were charged and found guilty of providing contraceptive information and advice to married persons. When the case came before the U.S. Supreme Court, it admitted that "the association of people is not mentioned in the Constitution nor the Bill of Rights."[21] The opinion of the Court then listed a number of cases in which rights explicitly guaranteed were found to generate implicit ones. "The foregoing cases suggest that specific guarantees in the Bill of Rights have penumbras, formed by emanations from those guarantees that help give them life and substance. . . . Various guarantees create zones of privacy," and marriage falls within one of those zones.[22] A law that forbids the use of contraceptives violates the privacy of marriage and is therefore unconstitutional, as is the application of a general statute that forbids giving information and advice on such use.

Justice Hugo Black had long been—and continued to be—an advocate of the proposition that the due-process clause was intended to incorporate all of the Bill of Rights. But he dissented vehemently from the opinion of the Court in this case, saying, "[o]ne of the most effective ways of diluting or expanding a constitutionally guaranteed right is to substitute for the crucial word or words of a constitutional guarantee another word or words, more or less flexible and more or less restricted in meaning." Such a word is privacy. "I get nowhere in this case," he said, "by talk about a constitutional 'right of privacy' as an emanation from one or more constitutional provisions."[23] He went on to conclude, "[t]he adoption of any such loose, flexible, uncontrolled standard for holding laws unconstitutional, if ever it is finally achieved, will amount to a great unconstitutional shift of power to the courts which will be bad for the courts and worse for the country."[24]

The great shift of power from legislatures to courts has continued apace and constitutes what could be called without exaggeration a change of regime. *Griswold v. Connecticut* was followed by a line of cases in which the Court decided that contraception was a right that did not belong to married couples alone but was an individual right independent of marital status.[25] A woman was determined to have a constitutional right to choose to abort her child,[26] whereas her husband and the father of her child has no legal right to prevent the abortion, since the state cannot delegate to him a power that it does not itself have.[27] These decisions spawned a host of subsequent cases concerning state and municipal laws that tested (usually unsuccessfully) the limits of the Court's concern for the primacy of individual choice.

In 1986, the Court upheld the constitutionality of a Georgia law making homosexual sodomy a crime.[28] As we shall see below, in 2003, the Court reversed that decision. But two opinions from *Bowers* are worthy of notice here. Justice Byron White, writing the opinion of the Court, explained:

> Despite the language of the Due Process Clauses of the Fifth and Fourteenth Amendments, which appears to focus only on the processes by which life, liberty, or property is taken, the cases are legion in which those Clauses have been interpreted to have substantive content, subsuming rights that to a great extent are immune from federal or state regulation or proscription.[29]

It is well known that Justice White dissented vigorously from the opinion of the Court in *Roe v. Wade* and subsequent abortion cases. But here, writing an opinion of the Court, he had to acknowledge that the Court had repeatedly accepted substantive due process—so that was a settled question. (As I once heard Dr. Leo Pfeffer say, "If the Court says something three times, then it is so.") Justice White went on to explain the nature of "rights not readily identifiable in the Constitution's text." One earlier decision of the Court had called them "those fundamental liberties that are 'implicit in the concept of ordered liberty' such that 'neither liberty nor justice would exist if [they] were sacrificed.'" Another case described them as those liberties which are "deeply rooted in this Nation's history and traditions."[30] Homosexual sodomy, he concluded, did not qualify for constitutional protection under these tests.[31]

Justice Blackmun responded for the four dissenters in a passage that was a classical statement of liberal individualism. He began by citing a series of cases in which the Court had found "that a certain private sphere of individual liberty will be kept largely beyond the reach of government." The heart of this argument in the present case is:

> We protect those rights [contained in the sphere of privacy] not be-
> cause they contribute in some direct and material way to the general
> public welfare, but because they form so central a part of an individu-
> al's life. . . . And so we protect the decision whether to marry precisely
> because marriage is an association that promotes a way of life. . . . We
> protect the decision whether to have a child because parenthood alters
> so dramatically an individual's self-definition. . . . And we protect the
> family because it contributes powerfully to the happiness of individu-
> als, not because of a preference for stereotypical households.[32]

With these words Blackmun denies that the family is a basic institution of society on whose health and well-being the common welfare depends, and he reduces it to a way of satisfying the psychological needs of individuals. He also implies that what makes a choice good is not that a good object has been chosen, but that the object is good precisely because it *has* been chosen:

> The fact that individuals define themselves in a significant way through
> their intimate sexual relationships with others suggests, in a Nation as
> diverse as ours, that there may be many "right" ways of conducting
> those relationships, and that much of the richness of the relationship
> will come from the freedom an individual has to *choose* the form and
> nature of these intentionally emotional bonds.[33]

The same attitude appears in a later case, *Romer, Governor of Colorado v. Evans*.[34] The citizens of Colorado had adopted an amendment to their state constitution that banned laws forbidding discrimination against homosexuals. The U.S. Supreme Court declared the Colorado amendment an unconstitutional violation of the equal-protection clause of the Fourteenth Amendment. First, the Colorado amendment imposes "a broad and undifferentiated disability on a single named group. . . . Second, its sheer breadth is so discontinuous with the reasons offered for it that the amendment seems inexplicable by anything but animus toward the class that it affects."[35] One is reminded of George F. Will's comment: "The fundamental goal of modern liberalism has been equality, and it has given us government that believes in the moral equality of appetites."[36] The liberalism of the Court's opinion is indubitable, but the Court's opinion is open to certain questions. Does the Constitution *require* the enactment of antidiscrimination laws? If not, why may the citizens of a state not decide against enacting certain antidiscrimination laws? And is it true that the equal-protection clause commands the people of a state to regard homosexual appetites as morally and legally equivalent to heterosexual ones? To press the question a bit further, does it require the states to recognize homosexual unions as marriages? If not, why not?

In 1997, the Court undertook another discussion of the scope of substantive due process and equal protection of the laws in two cases arising out of state laws prohibiting physician-assisted suicide.[37] The holding in the first case was that Washington's law did not violate the due-process clause; in the other case, it was that New York's law did not violate the equal protection of the laws clause. In each case, all the justices concurred in the judgment; but several concurring opinions suggested that in later cases they might perceive some right to assistance in suicide.

The most interesting aspect of the opinions is the justices' understanding of equal protection and, particularly, of substantive due process. The opinion of the Court in both cases was written by Chief Justice William Rehnquist, who stated what must now be taken as the Court's interpretation of due process: "The Due Process Clause guarantees more than fair process, and the 'liberty' it protects includes more than the absence of physical restraint. . . . The Clause also provides heightened protection against certain governmental interference with certain fundamental rights and liberty interests."[38] He then listed a string of earlier cases in which the Court had found such nonenumerated rights in the due-process clause. Then he added, quoting earlier decisions, "[b]ut we ha[ve] always been reluctant to expand the concept of substantive due process because guideposts for responsible decision making in this uncharted area are scarce and open-ended." We must therefore take care "lest the liberty protected by the Due Process Clause be subtly transformed into the policy preferences of the members of the Court."[39]

Justice David Souter, concurring in the judgment, took a broader view of the scope of substantive due process. He offered a "brief overview of its history," which is interesting as an exposition of how the judicial mind works when spinning out a body of constitutional law that gets far from anything to be found in the text of the Constitution.[40] Souter concludes, in a sentence that is pregnant with meaning: "The text of the Due Process Clause thus imposes nothing less than an obligation to give substantive content to the words 'liberty' and 'due process of law.'"[41] But, he insists, he does not assign to the Court the right to substitute its judgment for that of a legislature which has struck a balance between the competing claims of political contenders (normally the subject matter of politics), except when "it falls outside the realm of the reasonable."[42] Justice Souter therefore favors the development of substantive due process through what he calls the common-law method.[43]

Black's Law Dictionary describes the common law in these terms:

> As distinguished from law created by the enactment of legislatures, the common law comprises the body of those principles and rules of action, relating to the government and security of persons and property, which derive their authority solely from usages and customs of immemorial antiquity, or *from the judgments and decrees of courts recognizing, affirming and enforcing such usages and customs*; and in this sense, particularly the ancient unwritten law of England.[44]

But Justice Souter must know that in England no court can nullify an act of Parliament. The common-law method is simply inappropriate for American constitutional law.

Justice Souter's opinion is, of course, only the opinion of one member of the Court. But his description of how the Court ought to act is a fairly accurate depiction of the way it does act. In discovering a new unenumerated constitutional right, the Court customarily begins by citing a number of earlier decisions. The Court professes, as did Chief Justice Rehnquist and Justice Souter in their opinions in the case last discussed, to be restrained in the scope of its authority. But the justices are restrained only by the Court's interpretation of the limits of substantive due process, or by their sense of what the American people will tolerate. (For this reason the Court is highly unlikely to find a constitutional right to polygamy among consenting adults—but given its precedents, it could.)

The Court's view of the scope of its authority appears in full flower in the opinion written by Justice Anthony Kennedy in *Lawrence v. Texas*, a June 2003 case that struck down a Texas statute that had criminalized homosexual sodomy.[45] Our immediate concern is only to explain the basis on which the Court claimed the power to establish a constitutional right it had denied in *Bowers v. Hardwick* in 1986. The Court focused on the meaning of the liberty protected by the due-process clause of the Fourteenth Amendment. Echoing Justice Blackmun's dissent in the *Bowers* case, the Supreme Court of the United States declared in a truly remarkable passage:

To say that the issue of *Bowers* was simply the right to engage in certain sexual conduct demeans the claim that the individual [Hardwick] put forward, just as it would demean a married couple were it to be said that marriage is simply about the right to have sexual intercourse. The laws involved in *Bowers* and here are, to be sure, statutes that purport to do no more than to prohibit a particular sexual act. Their penalties and purposes, though, have more far-reaching consequences touching upon the most private human conduct, sexual behavior, and in the most private places, the home. The statutes do seek to control a personal relationship that, whether or not entitled to formal recognition in the laws, is within the liberty of persons to choose without being punished as criminals.[46]

But this is to say that all that matters is the personal sexual relationship, not the act in which it expresses itself. Furthermore, it is to say that the fact that persons have freely chosen it outweighs any social consequences that may flow from it. Yet extensive consequences do follow upon it—and were immediately demanded by homosexual activists on the very day the decision in this case was handed down. If prohibiting homosexual intercourse is equally demeaning to homosexual and heterosexual marital relationships, then why does "liberty" not require the equal legal status of same-sex and heterosexual marriage? Why should homosexual couples not have the same right to adopt and raise children? Why can the public schools not have their pupils read *Heather Has Two Mommies*? And why should heterosexual parents who want to prepare their little Heathers for heterosexual marriage have to allow her indoctrination into the equal value of homosexual relationships? Since the liberal mind can see only individual relationships, it can answer these questions only with "why not, if they have chosen each other?" But when did we all agree on that as a social norm?

The opinion of the Court detected "an emerging awareness that liberty gives substantial protection to adult persons in deciding how to conduct their personal lives in matters pertaining to sex."[47] It is true that a large number of states have repealed their laws criminalizing homosexual conduct between consenting adults in private. Yet it does not follow that the people of those states regard such conduct as a constitutional right. They may have done what they did because of a spreading "live and let live" attitude in a pluralistic society, or because they wanted to eliminate the police snooping involved in enforcing such laws, or because politicians are subject to constant pressure by groups that have money and are willing to contribute significant amounts to political campaigns. But in the eyes of the Court, this "emerging awareness" reveals a new frontier in substantive due process:

> Had those who drew up and ratified the Due Process Clauses of the Fifth Amendment or the Fourteenth Amendment known the components of liberty in its manifold possibilities they might have been more specific. They did not presume to have this insight. They knew times can blind us to certain truths and later generations can see that laws once thought proper in fact serve only to oppress. As the Constitution endures persons in every generation can invoke its principle in their search for greater freedom.[48]

The unspoken premise of the above passage is that the Supreme Court is peculiarly equipped to discern those principles by peering into the crystal ball of "liberty." It also assumes that an unelected and irremovable court is empowered to do the discerning.

Now we approach the political philosophy that is presupposed by judicial activism but is never articulated. Since it is taken for granted, as the intellectual air that we breathe in this country, its sources are not identified in the opinions of the Court. But those sources might even surprise some of the more activist justices, since the Court's habit is not to appeal to any philosophical sources for its premises but to refer to its earlier decisions: if we have decided that A, then B, then C are constitutional rights, surely we must do the same for D. The ultimate justification for the Court's decisions, in their minds, does not go beyond appeal to the nation's history and the idea of ordered liberty—and these mean what the justices say they mean.

The Court's interpretation of due process and equal protection has seen a fairly steady movement toward taking basic moral questions of public importance out of the democratic process and transferring them to the judicial process. This is not to say that the democratic process is always right—far from it. But what is left to the democratic process has at least this merit: that an issue can remain a subject of continuing debate and possible (usually gradual) change, whereas what the Court decides is announced as the meaning of the supreme law of the land, which is above political controversy. (On this point see the plurality opinion in *Planned Parenthood v. Casey*,[49] with its plaintive plea to be allowed to save the American people from themselves by taking danger-

ously controversial questions out of politics.) To the extent that the Court succeeds in imposing its will we no longer have a Constitution but a body of constitutional law spun by the Court from the concepts of liberty and equality.

Constitutional historian Leonard W. Levy has described—and praised—
the resulting situation:

> Excepting the commerce clause, which is the basis of so much congres-
> sional legislation, modern constitutional law is very much made up of
> Fourteenth Amendment cases. No part of the Constitution has given
> rise to more cases than its due process clause alone, and its various
> clauses taken together account for about half the work of the Supreme
> Court. The states in our federal system can scarcely act without rais-
> ing a Fourteenth Amendment question. The vast majority of all cases
> which concern our precious constitutional freedoms—from freedom
> of speech to separation of church and state, from racial equality to the
> many elements of criminal justice—turn on the Fourteenth Amend-
> ment. The history of its interpretation is, at bottom, the story of the
> two great subjects that bulk largest in our constitutional law: govern-
> ment regulation of the economy and individual rights.[50]

One may wonder whether all Professor Levy's cherished freedoms are either precious or constitutional, but his description of constitutional law today
is pretty accurate. As a colleague of mine has remarked, the liberal mind
conceives of civil society as a mutual nonaggression pact—hence the emphasis
on individual rights. But whence comes the thinking that leads to this heavy
emphasis on the individual's rights?

An obvious source is the social-contract theory that underlies so much of
liberal political philosophy. This theory issues from John Locke, and before
him, Thomas Hobbes and William of Ockham. Of Locke, Sheldon Wolin has
said, "[t]o the extent that modern liberalism can be said to be inspired by any
one writer, Locke is undoubtedly the leading candidate."[51] Locke is famous
as an apostle of natural rights—and that he was. But his epistemology and
metaphysics did not furnish an adequate foundation for a political philosophy
founded upon a common human nature.

Metaphysics is the part of any philosophy that deals with its most basic
conception of being: what is or can be. Epistemology is the part dealing with
what the human mind can know. Locke's philosophy could not admit knowledge of common natures because he was a nominalist. (The Latin *nomina*

means names: hence nominalism, the epistemology espoused by Locke.) In his major philosophical work, *An Essay Concerning Human Understanding*,[52] Locke says, "[m]etaphysical truth . . . is nothing but the real existence of things conformable to the ideas we have annexed to their names. This, though, seems to consist in the very beings of things yet, when considered more closely, will appear to include a tacit proposition whereby the mind joins a particular thing to the idea it had before settled with a name to it."[53] We do not know "the internal constitution and true nature of things, being destitute of faculties to attain it."[54] It is true that one never meets Humanity or Human Nature walking down the street, but only individual men, women, and children. But in a nominalist philosophy, we do not even recognize these individuals as unified by a common nature. We know them only as characterized as human by resemblance in their appearances—that is, as perceived by the senses—and distinguished as individuals by differences in the same. These sense impressions are combined by our minds to form nominal essences, or group names.

One begins to see the difficulty that Locke will encounter in trying to formulate a moral law based on the common-law nature of mankind. Nominal essences are not really inherent in things, then, but are abstract ideas that men make and "thereby enable themselves to consider things, and discourse of them, as it were in bundles."[55] But "universality belongs not to things themselves, which are all of them particular to their existence."[56] In saying this, Locke makes a basic move: only individual things exist, *therefore* only individual things are real. The general ideas by which we group them "are the inventions and creatures of the understanding, made by it for its own use."[57] A culture steeped in this epistemology will be an individualistic one.

Locke is even more a nominalist in his moral philosophy. The existing things to which we attach the names that are their nominal essences really exist. But "mixed modes"—the category into which virtues and vices fall—are entirely products of the human mind, with "no other sensible standard existing anywhere but the name itself." Moral disputes, therefore, concern only ideas about which people differ.[58] Thus, there is no room for a natural teleology by which human beings are oriented toward natural human goods: to goals inherent in human nature that are antecedent to choice, guide our choices, and impose moral obligations on us. To admit teleology in human nature would be to make the same move from an "is" to an "ought" that David Hume later said could not be made. But Hume arrived at that conclusion because he had inherited Locke's sensism and nominalism.

For Locke, the lack of natural human goods is not a problem because, philosophically, he is a hedonist. As he says,

> Things then are good or evil only in reference to pleasure or pain. That we call good, which is apt to cause or increase pleasure or diminish pain in us; or else to procure or preserve us the possession or preservation of any other good, or absence of any evil. And, on the contrary, we name that evil, which is apt to produce or increase pain or diminish any pleasure in us, or else to procure us any evil, or deprive us of any good.[59]

Since different people have different tastes, hedonism would—and in later times did—lead to a relativistic morality. But Locke was a Protestant who believed in God the Creator, as understood not by Aquinas but by William of Ockham, the principal founder of nominalism. God's law is supreme because it is His sovereign will and therefore "is the only true touchstone of moral rectitude." By it alone can men judge whether their actions "are like to procure them happiness or misery from the hands of the Almighty."[60] We remain, then, on the level of pleasure and pain, but in a universe ruled by God, who uses these impulses to get men to obey His will.

Locke is thus a voluntarist, yet also a rationalist in his fashion. In his philosophy, we know the world through the impressions it makes on our senses; and these are all impressions of singular and particular things. Yet we unite them in general ideas (nominal essences), so that for Locke the norm of rational judgment is our perception of the agreement or disagreement among reason's ideas. The world that reason knows is largely a world that human reason has constructed according to the laws of logic, of which mathematics is the best model. (An example Locke does not use but which may throw light on his thought states that, given the definition of a triangle, logic can work out the whole of trigonometry.) This, Locke believes, is enough to enable man to cope with the world and save his soul.

Locke believed in a law of nature, but one arrived at by perception of the agreement or disagreement among our ideas. On that basis, he surmised, one could build a law of nature: "The idea of a Supreme Being . . . and the idea of ourselves as understanding rational beings . . . would, I suppose, if duly considered and pursued, afford such foundations of our duty and rules of action, as might place morality amongst the sciences capable of demonstration."[61] According to John Dunn, Locke tried but "never completed any such demonstration," because "it is not in principle possible."[62] Given Locke's philosophical premises, it is indeed impossible. If we start with Locke's nominalism and hedonism, there is no common and knowable human nature and no moral teleology on which to base a natural moral law. Pleasure and pain are the motivating forces of human action, and these vary with individuals. We are then left with the priority of choice over nature, with a relativistic morality and a social contract in which individual consent is prior to and creates political obligation.

This view appears with starker clarity in *Leviathan*, a work by Locke's predecessor and older contemporary, Thomas Hobbes. Michael Oakeshott states, in the introduction to his edition of Hobbes's *Leviathan*:[63]

> Individualism as a gospel has drawn its inspiration from many sources, but as a reasoned theory of society it has its roots in the so-called nominalism of late medieval scholasticism, with its doctrines that the reality of a thing is its individuality, that which makes it *this* thing, and that both in God and in man will is precedent to reason. Hobbes inherited this tradition of nominalism, and more than any other writer passed it on to the modern world. His civil philosophy is based, not on any vague belief in the value or sanctity of the individual man, but on a philosophy for which the world is composed of *individuae substantiae*.[64]

Locke referred to Hobbes as "the justly decried Mr. Hobbes." But we find in Hobbes, in franker terms, the same nominalism, hedonism, voluntarism, and moral relativism that we have seen in Locke. In *Leviathan*, Hobbes argues for the necessity of absolute government (whether by a monarch or an assembly), but on the basis of a radically individualistic concept of human nature. For Hobbes, "the felicity of this life consisteth not in the repose of a mind satisfied. For there is no such *finis ultimus*, utmost aim, nor *summum bonum*, greatest good as is spoken of in the books of the old moral philosophers." Therefore, "I put it for a general inclination of all mankind, a perpetual and restless desire of power after power that ceaseth only in death." The reason for this is not a *libido dominandi*, a lust for domination, but that a man "cannot assure the power and means to live well, which he has present, without the acquisition of more [power]."[65] Men, he says, are sufficiently equal in physical and mental power that "the difference between man, and man, is not so considerable, as that one man can thereupon claim to himself any benefit, to which another may not pretend, as well as he."[66] Men's passions, chiefly greed and pride, lead them inevitably into conflict. In the absence of "a common power to keep them all in awe,"[67] they live in "a state of nature"—a state in which there is no peace, culture, or civilization and, in the famous phrase, in which "the life of man is solitary, poor, nasty, brutish, and short."[68]

Hobbes does not believe that such a state of nature once existed among human beings, at least not generally.[69] He is not describing a historically real state of affairs but pointing to man's selfish and competitive nature, which leads in that direction if not restrained by a sovereign power. For Hobbes, man is not a political animal designed by nature to live in a polis, as he was for Aristotle; he is rather a self-contained atom that crashes into other atoms in a "war of every man against every man."[70] Although such a war does not necessarily involve open violence, the nature of man persists even in an organized society that keeps civil peace. Most of the time, however, the society succeeds in protecting citizens against one another.

Hobbes's civil society is not founded on a teleological view of human nature, then. Rather, it is a way of escaping from the horror of the state that men are naturally in. In this state of nature, nothing can be unjust:

> The notions of right and wrong, justice and injustice have there no place. Where there is no common power, there is no law; where no law, no injustice. . . . It is consequent also to the same condition, that there is no propriety, no dominion, no mine and thine; but only that to be every man's that he can get: and for long as he can keep it. And thus much for the ill condition that man by mere nature is actually placed in; though with a possibility to come out of it, consisting partly in the passions, partly in his reason.[71]

It follows that there is no natural moral law: civil society, government, law, justice—all are creatures of convention, created by human wills obeying passions enlightened by the instrumentality of reason. "The passions that incline men to peace are fear of death; desire of such things as are necessary to commodious living; and a hope by their industry to obtain them. And reason suggesteth convenient articles of peace, upon which men may be drawn to agreement."[72]

Strange as it may seem to those who think of him only as an advocate of royal despotism, Hobbes's polity is a rights-based one. In the state of nature every man has a right to everything—in the purely negative sense that there are no moral or legal bounds to restrain him. This condition, however, is intolerable, and men understandably want to escape from it. But their "right of nature"[73] is nonetheless antecedent to justice and law, which are created by men's surrender of their original right to a governing authority. With the surrender motivated by the selfish passions of fear and desire, the purpose of the government to which they consent is to enable satisfaction of the passions to the greatest extent possible without men warring on one another.

Hobbes enumerates a number of "laws of nature" that must be observed if men are to create an ordered society in which they can pursue their private goals in peace. These laws dictate the necessity of every man surrendering "his original right to do what he please"[74] to a government that can impose peace by the threat of punishment. But the moral philosophy underlying this political purpose is hedonistic and therefore relativistic—one that varies according to times, places, and tastes. "*Good*, and *evil*, are names that signify our appetites, and aversions; which in different tempers, customs, and doctrines of men, are different: . . . 'Nay, the same man, in divers time, differs from himself,' about what he calls good or evil."[75] In the state of nature, therefore, "private appetite is the measure of good and evil: and consequently all men agree on this, that peace is good, and therefore also the way, or means of peace,"[76] i.e., the laws of nature as Hobbes understands them, because they are "the means of peaceable, sociable, and comfortable living." Private appetite remains the measure of good and evil, but within the boundaries required by peace. In this sense, then, one can say that Hobbes too is a founder of contemporary liberalism.

Michael Oakeshott has already been quoted as saying that individualism, as a reasoned theory of society, "has roots in the so-called nominalism of late medieval scholasticism, with its doctrines that the reality of a thing is its individuality, that which makes it *this* thing, and that both in God and man will is precedent to reason." An early-fourteenth-century Franciscan theologian, William of Ockham, has been called "the fountainhead of the terminist or nominalist movement"[77] and "perhaps the greatest logician of the Middle Ages."[78]

Turning briefly to Ockham, his basic move is from the proposition that only individual things exist to the proposition that only individual things are real. From this it follows that the categories in which we group things ("as it were in bundles," to use Locke's phrase) and the relations among them are mental constructs that we human beings create in order to introduce structure and intelligibility into the world in which we must live. As William of

Baskerville—the fictional monk who is Ockham's friend in Umberto Eco's novel *The Name of the Rose* (1983)—says repeatedly, "there is not order in the universe."

What he means is that we must constitute order in the universe because there is no order already there. There is no order implicit in the natures of things and accessible to human reason. According to Ockham, to assert that we can discern such an order and a natural moral law in it is to limit the supreme and unlimited power of God the Creator. We are indeed bound by the sovereign will of God as He has revealed it to us, but He could also have revealed a different will. Accordingly, no natural ends or purposes can impose moral obligations on human beings. We are indeed bound by moral obligations, but they are imposed on us by the sovereign will of God. The universe is composed of individual things; the order in which we group and regulate them is composed of constructs of our minds that we find useful. It is not based on common natures in things that we intuit. Likewise, "universal ideas," or class names by which we classify things, are not descriptions of real common natures; but we can use them for logical reasoning by which we can arrive at general conclusions. The ultimate reality is always individual things or persons, but we can use our definitions to relate them to one another in some kind of order. In human affairs, that order is not founded on the given nature of man but on the nominalist supremacy of will over reason in both God and man. Since relations among human beings are founded on subjective and variable judgments, the liberal tendency is to favor the claims of individual autonomy over the claims of the common good of society.

This nominalist epistemology has had a strong influence on theology, philosophy, and political and legal theory in the English-speaking world. It now appears to be accepted as dogma by many professors in our leading universities—particularly in the law schools. It has certainly affected the thinking of the U.S. Supreme Court, which has made the due process of law into an instrument for the enactment of a liberal political agenda. And it has successfully imposed this agenda on a passive and permissive populace. But we need not take this as a new birth of freedom. As the late George H. Sabine said, "[t]he absolute sovereign and omnicompetent state is the logical correlate of a society which consists of atomic individuals."[79] When liberalism has undermined the independence and authority of society's intermediate institutions, what is left but individuals and the state?

Part III

THE AMERICAN REPUBLIC:
DERAILMENT AND CRISIS

Religious Pluralism and the American Experiment: From Articles of Peace to Culture Wars

KENNETH L. GRASSO

In *The Basic Symbols of the American Political Tradition*, Willmoore Kendall and George W. Carey call attention to what is even today a frequently neglected feature of the ongoing American experiment in ordered liberty and self-government, namely, its religious dimension. Historically, they contend, the American people have understood themselves as a society through the prism of biblical ideas and imagery—in particular, through ideas and imagery deriving from the Book of Exodus. Indeed, they argue that while the American political tradition is careful to distinguish between religion and politics, at its very heart are found the "symbols" of "the Representative assembly deliberating under God; the virtuous people, virtuous because deeply religious and thus committed to the process of searching for the transcendent Truth."[1] And, if the point is not systematically developed, Kendall and Carey make clear that they are well aware that the American experiment in self-government and ordered liberty is also an experiment in religious pluralism.[2]

Now, it is a commonplace that one of America's most notable historical achievements has been the forging of a new and largely successful solution to the problem posed by religious pluralism. Although our political history has hardly been devoid of religio-cultural conflict, it is widely agreed that the American experience demonstrates that religious pluralism need not be politically debilitating, that it need not threaten the unity or vitality of the body politic.[3] It is widely agreed, in short, that the American experience shows that political stability does not presuppose religious uniformity.

Today, however, as James Davison Hunter has shown, a debilitating culture war is raging within the American polity.[4] Ultimately "religious" in nature and differing from past cultural conflicts in America by virtue of the
fundamental character of what is at stake, the emergence of this seemingly
"interminable" culture war would seem to raise grave doubts about the continuing viability of America's long-standing solution to the problem of religious pluralism. What I want to explore here are the nature of this solution
and the reasons for its contemporary collapse. Specifically, I want to suggest
that today's culture war must be seen against the backdrop of the breakdown
of the preconditions on which America's traditional solution to the problem of
religious pluralism had depended.

CIVIC UNITY AND RELIGIOUS INTEGRITY:
AMERICA AND THE PROBLEM OF RELIGIOUS PLURALISM

The obvious question concerns the nature of both the problem of religious
pluralism and the traditional American solution. Our starting point will be the
work of the thinker whose writings Kendall suggested should be "the take-
off point" for discussions of religion and American public life, John Courtney
Murray.[5] Religious pluralism, Murray writes, involves

> the coexistence within the one political community of groups who
> hold divergent and incompatible views with regard to religious ques-
> tions—those ultimate questions that concern the nature and destiny
> of man within a universe standing under the reign of God. Plural-
> ism implies disagreement and dissension within the community. But
> it also implies a community within which there must be agreement
> and consensus. . . . If society is to be at all a rational process, some set
> of principles must motivate the general participation of all religious
> groups, despite their dissensions, in the oneness of the community. On
> the other hand, these common principles must not hinder the mainte-
> nance by each group of its own different identity.[6]

The problem here is essentially twofold and revolves around the poles of
civic unity and religious integrity. On the one hand, it involves the establishment of civic unity, of a stable and unified body politic in the face of ir-
reducible disagreements on religious principle. Securing civic unity, in turn,
involves forging a consensus. This consensus, furthermore, cannot be mere-

ly procedural in nature. "No society in history," Murray writes, "has ever achieved and maintained an identity and a vigor in action . . . unless it has been sustained and directed by some body of substantive beliefs." But, given the stubborn fact of religious pluralism, neither can it encompass the totality of "theological truths that govern the . . . life and destiny of man." Rather, what is required is a consensus "operative on the level of political life with regard to the rational truths and moral precepts that govern the structure of the constitutional state, specify the substance of the common weal, and determine the ends of public policy."[7]

Such a consensus, Murray argues, performs a threefold function. It unifies the society, endowing it "with its vital form, its entelechy, its sense of purpose as a collectivity organized for action in history;" it "furnishes the standards according to which judgment is to be passed on the means that the nation adopts to further its purposes," or "what is called policy"; and it establishes "a common universe of discourse in which public issues can be intelligibly stated and intelligently argued." Forging such a consensus, while disagreeing on ultimate questions, is no simple matter.[8]

On the other hand, the fact of religious pluralism has profound implications for the character of civic unity and the consensus on which it rests. The unity must be "a unity of a limited order" (extending only to civil in contrast to religious matters) and "must not hinder the various religious communities . . . in the maintenance of their own distinct identities." Likewise, "the public consensus on which civil unity is ultimately based, must permit to the differing communities the full integrity of their own religious convictions." Solving the problem of religious pluralism thus involves securing civic unity while respecting and safeguarding the integrity of various religious traditions embraced by the populace. "There is," as Murray dryly notes, "no small problem here."[9]

Like the problem itself, "the American solution to the problem put by the plurality of conflicting religions within the one body politic" is two-pronged. Despite its religious pluralism, America has historically had "a public consensus," "a public philosophy" embodying not just the procedural norms enshrined in the Constitution but a whole constellation of political principles (e.g., limited government, government by the consent of the governed); moral principles (e.g., the existence of a universal moral law); metaphysical principles (e.g., the origin of this moral law in "the eternal reason of God," etc.); epistemological principles (e.g., the accessibility of this law "to the reason of man"); and theological principles (e.g., the sovereignty of God over all aspects of human life).[10]

The second element in America's traditional solution, Murray argues, were "the articles of peace" that found "legal" expression in the religious provisions of the First Amendment. This element represented "a special embodiment, adapted to the peculiar genius of American government and to the concrete conditions of American society" of "one of the central assertions" of the "Western tradition of politics," namely, the "distinction of church and state." These provisions constitute a "self-denying" ordinance through which "the American people exempted from their grant of power to government any power to establish religion or prohibit the free exercise thereof." Their effect is to limit the scope of the unity of the body politic. "The unity asserted" by the American motto, "E pluribus unum," writes Murray, "is a unity of a limited order. It does not go beyond the exigencies" of civil matters. Although it "is a good place to live," America "is not a church, whether high, low or broad." Rather, "it is simply a civil community whose unity is purely political" extending only to "the pursuit of certain enumerated secular purposes." "To say that the purposes are secular," he is at pains to stress, "is not to deny that many of them are also moral."[11]

By limiting the scope of civic life and the consensus on which it rests, these provisions rendered the unity of the American polity consistent with the demands of religious integrity. Indeed, by excluding "religious differences from the area of concern allotted to government," they have "strengthened" the body politic by keeping these differences from becoming occasions of political division and conflict.[12]

Why does Murray describe these provisions as "articles of peace"? He does so, to begin with, by virtue of the pragmatic character of the concerns in which they originated. "Like the rest of the Constitution," he wrote, they "are the work of lawyers, not of theologians or even of political theorists." Nor were they the product of "a sectarian concept of religion and of the church." These clauses reflected America's commitment to "the method of freedom" and to "a government of limited powers." Yet they also "were the twin children of social necessity, the necessity of creating an environment, protected by law, in which men of differing religious faiths might live together in peace."[13]

Confronted with the religious pluralism that was America's "native condition" and committed to freedom and limited government, the American people responded by sharply limiting the powers of the state in religious matters. Rather than have the government represent one of "the versions" of "transcendental truth . . . current in American society," it would be limited to representing "the commonly shared moral values of the community" and "the supreme religious truth expressed in the motto on American coins 'In God we trust.'" In the face of America's religious pluralism, "any other course . . . would have been disruptive, imprudent, impractical, indeed impossible."[14]

They are "articles of peace," furthermore, because of the role they have played historically. If these clauses have been able to command "the common assent and consent of the whole citizenry" of our religiously divided society, this is because their "content" has been understood as "simply political" rather than religious in nature. Given America's religious pluralism, if these provisions were understood as answering any "of the eternal human questions with regard to the nature of truth and freedom or the manner in which the spiritual order of man's life is to be organized or not to be organized," they would be incapable either of securing civic unity or safeguarding religious integrity, they would have been a source of division, and their acceptance would have required that some religious groups compromise the integrity of their distinct religious convictions and ways of life. Their historic ability to secure the free assent of our religiously divided populace attests to the fact that the religious provisions of the First Amendment have been understood as embodying not "sectarian tenets," but a commitment to public peace and the idea of a free people under a limited government.[15]

THE CONDITIONS OF CONSENSUS

To appreciate why the solution he celebrates is no longer working, it is necessary to explore something that Murray's analysis fails to bring into focus, namely, the preconditions (both cultural and political) on which the solution he celebrates depended for its viability. As we have seen, far from being merely procedural in nature, the consensus that historically united the American body politic encompassed a wide array of substantive political, moral, metaphysical, epistemological, and theological principles. Our ability to create and sustain such a consensus points to the existence of a common cultural horizon, a common worldview. This raises a number of obvious questions about the nature and origins of this horizon, as well as how its existence can be reconciled with the far-reaching religious pluralism characteristic of American society.

Light can be cast on these questions by returning to the second element in America's traditional solution: "the articles of peace" that receive "legal form" in the religious provisions of the First Amendment. Far from embodying "sectarian tenets," Murray insists that "these constitutional clauses have no religious content."[16] Gerard V. Bradley points out, however, that this claim is at odds with the thrust of Murray's own analysis.[17] As Murray reiterates, the American solution presupposes the idea of the distinction between church and state, an "ancient distinction" that was "one of the central assertions" of the "Western tradition of politics."[18] The origin of this now "traditional distinction," in turn, is to be found in the "revolutionary" distinction between "the spiritual and temporal orders and their respective jurisdiction" and "the dualism of two hierarchically ordered forms of social life" toward which it points. This dualism represented "Christianity's cardinal contribution to the Western political tradition."[19]

Insofar as the distinction between church and state presupposed by the American solution to the problem of religious pluralism is "historically unique" to Christianity, as Bradley observes, it follows that this distinction is "thinkable only where men inhabit a particular historical context," a historical context "penetrated by Christianity." "The religion clauses," therefore, "are a Christian artifact. This is not to suggest that only Christians can enjoy the religious liberty they promise, but rather that a Christian worldview produced them." Absent a historical context "penetrated by Christianity," we lack the "categories" that render the religious provisions of the First Amendment not "just desirable but conceivable."[20]

ARTICLES OF PEACE, ARTICLES OF FAITH

At this point, we are in a position to appreciate the nature and origins of the common cultural horizon against which the traditional American solution to the problem of religious pluralism unfolded. It was a cultural horizon shaped in critically important ways by Christianity and the far-reaching revolution in social and political life it inaugurated. It is Christianity's formative influence on American culture that explains our access to the distinction between church and state presupposed by our "articles of peace." As Os Guinness notes, these articles of peace "derive from articles of faith."[21]

Christianity's formative influence on American culture also played a decisive role in the public consensus discussed earlier. It helps explain both our ability to forge such a public consensus and the substantive content of that consensus. Our agreement about the political and moral truths that should govern public life was rooted in a prior religious consensus. Tocqueville's *Democracy in America* offers what is perhaps the classic account of this religious consensus and its political consequences. In America, he wrote, "Christianity reigns . . . by universal consent." Indeed, it reigned not as a "philosophy which has been examined and accepted," but as "a religion believed in without discussion," as "an established and irresistible fact." And, having "accepted the main dogmas of the Christian religion without examination," Americans embraced "in a like manner a great number of moral truths derived therefrom and attached thereto." Thus, he concludes, public life unfolds within the broad framework provided by these moral truths. "While the law allows to the American people to do everything, there are things which religion prevents them from imagining and forbids them to dare."[22]

This religious heritage also encompassed a shared political orientation. The early English settlers brought to the New World, Tocqueville writes, a variety of Christianity that "can only" be described "as democratic and republican." Furthermore, because it was "almost as much a political theory as a religious doctrine," it strongly "favored the establishment" of democratic political institutions. The resultant "social theory" was absorbed by the other varieties of Christianity that settled here so that "there is not a single religious doctrine in the United States hostile to democratic . . . institutions." When it comes to politics, "all the clergy . . . speak the same language." If despite their myriad political disagreements, Americans nevertheless "agree about the general principles that should rule human societies," this agreement stems to an important degree from their shared religious convictions.[23]

The obvious question here is how such a common cultural horizon rooted in a common religious orientation is possible given the religious pluralism that has traditionally characterized the American polity. The answer is to be found in the nature and limits of this pluralism. The America of the founding era, it is true, contained a rapidly proliferating multiplicity of religious communities, and interreligious relations were by no means always friendly. Bitter theological disagreements and rancorous religious antagonisms were a fact of life. Nevertheless, as Tocqueville pointed out, although there existed "an innumerable multitude of sects" in early America, "they all" belonged "to the great unity of Christendom." While these sects differ "in the worship they offer to the creator," they "all agree in the duties of men to one another" and preach "the same morality in the name of God."[24]

Here James Davison Hunter's work can be of assistance to us. "At the time of the first census in 1790," he notes, "Catholics comprised only about 1% of the total population." Jews and other non-Christians composed an even smaller percentage of the population. A cursory examination of American public life in theater, moreover, reveals that "a measure of cultural consensus" really existed. For "the language and ideas of [a] common Protestantism" supplied "a vision" that informed "all of the major institutions of public life." "Both in population and character," Hunter concludes, "America [at that time] was indisputably Protestant."[25]

In the course of the nineteenth and twentieth centuries, of course, this situation changed. As Hunter observes, the numbers of non-Protestants gradually increased so that by the early 1950s, Catholics constituted roughly 20 percent of the population (thereby becoming America's "single largest denomination") and Jews 2.5 percent of the population. The expansion of American pluralism beyond the borders of Protestantism, however, did not mean the loss of a common cultural horizon, but its transformation. As Hunter has pointed out, "a broader Judeo-Christian consensus" emerged, supplying "the cultural cement in American public life." This new consensus was made possible by common acceptance by "all the major players of . . . the suppositions of a biblical theism" that not only provided a common "language" for "public discourse" but "common ideals" for "public life" as well. If this consensus was somewhat thinner than the "pan-Protestant" consensus that preceded it, it was nevertheless far from merely procedural in nature, encompassing as it did a broad substantive agreement concerning the nature of man, the nature of the human good, and the basic structure of social relations that should inform human life.[26]

A common cultural horizon was possible despite America's religious pluralism precisely because of the decidedly limited character of this pluralism. Until quite recently, as Francis Canavan has written, "lush as the variety of creeds [in America] may have been," the fact is that "all of the religions that had adherents numerous enough to matter shared a common Judeo-Christian tradition" and "held the Bible in common." In most respects—particularly regarding "matters of public concern"—the religions of America "taught substantially the same moral code." Holding in common the Ten Commandments, they espoused the "same biblical morality." The type of pluralism that traditionally prevailed in America was a pluralism of "a multitude of religious branches that sprang from a common stem," a pluralism that existed in the overarching context of a shared adherence to the Judeo-Christian tradition.[27]

In the context of this pluralism, much could be taken for granted.[28] The meaning of such key terms as "religion," "church," "state," "secular," and "sacred," for example, were largely unproblematic. Likewise, the moral agreement between the major religious communities on questions of morality made it possible to distinguish "public morality" from "sectarian" doctrine, and to agree on the theological, moral, and political affirmations that would inform public life. At the same time, it was the shared commitment of the overwhelming majority of these religious groups to the distinction between church and state, and the insistence on the limited character of government's role in the overall economy of social life that issued from that commitment, which ultimately made possible the construction of a public order within which each of them could maintain its own distinctive identity and way of life.

THE TRADITION OF REASON

This common religious tradition was not the only source of a common cultural horizon. As Kendall and Carey remind us, the American political tradition drew on both revelation and reason, on both the religious and philosophic traditions of the West.[29] This common cultural horizon reflected not merely a shared religious orientation, but a commitment to a particular version of the natural-law tradition. This horizon reflected a commitment to, in Carey's words, "an objective moral order" accessible to human reason.[30] As one influential early American sermon put it, "a special revelation from heaven" was not needed to "teach us" the basic principles of moral and political order, because "the plain dictates of that reason and common sense with which the common parent of men has informed the human bosom" will suffice.[31] This moral cognitivism received expression in the Declaration of Independence's ringing affirmation of the existence of a body of "self-evident" moral "truths," of what it calls "the Laws of Nature and Nature's God." It also found expression, as Carey observes, in the insistence in *The Federalist Papers* that "concepts such as 'the permanent and aggregate interests of the community' . . . and 'justice' have existence and meaning quite apart from that which any majority or minority may assign to them."[32]

At the same time, understanding reason and revelation to be in harmony, this horizon saw the moral truths embodied in natural law as broadly congruent with traditional Judeo-Christian morality. One can't but think here of Jefferson's affirmation that the "code of morals" taught by Jesus "was the most benevolent and sublime . . . which has ever been offered to man."[33] As Thomas A. Spragens has pointed out, however much the version of natural law embraced by America might bear the imprint of the Enlightenment in its epistemology and metaphysics, its normative moral content consisted largely in "the traditional values of the classical and Christian tradition."[34]

The pervasive influence of this version of natural law generated widespread confidence that the core principles of morality were accessible to human reason and that they did not rest on revelation alone or depend for their credibility on distinctively Christian articles of faith. Given its affirmation of the harmony of the dictates of natural reason with at least the broad outlines of the Judeo-Christian ethic—not to mention biblical theism's role in laying the cultural and intellectual groundwork from which it emerged—it is appropriate to refer to America's core principle as the Judeo-Christian natural-law tradition. And this tradition made it possible for those who did not accept Christianity to nevertheless embrace the bulk of the moral code that had been developed under its auspices. Thus, as Canavan remarks, while the American proponents of "Deism, or natural religion as it was often called, rejected revelation as superstition" and argued for a morality grounded in reason alone, the "natural morality" they championed "did not differ dramatically from biblical morality on matters of public concern" and "was in fact a secularized version of traditional Christian morality."[35] And, as Henry May remarks, even "those Americans of the village atheist tradition" have "usually [been] anything but skeptics about moral values." They have "often" espoused a "morality . . . not very different from that of the clergy" they baited.[36]

In the face of America's far-reaching religious pluralism, the Judeo-Christian natural-law tradition was a powerful source of moral—and, insofar as it involved a natural theology, religious—unity. It not only created a large measure of common ground between those who embraced biblical theism and those who rejected it, but also established what George Weigel terms a common moral vocabulary and "grammar"—an "intellectual template"—making possible "disciplined, ecumenical, and publicly accessible moral argument over the right ordering of our common life."[37] It made possible, in other words, a common universe of discourse in moral conversation between the adherents of differing religious traditions, in which moral disagreements could be intelligibly articulated despite religious pluralism.

POLITICAL AND CONSTITUTIONAL PRECONDITIONS

As important as it was, this religio-moral consensus was hardly the only condition on which the American solution to the problem of religious pluralism depended for its workability. It also depended on an array of political preconditions. We can do no more here than briefly mention some of the principal ones. The first of these concerns was the size and scope of government. If the night-watchman state of classical-liberal theory never existed in America, the fact remains that for most of our history government played a relatively limited role in the overall economy of American life. The political theory of the American founding, as Carey reminds us, "presupposes what can be termed a low-key or relatively passive government."[38] As Harold J. Berman points out, "in 1787 and for many decades thereafter," in areas such as education, "poor relief, health care, and other forms of social welfare, the role of government at all levels, local as well as state and federal, was minimal" and possessed "an auxiliary" character.[39] Its job was to assist and supplement the work of other nongovernmental institutions that were understood to have the primary responsibility for meeting social need in these areas.

In the present context, what is important about this state of affairs is how it contributed to the workability of our religiously pluralist society. As Canavan observes, "a state that acts vigorously on a number of fronts to promote people's welfare must have some conception of what that welfare is." By confining governmental action to "areas of common material concern about which general agreement can be assumed, e.g., paving the streets and providing protection against fires," the sharply limited role played by the state acted to reduce the occasions of religiously grounded disagreements on law, politics, and public policy.[40]

The second of these preconditions concerns the character of American federalism. For most of our history, federalism was understood as meaning, as *The Federalist Papers* put it, that "the jurisdiction [of the central government] extends to certain enumerated subjects only," while the states possess "a residuary and inviolable sovereignty over all other subjects."[41] Under this understanding of federalism, as Justice Story observed, "the whole power over the subject of religion" was "left exclusively to the state governments."[42] The powers reserved to the states, furthermore, were understood as including what came to be called the police power, namely, the power to enact laws protecting public health, safety, and morality. Each state was understood as entitled to handle questions of church-state relations, religion and public life, and public morality in the way it thought best.

As Kendall points out, this meant that the traditional understanding of federalism prevailed on the highly sensitive question of religious observances in the public schools. There was "no general rule," no national standard, "except" allowing "the local community to decide." By the mid-twentieth century, the policies adopted by different local communities ran the gamut from the "virtual exclusion of religious observances" to the allowance "of a wee little bit of religious observances" to the allowance of "quite a bit of religious observances."[43] Federalism was traditionally understood to extend to the states and localities this same latitude regarding other aspects of religion and public life and the whole area of public morality.

What Canavan observes regarding laws governing public morality is true for laws governing the questions of church-state relations and religion and public life as well. Such laws normally require "the support" not just of "a bare majority" but a broad-based consensus. "A bare majority," he writes,

> suffices to enact a tax law or to pass a measure for constructing highways. Such decisions, once made, are usually accepted by the defeated minority with more or less good grace. But a law that seeks to establish a moral standard of conduct cannot be enforced if it is not supported by the moral beliefs of the larger and sounder part of the community. This is what is meant here by the consensus by which laws for the protection of public morals must be supported. It is not unanimity. But it is a measure of agreement great enough that one can say, in a meaningful sense, that the laws represent the conscience of the community and do not merely impose the moral judgment of one part of it on the rest.[44]

In a religiously pluralistic polity such consensus may not always be easy to achieve. Federalism, however, made the task immeasurably easier. It did so, to begin with, by, in Carey's words, "removing certain sensitive concerns from the national political sphere," thus sparing us the unenviable task of forging policies on these matters capable of commanding a consensus in our highly pluralistic society. The First Amendment's religious provisions, for example, removed "explosive issues involving the rights of conscience from the arena of national politics."[45]

At the same time, it left the responsibility of forging such policies in the hands of states and localities, whose more homogeneous character greatly increased the chances of success. Americans, as Kendall remarks, have not only historically been divided on religious questions, but have been divided "spottily" on them.[46] Something similar might well be said about issues of public morality. It is one thing, for example, to devise a policy on religious observances in the public schools or the laws regulating marriage capable of securing the support of a broad-based consensus in Peoria. It is an altogether different—and far more difficult—thing to devise policies on these topics capable of generating such a consensus in both Peoria and San Francisco.

This is not to suggest, it should be emphasized, that federalism was some type of panacea. To say that the more homogeneous character of states and localities increased the likelihood of consensus isn't to say that it guaranteed such consensus. Some states and localities might be as bitterly divided on such questions as the nation as a whole. The nature of some of these questions and the postures assumed by their partisans, moreover, may make their complete localization impossible.[47] Nevertheless, as David Gelernter has pointed out, federalism historically acted to supply "the expansion joints" that made "America supple rather than brittle," that made America "a bridge" capable of riding "out hurricanes without falling to pieces" because it was capable of sustaining "enormous twisting, turning, and tearing forces without cracking."[48]

The third of these preconditions concerns the impact of certain traditional constitutional understandings on the making of law and policy in the areas of church-state relations, religion and public life, and public morality. The religious provisions of the First Amendment, for example, were generally interpreted in an "accomodationist" or "nonpreferentialist" fashion. They were generally understood, in other words, as, within certain broad limits, allowing government "to accommodate the religious needs of the people" and indeed to aid religion on a nonpreferential basis. At the federal level, this understanding has historically found expression in such long-standing features of American public life as chaplaincies in the armed forces, the motto "In God We Trust" on our currency, the tax-exempt status of religious institutions, legislative chaplaincies, prayer at legislative sessions, and Thanksgiving Day proclamations.[49]

As John Witte has shown, while state constitutional law on the subject of religion varied, for most of our history state constitutional provisions on religion were generally understood in an accommodationist or nonpreferentialist manner. Indeed, for most of our history "the dominant pattern" of "religious rights and liberties" in the states was "a general freedom of private religion" combined with "general patronage" of "a 'public' religion that was generally Christian, if not Protestant in character."[50] States and localities also "afforded various forms of aid to religious groups," including subsidies to frontier missionaries, funds for Bibles and liturgical books, property grants and assorted subsidies, and tax exemptions. Mandatory courses in the Bible and religion, prayer, and compulsory attendance in worship services were common in public schools and universities.[51]

Finally, as Witte also notes, state governments had not been shy about employing their police powers to proscribe (among other things) polygamy, prostitution, pornography, and certain sexual acts as well as gambling, lotteries, and fortune-telling. They also required governmental institutions such as schools, prisons, reformatories, orphanages, and asylums to actively propagate certain moral principles.[52]

The cumulative effect of these constitutional understandings was to entrust the making of public policy on matters of religion and public life and public morality to the normal political process, rather than seeking, as Carey puts it, "to constitutionalize them."[53] Neither the federal constitution nor the state constitutions were understood as mandating one particular set of public policies in these areas. On the contrary, they were understood as giving government a broad (albeit, of course, not unlimited) latitude to establish whatever public policies it thought best suited, at any given time, to advance the public good.

An accomodationist understanding of the First Amendment, for example, doesn't mandate such practices as the provision of chaplains for the armed forces or the commencement of legislative or judicial sessions with prayers. It simply affords government the option of establishing such practices if it so chooses. Likewise, a nonpreferentialist reading of state constitutional provisions on church-state relations doesn't require such practices as the commencement of school days with prayer or Bible reading or the posting of the Ten Commandments or Bible verses on public property. It simply affords state governments the option of establishing such practices. Similarly, the traditional understanding of the police power didn't mandate the establishment of local laws proscribing sodomy or obscenity, but simply afforded local government the option of establishing such laws if they so chose.

How did this state of affairs contribute to the workability of America's traditional solution to the problem of religious pluralism? To begin with, the effect of leaving these questions in the political arena rather than constitutionalizing them was to give government the flexibility necessary for the creation of policies capable of commanding broad-based support and thereby securing civic peace and unity. Secondly, it gave government the flexibility to regularly revise public policies in these areas in light of changing circumstances and public attitudes. Insofar as these policies were not understood as constitutionally mandated, they were not understood as being, as it were, set in stone.

Thirdly, not constitutionalizing these questions had the effect of entrusting policymaking in these areas to the legislature rather than the courts, to the legislative rather than the judicial process. This is significant for several reasons. Legislatures, as Charles S. Hyneman points out, are designed in a manner that places their members under great pressure to act in accordance with "the expectations and preferences of the population." Placing them in "unrestrained" contact "with their constituents" and the "forceful demands" of "people who favor and oppose any contemplated action" situates them "in a favorable position for reading" these expectations and preferences. Legislative determinations on matters of public policy have what Hyneman calls "a tentative, experimental" character. They are not designed to endure "for the ages," as it were, but to be periodically altered in light of ever-changing circumstances and needs.[54]

Finally, as Hyneman reminds us, legislating does not consist in the drawing of inferences from abstract principles; it involves the drafting of legislation capable of commanding not only the assent of a majority of the legislators, but the type of broad popular support necessary for the legislation's successful implementation.[55] Compromise and coalition-building thus figure centrally in the legislative process.

By entrusting the responsibility for policymaking in these areas to the legislature, our traditional constitutional order entrusted it to an institution designed to be extremely sensitive to public opinion and well equipped to gauge the intensity with which various views are held (and thus with the social costs involved in enacting and enforcing a particular piece of legislation). In a legislature's decision-making process, compromise and coalition-building figure centrally, and its enactments are intended to be periodically revised in light of new circumstances and needs. It is a branch of government well suited to devise policies capable of commanding broad popular support in a religiously divided society.

FROM ARTICLES OF PEACE TO *KULTURKAMPF*

What triggered today's culture wars, I would suggest, was the erosion of the cultural and political preconditions just outlined. The past century has witnessed a massive expansion in the size and scope of government at all levels. As Ballard C. Campbell observes, whereas prior to the end of the nineteenth century "government performed a limited range of functions and rarely intruded into everyday life," today "the public sector manages an immense array of programs that affect all aspects of society."[56] As a result of the New Deal and Great Society, as George Carey has pointed out, the "protective, limited, and relatively inactive government"[57] bequeathed to us by the founders has been supplanted by an activist welfare state charged with "providing for the security and well-being of its citizens" and discharging a wide array of functions that had in "prior times" been discharged by "individuals. communities and private charities."[58]

Whatever one thinks of this development as a matter of social policy, its effect has been to intensify social conflict and to help trigger today's *kulturkampf*. Given that a religiously pluralist polity is not going to be able to secure a consensus on the religious and moral norms that should govern every aspect of human social life, it follows that the more areas of life the state becomes active in, the more the possibilities for religiously grounded social conflict increase. Thus, the gradual expansion of the role of the state in American life, its gradual expansion beyond areas of common material concern, has acted to make an increasing number of religio-moral disagreements publicly relevant and has thereby generated a host of new political issues.

The essential dynamic here is illustrated by the first of the areas into which government moved in a major way, namely, education. It is no accident that once government began to play a major role in the area of education, the questions of what (if any) religious observances are appropriate in public schools, what (if any) types of religious and moral instruction are appropriate, what worldview the curriculum should embody, and the propriety of the use of tax dollars to fund religiously affiliated schools quickly emerged as hotly contested political issues. It is no accident, in other words, that the movement of government into the field of education has been followed by a seemingly unending series of "school wars." The simple fact is that the citizens of our religiously pluralistic society disagree about the nature of the religio-moral vision that should inform education. Governmental involvement in educa-tion—particularly if it involves the establishment of a common educational system encompassing a common curriculum and common rules regarding religious observances—necessarily will spur political division.

The same is true in other areas. Our religiously pluralistic society disagrees about the moral permissibility of a host of medical practices such as abortion, contraception, and embryonic stem-cell research. Once government begins to play a major role in the provision of health care, questions such as whether taxpayers should fund morally controversial medical practices (e.g., contra-ception, abortion, and embryonic stem-cell research), whether "private" and even religiously affiliated healthcare providers (e.g., hospitals and pharmacies) should be compelled to provide morally controversial forms of medical care, and whether private and even religiously affiliated institutions (e.g., schools, charitable groups, businesses) are obligated to cover such forms of care in the insurance coverage they are obligated to provide to their employees will in-evitably become divisive public issues.

THE NEW CONSTITUTIONAL ORDER

The past century has also witnessed what Gelernter terms "the collapse of federalism."[59] As Carey notes, an expansive interpretation of the commerce clause, federal grants-in-aid to state governments (or, more specifically, the federal control that comes with their acceptance), and, most importantly, the rulings of federal courts have caused a massive expansion of federal power and a dramatic decline in the power and autonomy of state governments. The result has been a transformation of our federal system and the loss on the part of "localities of their authority to handle matters at the very core of their be-ing."[60]

In the area of religion and public life, the decline of federalism has mani-fested itself in the application, by the Supreme Court, of the religious provi-sions of the First Amendment to the states (via the due-process clause of the Fourteenth Amendment). It is only a slight exaggeration to suggest that the effect of this process has been to transfer authority over the whole area of church-state relations from the states to the federal government (in the form of the federal judiciary) and to replace state and local policies in this area with a uniform national policy. A similar process of "nationalization" has gradually occurred in the area of public morality. One thinks here of court rulings dealing with obscenity, vulgar speech, contraception, abortion, and sodomy.

The effect of this has been to sweep away state and local policies that enjoyed long-standing and widespread public support. It has also been to deprive us of, in Gelernter's phrase, the "escape valve" that federalism had traditionally offered to "poisonous polarization" and to confront government with the virtually impossible task of having to forge policies capable of a broad-based national consensus.[61] The *kulturkmpf* engulfing our polity and the bitter polarization it reflects provide clear evidence of its failure to do so. As Robert F. Nagel notes, by nationalizing "abortion policy," for example, the Court "dramatically raised the moral and political stakes all around, thereby fomenting the very political stridency" that finds expression in today's "culture war."[62]

Finally, the constitutional revolution that emerged in the course of the twentieth century involved not just the replacement of state and local policies in the areas of church-state relations and public morality with a uniform national policy, but their replacement with a judicially imposed national policy understood to be mandated by the Constitution itself. Its effect was not just to nationalize public policy in these areas but to constitutionalize, and thus, as it were, "judicialize" it.

The consequences of this were far-reaching. It created a situation in which, rather than reflecting adjustable prudential judgments about the demands of the common good and public peace at a given moment in time, public policy was to reflect immutable and inviolable constitutional principles that trumped such prudential considerations. It thus had the effect of denying government the flexibility to adopt policies based on considerations of public peace, civic unity, and the like, and to revise these policies as changing circumstances and public attitudes dictated. It also effectively transferred responsibility for the making of policy in these areas from the legislature to the courts (thereby, in Corwin's famous formulation, transforming the United States Supreme Court into a "national school board").[63] In doing so, however, it transferred it to an institution significantly less equipped to successfully navigate the treacherous waters of policymaking in a pluralist society.

To begin with, as Hyneman reminds us, in sharp contrast to legislatures, courts are designed in a manner to insulate them from the "political vortex," to insulate their members from both direct popular control and the direct pressure of public opinion. Judges do not experience the type of "unrestrained" contact with the public that legislators do. Unlike legislators, judges "do not [have to] fight an election campaign" and "pressure groups do not flood . . . judges with telegrams from constituents, lay down ultimatums in public hearings, or threaten reprisals if decisions go against them." As a result, they are less equipped than legislators to grasp public expectations and preferences.[64] As Carey notes, courts have "no reliable means to gauge the relative intensity of the interested parties, what the reactions will be to any given pronouncement, or, *inter alia,* what obstacles are likely to arise in its execution."[65]

Secondly, and again in sharp contrast to legislatures, the job of courts is not to devise public policies capable of securing the common good of a particular concrete community at a particular moment in time, but to interpret laws, or, in this case, the Constitution. Unlike the enactments of legislatures (which are meant to be revisited and revised in the light of changing conditions), such interpretations are meant to have a final and definitive character. Thus, as Carey observes, "once having embarked on a path," courts "can pull back or reverse" themselves "only at great cost" to their "prestige and the principle of the rule of law."[66] Such rulings are supposed to be exercises in judgment based on historical research and legal reasoning, not products of negotiation and logrolling designed to secure popular support or prudential judgments regarding such things as the state of public opinion, the demands of public peace, and the urgency of competing social needs.[67]

The cumulative effect of constitutionalizing and "judicializing" issues of religion and public life and public morality is to greatly reduce the prospects for policies capable of commanding broad-based support in a pluralistic society and thereby defusing religio-moral conflict.

THE NEW PLURALISM AND THE COLLAPSE OF THE HORIZON

As important as these political changes have been, even more important has been the cultural transformation that America has experienced. A profound change has taken place in the character of American religious pluralism. Here again, Hunter's work is instructive. In the past few decades, the numbers of Muslims, Hindus, Buddhists, and adherents of other non-Western religions have "grown prodigiously." Islam, for example, has become "the eighth largest denomination in the United States—even larger than the Episcopal church, the Presbyterian Church, U.S.A., the United Church of Christ or the Assemblies of God."[68]

These same decades have also witnessed a dramatic expansion in the portion of the population professing "no particular religion or religious affiliation." Growing from 2 percent to 11 percent of the population in the years between 1952 to 1982, those whom social scientists label "secularists" now "represent the fastest growing community of 'moral conviction' in America." In terms of the influence of this development on the character of American pluralism, just as significant as the growing number of secularists has been their distribution. Inasmuch as they are disproportionately represented among "the intellectual classes, broadly understood—those who derive their livelihood from the knowledge sector—whether they be professors, journalists, media elites, lawyers or educators," they are an even greater factor in the shaping of our culture than their numbers alone would suggest.[69]

Equally important has been the polarization of Catholicism, Judaism, and the various Protestant communions into "orthodox" and "progressive" camps. What divides these camps "are two distinct conceptions of moral authority," two distinct conceptions of "the basis . . . on which people [should] determine whether something is good or bad, right or wrong, acceptable and unacceptable." Although they might disagree about the "specific media" through which it is communicated, the orthodox are united by a "commitment . . . to an external, definable, and transcendent" source of moral authority. Believing that moral truth is not created by human beings but discovered by them, the orthodox are committed to the existence of objective, unchanging, and universally obligatory moral norms.[70]

If traditional forms of Judaism, Catholicism, Protestantism, and natural-law theory reflect an "orthodox" understanding of the nature of moral authority, progressivism originates in "the secular Enlightenment of the eighteenth century." In sharp contrast to the proponents of orthodoxy, progressivists are committed to the denial of the existence of any external and transcendent source of moral authority. On the contrary, they insist that "moral truth is perpetually unfolding; that moral truth is a human construction and, therefore, is both conditional and relative; and that moral truths should reflect ethical principles that have the human good as their highest end." This view of moral truth as something we created (either through some form of "self-grounded rational discourse" or "personal experience") rather than discovered is linked with a celebration of individual "autonomy," with a celebration of the right of each individual to choose his or her own values or way of life. In this view, "the liberated individual . . . becomes the final arbiter of moral judgment."[71]

This progressivist vision commands the allegiance not just of secularists, but of a significant portion of religious believers in contemporary America. Indeed, "progressively oriented Protestants, Catholic, Jews" find that they "share more in common . . . culturally and politically" with secularists "than they do with the orthodox members of their own faith tradition."[72]

These developments fundamentally change the character of American religious pluralism. Their effect has been to replace a real but limited religious pluralism, whose constituent parts were united by a common allegiance to biblical theism—by a common allegiance to a particular form of orthodoxy, namely, to the Judeo-Christian tradition—with a far deeper, far more radical pluralism. The broadening and deepening of American religious pluralism over the past half-century, in short, has issued in nothing less than what Hunter terms "the collapse of the long-standing Judeo-Christian consensus in American life."[73] We are no longer united in a commitment to the orthodox understanding of the nature of moral authority, much less to the version of it embodied in biblical theism. Simultaneously, insofar as what we have called the Judeo-Christian natural-law tradition embodied an orthodox understanding of the nature of moral authority, the ascendancy of progressivism to the status of major cultural force has effectively undermined our shared cultural allegiance to it as well.

The result of these developments has been a transformation of our moral culture. In sharp contrast to the moral cognitivism that prevailed in earlier eras of American history, our culture has increasingly come to be characterized by what Alasdaire MacIntyre terms moral "emotivism": the view that moral judgments are ultimately expressions of "arbitrary will and desire," are "*nothing* but expressions of preference, expressions of attitude or feeling."[74] We have also seen the rise of a new, post-Judeo-Christian moral orientation that Carey labels "secular, scientific humanism." At the heart of this orientation is a commitment to a "crude utilitarianism," "moral and ethical relativism," "virtually unbridled liberty," and "egalitarianism."[75]

Biblical theism and the Judeo-Christian natural-law tradition were the twin pillars on which the common cultural assumptions undergirding our traditional solution to the problem of religious pluralism rested. Not only has their collapse issued in the disintegration of this horizon, but the very pluralism that caused their collapse precludes the formation of a new one. We have ceased to agree about what a human being is, about what is good and bad for human beings, and about what structure of relationships should inform human life in society. The result is not only the emergence of a whole array of highly divisive "social" issues (e.g., abortion, homosexuality, religion and public life) but an ongoing conflict regarding the moral and spiritual ethos that will inform our public life, the moral and spiritual substance that will animate the American democratic experiment.

This conflict differs from the culture wars that America has experienced in the past, as Hunter points out, because of what is at stake. Previous cultural conflicts took place "within the boundaries of a larger biblical culture." They concerned which version of "biblical theism" would inform America's public culture.[76] What is at issue in today's *kulturkampf,* in contrast, is nothing less than which of two "fundamentally different understandings of being and purpose," which of two dramatically "differing worldviews" encompassing "different ways of apprehending reality, of ordering experience, [and] of making moral judgments" will dominate American public life: progressivism or the version of orthodoxy embodied in the Judeo-Christian tradition.[77] Unlike past cultural conflicts, what we experience today is not a conflict between between different forms of the same religious tradition (i.e., biblical theism), but a conflict between fundamentally opposed religious visions.

Against this backdrop, it becomes possible to appreciate the intractable nature of this culture war. If this conflict has an "interminable character," this is not merely because of the intensity of the partisans on each side or the fact that both command the support of sizable segments of the populace. Rather, it is because of the radically different moral, intellectual, and spiritual universes inhabited by each. The effect is to deprive them of a common moral language and vocabulary in which to discuss their differences and a common moral ground upon which to resolve them. Under such conditions, dialogue, much less compromise, becomes "a virtual impossibility."[78]

CONCLUSION

Insofar as progressivism originates in the Enlightenment, as Hunter observes, today's *kulturkampf* pits the champions of traditional Christianity and Judaism against the proponents of "the secular Enlightenment" and "its philosophical aftermath" as expressed in the work of thinkers like "Nietzsche and Rorty."[79] It pits the champions of what David Novak describes as the "theonomous" vision of the nature of moral authority,[80] the human person and the human good embodied in traditional Christianity and Judaism, against the proponents of the Enlightenment's affirmation of human autonomy.

There is of course no small irony in this state of affairs. In early America, Christianity—or at least Protestantism—and the Enlightenment tradition were, as George Marsden observes, "almost always seen not as contradictory but as complementary."[81] The heirs of Luther and Calvin and the devotees of the English and Scottish Enlightenments made common cause in the launching of the American republic. What made this harmonious relationship possible, however, was the conservative form—as evidenced by the embrace even by deists in the founding era of both moral cognitivism and a secularized version of traditional Christian morality—the Enlightenment took in the English-speaking world.[82]

Ideas, however, have consequences. As the inner dynamism of the ideas constitutive of the Enlightenment as a distinctive intellectual tradition unfolded, and as the cultural forces that in the English-speaking world had acted to blunt the impact of these ideas weakened, Enlightenment thought moved in progressively more radical directions.[83] It moved progressively away from the Judeo-Christian ethic and progressively toward an ethic of radical human autonomy. The result of this radicalization of the Enlightenment and the wholesale conflict with the Judeo-Christian tradition is the culture war we witness around us. Today's *kulturkampf*, ironically enough, signifies the dissolution of the very cultural alliance that helped launch the American experiment in self-government and ordered liberty.

Where then does this leave us? It leaves us, I would suggest, with an insoluble problem for the simple reason that the very same political, constitutional, and cultural developments that have caused the collapse of our traditional solution to the problem of religious pluralism would appear to make a new solution impossible. Given contemporary cultural, political, and constitutional realities, it is difficult to see how we can succeed in simultaneously securing civic unity and safeguarding religious integrity. Indeed, these realities might well make it impossible to do either.

How can we forge the type of robust overlapping consensus about the moral and political principles that should inform our public life we once had, and upon which our body politic's unity and vitality depend in the face of the new, more radical type of pluralism that exists today—a pluralism encompassing fundamental disagreements about the nature of man and the human good?

How can we forge new articles of peace that command the common assent of the whole citizenry in the absence of shared articles of faith? How can we embrace the movement of government into ever more areas of life—thus transforming more and more moral issues into political issues—without thereby intensifying religio-moral strife? How can we nationalize, constitutionalize, and, as it were, "judicialize" public policy on matters of religion and public life and public morality without thereby denying government the flexibility it needs to effectively defuse religio-moral strife in a highly pluralistic society?

What we can expect for the foreseeable future, I would suggest by way of conclusion, is a continuing descent into the morass of the procedural republic and the debilitating strife of the ongoing cultural war. The implications of this state of affairs for the future vitality of the American democratic experiment are, to put it mildly, disconcerting. If I have no solution to the problem which troubles us, I do offer one modest suggestion. My suggestion is that we honestly and forthrightly acknowledge the fundamental nature of our differences. It does us no good to try to avoid the difficult and fundamental decisions we face either by denying the depth of our disagreements or seeking to evade them through specious appeals to the ideal of governmental neutrality on the question of the human good. Forthrightly engaging our differences is not, I would stress, some type of panacea and in the short run might even exacerbate our difficulties. Nevertheless, it is only by openly acknowledging the nature of the problem that confronts us that we can begin the type of sober reflection and serious argument the gravity of our situation warrants.

Horizontal and Vertical Consolidation of the United States into an Administrative State

JOHN S. BAKER, JR.

The "administrative state" formed by a large federal bureaucracy represents a challenge to the Constitution's structure of federalism and separation of powers.[1] Although these constitutional restraints have prevented the administrative state from completely consolidating power, the changed character of the Senate following the Seventeenth Amendment both weakened federalism and disrupted separation of powers. The Seventeenth Amendment, by providing for the popular election of senators, made the popularly elected officials less responsive to state governments. The states thus gradually lost much of their protection against the federal government ("vertical federalism"), as well some as of their protection against each other ("horizontal federalism"). This structural shift has not only 1) greatly enhanced the power of the federal government vis-à-vis the states; but has also 2) disrupted the horizontal balance among the states; and 3) given rise to a de facto national police power usurping the police powers of the states and consolidating them in the federal government.

Those promoting an administrative state have believed, in accord with Woodrow Wilson, that the Constitution's system of divided powers illegitimately restricts the democratic will.[2] In the 1930s, they targeted the Supreme Court because it impeded the democratic will by declaring several important pieces of federal legislation unconstitutional.[3] The first obstacle, however, to creating the administrative state was not the Court, but the Senate. Without a popularly elected Senate in place, the New Deal legislation, transferring power from the states to administrative agencies, would not have been enacted in the same form. Also, a popularly elected Senate, freed from possible reprisals from state legislatures, became more disposed to the nomination and confirmation of Supreme Court justices who would be more inclined to uphold the constitutionality of federal legislation that infringed the power of the states. This change in the character of the Senate and its effect on the character of the federal judiciary have altered both vertical and horizontal federalism.

Congress's treatment of social/moral issues, such as gambling, reflected the impact of a more democratized Senate in creating national police powers. Prior to the change in the Senate, Congress's early responses to gambling operated *procedurally* to protect states from each other. When a single state was exporting gambling to other states, Congress passed legislation that prevented commerce in gambling from moving across state lines. Congress did not act *substantively* to outlaw gambling as such. Congress protected the laws of all states, by both preventing one state from interfering with the anti-gambling laws of other states and by leaving states that so desired to legalize gambling within their own borders. Congress prevented the spread of what many considered to be a "disease" by isolating or quarantining it.[4] As the Senate became more responsive to democratic impulses, however, Congress's "morals" legislation became more expansive and substantive.

That Congress initially addressed "morals" issues only procedurally, without claiming the authority of a general police power, demonstrates that the post–Civil War amendments, by themselves, did not change the nature of federalism to the extent that some like to claim. Those constitutional amendments addressed particular problems in the original structure of federalism that had allowed states to protect slavery. In other matters, however, national power was still limited in a manner that respected both the vertical and horizontal dimensions of federalism. The continuing vitality of federalism, even after the Civil War, was reflected in a statement by Salmon Chase, an opponent of slavery and member of President Lincoln's cabinet, who as chief justice wrote in *Texas v. White*[5] that "The Constitution, in all its provisions, looks to an indestructible Union, composed of indestructible States."[6]

DISRUPTION OF THE HORIZONTAL
AND VERTICAL BALANCE OF FEDERALISM

In a confederation, the organizational model is broadly horizontal and, at most, only modestly vertical or hierarchical. In a unitary state, the structure is just the opposite. According to *Federalist* 39, the United States Constitution creates a compound of the two. The great difficulty in a federal state, therefore, is maintaining the balance between the horizontal (state-to-state relationships) and vertical (federal-government-to-state relationships) dimensions and avoiding both secession and consolidation into a unitary state.

According to the Antifederalists and their intellectual heirs, the protection of the states died with adoption of the Constitution and the end of the Confederation. In fact, however, the Constitution permitted a minority of states, through senators elected by their own legislators, to block any legislation. Nevertheless, during the period prior to the Civil War, John C. Calhoun of South Carolina argued for even greater protection of state interests through what he called "concurrent majorities."[7] This would have meant that each part of the national community affected by legislation would have had a veto power. If implemented, sections of the country would have had the power to nullify decisions approved by majorities in Congress. Calhoun and other senators from the South were resisting the eventuality that with the addition of more senators from new nonslave states the senators from the South would not be able any longer to block legislation deemed detrimental to their interests.

The two houses of Congress reflect the dual dimensions of horizontal and vertical federalism. The House is nationalist in orientation because apportioned according to population; the Senate is (con)federal because representation is allocated equally among the states, without regard for population. The Senate is supposed to provide protection for the states. The Constitution deprives the states of control over their borders. Therefore, they are vulnerable to each other by being unable to close their borders. While each state can prohibit particular conduct, none can prohibit transportation into the state of the means for carrying on the illegal activity. As a result of the open-borders structure of federalism, interstate conflicts have occurred on the moral/religious issues of slavery, alcohol consumption, and gambling.

The conflicts over each of these social issues involved a morally significant action tied to a commercial transaction. These issues, at different times, have divided the U.S. between slaveholding and nonslaveholding states; "wet" and "dry" states; and still between gambling and nongambling states. For a time on slavery and alcohol (prior to Prohibition) and still on gambling, the federal government legislated procedurally to control only the interstate movement of the activity. That left the states free to legislate on the substance of the law pursuant to their police powers. Eventually with slavery and for a period of time with alcohol during Prohibition, a national substantive solution came about through a constitutional amendment.

When national substantive law—by constitutional amendment, congressional legislation, or Supreme Court decision—resolves a controversial issue, national action generally changes the balance of federalism in favor of the federal government. There is a tendency to think of all national action as antithetical to federalism, when in fact national procedural law can serve to protect and reinforce the horizontal dimensions of federalism. Issues of vertical federalism arise when the Congress legislates *substantively* on matters that are then matters of state law. Horizontal federalism, on the other hand, involves the relationship between and among states and their legal regimes. Within a federal system, conflicts will occur in legal matters involving more than one state, which are similar to the conflicts that occur from state to state in matters of private international law. As reflected in the full faith and credit clause, the privileges and immunities clause, and the extradition clause,[8] the Constitution requires cooperation *procedurally* among states in order to bring about equal treatment for them and their citizens.

The Impact of a Democratized Senate on Federalism

In providing for the election of U.S. senators directly by the voters of each state, the Seventeenth Amendment eliminated the voting role of the state legislatures. Ironically, this change was driven by state legislatures, which obviously did not understand the protection they were giving away. While the amendment increased the democratic character of the Senate, it decreased its federal character.[9] The Great Compromise, also known as the Connecticut Compromise, of the Constitutional Convention provided that the Senate represented the states as states—a partial continuation of the principle of representation under the Articles of Confederation. Prior to the Seventeenth Amendment, senators more clearly represented the "states as states" because they were elected by, and responsible to, state legislatures. The electoral base of the Senate made the states a constituent part of the Congress. Senators who owed their election to state legislatures were naturally responsive to those legislatures. With direct, popular election of senators, the status of state governments at the national level has been reduced to that of other lobby groups. The states and their elected officers have found themselves competing with the various associations that lobby in the nation's capital. Moreover, since the states can no longer automatically block legislation, they tend to act like other lobby groups in that they seek financial subsidies. Instead of operating as a check on federal power, as described in *Federalist* 51, the states have contributed to the centralization of power through requests for federal funding and agreeing in return to be subject to federal regulations attached to the funding.

As long as the Senate represented the states, a minority of states could block any legislation or judicial nominations they deemed detrimental to their interests. Indeed, that reality was responsible for the standoff over slavery which led to the Civil War. The post–Civil War amendments modified the situation only regarding basic civil rights. Congress was still able to centralize only on those matters that advanced the general interest of the states. Congress's ability to centralize power over the objections of many states came only when senators, like members of the House of Representatives, became popularly elected. As explained in *Federalist* 39, the Constitution's provision for popular or democratic election reflected the national or consolidating side of the compound republic, in contrast to the federal side, which was originally the basis for representation in the Senate.

When, during the 1930s, Congress expanded federal power, it also created new administrative agencies. For Congress to pass so many new laws, it needed the kind of assistance that could only come from administrative bureaucracies. Increasingly, Congress "delegated" much power to the administrative agencies in the form of rule making. This movement reflected progressive opinion that technical experts should govern. In the view of this writer, this delegation conflicted with separation of powers and federalism. Moreover, for a central bureaucracy to micromanage local affairs clearly represented the opposite of the principle of political accountability. The fact that, with two isolated exceptions,[10] constitutional attacks on Congress's delegations to administrative agencies have failed proved that the judiciary cannot be expected to stop the consolidation of federal power.

As a result of direct popular election of senators, both houses of Congress have come to be aggressive delegators and centralizers of power. Without the Seventeenth Amendment, federal actions that became commonplace, such as "unfunded mandates" (legislation or administrative rules requiring actions by the states without providing the funding) and preemption of state laws, would have been either unthinkable or rare. Although it is still relatively difficult to enact federal legislation, that is attributable to the remaining structural differences between the two houses and to the competition among factional inter-ests, as discussed in *Federalist* 10. Nevertheless, the modern Senate functions much less like the upper house of the eighteenth century British Parliament, as some of the founders expected it to operate, and less like the body of statesmen observed by Tocqueville in the 1830s.

The rise of the administrative state through a more democratized Senate has actually brought with it a decline in democratic accountability. Although populists and democrats regularly complain about the complexity of the legal system in the United States, they are constantly urging some kind of change that, of course, requires new legislation. Indeed, it is deemed to be an indict-ment of Congress if it is labeled "do nothing," i.e., if it does not pass a great deal of legislation. The more legislation Congress enacts, the more benefits it passes out to voting constituencies and to lobbyist-contributors. In the course of effecting these transfers of wealth, Congress has passed legislation its mem-bers cannot possibly read because there is so much of it. Congress could not enact so much legislation if its members carefully considered the laws being enacted. In order to be "productive," Congress needs a large bureaucracy to "fill in the details" not addressed in the legislation. Thus, Congress's lawmak-ing power is effectively given to unelected civil servants who govern through administrative rule making.

Ideally, the system of separation of powers should prevent legislation from being easily enacted or readily delegated to administrative agencies. Despite the increased volume of legislation, institutional and procedural obstacles still force some deliberation in Congress as part of the system of internal checks and balances. Ultimately, Congress is influenced by the fact that legislation, once enacted, leaves its control because an independent executive has the power to implement it as he sees fit. If members of Congress fear that the pres-ent or a future president might administer a law differently from the way they would want, then it behooves Congress to tie the executive down with clear language that strictly limits his discretion.

Congress crafted the administrative state to allow it to increase the scope of federal legislation without actually ceding control over policymaking to the executive. Congress has delegated while avoiding the constraints of separation of powers by employing certain constitutionally questionable innovations. Congress has done so through the "fourth branch of government," which consists of "independent" administrative agencies. Like courts in England, these agencies are "independent" of the executive, but not entirely so from the legislative branch. Generally, Congress has pursued its purpose by unconstitutional attempts to remove the president's power to make appointments and/or by court-sanctioned limits on his power to remove appointees.

The Preemption Doctrine and Concurrent Powers

Congress has increasingly used the preemption doctrine to consolidate federal power in noncriminal matters. Preemption refers to the displacement of state law by federal law. Generally, the issue involves a matter of statutory interpretation. That is to say, assuming the constitutional validity of a particular federal law, the issue concerns whether the Congress intended to supplement or supplant state law. Often, continued validity of state law after the enactment of federal law on the same issue is a matter of judicial interpretation.

The preemption doctrine is a gloss on the text of the Constitution; the Constitution contains no "preemption clause" as such. Rather, Article VI contains the supremacy clause, which provides that the Constitution, federal statutes passed pursuant to it, and treaties are the supreme law binding judges in every state, "the Constitution or laws of any state to the contrary notwithstanding." On its face, the supremacy clause only displaces state law to the extent that state law conflicts with federal law.

The Marshall Court set the foundation for federal-state relations in its great supremacy-clause cases, most notably *Martin v. Hunter's Lessee*,[11] *Gibbons v. Ogden*,[12] and *McCulloch v. Maryland*.[13] These cases involved federal statutes determined to be constitutional, which in each case conflicted with a state statute and/or court decision. Given a conflict between federal and state law, both could not prevail. The supremacy clause and common sense, according to *Federalist* 32,[14] dictated that valid federal law must prevail.

The modern preemption doctrine expands well beyond the Marshall Court's supremacy-clause jurisprudence. Under the modern doctrine, state law may be defeated even when there is no direct conflict, and even though Congress has not explicitly expressed its intent to preempt. Preemption has been applied to situations in which a court determines that: 1) the federal law "occupies the field" (*Hines v. Davidowitz*);[15] 2) federal law demonstrates the need for uniformity (*Jones v. Rath Packing Co.*);[16] or 3) state law *might* impede the federal law (*Pennsylvania v. Nelson*).[17]

When the Supreme Court invalidates state law in the absence of a direct conflict, it does so on the basis that *Congress intends* preemption. Apart from wondering how it is that Congress can preempt state law if no direct conflict exists, one might suppose that if Congress intended to preempt, it would say so. If Congress routinely fails to state expressly its intent to preempt, the natural inference would seem to be that Congress has no such intent. If the federal courts were genuinely concerned about federalism, not to mention separation of powers, they would adopt rules requiring Congress to express clearly its intent to preempt, just as the Supreme Court requires an express statement for legislation to be retroactive.[18]

The Supreme Court does not, by its own admission,[19] have clear rules for interpreting the intent of Congress regarding preemption. Therefore, if Congress wishes its intent to be clearly understood by the courts, the most sensible thing for it to do is to create rules of construction. The only approach consistent with our federalism is a provision that neither a statute nor an administrative agency can preempt state law unless the congressional "statute expressly so states."

Without the gloss of the preemption doctrine, the supremacy clause alone suffices for protecting federal power in areas of concurrent powers when state and federal power come into conflict. The basic premise of the Constitution is that unless otherwise clearly indicated, the powers of the federal government are *concurrent* with those of the states. According to *The Federalist Papers*, federal law is exclusive in relatively few matters.[20] *Federalist* 32 lists only three such situations:

> where the constitution in express terms granted an exclusive authority to the union; where it granted, in one instance, an authority to the union, and in another, prohibited the states from exercising the like authority; and where it granted an authority to the union, to which a similar authority in the states would be absolutely and totally *contradictory* and *repugnant*. I use these terms to distinguish this last case from another which might appear to resemble it; but which would, in fact, be essentially different: I mean where the exercise of a concurrent jurisdiction, might be productive of occasional interferences in the *policy* of any branch of administration, but would not imply any direct contradiction or repugnancy in point of constitutional authority.[21]

Given concurrent jurisdiction, conflicts between federal and state law are inevitable. It is for that very reason that the Constitution includes the supremacy clause. Many, but not all, conflicts can be avoided in the course of the legislative process. Even if it tried to do so (which it does not), however, Congress would not be able to discover every actual or potential conflict. Federal-state conflicts arise, as in all legislation, through unanticipated circumstances. When direct conflicts do occur, the supremacy clause makes federal power controlling. When, however, no direct conflict occurs, the preservation of the concurrent jurisdiction of the states should require that the supremacy clause *not* be applied to block state laws. In other words, the so-called preemption doctrine represents a judicial intrusion on state power through the expansion of the supremacy clause.

The norm is for federal and state law to coexist. When a conflict occurs between the two, state law must yield under the supremacy clause. The conflict does not displace state law completely, but only to the extent necessary to avoid the conflict. Nevertheless, the Constitution rejects the confederal model of a central government governing state governments. As a result, Congress is prevented from directing the states on how to legislate, or ordering the state officer to implement federal legislation. In this, the U.S. differs markedly from the European Union, which provides for directives and other orders to the constituent governments.

The Constitution has always allowed Congress indirectly to limit state power without displacing state law or issuing directives to the state. As explained in *The Federalist Papers*, the federal system is designed with the recognition that states have and will continue to enact some unjust laws. As mentioned at the beginning of this chapter in connection with "morals" legislation, the federalist solution is not to displace state law, but when necessary to isolate or quarantine "problems" to a particular state. As stated in *Federalist* 10:

> The influence of factious leaders may kindle a flame within their particular states, but will be unable to spread a general conflagration through the other states: a religious sect may degenerate into a political faction in a part of the confederacy; but the variety of sects dispersed over the entire face of it, must secure the national councils against any danger from that source: a rage for paper money, for an abolition of debts, for an equal division of property, or for any other improper or wicked project, will be less apt to pervade the whole body of the union than a particular member of it, in the same proportion as such a malady is more likely to taint a particular county or district than an entire state. . . .

> In the extent and proper structure of the union, therefore, we behold a republican remedy for the diseases most incident to republican government.[22]

Since the democratization of the Senate, the Congress has favored centralization through substantive law over procedural protection of and through horizontal federalism. Congress's broad use of the commerce clause, its delegation to administrative agencies (especially "independent agencies"), and its increased use of preemption have expanded the capacity for centralized policymaking. Congress has more recently even attempted to force the states to act as its agents in a manner similar to the mechanisms available to the European Commission. But in *New York v. United States*[23] and *Printz v. United States*,[24] a majority of the Supreme Court declared unconstitutional attempts by Congress to force state officials to administer federal laws. Congress has also attempted unsuccessfully to force states to follow its will by subjecting the states to lawsuits by individuals for violating federal law. Again, the Supreme Court has upheld constitutional protection for the states by upholding state-government sovereign immunity against lawsuits by individuals.[25] As long as Congress cannot actually force the states to do its will, as the European Union does to its member countries, it has had to rely on the "carrot" of grants to the states. By imposing substantive conditions on the grants, Congress and administrative agencies are able effectively to dictate a national policy even though they lack power that authorizes them to set a national policy directly in areas such as education.

FAILURE TO MAINTAIN THE
HORIZONTAL BALANCE AMONG THE STATES

While Congress has been consolidating its own powers, it has generally failed to act in areas where its action could protect federalism. That is to say, Congress's inactivity on some issues has allowed states to encroach on each other in ways inconsistent with horizontal federalism. Specifically, Congress has failed to set rules governing choice of law. The issues of choice of law, or private international law, inherent in legal relations between sovereign states, affect legal relations even more so in a federal state. Historically, "federalism" derives from the use by the ancient Greek cities of compacts, covenants or agreements to create leagues. The U.S. Constitution transforms what was a (con)federal compact among individually sovereign states into a federal state.[26] Unfortunately, Congress has left conflict-of-law issues almost completely to the federal courts, which have followed academic advocacy to undermine federalism by allowing some states (especially in tort litigation) to impose their law, in effect, on other states. By failing procedurally to protect some states from other states, Congress is then urged to act substantively by nationalizing certain areas of law, such as product-liability laws.

Conflicts-of-law scholarship, which includes "choice of law,"[27] is a particularly esoteric subject that has been described as a "dismal swamp."[28] A field once dominated by clear, if not completely satisfactory, rules has generated intellectual and litigious chaos as a result of the influence of legal realism.[29] Unfortunately, the intellectual chaos in the field of conflicts has obscured and undermined the clear *logic* in the relationship been federalism and territorially based choice-of-law rules. As Justice Joseph Story made clear in his famous *Conflicts of Law* (1834) treatise, issues involving conflicts of law and choice of law are especially important in the American federal system.[30]

The modern Supreme Court, however, has given very modest constitutional oversight to choice-of-law questions.[31] Within very broad limits under the due process and full faith and credit clauses, the Court has allowed states to choose the law to apply in cases involving parties from different states. As argued by Professor Douglas Laycock, however, the current choice-of-law regime violates the principle of equality as between states and between citizens of different states.[32] He contends that the privileges and immunities and full faith and credit clauses of Article IV of the Constitution, together with the federal structure of the Constitution, *require* national choice-of-law rules adopted either by Congress or the Supreme Court.[33] Regardless of whether choice-of-law rules are constitutionally *required*, it is sufficient for present purposes to build upon the proposition that Congress has the constitutional power to implement a national set of choice-of-law rules, and that some set of rules is very much needed in order to protect the integrity of the law of the states.

Full Faith and Credit and Privileges and Immunities Clauses

In terms of horizontal federalism, the Constitution contains several mutually reinforcing provisions: diversity jurisdiction, the privileges and immunities clause, and the full faith and credit clause. The two clauses are found in Article IV, along with other provisions that reinforce horizontal federalism.[34]

Together they provide the constitutional authority for addressing issues related to choice of law. Choice-of-law issues, however, have neither been coherently resolved by the Supreme Court nor been the subject of comprehensive congressional legislation.

The full faith and credit clause applies to "public Acts" and "Records," as well as "judicial Proceedings." Article IV, Section 1 provides:

> Full Faith and Credit *shall* be given in each State to the public Acts, Records, and judicial Proceedings of every other State. And the *Congress may by general Laws prescribe* the Manner in which such Acts, Records and Proceedings shall be proved and *the Effect thereof.* (Emphasis added.)

While the clause mandates ("shall") that each act, record, or proceeding be given "full faith and credit," it also allows ("may") congressional legislation regarding proof and effect. Although Congress has not yet done so, "almost everyone agrees that [Congress's power to specify the "Effect" of sister-state law] includes the power to specify choice-of-law rules," writes Laycock.[35]

Diversity jurisdiction, the privileges and immunities clause and the full faith and credit clause make it possible to resolve interstate conflicts on the basis of equality between states and between their citizens. In *The Federalist Papers*, Hamilton explains diversity jurisdiction as being necessary to implement the privileges and immunities clause.[36] That may seem to be a doubtful assertion, because for a specific challenge based on the privileges and immunities clause, Article III's federal-question jurisdiction would suffice. According to Professor Laycock, however, Hamilton means "that the Privileges and Immunities Clause is at issue in every diversity case."[37] That is to say, "Hamilton's argument makes sense only if he means that in any litigation, arising under any law, *discrimination in the administration of justice* against a citizen of a sister state would violate the Privileges and Immunities Clause."[38]

Hamilton's linkage between diversity jurisdiction and the privileges and immunities clause naturally leads to the full faith and credit clause. On the one hand, a state must extend the privileges and immunities of its own laws to citizens of other states. On the other hand, states must give full faith and credit not only to judicial proceedings but also to "Acts" and "Records" of other states. Obviously, some method is required to determine when a state may or must apply its own law, and when it may or must apply the law of another state.

Congress has paid little notice to its power under the full faith and credit clause to regulate choice of law and thus strengthen the horizontal dimension of federalism. Unlike Congress's exercise of other powers, this exercise of power would strengthen, rather than erode, the power of each state. Congress's ability to prevent some states from effectively imposing their laws on others is clearly the basis for its enactment of the "Defense of Marriage Act (DOMA)."[39] That act authorizes states *not* to give "full faith and credit" to "same-sex marriages" enacted by the laws of any other state. In the absence of such legislation, states might have to give full faith and credit to the acts of states authorizing such "marriages."

The meaning of the term "full faith and credit," except as to judgments, has not been refined through litigation. The purpose of the full faith and credit clause, however, "is to make it easier for a state to regulate its own affairs, not to enable it to fiddle with the affairs of others."[40] Nevertheless, arguments have been put forth that the full faith and credit clause would require states to recognize "same-sex marriages" permitted in other states. In reaction to that possibility, Congress invoked the clause to enact DOMA. By so doing, Congress has attempted to isolate a state, at least to the extent of confining the "Effect" of a certain "Act" to that state. While scholarly opinion is divided on the constitutionality of DOMA, Congress certainly does have the power to adopt general rules regarding choice of law.

Inter-Jurisdictional Relationships

From a national perspective, the disagreements about state law (whether tort law or laws pertaining to marriage) need to be understood in terms of the two faces of federalism. Within their borders, states are free to shape their own substantive and procedural law generally as they deem best. Depending on their constitutions and legislation, states take various approaches in allocating responsibility to the legislature, the judiciary, and juries to determine outcomes. However a state does so, the Constitution contemplates limits on the reach of a state's law.[41] By its nature, the constitution of a federal state must be designed to protect some degree of independence for each state, not only from the national government, but also from each of the other states. The Constitution deprives states of the sovereign power to control their borders through specific prohibitions against conducting foreign affairs, regulating trade, and waging war. Having lost control of their borders, states become vulnerable to the practices of other states. The Constitution must, and does, provide protection in the event one state legislates or acts in ways that damage other states. When one state has a particular cause of action against another, it can invoke the Supreme Court's original jurisdiction. This is a substitute for resorting to war. In addition, two or more states may want to settle their disagreements cooperatively through some kind of agreement. The Constitution also allows, but only with the consent of Congress, states to enter into compacts with each other.[42]

The Constitution thus provides various "federal" solutions to maintain harmony and equality among the states. This horizontal federalism constitutionalizes the well-known maxim, which is also at the foundation of international law, to "do unto other (states) as you would have them do unto you." The Constitution borrows this principle of comity among nations from international law but extends and enforces it. Whereas comity is a matter of policy, the Constitution *requires* it, obligating the states to extradite prisoners to other states, to give full faith and credit to the judgments and acts of sister states, and to extend to citizens of other states the privileges and immunities afforded their own citizens.

By opting for a federal system rather than a unitary state, this country's founders were preserving a form of plural jurisdiction. The operation, in every state, of the federal and state law and a dual court system creates a dualism of jurisdiction. Together, the fifty states produce a pluralism of jurisdiction and law. This pluralism reflects the framers' concept of protecting liberty by limiting power in multiple ways.[43] Indeed, diversity jurisdiction, which was created to protect those who are not citizens of the forum state, guarantees a certain amount of "forum-shopping" in suits between citizens of different states. Initially, if they meet the jurisdictional amount, plaintiffs can choose to sue citizens from other states in either state or federal court. If suit is filed in state court, the defendant(s) may be able to remove to federal court. This kind of "forum-shopping" is part of the Constitution's design to protect liberty.

Personal Jurisdiction

At the time of the founding, the judicial system could fairly well operate without Congress legislating choice-of-law rules. The relatively low level of interstate commercial activity, not to mention the relatively low level of litigation, meant that the need was not as great as it is today. Nevertheless, Justice

Story filled the need with his treatise. Both the situation in the country and the general understanding of conflicts reinforced the federal principle of territoriality. Moreover, the rules governing personal jurisdiction were also tied to territoriality. These principles were clearly stated in the long-controlling, but since overruled and much vilified, 1877 case of *Pennoyer v. Neff.*[44]

It has been said that "*Pennoyer v. Neff established* the principle that in the absence of a waiver the presence of defendant within the state was a necessary prerequisite to a court's asserting personal jurisdiction over him."[45] In fact, however, general rules regarding jurisdiction had long been established in the common law. In actions involving real property and in mixed actions, jurisdiction was confined to the site of the real property; in personal actions, such as torts, jurisdiction was proper wherever the defendant was found.[46] As is apparent from a comparison of the language from *Pennoyer* and language from Justice Story's *Conflicts,* personal jurisdiction, like choice-of-law issues, was tied to the fundamental principle of territorial sovereignty.[47]

While the choice-of-law issue is distinct from the question of personal jurisdiction, both come under the subject of conflicts of law. In the United States into the twentieth century, both matters were controlled by the principle of territoriality. Moreover, in *Pennoyer* the Supreme Court stated its understanding that the recently enacted Fourteenth Amendment due-process clause was consistent with the territorial principle of personal jurisdiction.[48] Later constitutional and nonconstitutional theories, which give minimal regard to territoriality, shifted to a more subjective basis labeled "contacts analysis."[49] The Supreme Court broke the link between due process and the territorial principle. As a result, the Court drained the full faith and credit clause of much meaning as to acts, although it has continued strictly to enforce the "judgments" dimension of the clause. Except for DOMA, Congress has not legislated on the "acts" aspect of the clause.

THE GROWTH OF A NATIONAL POLICE
POWER USURPING STATE POLICE POWERS

Over the last century, Congress's creation of national police power has gone largely unnoticed. When exercising its power against gambling under the commerce clause in 1895, Congress did not displace state law, but rather simply limited its reach to its own borders. Unfortunately, the Supreme Court took a much broader view of congressional power. The Court posited a general, national police. Ever since, Congress has been expanding federal criminal power. As applied to criminal law, Congress has acted contrary to the basic principle that police powers rest with the states.[50]

"More than 40% of the federal criminal provisions enacted since the Civil War have been enacted since 1970,"[51] according to an American Bar Association task force. The pace has only accelerated in the years since. "All signs indicate that the federalization trend is growing, not slowing, in fact as well as perception."[52] No one knows exactly how many federal crimes exist because it is impossible to get an accurate count. Previous estimates of approximately 3,000 federal crimes have become dated due to the surge in federal criminalization during the last sixteen years.[53] Depending on how one treats federal regulations, that number can skyrocket. Nearly 10,000 regulations carry some sort of criminal or civil penalty.[54] "Whatever the exact number of crimes that comprise today's federal criminal law, it is clear that the amount of individual citizen behavior now potentially subject to federal criminal control has increased in astonishing proportions in the last few decades."[55]

If, despite the growth of federal criminal law, the states still prosecute all but a small fraction of criminal cases, it might seem that the federalization of crime has practically little effect and is therefore of little concern. The point, though, is only partly that the claimed benefits of federalization are illusory. If federalization were simply ineffectual, it would only involve a waste of time and resources no worse than many other programs of the federal government. On the contrary, the overall ineffectiveness of federal criminal law vis-à-vis local crime only magnifies its dangerous potential. Although federal law enforcement has had very little impact on local crime, federal law-enforcement agencies can apply tremendous power against particular persons and corporations on whom they set their sights.

Every time Congress passes a new criminal statute, or a federal court expands an existing one, the jurisdiction of federal law enforcement increases. Each increase means that some federal agency somewhere has more power to investigate some conduct, or some aspect of that conduct, that it could not have investigated otherwise. That investigative power will be used to determine, for purposes of arrest or indictment, whether there is probable cause to believe that a crime has been committed. As a result of the surge in federal criminalization over the past two to three decades, the traditional notion that federal law-enforcement agencies have only limited powers has ceased to reflect the reality. Instead, the working assumption has become that collectively the agencies of the Justice Department, Treasury, and Postal Service can investigate anything and anyone that they decide to.[56] Almost every kind of crime is potentially a federal crime.

The Commerce Clause and Police Powers

The federalization of crime through the commerce clause has been made possible in large part by a failure to distinguish between *regulating commerce* and *punishing crime*. During the second half of the nineteenth century, Congress and the individual states began to apply criminal sanctions to economic regulations.[57] Notable examples included the Interstate Commerce Act[58] and the Sherman Anti-Trust Act.[59] These "regulatory" offenses differed from "true" crimes, as has since been recognized, in that they did not involve moral stigma but were designed to force compliance with regulations.[60] The Supreme Court, however, did not make such distinctions when addressing the commerce clause in the 1890s and later.[61]

Indeed, in the first significant commerce clause case related to crime, *Champion v. Ames*,[62] the Court confused regulating commerce and exercising the police power. Congress enacted legislation to protect states where gambling was prohibited (which was all but one) by prohibiting the shipment of lottery tickets across state lines. Congress did not outlaw gambling or the sale of lottery tickets; it merely prevented the movement of lottery tickets from the one state where they could be legally purchased into other states. The Supreme Court upheld the act as a constitutional regulation of commerce in lottery tickets by restricting their sale within the borders of the one state. Unfortunately, the Supreme Court went further and posited a general police power in Congress to criminalize certain conduct.[63] As I have explained in greater detail elsewhere,[64] the Supreme Court's decision initiated confusion between Congress's undeniable power to regulate commerce among the states and the police power of defining, prosecuting, and punishing crime.

During the Roosevelt administration in the 1930s, Congress heavily regulated the economy under the commerce clause. Following some cases voiding key components of the New Deal, the Supreme Court eventually validated most of this regulation, laying the groundwork for the later expansion of national police powers.[65] Still, congressional inertia and concerns for federalism inhibited rapid expansion of federal criminal law and jurisdiction. That changed about 1970, when Congress and the executive branch began to show greater willingness to extend the federal police power into areas of traditionally local concern due to mounting public pressure for the government—state or federal—to "do something" about crime, with little thought about federalism.[66]

When Congress began to federalize more crimes, it relied on the fact that, since the famous 1937 case of *NLRB v. Jones & Laughlin Steel*,[67] the Supreme Court had—until *U.S. v. Lopez* in 1995[68]—upheld virtually every congressional act under the commerce clause. The vast majority of cases at least involved commerce, not crime. Nevertheless, prior to *Lopez*, the Court had not invalidated any federal criminal statutes under the commerce clause, even though it tended to give narrow constructions to federal criminal statutes prior to 1970.[69] With *Perez v. United States* in 1971,[70] the Court seemed to allow Congress as much deference in defining and federalizing crime as it had allowed concerning regulations of commerce. In *Perez*, the Court upheld application of a federal "loan-shark" statute to local acts without any showing of any relation to interstate commerce. The Court considered it sufficient that the activity was part of a class of activities that Congress had targeted as having affected commerce through organized crime.

Law Enforcement within a Federal System

The Constitution's failure to provide a general federal police power is neither accidental nor irrational; it corresponds to traditional American concerns about protecting the liberty of individuals. Contrary to some misconceptions, and despite its problems, state law enforcement not only remains quite capable of responding to local crime problems, but also can do so much more effectively than federal law enforcement. The strengths and weaknesses of state and local law enforcement result from its organization on a local basis. Efficiency experts may find much to fault in the criminal-justice system, precisely because it is not systematized on any uniform basis. That critique, however, can be made against virtually any aspect of federalism, including the very existence of separate states. Experts in mergers and acquisitions can presumably make a case for why all state governments should be eliminated or centralized under the national government. In the opinion of the founders, however, self-government is necessarily inefficient in that ordinary citizens, rather than only experts, participate in the business of government. The framers built certain inefficiencies into the Constitution as protections for liberty. Even if efficiency were more important than liberty, nothing about the local crime problem suggests that centralization of power in federal law enforcement can produce greater efficiencies than the local organization of law enforcement. Certainly, from the perspective of citizens who are the victims of crime, local law enforcement needs to be the most efficient in protecting them.

While the federal government has an important role in protecting the public, that role falls within its enumerated powers under the Constitution. Its most important duty, one that only it can execute, is the defense of the country against foreign aggression. Principally, such aggression and our response to it has been military. Foreign aggression, in and outside of war, also takes the form of espionage. When espionage occurs within the United States, such aggression becomes a law-enforcement problem. The U.S., at least prior to the terrorism of September 11, 2001, has traditionally drawn the distinction, which some nations do not, between the military and law enforcement, and between external and internal threats to peace. Unlike some nations, the U.S. has not in the past used military force to maintain the peace at home.[71] Only in the case of domestic disorder (as opposed to insurrection against the United States or invasion of a state or the United States) does the Constitution provide for the use of federal power to maintain order within the states—and then only at the request of a state's legislature (or, if the legislature cannot be convened, of the state's governor).[72] This distinction between complete central control over military power and minimal internal police power comports well with the distinction between the external sovereignty and the distribution of sovereign powers internally in a federal state.

The nature of the federal system is such that some legitimate overlap will necessarily exist between federal and state law on criminal-law matters. Confusion naturally arises as to how to differentiate between what is properly federal and what is properly left to the states. There can be no doubt, however, that in the current state of affairs, federal criminal law has gone well beyond any legitimate overlap; it now almost completely duplicates state criminal law.[73]

CONCLUSION

The administrative state represents the very consolidation of power opposed by all the founders—Federalist as well as Antifederalist. An administrative state is normally the byproduct of a unitary sovereign. In the U.S., however, the administrative state has been crafted as an attempt to displace a system of divided powers. The constitutional system assumes that only the people are sovereign, not any institution of government. Those who exercise sovereign powers delegated by the people to the federal government, however, have often not accepted this view. Instead, they have worked to increase their power in the name of making the U.S. government "more efficient" by building up an administrative state.

Democratic government, of course, is inherently inefficient if it operates under the rule of law. In the U.S., the rule of law is embodied in a constitutional structure of federalism and separation of powers. Popular majorities or technical elites may be very efficient in effecting their own will—if only freed from the institutional and structural restraints of the Constitution. In the process of consolidating their power, those factions will also be very efficient in suppressing the liberty of their opponents, as *Federalist* 10 teaches.

The Rule of Men:
How Caring Too Much about Important
Things Is Destroying Constitutional Law

WILLIAM GANGI

In the United States today, constitutional scholars are bitterly divided. The vast majority (including the faculties of our most prestigious law schools and political science departments) champion what is sometimes called "non-interpretivism." The proponents of this view celebrate a series of landmark judicial decisions that further the causes of individual freedom and equality while viewing much of the Constitution as ambiguous, open-ended, and malleable. They call on the judiciary to actively pursue the goal of eliminating discriminatory barriers and expanding personal liberties.

Their "interpretivist" opponents, in contrast, are a small, isolated, and embattled minority. As George W. Carey points out, they: 1) contend that constitutional interpretation must be informed by the ratifiers' understanding of the meaning of the Constitution; 2) insist that many of the landmark decisions of the past half-century are illegitimate because in these cases the Supreme Court has been acting *ultra vires*, beyond the scope of its constitutional authority; and 3) fear that over the past half-century the courts have assumed a new role incompatible with both our constitutional tradition and the principles of republican government. Indeed, as Carey observes, they wonder whether the ascendancy of noninterpretivist jurisprudence has not made the Constitution "a dead letter."[1]

Noninterpretivists reject these concerns as exaggerated. Interpretivists, they contend, ignore the fact that over the past fifty years greater judicial involvement in public policymaking has produced many positive results. They argue that throughout our history disputes over the content and application of constitutional principles have always existed—disputes sometimes more vehement than those of today. Interpretivists neglect to mention, they further contend, that the process of constitutional adjudication remains largely unchanged: litigants file suits, district-court judges preside over trials and render opinions, and appeals proceed as they always have. The Supreme Court remains, as the Constitution's framers intended, the court of last resort and, as before, astute scholars analyze and comment upon the Court's work. Once differences in time, circumstances, and ideology are accounted for, noninterpretivists assert the Supreme Court continues to play its traditional role. Constitutional law, they conclude, is alive and well.

Those of us who are interpretivists, however, disagree. We insist that beneath the veneer of continued normalcy the discipline has been shorn of substance, and that self-government has been replaced by de facto judicial governance under the guise of constitutional interpretation. We believe that the courts have assumed a new and revolutionary role that, as Carey points out, raises "regime questions"—fundamental questions about the very "character of our constitutional order,"[2] questions about the proper role of the Constitution and courts, and the "dynamics and operations" of our "constitutional institutions and processes."[3] While acknowledging that some of the concerns that have motivated noninterpretivist jurisprudence (e.g., racial equality) are laudable, we believe that this jurisprudence has endangered other important values (e.g., federalism and self-government).[4]

The remainder of this essay is divided into four parts. Part I reviews the nature of the disagreement between noninterpretivists and interpretivists, explores the concerns that have driven noninterpretivist jurisprudence, and offers several criticisms of interpretivism. Making the case that noninterpretivism has destroyed the integrity of constitutional law and undermined democratic governance, it argues that by caring too much about certain important things—legitimate concerns and values—this jurisprudence has distorted constitutional law, endangered democratic governance, and diminished the competence of both the federal and state governments. Part II continues the critique of noninterpretivism, maintaining that, for a variety of reasons, the judiciary is ill-equipped for the task of public policymaking. Part III discusses some of the issues that must be addressed and tools that must be acquired before a refounding of constitutional law can take place. Finally, Part IV offers some conclusions and a proposal.

I

When examined in toto, noninterpretivism's constituent premises are integrated, complex. and comprehensive. Succinctly put, they contend that the ratifiers' understanding of the Constitution should no longer be determining, and that every generation is entitled to reinterpret the Constitution to suit its needs. They further contend that in modern America the responsibility for this task of reinterpretation necessarily falls to the judiciary.

After World War II, for example, there existed a stark contrast between the ideals Americans professed in their conflict with the Axis powers and realities of American life such as racial segregation, inadequate state systems of criminal justice, and continued gender discrimination. In all these areas, Congress and the state legislatures had refused to enact meaningful reforms. The simple fact was that the legislative and amending processes had proved far too cumbersome to be of any practical use. With regard to minority rights, our democratic institutions had proved themselves inadequate. Something had to be done about this state of affairs before further damage, and perhaps even civil unrest, ensued.

The judiciary, particularly the Supreme Court, bridged the gap between our ideals and existing realities by stepping into the political vacuum created by the unresponsive political branches. The Supreme Court became our nation's moral conscience and actively pursued an ambitious agenda of social reform. It acted boldly, noninterpretivists claim, because judges could do the "right thing" without fear of losing their jobs. For more than fifty years, Supreme Court decisions have changed public policies for the better; because of these decisions, American life conforms more closely than ever before to the ideals of freedom and equality that constitute our highest commitments as a people. Almost single-handedly the Supreme Court has erased our nation's past failures, transforming the law to make us more the people we had professed to be. Noninterpretivists urge the justices to make decisions that will continue that legacy—encouraging us to become more the people we *ought* to be.

To achieve these long-overdue reforms, two generations of Supreme Court justices have created doctrines such as, but not limited to, fundamental fairness, liberties essential to a scheme of ordered liberty, evolving standards of decency, a variety of nexus and balancing tests, intriguing phrases (including penumbras and emanations, vagueness and overbreadth), expectations of privacy, excessive entanglement, and grossly disproportionate. Admittedly, some of these doctrines are snazzy and have a modicum of interpretive merit, but more often than not they have little substance outside of the policy predilections that inspired them. Far too often, these doctrines ignore the framers' design, historical facts, and long-standing legal precedents and doctrines. Far too often, they subordinate constitutional interpretation to personal assessments of what the American people need or should desire.

As Wallace Mendelson points out, the modern Supreme Court has instituted "more and more devious [doctrines and] slogan[s]" that have created "fairy tales" that "obscure (for lesser minds)" the fact that what has occurred are "raw exercise[s] of judicial fiat."[5] When all is said and done, noninterpretivists read the Constitution in an open-ended fashion, insisting that what were once clearly understood constitutional meanings are now ambiguous, so as to permit judges to substitute their policy preferences for those of legislators and thus to secure what they view as morally superior results.

Noninterpretivism does not only wreck constitutional law by untethering it from the original intentions of the framers; it also has undermined democratic government. Over the past fifty or sixty years, noninterpretivist jurisprudence has evinced a disturbing pattern of rights redefinition, creation, and expansion, the cumulative effect of which has been to markedly reduce the scope of the American people's right to self-government. Even if, for argument's sake, we concede that noninterpretivism's public-policy preferences are morally superior or otherwise preferable to those presently operative in our society, by what right do judges substitute their policy preferences for those of legislators or voters?

Noninterpretivists display an incredible moral arrogance, not to mention a profound lack of confidence in the American people. "Being terribly sure that they are right and everybody else not only wrong, but wrong because of their wickedness and perversity," as Willmoore Kendall and Carey write, they are unwilling to wait "for the deliberate sense of the community" to coalesce around their program or "to content themselves" with a "process of persuasion and conviction."[6] They redefine republicanism so as to render popular consent irrelevant to the legitimacy of their public-policy agenda. The cumulative effect of this jurisprudence has been to erode the competence of both the federal and state governments and to diminish the ability of the state to protect and promote certain critically important social goods. A quick look at some areas of public policy that have been influenced by noninterpretivist jurisprudence will illustrate this point.

Take, for example, the whole question of racial equality. *Brown v. Board of Education* is perhaps the most influential case decided by the Supreme Court in the twentieth century.[7] It stands for the principle of equal treatment of all races. The Court's immediate concern had been with segregated schools, but *Brown* certainly helped create the climate that, a decade later, made possible the passage of the Civil Rights Act of 1964. Over time, furthermore, it undoubtedly contributed to Americans becoming more sensitive to other forms of discrimination as well. Many noninterpretivists proudly locate the birth of modern judicial review in *Brown,* and insist that it has played a critical role in the shaping of contemporary American political culture, causing Americans to care more deeply about all types of discrimination than ever before.

But things change. Under judicially forced busing, school desegregation soon metamorphosed into affirmative action, then into the far more complex issue of reverse discrimination, and more recently still, the issue of school vouchers (which at least indirectly contains a race component). To one degree or another, race issues persist in public education and plague our public schools, particularly in urban areas. One substantive concern is the disproportionately high dropout rate among black male high school students, which in turn limits the number of black males in college, graduate, and professional schools. That, in turn, eventually hampers black job opportunities and upward mobility.

Confronted with this situation, some educators argue that the dropout rate among black males is high at least partially because they lack appropriate role models. They urge that some *public* funds be expended to create all-black male high schools where a disciplined atmosphere, vigorous curriculum, and black male teachers might reduce the dropout rate. Would such an experiment work? I don't know. Is it worth a try? I think so. It may not be the only proposal, or the best one, but how can we know how effective it might be unless we give it a try? Would not such public funding run afoul of the very principles established by *Brown*? Some scholars argue that it would not because the Fourteenth Amendment does not prohibit *beneficent* discrimination. Other scholars insist that such a distinction only encourages racial divisions.

My point is this: race-discrimination issues (and for that matter gender and sexual-orientation ones) are complex—indeed, far more complex today than when *Brown* was decided—and public opinion is far more fragmented. Clearly, obvious solutions do not exist for each of these issues; they remain questions about which reasonable people can disagree. And surely the pro-

225

found disagreements surrounding them aren't going to be resolved by judicial fiat. Judicial pronouncements, however, have constrained legislative options.[8] In attempting to impose a single *national* solution, haven't these decisions deprived us of one of the benefits of a federal system, namely, state experimentation? *Brown* contributes to legislative incompetence today because in the name of a vague legal principle legislative creativity has been inhibited.

Something similar is true in the area of procedural rights. Such rights, of course, revolve around the question of how executive and judicial officials must proceed before doing something, such as with respect to the treatment of criminal defendants. For more than forty years, the principle that "the quality of a nation's civilization can be largely measured by the methods it uses in the enforcement of its criminal laws" has dominated contemporary criminal constitutional law.[9] The Supreme Court has insisted that Americans ought to care about protecting defendant's rights because, first, citizens ultimately have more to fear from abusive police conduct than they do from criminal activity; and second, because one day we might find ourselves in the position of a criminal defendant. Accordingly, noninterpretivists celebrate those Supreme Court decisions which have secured such rights, particularly among the disadvantaged and racial minorities.

Leaving aside the various historical and theoretical objections that have been raised to the Court's jurisprudence in this area,[10] it's clear that these precedents have diminished legislative competence, as well as contracted the ability of government to protect the life and property of citizens. Take, for example, the issue of profiling. Courts uniformly condemn racial profiling, claiming that under the "strict scrutiny" doctrine used by the judiciary such profiling constitutes an unreasonable search and seizure. At best, courts have reluctantly approved police profiling techniques designed to identify, for example, behavior patterns of potential drug smugglers (e.g., repeatedly flying to particular locations, paying cash for their tickets, and seldom checking in luggage).[11]

While the Bill of Rights has always been understood as placing restrictions on governmental conduct, it has not historically been understood as requiring the suspension of common sense.[12] Is it certain that profiling is always wrong? Given the terrorist threat, might a reasonable person conclude that there are circumstances in which such profiling, even if it had a racial or ethnic component, might be necessary to public safety? To qualify as "reasonable" must such searches be 100 percent effective? 90 percent? 80 percent? By depriving the legislative and executive branches of this weapon, might the courts not be endangering American lives?

More importantly, who should make the determination of whether, and under what circumstances, such techniques should be permissible: the president and Congress—officials accountable to the voters—or life-tenured judges? Who should be responsible for striking the balance between the various values involved? Is it not clear that the vast majority of Americans believe that the airport security measures adopted in the wake of 9/11 are necessary to public safety? Do you doubt for a moment they would still be in place if a majority of citizens considered them unreasonable? What happens, moreover, if a court strikes down a security measure as unreasonable, and after some incident, like that of September 11, 2001, an investigation concludes that had the security measure been in place, the incident would have been prevented? Unlike elected officials, judges cannot be held accountable at the polls. Lack of common sense, stupidity, and an overzealous commitment to individual rights, after all, are not impeachable offenses.

Questions of substantive rights raise similar concerns. First Amendment rulings concerning freedom of speech are a case in point. Of all the provisions of the Bill of Rights, noninterpretivists hold none in higher esteem than those of free speech and press. Viewing these rights as at the very heart of American freedom, noninterpretivists insist that they constitute nothing less than preferred freedoms. If *Brown* is one leg of the three-legged stool justifying modern judicial power, the First Amendment is certainly one of its other legs.[13] We care deeply about the First Amendment.

Putting aside the powerful historical objections that have been raised to the Supreme Court's interpretation of the First Amendment's guarantee of freedom of speech,[14] its rulings in this area have diminished governmental competence. The fact is that in perhaps no other area have legislative hands been more often tied. For our purposes here, I'll focus on the case of *Texas v. Johnson*, in which the Supreme Court declared unconstitutional state statutes prohibiting the burning (desecration) of the American flag.[15] The Court cited precedents that had held that the First Amendment not only protects "speech" but expressive conduct as well.[16]

Here again, what I want to call attention to is this decision's impact on the whole question of governmental competence. In *Texas v. Johnson*, as in every other First Amendment case I have examined, not one justice demonstrated more than the most elementary appreciation of symbols and their role in political life.[17] They all have ignored the whole body of scholarship that insists on the central role played by symbols in constituting and uniting a body politic. Stable and enduring political orders, as Kendall and Carey observe, are "more than *merely* external relations of command and obedience." Rather, they are "little worlds of meaning" in which a people, through an apparatus of "symbols," "myths," and "rites," express self-understanding as a people. Thus, "all societies think of themselves, once they begin to think of themselves at all, as representing a truth, a meaning, about the nature and destiny of man."[18] Whoever defines a society's symbols defines that society.

Seen against this backdrop, the American flag emerges as an important symbol of our national identity, our values as a people, our shared history and communal solidarity. Seen as a public-policy question, it pits these values against the value of what has come to be called "expression" or "symbolic speech." Leaving aside, once again, the question of in whose hands the framers placed the responsibility for balancing these values, what needs to be asked is this: Which branch of government is better equipped to balance these values—the legislature or the courts? Aren't public-policy resolutions that require such balancing at the very heart of politics? Isn't that what lawmaking is all about? Shouldn't the same body that is authorized to make and declare war, and thus to place the lives of American sons, daughters, fathers, and mothers on the line by sending them into combat, have the responsibility for determining how best to protect the symbols of the nation for which it is asking Americans to risk their lives? By tying the hands of Congress and state legislatures on the matter of flag burning, haven't the courts diminished their ability to foster essential values such as patriotism and communal solidarity?[19]

II

Even a casual reading of the Constitution reveals that it places Congress, as the body responsible for the making of laws, at the center of the compound republic. In sharp contrast to the founders, noninterpretivists seek to limit the scope of self-government by transferring to the courts a significant part of the lawmaking authority the Constitution conferred upon Congress. They do so in the conviction that judicial deliberation will produce better policy outcomes than legislative deliberation.

This contention is, to say the least, problematic. The making of public policy—law—is an imprecise and very complex business. It is shaped by self-interest as well as concerns about justice, rights, and the general welfare; and it involves balancing a wide array of competing values and interests, as well as ranking a host of competing goods (e.g., individual freedom versus national security). At the same time, it requires knowledge of existing social conditions, the nature and direction of social change, particular social problems, the various policy options, and the costs and likely consequences of each. Inasmuch as one of the constants of social life is change, lawmaking involves the continual adjustment of existing policies in the light of shifting social and economic conditions, new knowledge, and new policy alternatives. Ultimately, good governance, like virtue, exists in an unnamable mean that is the object of deliberation.

As Carey points out, there is no reason to believe that judges are better "suited for this task" than legislators. To begin with, "legal training scarcely provides the breadth of knowledge in fields such as philosophy, history, the sciences and the social sciences necessary for this mission."[20] Nor is there any reason to believe that judges are better equipped than legislators to sort out the constantly changing flux of problems, demands, and options that confront policymakers; to balance competing values; or to continually adjust policies to stay abreast of ever-changing conditions or circumstances.

If anything, being unaccountable at the polls renders judges ill-equipped for this task. It acts to insulate them from shifting social, economic, and political currents and public, as opposed to elite, opinion. It's no accident that at momentous turns in American history (e.g., the conflicts over slavery and industrial capitalism), judges resisted change, exacerbated economic and social strains, and rendered the national and state governments incapable of meeting the crisis they confronted because they read their own policy predilections into the Constitution. Throughout our history, it has been legislators who have adapted law and public policy to changing circumstances. They did so or they lost their job.[21]

Likewise, the nature of the judiciary renders it less suited than the legislature to address a central problem of democratic theory: the intensity problem. Disagreements about public policies habitually divide a people; and when these divisions become particularly intense they threaten the ability of the majority to secure the cooperation of the minority without the widespread use of coercion, thereby undermining the vitality and stability of democratic government. As Kendall and Carey point out in their classic analysis, this problem was (and still is) largely neglected in contemporary democratic theory.[22]

The founders' appreciation of this problem finds expression in the distinction drawn by "some of the delegates" to the Philadelphia Convention "between 'temporary' or 'snap' or 'frivolous' majorities on the one hand and what we may call 'serious' or 'deliberate' majorities on the other." Their appreciation also helps explain why "the Convention . . . wrote into the Constitution severe limitations upon temporary majorities, and left the path to the statute-book open only to serious, deliberate majorities, that is, majorities able to keep themselves in being long enough to gain control of both houses of Congress, of the Presidency, and of the Supreme Court."[23] In the founders' model of democratic government—in what might be called "Madisonian democracy"—legislative deliberation plays a critical role in establishing the type of consensual decision making required in order to address the intensity problem.[24] To understand why, it is necessary to appreciate that the consensus building required in order to solve the intensity problem has a variety of preconditions. Each group, for example, must assess the intensity of its members on particular issues and assess as well the intensity of its opponents. Doing the latter involves distinguishing between real intensity and manufactured intensity. (Groups will frequently fake a nonexistent intensity in a calculated ploy to obtain some advantage.) Without such skills groups would neither be able to prioritize what they want nor evaluate what the other groups may or may not be willing to give in order to obtain their cooperation. When the ability to accurately make such assessments is lacking, prospects for serious miscalculations increase, as do the prospects for polarization, civic strife, and even violence or civil war.

Another precondition is the presence of a significant number of citizens who do not feel intensely about a particular issue. Why is the presence of a body of relatively "apathetic" citizens so essential? A simple example will aid us here. A group of friends are discussing what they might do one evening and one member suggests, "Let's go to restaurant 'Z,'" only to find there is no clear-cut majority. While some are intensely for or against the suggestion, others in the group remain indifferent. Assume the group adopts majority rule as a fair basis for reaching a decision. In the absence of a clear majority, the relatively indifferent group members are in a position to play a key role in fostering consensus.

These members can approach the issue in a cooler manner than their more committed compatriots (whose very intensity may produce a certain lack of perspective). Yet insofar as both sides need them, they are in a position to demand concessions in exchange for their support. They might, for example, agree to restaurant "Z" if the supporters of this idea agree to let those who were adamantly opposed to this choice have their way next week (perhaps on an entirely unrelated matter).

Yet another precondition is a citizenry that approaches politics in a non-ideological fashion and exhibits a willingness to compromise. In a citizenry whose members believe that tempering one's principles is *itself* unprincipled or illogical, and who insist on carrying their principles through to their logical conclusion, compromise is going to be extremely difficult if not impossible. Consensual politics requires citizens who are willing to be guided by something other than the sheer logic of their premises, who value goods like unity and stability more than ideological consistency; it requires people who are willing to temper their convictions in the interests of consensus and civic amity.

The Madisonian model is designed to handle intensity issues because, by relying on the legislative process rather than elections to decide issues of public policy, it slows down the decision-making process and makes elections revolve around which candidate will participate in a deliberative process rather than determining the specific outcomes of various public-policy issues. It creates conditions whereby the contending parties can accurately gauge each other's intensity. As Kendall and Carey note, "by spreading actual policy decisions out over a period of many months or even years" and by having them made by individuals who have "maximum opportunities to know and understand one another, to 'feel each other out,' and thus to arrive at correct reciprocal anticipations," the possibility of serious miscalculations triggering civic conflict are greatly reduced.[25]

At the same time, the pluralism flowing from the extended character of the Madisonian republic creates a situation in which citizen opinion will frequently fragment. This fragmentation further slows the decision-making process, both giving some partisans a chance to calm down (thereby removing passion from the process) as well as affording the opportunity for groups that ordinarily do not see themselves as allies to come together.

Since most citizens will rarely feel intensely about more than a few (if any!) of the infinite number of policy issues confronting our society, a situation is created in which the balance of power on any given issue is in the hands of the relatively indifferent (relatively apathetic) citizens. The cumulative effect of this is to ensure that "cooler heads" prevail and to encourage compromise.

Under such conditions, groups have an incentive to put their cards on the table and set a reasonable "price" for their support, because if that price is set too high or all compromise is rejected on the basis of some "principle," the reality is that a majority may coalesce without them! So instead of perhaps getting *something* for joining a coalescing majority, they may well be totally ignored. The majority, after all, rules. Groups that refuse to compromise out of stubbornness, or that believe tempering one's principles is unprincipled or illogical, will generally find themselves condemned to political irrelevancy.

Further incentives to compromise are created by the nature of the political institutions at the center of the Madisonian model. As Kendall and Carey observe, in the United States governmental action requires a consensus, not only between the houses of Congress but "among the three branches" of government, because "the branches represent different constituencies out among the people."[26] These incentives toward compromise are augmented by the constitutional morality inculcated directly and indirectly by the Madisonian model, "a morality of conciliation, moderation, and, above all, deliberation."[27]

Making the legislature the central political institution and relying on legislative deliberation for the making of public policy, the Madisonian schema encourages consensus-building, negotiation, and horse-trading among competing groups and interests. While safeguarding the principle of majority rule, it establishes a system in which preferences are "weighed as well as counted, and weighed in such a manner that the heavier ones tip the scale more than the lighter ones."[28] Thus, "the normal legislative act is in America, and always has been, a 'deal' hammered out, in the course of lengthy deliberation and negotiation between majority and minority, and by no means the act that the majority, had it consulted its own views and wishes, would have put on the statute book."[29]

In contrast to the legislature in the Madisonian model, judicial deliberations to which the proponents of noninterpretivism entrust policymaking have no reliable means of measuring intensity, "Unlike the Congress," as Carey writes, unelected judges have "no reliable means to gauge the relative intensity of the interested parties, what the reactions will be to any given pronouncement or, *inter alia*, what obstacles are likely to arise in its execution."[30] They have no reliable means of doing so because their small size and mode of selection combined with the norms governing their dealings with political actors collectively assure that the judiciary neither represents as broad a cross-section of views on any given policy question as does the legislature nor provides a forum in which representatives of different views can feel one another out and thus arrive at correct "reciprocal anticipations." The very way in which judges are insulated from the type of political pressures to which legislators are subject, in short, renders them incapable of measuring properly the intensity of the various groups whose demands they must address.

Even if they could measure it as well as the legislature, the nature of the judiciary precludes the type of negotiation and horse-trading employed by legislatures in the making of public policy—negotiation and horse-trading that allows the legislature not only to gauge the intensity of the various parties, but to take it into account in the creation of public policy. Judicial determinations, after all, are supposed to proceed in a straightforward and logical way from constitutional principles. Once the courts have announced that the Constitution requires or prohibits some particular course of action on a matter of public policy, it is far more difficult for them to change course than it is for a legislature to revise its approach to some area of public policy. A legislature can simply announce that circumstances have changed, an existing policy isn't working, or new facts have come to light. "Once having embarked on a path," as Carey writes, a court "can pull back or reverse itself only at great cost to its own prestige and the principle of the rule of law."[31]

It might be objected that courts could rely on polls to measure intensity. Today's more sophisticated polls include so-called intensity scales.[32] But polls only record first impressions; and such impressions are more often than not tied to our existing attitudes, steeped in emotions only too susceptible to manipulation. The simple choice of wording, for example, can easily skew a poll's outcome. We don't take polls, then ask the respondents to examine all the pertinent evidence, and repoll them to see if their opinions have moderated. Polls, furthermore, must include a finite scale of responses because they could not possibly anticipate or encompass the variety of human choices on even the simplest subject. (Wait in line at the local Starbucks and just listen to the variety of coffee preferences!) And as far as measuring intensity is concerned, how can polls possibly distinguish between real and "manufactured" intensity?

Finally, while polls can record initial voter preferences, decision making based on such preferences alone is the antithesis of the Madisonian model of democracy. While in a well-constructed popular government such sentiment would serve as an initial political focal point for political decision making, it could hardly be the last word. On the contrary: if democratic government is to be good government, it is necessary, in Madison's words, "to refine and enlarge public views" through deliberative processes, to produce public policies that reflect not simply the initial will of the people, but rather "the deliberate sense of the community."[33] To rely on polls to guide judicial policy-making is to embrace what the framers studiously attempted to avoid: the direct injection of passion into the making of law and public policy.

III

The restoration of America's traditional constitutional order will require a revolution in our thinking about a variety of important topics. To begin with, it will involve a return to the founders' understanding of the nature and limits of judicial power. Interpretivists and noninterpretivists agree that the government established by the Constitution is a limited one, that it "contains certain specified exceptions to the legislative authority." They also agree both that it creates a life-tenured judiciary, and that judicial review is "essential" to the preservation of those limitations.[34]

Interpretivists, however, maintain that in accepting judicial review the framers never authorized judges to impose *their* sense of wisdom or morals on the people, or to expand the restrictions on Congress and the president contained in the Constitution, or to create new rights. As Carey points out, the founders' understanding of judicial review is articulated in *Federalist* 78, which,

> when read in its entirety . . . amounts to a perfectly sensible statement with which few, if any, would seriously disagree, given the fact that we have a written charter of government. To note, as Hamilton does, the feebleness and weakness of the judiciary, the fact that it cannot take any "active resolution whatever," that it is to be a passive institution exercising only JUDGMENT, that its powers extend to declaring acts of the legislature unconstitutional only when contrary to the "manifest tenor" of the Constitution . . . that it can only use this power when there is an "irreconcilable variance" between the statute and the Constitution, and finally, that it is "indispensable" that it be "bound down by strict rules and precedents," hardly lends support to the thesis that he sought to vest the judiciary with the kind and degree of powers that modern-day "judicial activists," among others, impute to it.[35]

Noninterpretivists, in short, tend to forget that the framers' understanding of judicial review was a strictly limited one. Instead, they hop-skip-and-jump from the premise that judicial review is necessary to a regime of limited government to the utterly unfounded conclusion that the contemporary role played by the Supreme Court is *consistent* with the ratifiers' design. In contrast, as Carey shows, the founders' understanding of judicial review differs sharply from noninterpretivist claims of "judicial *supremacy*."[36] The framers, as Carey explains, assumed that judicial review would be employed to "nullify only obvious . . . violations of the Constitution."[37] They also assumed that the judiciary would be "beyond comparison the weakest of three departments of power" and that judges would use traditional canons of statutory construction.[38]

Finally, they assumed that if judges strayed too far from their interpretive responsibilities, Congress could limit appellate jurisdiction, reduce the budget of the judicial branch (but not the salary of judges), regulate how courts conduct their business, or, ultimately, impeach them. The powers exercised by the courts are delegated to them by the American people. When the courts violate the terms of their contract with the American people by exceeding the limits of their powers, as Carey writes,

> our obligation to respect or obey its power of judicial review is severed, and the other branches of government, principally the Congress, are entitled, nay *obliged*, to use the constitutional means at their disposal to curb, regulate, and control the Court in such manner as to compel conformance with the terms of the contract. This line of reasoning is but a corollary of the line of reasoning by which courts lay claim to the power of judicial review. The Court is equally obliged as a creature of the Constitution not to overstep its bounds or exceed its constitutional authority. To argue otherwise would be to say that the Court endorses judicial supremacy.[39]

To conclude, as many noninterpretivists imply, that by authorizing judicial review somehow the ratifiers signaled a repudiation of the republican character of the government they had created is patently absurd. As *Federalist* 78 observes, judicial review does not presuppose the "superiority of the judicial to the legislative power," but rather the superiority of "the power of the people . . . to both."[40]

While the noninterpretivist defense of the modern judicial role is sophisticated, it nevertheless marks a fundamental break with the American constitutional tradition. To restore that tradition it is necessary to recover the framers' understanding of the nature and limits of judicial power in a constitutional republic.

The reestablishment of our traditional constitutional order also will involve a recovery of the American political tradition. Noninterpretivist jurisprudence emerges against the backdrop of a reading of the American political tradition that insists that its highest commitments were to individual freedom and equality. As Kendall and Carey have shown, however, the American political tradition as it unfolds from the Mayflower Compact through the Bill of Rights is not one of individual rights and equality, but one of self-government and legislative supremacy.[41] The essential nature of the tradition is illustrated by one of its foundational documents—the Massachusetts Body of Liberties (1641).[42] This document, Kendall and Carey write, does not speak "in terms of individual rights; or at least not in terms of individual rights against the legislature." On the contrary, when in this document the people "put into words the liberties, immunities, etc., that they understand themselves as entitled to . . . what they lay claim to is . . . the rights of being governed by their own representatives, the rights of self-government."[43]

While this tradition allows considerable room for individual rights, those rights traditionally have been of a *procedural* nature—most notably aimed at the executive and judicial abuses common in the course of English history. The Massachusetts Body of Liberties, as Kendall and Carey observe, contains "no hint . . . of any right *against* the legislature." From its perspective, "the rights that individuals ought to have are, neither more nor less than those required . . . by the common good."[44] Indeed, in the areas that noninterpretivists today consider particularly sensitive one finds "escape clauses" empowering the legislature (that is, the Massachusetts General Court) to make exceptions to the general application of certain remedies (i.e., liberties).[45] For example, it affirms that

> no man shall be forced by Torture to confesse any Crime against him-
> selfe nor any other unlesse it be done in some Capitall case, where he
> is first fullie convicted by cleare and sufficient evidence to be guilty,
> After which if the cause be of that nature, That it is very apparent there
> be other conspiratours, or confederates with him, Then he may be tor-
> tured, yet not with such Tortures as be Barbarous and inhumane.[46]

As this suggests, the Body of Liberties recognizes what today we still instinctively know (once inoculated against contemporary rights rhetoric): that few, if any, rights can exist in all times and circumstances. Liberties always require a balancing of competing concerns. And as far as the question of who should do the balancing is concerned, the people of Massachusetts are emphatic in insisting the responsibility rests with legislators.

Now, there is some truth in the proposition that the approach represented by the Massachusetts Body of Liberties changed once equivalent "liberties" became constitutionalized. Constitutional provisions, it is clear, stand on higher ground than congressional statutes. But what type of change does this represent? As Kendall and Carey show, the Constitution remains firmly rooted in the very political tradition of which the Body of Liberties is an expression; and, as *The Federalist Papers* insist, "in republican government, the legislative authority necessarily predominates."[47] In a nutshell, as important as individual rights were to those who ratified the Constitution and Bill of Rights, they did not singularly or collectively supercede the right of self-government—which, after all, ultimately is the right to create and define individual rights, both statutory and constitutional.[48] While it is true that Congress was bound to respect the particular restrictions contained in the Constitution and Bill of Rights, it is also true that these rights were understood historically in ways that allowed the government broad latitude to act to protect and promote the general good, and that Congress played an important role in defining their nature and scope.[49]

Finally, and perhaps most importantly, the restoration of the American constitutional tradition will require the renewal of scholarship on the origins and meaning of the Constitution's provisions. More than ever, scholars today have enormous difficulty mastering a specialized field. The problem is not simply unparalleled access to materials in any one specialty, or even in one discipline; it is the need to grasp the relationship between one's specialty and the general discipline, and then between one's general discipline and allied fields.

All scholars, furthermore, must separate important from unimportant in-formation, and to do that, they—explicitly or implicitly—employ criteria of inclusion or exclusion. These criteria vary over time. More often than not, to one degree or another the criteria used by one generation of scholars are eventually found either partially or wholly defective by succeeding generations. Later scholars generally conclude that their predecessors relied too heavily upon incomplete or insufficient data, or made unwarranted assumptions. What this underscores is that scholarship is influenced by the climate of opinion and the body of largely unexamined assumptions within which it unfolds. Indeed, it is from this climate that we draw our criteria of inclusion or exclusion, just as it was from the intellectual climates of their eras that previous generations of scholars drew the unwarranted assumptions that vitiated their work.

For several generations, historical scholarship on the origins and meaning of the Constitution's provisions has occurred within a climate of opinion in which it was taken for granted that the highest commitment of the Founding Fathers and the political order they launched was to the values of individual rights and equality—and that American history is a tale of progress, the story of the increasing actualization, dissemination, and expansion of these values. These assumptions could not but influence scholarship.

Take, for example, the case of a contemporary scholar who decides to investigate how one or another eventual provision of the Bill of Rights had been understood during the American Revolutionary period.[50] Given the assumptions on which he operates regarding the values to which the founders were dedicated, the scholar may ignore or give short shrift to aspects of the historical record incompatible with these assumptions. Given his assumptions about the progressive unfolding of American history, moreover, in studying primary sources, it will be difficult for him not to allow his understanding of these sources to be affected by how the provision in question came to be understood *after* the Revolutionary period—perhaps very long after. This scholar's conviction that American history is a tale of unfolding and increasing liberty may well lead him to interpret the historical materials in such a way as to emphasize only those aspects of the historical record consistent with how the right later came to be understood.

In short, it is quite natural for a scholar who views history as a progressive evolution to smooth out (why confuse the reader?) rough edges (inconsistencies) in order to demonstrate that the continuity was "natural"—nay, almost *inevitable*. History thus takes on the characteristics of any good novel. The historical record is cherry-picked to identify the seeds that eventually grow and bear fruit in the form of the rights championed by noninterpretivist jurisprudence.[51] Such scholarship influences court decisions, which in turn influence later scholarship—and so on.

My point is this: for scholars to take a phrase from the Constitution, like, say, "due process of law," and retroactively read into it their current understanding of that phrase—without trying to carefully ascertain what those words meant at the time the Constitution was written—is fraught with danger. They might use wonderful "logic" to explicate what protections that phrase could or should guarantee today, but this logic must be recognized for what it is: the means by which scholars and judges inject their own predilections into constitutional law under a pretense of "interpreting" the Constitution. Such an approach is inadequate—regardless of how clear the meaning of the word or phrase appears to be, or how natural the consequences appear to their advocates.

Before students can determine what the ratifiers of the Constitution intended by the words they used, the words must be placed in context. Historical studies purporting to provide that context should possess at least four characteristics:

1. They must attempt to understand the words and phrases employed by figures in earlier periods of our history as they were understood by those figures themselves.

2. It should not be assumed that the way in which phrases and principles were understood at some later period of history reveals how these phrases were understood during some earlier era.

3. If, during the period studied, the principles or words had several usages, scholars should determine which understanding *dominated*. They shouldn't automatically assume that the usage that prevailed later in our history was originally the dominant one.

4. Perhaps most importantly, scholars should test the word's *alleged* meaning against *actual practice*. Scholars, as Kendall and Carey remind us, should not be satisfied with logical explications: they must zero in on a people's *actions*. These actions provide crucial context for the interpreter, just as, in adjudication, concrete facts provide a more appropriate setting than do hypotheticals. Students should be leery when discrepancies between belief and action are characterized as ignorance of the words' "true" meaning, or are due to the people's alleged hypocrisy.[52]

The operating premises of interpretivist jurisprudence—its insistence that we must understand the provisions of the Constitution as they were understood by the framers and ratifiers—is dependent upon the work of historians. Regrettably, for the reasons just noted, the available historical scholarship often is unreliable—uncritically biased in favor of progressivist or personal-rights assumptions. This is not to suggest that interprevists must ignore this scholarship but rather that they must treat it gingerly. At the same time, they must resist the urge to throw the baby out with the bath water, because even scholarship distorted by flawed assumptions will often contain important insights. Ultimately, however, the restoration of our constitutional tradition will involve an immense amount of new and better historical scholarship.

IV

The ascendancy of noninterpretivism has succeeded in transforming judicial review into a doctrine of judicial supremacy, and in converting a Constitution intended, in law professor Larry Kramer's words, to "regulate and restrain the government" into one in which the Supreme Court "restrain[s] the people."[53] As a result, the Court is not only now sitting as a continuing constitutional convention, but it has the authority to ratify its own proposed amendments. Instead of providing elected representatives with broad discretion to adopt the polices they believe best suited to advance the general welfare and to change these polices when they believe circumstances dictate, what Carey describes as the "new regime" created by the ascendancy of noninterpretivism drastically restricts that discretion by elevating to constitutional status their own public-policy preferences.[54]

Confronted with this state of affairs interpretivists remain on the defensive. Their goal is to seize control of the judiciary. Yet they also react to specific judicial usurpations. Some take issue with the judiciary's expansion of personal liberties and creation of heretofore unknown rights; others object to judicial assaults on existing cultural mores. Minimally, interpretivists wish to prevent new usurpations from occurring. At their most aggressive, they want to reverse decisions they find distasteful. They tend to focus on the specific public policies mandated by the courts while giving short shrift to the broader issue of legitimacy.

The net result of their strategy, however, has been to make judicial appointments more contentious, with each camp fearing control of the judiciary by the other. Legislative resistance to judicial usurpations—by such traditional means as slashing judicial appropriations, or the removal of Supreme Court appellate jurisdiction, or commencing impeachment proceedings against judges and so on—either are no longer attempted or, in the specific context in which they occur, seem excessively partisan. Occasionally, interpretivists advocate issue-oriented constitutional amendments. Whatever merit they may have, these strategies have never addressed the noninterpretivist legacy—the transformation of our government into a judicial oligarchy. Nor have they challenged the legitimacy of the new constitutional order it has produced.

Traditional congressional tools of resistance have lost their potency, not because they would be ineffective if invoked, but because a majority of Congress has accepted the idea of judicial supremacy. Today, Congress lacks the strong institutional consciousness upon which the framers so depended. Members have chosen to ignore what Kramer describes as "the Court's self-aggrandizing tendencies" and the growing elitism "among lawyers, judges, scholars, and even politicians" who believe "that ordinary people are foolish and irresponsible when it comes to politics," a belief which is "grounded less in empirical fact or logical argument than in intuition and supposition."[55] In sum, Congress today is ill-equipped to preserve and defend our republican regime.

It certainly is an odd state of affairs. The framers, by birth aristocrats and among the intelligentsia of their day, had greater faith in the constitutional structures they created, as well as in the people, than do their congressional successors. Even in the 1930s, the progressivists—beyond any question, part of the intelligentsia of their day—never dreamed of circumventing elected officials. At least *initially* they concentrated their efforts on halting illegitimate judicial vetoes of legislative economic proposals. Felix Frankfurter, for example, as a private citizen sought political remedies, and as a justice of the Supreme Court advised that "[t]he Court is not saved from being oligarchic because it professes to act in the service of humane ends."[56]

Today the situation could not be more different. Our intelligentsia, including elected officials, has become part of the problem—not a potential solution. It evinces an unprecedented lack of faith in the political judgment of the American people, standing idly by as members of the judiciary claim to know what is best for them. Worst of all, our intelligentsia refuses to acknowledge that under the guise of constitutional interpretation the policy preferences of nonterpretivists, a majority of justices, and some legislators are being imposed by judicial fiat on the American people.

The complicity of the legal profession in this state of affairs is particularly disturbing. Lawyers have increasingly abandoned the Constitution, as well as the tools of their craft, while acquiescing in their elevation to priestly status by the new order. The ratifiers thought the legal profession essential to preserving and protecting the regime from momentary passions, thus better securing the rule of law.[57] Too many lawyers today have shamefully abandoned the founders' intentions. Instead, they champion—or at least acquiesce in—the replacement of a government of law by the rule of men.

Given how enamored our intelligentsia has become of judicial power, it will be exceedingly difficult to prevent further usurpations, much less reverse previous ones. The interpretive tools employed by noninterpretivists and their supporters are inherently expansive. Fertile imaginations will continue to create new rights (e.g., privacy) and to redefine constitutional phrases (e.g., freedom of speech). And once the judiciary has embraced these innovations, logic will brush aside competing values not enjoying constitutional status, or else the Court will fabricate yet another so-called "balancing test" to mask the majority's imposition of its policy predilections. Whether created out of whole cloth or simply redefined, such "rights" will inevitably take on a life of their own, thereby drawing the judiciary ever deeper into areas traditionally reserved to the legislature. Considerations such as the republican character of our regime, our tradition of self-government (which in fact placed most of the responsibility for the determination of the nature and scope of individual rights in the hands of the legislature), or the framers' understanding of the limited scope of judicial review will simply disappear from view as the logic of "rights" asserts itself.

It is true that on occasion the Court has been forced to retrench so as to avoid generating so much political hostility that its new role would be threatened. One thinks here of its decisions concerning the establishment clause, the rights of criminal defendants, the death penalty, and abortion. But such retreats are merely tactical and provide only a temporary respite. Over the past forty years, no majority of the Court has foresworn expansionary and illegitimate noninterpretivist premises. Sooner or later, the inner dynamism of noninterpretivist jurisprudence will assert itself, driving the Court to create and secure new rights or expand old ones.

Where does this leave us? There is no way to predict the ultimate outcome of this clash over the nature of constitutional law and republicanism. Already a minority, the interpretivists may simply fade away because they cannot attract sufficient numbers of adherents to remain a force on the intellectual or political scene. Yet interpretivism may undergo a revival if the Court majority misjudges popular hostility to its latest public-policy decisions. And it is always possible that implementation of noninterpretivism's current reform agenda may cause its support to decline or that the emergence of new or more complex issues may introduce divisions into the ranks of its supporters.

Perhaps the most disturbing aspect of this state of affairs is the steadfast refusal of the noninterpretivists to openly acknowledge to the American people what has occurred, and to seek their consent to the far-reaching constitutional revolution that they have wrought. They should at least be as frank as the framers were and ask the people to formally ratify a change they so obviously favor: the transformation of our form of government from a republican one to a judicial oligarchy. While the American people are perfectly entitled to embrace a judicial oligarchy, they and their elected representatives cannot ignore the constitutional requirement that they do so by formal amendment.

Curiously, given that their political theory is often attacked as antidemocratic, the ratifiers were concerned about the possibility of public officials becoming insulated from public opinion. Accordingly, although it has never been invoked, they included in the Constitution a method of amending the document that does not require the approval of Congress. The pertinent portion of Article V provides that "[t]he Congress . . . on the application of the legislatures of two thirds of the several states, shall call a convention for proposing amendments, which . . . shall be valid to all intents and purposes, as part of this Constitution, when ratified by the legislatures of three fourths of the several states, or by conventions in three fourths thereof."

While this method should not be used lightly and is fraught with danger,[58] the situation created by the ascendancy of noninterpretivism may require its invocation. Perhaps in this way we may close the gap between the Constitution ratified by the American people some two hundred years ago and the new one that has emerged under the impact of noninterpretivist jurisprudence. As a people, we have the right to declare whether we prefer the rule of law or the rule of men, the rule of the many or the rule of the few.

243

The Crisis of the American Political Tradition

E. ROBERT STATHAM, JR.

*The document crafted by our Founding Fathers in Philadelphia
over the course of the summer of 1787 is a dead letter.[1]*
—George W. Carey

The American political order is experiencing a constitutional crisis, one that, at its root, is a crisis of public philosophy.[2] As Walter Lippmann pointed out in his classic work *The Public Philosophy* (1955), there is "mounting disorder in our Western society," as we are in the process of losing "our great traditions of civility, the liberties Western man had won for himself after centuries of struggle and which are now threatened by the rising tide of barbarity."[3] This tide of barbarity arose from a "functional derangement of the relationship between the mass of the people and the government," where mass democracy supersedes and destroys the original animating intellectual and moral foundations of free and constitutional living.[4] Evidently José Ortega y Gasset's *Revolt of the Masses* (1929) is now in full swing.[5] In Lippmann's estimation, "a mass cannot govern," and

> [w]here mass opinion dominates the government, there is a morbid derangement of the true functions of power. The derangement brings the enfeeblement, verging on paralysis, of the capacity to govern. This breakdown in the constitutional order is the cause of the precipitate and catastrophic decline of Western society.[6]

America's constitutional crisis, which is in no small way a symptom of the decline of Western civilization, is largely found in the replacement of the culture and forms of constitutionalism with the culture and informality of mass democracy. One of Carey's most important contributions to American political thought is his perspicacious diagnosis of this crisis.

I

Aristotle, in *The Politics*, begins by asserting that "every state is a community of some kind, and every community is established with a view to some good."[7] Carey (along with Willmoore Kendall) has pointed out that the American political tradition "is now a problem where it was not a problem before," raising questions regarding who and what we are as a people.[8] Directly, the traditional is no longer clearly associated with the good in contemporary America. Since every community is rooted in certain specific traditions that are, in the Aristotelian sense, aimed at a view to the good, America is indeed experiencing a disconnect, if not derangement, between the people and their original constitutional order.[9] The primary expression of this problem is the growth of mass democracy, which is a perversion of the constitutionalism of the American founding.

In Aristotelian terms, the American constitutional order, as it was founded, was a just form of the rule of the many.[10] It allowed for the indirect, filtered rule of the people via a written constitution that incorporated the principles of the separation of powers, checks and balances, federalism, and republicanism, all within the context of limited government. It fulfilled the role dictated by the abiding concern Madison expressed: "In framing a government which is to be administered by men over men, the great difficulty lies in this: you must first enable the government to control the governed; and in the next place oblige it to control itself."[11]

Today the government no longer controls the governed, or itself. This indicates a lack of self-government, one of the cornerstones of our constitutional order, and thus a serious problem of liberty.[12] To reiterate, our constitutional order has lapsed, ever so progressively (a term that Professor Carey is fond of utilizing in the appropriate "negative" sense), into the perverted form of the rule of the many, a mass democracy.

Carey pinpoints the causes for the crisis of the American political tradition at a level deeper than that of mere political machinery. In this he follows Eric Voegelin, who argued that human society "is illuminated through an elaborate symbolism" that provides its meaning.[13] The "self illumination of society through symbols" is an integral part of social reality, even "its essential part," since through symbolization members of society "experience their human essence."[14] The American political tradition is grounded in just this kind of symbolism, Carey argues, and it is this symbolism that has suffered serious damage.[15]

The basic symbols of the American political tradition have been transformed by ideological symbols that represent the antithesis of the original constitutional order, symbols specifically generated by progressive-Enlightenment thought and that produce mass democracy. Carey notes this in asserting:

> Our political tradition, as it is embodied in the Philadelphia Constitution of 1787 and the premises on which it is fashioned, has been under a sustained attack. . . . [W]hat is more, enlightenment ideology so thoroughly permeates our entire culture that certain of its principles are now unquestioned components of our social and political landscape. As a consequence, significant aspects of this ideology have been tacitly accepted by sizeable proportions of the population. They have become a part of our "civil theology," so to speak.[16]

Carey finds that modern progressivism was "born out of the fanaticism of the French Revolution."[17] Indeed, there is a direct connection between modern progressive ideology and French Jacobinism.[18]

Once again, Walter Lippmann provides us with an important insight into the ideology propagated by Jacobinism:

> Like Saint Paul, the Jacobins promised a new creature who would "be led of the spirit" and would not be "under the law." But in the Jacobin Gospel, this transformation was to be achieved by the revolutionary act of emancipation from authority. The religious end was to be reached, but without undergoing the religious experience. There was to be no dark night of the soul for each person in the labor of his own regeneration. Instead, there were to be riots and strikes and votes and seizure of political power. Instead of the inner struggle of the individual soul, there was to be one great public massive, collective redemption.[19]

The dominant characteristics of the Enlightenment ideology that has undermined the American political tradition are grounded in a hypervaluation of democracy over against the structures and principles of a limited constitution. In Alexis de Tocqueville's estimation, democracy tends to produce a greater love of equality than of liberty and law, so that in America, equality is the people's idol.[20] Democratic peoples' passion for equality is "ardent, insatiable, incessant, invincible," to the extent that "they call for equality in freedom, and if they cannot obtain that, they still call for equality in slavery." They will "endure poverty, servitude, barbarism, but they will not endure aristocracy."[21]

Carey, consistent with Tocqueville and Lippmann, finds an overvaluation of equality in our constitutional order that leads to the attempt to "reduce men as far as possible to the condition of sameness."[22] What is more, this radical egalitarianism produces a "perverse form of relativism that exalts equality" or "transforms equality into the common good or the true interest of society," but which also dogmatically holds that there is no such thing as a national interest or a common good.[23]

II

One of the most important insights that Carey provides us regarding our political tradition is the understanding that "constitutions play a limited role in fostering and nourishing communities."[24] Put differently, constitutions do not create communities, communities create constitutions. It is in communities, at the most basic levels of society, that we find the traditions and customs that are conducive to limited self-government. On this score, Tocqueville pointed out in his classic work *Democracy in America*:

> I am convinced that the most advantageous situation and the best possible laws cannot maintain a constitution in spite of the customs of a country. . . . So seriously do I insist upon this head that, if I have hitherto failed in making the reader feel the important influence of the practical experience, the habits, the opinions, in short, the customs of the Americans upon the maintenance of their institutions, I have failed in the principal object of my work.[25]

It would appear that the decline of the American political order is rooted in large part in the decline of the customs and traditions of the American people. This question leads us to a consideration of the intellectual and moral foundations of the American polity.

The American Constitution establishes the rule of law for the purpose of institutionally and structurally regulating self-interested human nature in the service of the public good.[26] In this regard the Constitution is a brilliant success. However, as Carey points out, the American framers presupposed that a certain degree of public virtue would exist in the citizenry in order to maintain constitutional order. This is not to say that the framers formally required observance of the morality necessary for the perpetuation of the constitution they founded.[27] While the American founding was a dramatic and marked success in establishing the rule of law and, therefore, in creating the conditions of negative liberty (freedom "from" tyranny and anarchy), there is reason to believe that that founding is, nevertheless, incomplete.[28] A people cannot live freely without living virtuously.[29] What is apparently missing in the American sociopolitical landscape is the sufficient and necessary cultivation of public virtue, of the customs and traditions of individual and communal self-government that the founding generation practiced so well but neglected to institutionalize, either constitutionally or in the form of an ethical treatise of some kind.[30] For this reason Carey raises the following concerns:

> How or by what means did the Framers believe the virtue necessary for the system would be cultivated and maintained? How, in other words, did they suppose the moral character and virtue of the people, so essential for republican regimes, could be maintained at sufficient levels so that the regime might endure for the ages? There is no easy answer to this question. We find no constitutional provision relating to, say, education that might bear upon this question.[31]

Neither do the authors of *The Federalist Papers* provide answers to the question of how to maintain the virtue necessary for the regime. Unfortunately, their work "offers no solutions, plans, or regime for inculcating or maintaining the requisite virtues."[32]

In his thorough and penetrating analysis of *The Federalist Papers*, Carey finds that Publius did not provide for the nurturing of opinions of the citizenry in order to promote a more cohesive and cooperative society. Neither did Publius provide the means by which the passions of the people could be moderated by educating and otherwise inculcating the citizenry with sufficient virtue. Moreover, he did not devise an appropriate mechanism to develop the intellectual and moral potential of future generations.[33] From these observations it is clear that Publius's conceptual framework is Enlightenment-based and not particularly congruent with the directives of classical political philosophy.[34] In this way there is a distinct separation between government and the people, between the Constitution and society in the American political order.[35] In the end, Carey finds that *The Federalist* "does not constitute a comprehensive and systematic discourse in political philosophy," as it leaves "the intellectual and moral development of individuals to society" and largely outside of the range, scope, and sphere of the Constitution.[36]

III

Why has the Constitution, with its incorporation of the tenets of the separation of powers, checks and balances, federalism, and republicanism (all within the framework of a sober understanding of human nature), failed to prevent the deleterious effects of democratization? It would appear that without a principled justification, the rule of law (the Constitution) becomes meaningless and impotent.[37] While the constitutionalism of *The Federalist Papers* provides a forceful, practicable remedy for the problems of democracy that derive from the pernicious aspects of human nature (mainly passionate self-interest), it does not present an exhaustive, normative defense of the regime it recommends.[38] Put differently, the Constitution preserves negative liberty (liberty from tyranny and anarchy) but does not provide a political-philosophical explication of constitutional justice in the positive sense (freedom "to").[39]

There is a necessary connection between politics and philosophy, between the law and reason, between the Constitution and wisdom. In our time, however, political philosophy "is in a state of decay and perhaps putrefaction."[40] The decline of political philosophy in our time is, therefore, directly linked to the decline of the American constitutional order. How is this so? The relation is essential since the law (Constitution) must be grounded in a transcendent standard if it is to be meaningful and authoritative.[41] And the transcendent standard of constitutionalism can only be ascertained by political philosophy, since there is a necessary relation between reason and right or justice. The transcendent standard for the rule of law is natural right and the foundation of natural right is reason.[42] There is an essential connection between the *eidos* (the form) and character of a political order, and the end to which that order is dedicated.[43]

The Constitution serves institutionally and externally to regulate passionate self-interest. It regulates human behavior externally for the purpose of preserving (negative) liberty. It does not address the internal character of the citizens upon which the intellectual and moral foundations of the order rest.

Neglect of the souls of individuals (the inner self) inevitably declines into "permissive egalitarianism" where what is secured and upheld is not conscience or reason, but the individual with his urges.[44] Permissive egalitarian democracy protects the free, equal, and relatively unrestrained pursuit and realization of the passions. And where the passions predominate, individuals engage in a seemingly infinite variety of sensually exciting activities: "having fun," "making contacts," "going places" (i.e., entertaining themselves).[45] The production of a sphere of freedom absent moral and philosophical directives protects individuals in a quasi-animal condition where the emotions and instincts dictate behavior, little restrained by either law or reason.[46]

Carey argues that the framers of our constitutional order took for granted that "the family, church, and communities, the most basic human associations, would produce the morality needed for the constitutional system to operate as intended."[47] But these associations and social institutions have atrophied over time from the "expansion of governmental powers and their centralization in the national government."[48] Why? Carey finds the answer in the evolution and ultimate dominance of the ideology of progressivism.[49] He specifically indicts the core beliefs, assumptions, and objectives of the work of Herbert Croly and his *The Promise of American Life* (1911). Croly believed that the American system of government could provide the greatest hope for excellent worldly life, for "heaven on earth," as it were. Through a concentration of power and wealth in the national government, most human problems could be overcome, from Croly's perspective.

The key elements of progressive ideology are: secular humanism that is grounded in "this-worldliness"; belief in the infinite, progressive malleability of human nature and the placing of humanity at the center of the universe; egalitarianism, which sees the need to equalize human conditions while leveling differences (particularly natural differences, including differences of merit) and also seeks to redistribute wealth throughout society; and centralization, which transforms public policymaking by placing it predominantly at the national level at the expense of local self-government.[50]

Carey finds that the Constitution and the objectives of progressivism are incompatible.[51] The Constitution, he writes, is "not an ends oriented document," but only a means, an instrument for preserving the liberty of the people and for assisting them in making decisions.[52] Again, the framers created a constitutional order that would negate the pernicious aspects of human nature (a fixed nature), thereby preventing tyranny and anarchy, but leave positive

self-government to the people, largely outside the sphere of the formal institutions of government. Thus, while the principal mission of constitutional
government is not "positive" in nature, the assumptions and goals of progressivism are "positive" and "ends" based.[53]

IV

What are the positive ends of free and constitutional living if they cannot be
found in the objectives of progressivism? Here we need to define the concept
of public virtue in a constitutional order and to determine the appropriate
structural, institutional, and environmental conditions conducive to the cultivation and perpetuation of such. Now, in Western civilization there are two
basic groundings or orientations regarding virtue. One approach is given to us
by the tradition of classical political philosophy that was initiated by Socrates
and continued by Plato and Aristotle. The other orientation is provided by
the Judeo-Christian tradition that is first and foremost grounded in the life
and teachings of Jesus Christ, but which is, broadly speaking, the biblical
tradition. The American founding incorporated both of these traditions: the
Constitution is the product of reasoned deliberation and discourse regarding
the political, and that same Constitution protects religious faith and conduct.
Public virtue in the American political tradition may therefore be defined in
terms of reason and/or revelation.[54]

Traditionally, Carey points out, "the breeding ground for virtue and morality was the family, the church, voluntary associations, and the community."[55] This kind of virtue is largely of a religious nature, and to be sure, dogmatic religious belief may play a formative and important role in democracies.
Tocqueville astutely pointed out that men need dogmatic belief, and that of
all the kinds of dogmatic belief, "the most desirable appears to be dogmatic
belief in matters of religion."[56] In his estimation, "men are immeasurably interested in acquiring fixed ideas of God, of the soul, and of their general duties to their Creator and their fellow men"; such ideas are crucial because to
submit to "doubt on these first principles would abandon all their actions to
chance and would condemn them in some way to disorder and impotence."[57]
He finds that fixed general ideas respecting God and human nature should be
recognized as a principle of authority in society, as they are indispensable to
all.[58] And the reason for this is that

[t]he greatest advantage of religion is to inspire diametrically contrary principles. There is no religion that does not place the object of
man's desires above and beyond the treasures of earth and that does
not naturally raise his soul to regions far above those of the senses. . . .
Religious nations are therefore naturally strong on the very point on
which democratic nations are weak; this shows of what importance it
is for men to preserve their religion as their conditions become more
equal.[59]

Dogmatic religious belief is especially useful in democratic societies like postmodern America. It provides sociopolitical cohesion and authority in a way
that is not possible through the national political process. And it serves as a
restraint on human passions, passions that can and do serve to undermine
liberty and the rule of law.

Unfortunately, as Carey has noted, the Enlightenment ideology of the
American experiment has placed considerable emphasis upon science, and
subsequently upon progress, this-worldliness, and material prosperity in the
here and now. Science, in presuming that all human values are of equal worth
(since science cannot pronounce authoritative judgement upon values), leads
to the relativism that is so destructive of principles, particularly liberty and
law. Revealed religion has for this reason suffered considerable opposition
over time, and not without deleterious consequences. If a democratic people
loses their religious faith, what replaces that faith?

The tradition of classical political philosophy is also in disrepair, and
for similar reasons. Enlightenment ideology has placed great emphasis upon
utilizing the scientific method (broadly conceived) in the study of society,
politics, and public policy. And yet, these studies are necessarily evaluative in
nature, requiring the assistance of theory or philosophy (the reasoned pursuit of knowledge and ultimately wisdom). Indeed, Carey has demonstrated
that the scientific study of politics "leads straightway to relativism, to the
conviction (unproven, of course) that there can be no provable hierarchy
of values."[60] Behaviorism dominates in the American study of politics, and
"its secularism will exclude exploration of man's relation to the transcendent" (religiously and philosophically). Moreover, "its lack of openness to
the whole of man's being and experience precludes it from ever being" truly
scientific.[61] Carey finds that the American scientific study of politics actually
serves as a mask to shield the fact that American political scientists have ac-

cepted Enlightenment ideology and its "isms" (multiculturalism and feminism in particular).[62]

A pertinent and unavoidable question arises regarding the role of reason in contemporary America. The classical, if not Socratic, way of life is quite nearly nonexistent in contemporary America. And yet, as Mordechai Roshwald argues, "Socrates points to the importance, the overriding importance, of the improvement of the soul." And "the soul is essentially, or at least primarily, reason." From the view of classical political philosophy, "the thinking, the rational capacity of man, is the center of his being, and as such requires and deserves attention and care."[63] Without this at once moderating and informing influence, is not the American constitutional order merely a regime of commerce, politicization, and sheer interest?

So it is clear that the two sources of public virtue in America and the West are religious and philosophic, both of which are transcendent. It is also evident that both of these sources are in either decline or disrepair as a result of Enlightenment ideology. Concomitantly, it is apparent that progressivism and its emphasis upon the centralization of political power in the state have produced structural, institutional changes in society that make the cultivation and perpetuation of public virtue precarious. The problem is, on the one hand, spiritual and intellectual, and on the other, social and political. With respect to the latter, reference can and should be made to Robert Nisbet, who argues that "certain profound dislocations in the primary associative areas of society, dislocations that have been created to a great extent by the structure of the Western political state," are responsible for our current crisis.[64] Nisbet finds (as does Carey) that "family, local community, church, and the whole network of informal interpersonal relationships have ceased to play a determining role" in our society.[65] What has been lost is "community" and "self-government," both of which are found in "intermediate associations."[66]

We are thus brought back to the increasing democratization of the American constitutional order. Enlightenment ideology is the intellectual companion of democratization. The two transcendent sources and companions of constitutionalism are, for this reason, in disrepair. Democracy is the perverted form of the rule of the many precisely because it represents the rule of the many over and against the few, under the presumption that the decision of the majority is, in and of itself, just. But the framers of our constitutional order understood only too well this problem of democracy. When the majority rules in its own interest, it might very well be ruling in "its own interest" tyrannically, since the "public interest" may or may not be determined numerically, either by the majority or a minority of the whole.[67] The democratization of the American political order thus occurs through the creation and existence of democratic masses and an associated ideology (progressivism) that at once "atomizes social and cultural relationships" and then rescues the masses "by leading them into the Promised Land of the absolute, redemptive State."[68]

It would appear that democracy is essentially degenerative. This is why Bertrand de Jouvenel considers democracy in totalitarian terms. The "democratic principle's degeneration is psychological: conceived at first as sovereignty of the law, it triumphed only when it had come to be regarded as sovereignty of the people."[69] Democratic governments are not the "abiding place of liberty" since the *power* of the people is not synonymous with the *liberty* of the people.[70] Indeed, Jouvenel finds that in democracies, law and liberty are perpetually in conflict with the absolute sovereignty of the people.[71] In this way, the tangible, practical effects of the democratization of the American constitutional order are found in popular sovereignty. Popular sovereignty has a fundamental defect:

> There are no institutions on earth which enable each separate person to have a hand in the exercise of Power, for Power is to command, and everyone cannot command. Sovereignty of the people is, therefore, nothing but a fiction, and one which must in the long run prove destructive of individual liberties.[72]

Democracy is despotic. In the name of the "general will" it "crushes each individual beneath the weight of the sum of the individuals represented by it" and "oppresses each private interest in the name of a general interest which is incarnate in itself."[73]

But modern democracy is despotic in totalitarian fashion. This derives from an important observation: the masses "neither should nor can direct their own personal existence, and still less rule society in general."[74] José Ortega y Gasset understood the problem of modern democracy as "the accession of the masses to complete social power," and he associated this phenomenon with the term "hyperdemocracy."[75] In his estimation: "The old democracy was tempered by a generous dose of liberalism and of enthusiasm for law. . . . [T]oday we are witnessing the triumphs of a hyperdemocracy in which the mass acts directly, outside the law, imposing its aspirations and its desires by means of material pressure."[76] And Ortega y Gasset did not have a high estimation of America in this regard, since in his view "America is, in a fashion, the paradise of the masses."[77]

The rule of law and liberty requires something that cannot be found in democracy. Democracy in a constitutional order is intended to be regulated, filtered, qualified, and limited by the rule of law. But this is what is missing. The existence and predominance of mass man and the relativistic Enlighten-ment ideology of radical egalitarianism that he values above all else suggest that Ortega y Gasset was correct in noting that the dominant characteristic of our time is that of the commonplace and the average, as the "mass crushes beneath it everything that is different, everything that is excellent, individual, qualified, select."[78] The lapse from constitutional democracy to hyperdemoc-racy is a lapse into barbarism.

Ortega y Gasset points out why democracy cannot but destroy society, observing that "human society is always, whether it will or no, aristocratic by its very essence."[79] A regime that maintains the ultimate sovereignty of the populace is an order in which we see, in Jouvenel's words, "an emergence of a despotism, of a regime from which law and liberty have taken flight."[80] To reiterate, a mass cannot govern itself or rule society because it is, by definition, unqualified and incapable of doing so.

In what way is society essentially aristocratic? In the thought of Ortega y Gasset:

> Society is always a dynamic unity of two component factors: minori-ties and masses. The minorities are individuals or groups of individuals which are specially qualified. The mass is the assemblage of persons not specially qualified. By masses, then, is not to be understood solely or mainly, "the working masses." The mass is the average man . . . man as undifferentiated from other men.[81]

What differentiates minorities from the masses is excellence. And that ex-cellence is most evident in the quest for, and perpetuation of, "ideas." Ideas are the standards, the principles upon which culture rests.[82] Ideational standards or principles are the preserve of those of qualification, of excellence, as a re-sult not of natural superiority, but of labor, most importantly the labor of the mind. The masses accept themselves, ready-made, and consider themselves to be perfect, with their own fixed ideas that they have received but have not refined or worked for (e.g., enlightenment ideology: multiculturalism, radical egalitarianism, feminism). Rule by the masses is the rule of the vulgar, of the undifferentiated, of unreason.[83] Absent are the ideas, the standards, the principles of civilization. Culture is the cultured man writ large.

There are two ultimate, fundamental ideational standards for Western civilization and the American political order: reason and revelation. And these standards are represented, humanly speaking, by elite minorities (either intellectual or religious). In Carey's estimation, these elites have either fallen under attack, or they have acquiesced in Enlightenment ideology, thereby relinquishing their position of notable excellence in society.[84] Carey highlights Father John Courtney Murray's observation that

> [i]t is the "wise and honest," the few who possess not only knowledge but also "rectitude of judgment" who must take the lead. . . . It is their function to explain the public "consensus" to those of "lesser reflective capacity," i.e., to those who, though "incapable of the careful inquiry" underlying the conclusions of the wise and honest, can comprehend "the reasonableness of (these) conclusions."[85]

Unfortunately, as Carey points out, it is distressingly evident that while the public philosophy depends so largely on the educated religious and intellectual elite, these same elites have become highly influenced by Enlightenment ideology, particularly the influences of relativistic postmodernism.[86] The elites have succumbed to, even become a part of, the masses, in the "counterculture," or the anticulture, of unreason.

V

Carey asserts that the American political tradition and its perpetuation require the "cultivation of man's higher nature."[87] The "pursuit of happiness" that Thomas Jefferson asserted to be a right by nature in the Declaration of Independence is, therefore, in need of definition and qualification. That definition and qualification is found in the term "culture." The American constitutional order (liberty and law) is in need of an associated culture of public virtue. Liberty of conscience, which is protected by the Constitution and which provides, most importantly, for the pursuit of happiness in terms of religious belief and reasoned conviction, is being depreciated by Enlightenment ideological dogma and the hyperdemocratization of America.[88]

There are but two ways (not necessarily mutually exclusive) in which our higher natures may be cultivated: reason and/or revelation.[89] Both of these pursuits are transcendent in that they move beyond the concrete existence of this world and the Constitution and point toward the inner self. Because these sources are transcendent, they provide the appropriate means for the cultivation of our higher natures, for the creation and perpetuation of public and private virtue. From the perspective of reason, virtue is the examined life (the Socratic life). From the perspective of revelation, virtue is faith and obedience to divine commands.

Both the life of reason and the life of revelation foster virtue and community. The customs and traditions of civility are transmitted from generation to generation in communities of reason (colleges and universities) and communities of faith (churches). This is why the loss of a sense of community in contemporary America derives to a large extent from the decline of reason within the university (having been replaced by Enlightenment ideology, e.g., science and postmodernism) and the depreciation of dogmatic religious worship and belief. Community occurs when citizens gather together to either pursue wisdom or renew their faith. At present, citizens still gather together, but without the appropriate motives.

Friedrich Nietzsche saw deeply into our age and its conditions in his essay "The Madman":

> God is dead. God remains dead. And we have killed him. How shall we, the murderers of murderers, comfort ourselves? What was holiest and most powerful of all that the world has yet owned has bled to death under our knives. Who will wipe this blood off us? What water is there for us to clean ourselves? What festivals of atonement, what sacred games shall we have to invent? Is not the greatness of this deed too great for us? Must not we ourselves become gods simply to seem worthy of it? . . . What are these churches now if they are not the tombs and sepulchers of God?[90]

Nietzsche's insight points toward a massive turning away from a cornerstone of transcendent authority that is hardly possible of human replacement: the role of divine revelation, of God in our public and private lives. It simply is not possible to overestimate the void that has been left by the American citizenry's relinquishment or discarding of faith, only to replace it with a different faith in Enlightenment science and secular ideology. If God is dead, so then is the public virtue and community that dogmatic religious belief and practice engender.

Note the extent to which reason (philosophy, or the Socratic pursuit of wisdom) is dead also. What are these colleges, these universities now if they are not the tombs and sepulchers of reason? The primary source of Enlightenment science and secular ideology is American colleges and universities. It can be stated with certainty that neither the life of faith nor the life of reason is pursued or supported in the contemporary university. Reason has been conspicuously ostracized. The pursuit of wisdom has been widely considered to be an outdated waste of time. Indeed, philosophy has been replaced by the history of philosophy, suggesting that the endeavor is a matter of the past, and not the present and future. The concept of truth, of fixed, transcendent absolutes has been replaced by the now commonly accepted truth of the absolute absence of truth: relativism. It is for this reason that Allan Bloom noted that "almost every student entering the university believes, or says he believes, that truth is relative," and that what binds American students today is "their relativism and their allegiance to equality."[91] The American university has traded reason for sophistry.

Bloom understood the importance of the university in producing the best kind of community, seeing that "the real community of man . . . is the community of those who seek the truth, of the potential knowers, that is, in principle, of all men to the extent that they desire to know."[92] Moreover, he understood the extent to which the fate of the American political order rests on whether our universities can fulfill their real mission of seeking truth rather than the propagation of Enlightenment ideology.

> This is the American moment in world history, the moment for which we shall forever be judged. Just as in politics the responsibility for the fate of freedom in the world has devolved upon our regime, so the fate of philosophy in the world has devolved upon our universities, and the two are related as they have never been before. The gravity of our given task is great, and it is very much in doubt how the future will judge our stewardship.[93]

The role of reason in American life is dwindling, and yet, writes Roshwald, "the rational capacity of man, is the center of his being, and as such requires and deserves attention and care."[94] How many citizens, for example, "can define the meaning of justice, equality, democracy in a way that assures the inner consistency of the term," and "is it not easier to wave the banner of liberty than to explain what it actually means?"[95] Some serious "soulsearching, through strict reasoning, would do our reason good, would give us a sense of personal sincerity and honesty, and would have important social and public repercussions."[96] But for this to occur, the pursuit of wisdom, broadly speaking, would need to be revitalized in the contemporary university. Unfortunately, as Carey has pointed out, "the materials and resources (human and intellectual) necessary for the restoration of the public philosophy are simply not there."[97]

VI

The decline of the American political tradition stems from a crisis of public philosophy. There must be a structural change within the American constitutional regime, and there must be an associated change in the hearts, minds and souls of the American public. The structural change might well lay in a rethinking of the concept of federalism and the possible, qualified adoption of the principle of subsidiarity. And Enlightenment ideology must be tempered by a renewal of religious faith and experience along with a restoration of the role of civic education through the revitalization of political philosophy in contemporary America.

There are two aspects of the structural problem of the American constitutional order: increasing centralization of authority in the national government and a hyperdiversification of interests. Carey has expressed concerns and raised very pertinent questions regarding these structural problems. For example, he suggests that the Antifederalists' contention that a strong central government eventually would become coercive and despotic is perhaps sound in light of our contemporary experience.[98] And he has wondered whether Publius's extended-republic theory, which was intended to prevent majoritarian tyranny, might serve to "undermine the commonality necessary for the regime to operate without continual recourse to coercion," as there are

> limits to the kinds of interests the system can accommodate, much less protect and cultivate, without experiencing severe internal tensions that could well serve to undermine its foundations and effectivenes. . . . Publius' basic commitment to liberty and the diversity it nourishes poses a problem. This diversity may erode those elements of commonality that provide the basis for deliberation about the common good or help to secure the social unity and cohesion necessary for government to perform its delegated functions.[99]

The problem with centralization is that it conflicts with the republican principle of self-government. The national government was not intended to govern the localities in the variety of ways it does today. One possible solution for this problem would be the introduction and perpetuation of the principle of subsidiarity, which recommends that decision making and governance always be managed and effectively handled at the most local level first. Subsidiarity and republicanism are mutually compatible.[100] Americans would also be well served to return to their religious roots since a renewal of religious faith and experience is conducive to a refocusing of attention on the intermediate units and organizations of society that are so vital to republicanism and self-government.

The diversification of interests produced by the extended republic is partly, if not mostly, derivative of a near absence of civic education in America. Carey has pointed out that America is "losing its historic memory" and that the citizenry is woefully undereducated in terms of basic understandings of American history and politics.[101] It would appear that it is not simply, or even necessarily, the actual "size" of the nation that poses the problem, but the lack of a shared, common philosophical framework amongst the citizenry.[102]

The structural problem and the internal problem are in this way integrally interrelated. The problem of a missing philosophical framework (e.g., American history and politics, in principle and practice) has led to a hyperdiversification of interests and a responding centralization of authority in the national government. The crisis of public philosophy, of the *raison d'être* of the American political order, is in need of resolution if the American political tradition is to be conserved.

The "basic symbols of the American political tradition" must be made real to the American citizenry by way of political socialization in both public and private schools so as to reestablish what is "traditional amongst us."[103] Americans must concomitantly return to their religious underpinnings to find answers to their most pressing spiritual and emotional needs—needs that the national government, or even state governments for that matter, cannot possibly fulfill. In so doing, they will find that they can solve most of their problems by themselves, individually and in local communities.

Americans will need to deliberate upon the basic symbols of the tradition in colleges and universities. But in order for this to occur properly, they will need to have been socialized to understand those symbols. Morever, colleges and universities will need to recognize the importance of the pursuit of wisdom or truth and therefore reject some of the most pernicious elements of Enlightenment ideology, namely radical egalitarianism and relativism. In other words, the American political tradition needs to be restored, and then its cultivation and preservation will require political philosophy, particularly in terms of higher education. The American polity must recover its principles, both intellectual and religious. And then it must discover the beauty and re-fining elegance of daily conversation regarding virtue and the good.[104] To the extent that the best in us, humanly speaking, derives from the desire to know, we are bound together by a "common concern for the good."[105]

But this common concern for the good cannot guide us if that which is "traditional amongst us" is not firmly established. Carey's impressive, even imposing body of work has been directed largely toward a defense of the traditional elements and principles of our political order. For this, he is to be commended and honored, since without this firm foundation, the pursuit of the good would not only be impossible, but unthinkable. The best that is possible within us and amongst us cannot flourish and thrive without our Constitution and its associated public morality. Perhaps it would do us well to recall that Socrates, while accused of disbelief in the gods and of corrupt-ing the youth, and who was sentenced to death after his remarkable trial and *Apology*, nevertheless refused to flee Athens when the opportunity arose.[106] Political philosophy needs the city as much as the city needs political philoso-phy. In defending the Constitution and the basic principles of the American political order, Carey has laid the foundation for the responsible fulfillment of everything liberty, properly understood, is intended to provide.

Neo-Jacobin Nationalism or Responsible Nationhood?

CLAES G. RYN

The issue of peace or war in the third millennium will turn as in other times on the character, thought, and imagination of political leaders and their peoples. Some attitudes and kinds of conduct are inherently provocative and conducive to conflict, others are inherently peaceful and conducive to respect among nations and civilizations. An all-important question is whether the world's only superpower will impose on itself the limitations of what may be called responsible nationhood, or whether it will be governed by a desire for armed world hegemony and will adopt corresponding personality traits. The purpose here is to consider current trends in American foreign policy in relation to the requirements of responsible nationhood and peace. It will be argued that those trends, by themselves, point in the direction of an era of conflict, but that traditional American notions of constitutional restraint and corresponding notions of personal character are more compatible with—indeed, conducive to—peace. If America is to help defuse rather than aggravate international tensions it needs to recover some of that older identity.

A central idea behind the U.S. Constitution of 1787 was that human beings are members of a fallen race. They are also limited in wisdom and other abilities. They need to be humble in their self-assessments. They should aspire to self-discipline, show tolerance, and be willing to compromise. As no one person or group can have all the right answers, it is necessary, within limits, to respect the opinions of others and grant them leeway in living their own lives. The common good depends on a limiting of egotism. This view is closely connected to another idea of the Constitution, that the common good and liberty will thrive in circumstances of simultaneous unity and diversity, first of all among the several states but more generally among interests and persons. In the American context, *e pluribus unum* does not mean that unity requires the abolition of diversity. On the contrary, the term implies the beneficial interaction between them. States, counties, local communities, and individuals can, through the responsible exercise of freedom, contribute in their diverse ways to the good of the whole. This traditional American notion can be extended to international affairs and be translated into the kind of cosmopolitanism that is required for responsible nationhood and peace in a multicultural world. Unhappily, American foreign policy has moved in a much different direction.

In his 2000 presidential campaign, President Bush expressed strong reservations about nation-building and a generally interventionist foreign policy. He called for a more "humble" U.S. foreign policy. Only months later, in the aftermath of 9/11, he articulated a sharply different view. So great was the change that one has to wonder about the sincerity of his earlier stated views. September 11 deeply angered the president, and rightly so, but it is unlikely that this atrocity would have so transformed his thinking unless, despite his campaign promises, he was already under the influence of the ideology of empire that had long been propounded or treated respectfully by many of his advisors and political allies. This ideology justifies a greatly expanded role for America in the world. Though its advocates do not envision American occupation of large parts of the world in the manner of old-fashioned imperialism, they do aspire to American armed global supremacy and control.

After 9/11, proponents of this ideology were in a position to help shape the president's reaction to the attacks and help remove any inhibitions he might have had about an activist, interventionist foreign policy. Significantly, his response to the attack on America was never sharply focused on identifying the actual perpetrators and striking back at them. Instead, from the beginning, 9/11 became the occasion for promulgating a new, exceedingly ambitious foreign policy virtually the opposite of what the American people had been led to expect. The president set forth the new policy in a series of speeches and statements. America would not only launch a systematic campaign against world terrorism and strike preemptively against potential threats; it would also promote freedom and better governance in the world. The president would eventually call the war against Iraq the first step in "the global democratic revolution."

Neither an intellectual nor a historian, President Bush may have been unaware of the full significance of the new foreign policy that was urged upon him after 9/11. He was undoubtedly governed less by ideological considerations than by anger and nationalistic sentiment, perhaps also the thrill of employing the awesome power at his disposal. The same was probably true of Vice President Richard Cheney, another businessman–politician. But both of these leaders had advisors who had long espoused a new, far-reaching strategy for the United States and who argued for it in ideological terms. The same outlook was strongly represented at the Pentagon, though in the civilian, not the military, leadership. After 9/11, the president increasingly adopted the ideas and rhetoric of a large network of political intellectuals and activists inside and outside of the administration who were already advocating the ideology of American empire.

Though the ideology of American empire puts a particular emphasis on international affairs, it constitutes an entire worldview, including a conception of human nature and society. It is committed to what it variously calls "democracy," "freedom," "equality," and "capitalism." A prominent and distinctive feature of the ideology is that it regards America as unique among nations for having been founded on universal principles. The ideology charges the United States with remaking the world in the image of those principles. Its advocates are highly prone to moralistic rhetoric. They see themselves as noble champions of "virtue." In a world of great uncertainty and complexity, they demand "moral clarity" as well as great firmness in dealing with those who stand in the way of America's cause. In 2002, President Bush informed the U.S. Congress that the "Department of Defense has become the most powerful force for freedom the world has ever seen."[1]

There are great similarities between the proponents of the ideology of American empire and the Jacobins who inspired and led the French Revolution of 1789. Like today's advocates of American global supremacy, the Jacobins regarded themselves as champions of universal principles. Their slogan was "*liberté, égalité, et fraternité*." They fashioned themselves fighters against evil and called themselves "the virtuous." They demanded a society and world radically different from the existing one. The consequences for Europe and other parts of the world were protracted war and upheaval.

The thinker who most deeply influenced the French Jacobins was Jean-Jacques Rousseau (1712–78), one of the Western world's truly seminal philosophers. It was Rousseau who asserted, in *The Social Contract* (1762), that "man was born free, but he is everywhere in chains."[2] Man is naturally good, Rousseau asserted, but historically existing societies had warped and imprisoned him. Rousseau flatly rejected the classical and Christian notion that man has evil as well as good potentialities within him. Maximilien Robespierre (1758–94), the Jacobin ideologue and orator who became the leader of France, was especially enamored of Rousseau's ideas and believed that he was carrying them into practice. He and the Jacobins saw themselves as called to liberate man from all that oppresses him. President Bush's notion that America's military is the greatest force for freedom in history calls to mind Rousseau's infamous idea that those who resist what is right will have to be "forced to be free." The French Jacobins appointed France as humanity's savior; the new Jacobins have appointed the United States of America.

Two prominent American journalists and political activists, William Kristol and David Brooks, exemplify a common blending of ideological zeal with a kind of nationalism. "Our nationalism," they assert, "is that of an exceptional nation founded on . . . 'an abstract truth, applicable to all men and all times.'"[3] The new Jacobins want to replace the America of history, with its roots in classical, Christian, and British culture, with an America of their own, which is defined by ahistorical, allegedly universal, and rational principles, specifically freedom and equality. In their view, the United States is a liberating power, which overturns oppressive institutions and traditions. It has broken with the bad habits of the old, pre-Enlightenment Western civilization, and now its mission is to give all of humanity a fresh start. America should everywhere help sweep away archaic obstacles to democracy and progress.

As with all ideologies, advocates of the new Jacobinism differ with regard to the completeness and rigidity of their adherence to its tenets. The term "neo-Jacobin" here denotes individuals who are especially prone to neo-Jacobin thinking. It is understood that even they have disagreements among themselves and that some of them have views that balance or qualify their preponderant ideas. A special category of neo-Jacobins are the many individuals who have some basic beliefs that are ultimately incompatible with neo-Jacobin ideology but who adopt elements of the ideology anyway because they are unaware of the tension or because neo-Jacobin views are fashionable and known to benefit careers.

Because of their large and growing influence in the media and in the vast American foreign-policy establishment inside and outside of government, the new Jacobins were in a position to use 9/11 to advance their long-standing push for American empire. They could channel the anger of the American people. They were able to boost and redirect hard-line foreign-policy reflexes that had been developed in both of the two major parties during the Cold War but that now lacked a purpose. Many cold warriors, finding themselves without the old enemy of communism, discovered in the neo-Jacobin goal of democratizing the world a new justification for exercising American power. Neo-Jacobinism could be all the more easily disseminated because its notion of America's mission had antecedents in American politics. President Woodrow Wilson comes especially to mind. It was he who told the U.S. Congress in 1917 that "the world must be made safe for democracy." America was called to help achieve that goal because of its special moral status.[4]

Neo-Jacobin ideology makes far-reaching claims for America. Not only is America based on universal principles; it is also called to spread its values to the rest of the world. The late University of Chicago professor Allan Bloom (1930–92), a leading disciple of the late German-American political theorist Leo Strauss (1899–1973), argued in a best-selling book, *The Closing of the American Mind* (1988), that "the American project" was for all people. "When we Americans speak seriously about politics, we mean that our principles of freedom and equality and the rights based on them are rational and everywhere applicable." World War II was, in Bloom's view, not merely a struggle against a malevolent enemy. It was "really an educational project undertaken to force those who did not accept these principles to do so."[5]

If America represents universal right, it stands to reason that she should insist on having her way. President Bush seemed to give voice to just this kind of thinking when he said, "There is a value system that cannot be compromised, and that is the values we praise. And if the values are good enough for our people, they ought to be good enough for others."[6]

In the view of the new Jacobins, only democracy, as they define it, answers to a universal moral imperative. Other forms of rule are illegitimate. American foreign policy should therefore advance the cause of democracy. We may call this element of neo-Jacobin ideology "democratism." Its tenets are so often repeated in American public discussion that they might appear to be self-evident truths.

A large number of political intellectuals have long pushed for this kind of foreign policy. They include William Bennett, David Brooks, Robert Kagan, Charles Krauthammer, Irving and William Kristol, Michael Ledeen, Joshua Muravchik, Michael Novak, Richard Perle, Norman Podhoretz, Benjamin

Wattenberg, and Paul Wolfowitz. All of them are, though not in identical ways, strongly prone to neo-Jacobin thinking. In spite of the fact that they stress the need to remake the world, they are widely known as "neoconservatives." Individuals so described are generally Cold War, anticommunist liberals who have become disgruntled with the Democratic Party because of its pacifist leanings and continuing leftward drift. Some of them have gravitated towards the Republican Party and tried to move that party towards acceptance of large federal government and an assertive foreign policy. Among the many leading American newspapers and magazines that push or are highly receptive to this foreign-policy stance, especially in their editorial and commentary sections, are the *Wall Street Journal*, the *Washington Post, Commentary,* the *Weekly Standard, National Review,* the *New Republic, Newsweek, Time,* and *U.S. News and World Report.* Think tanks and other organizations that lean heavily in the direction of a neo-Jacobin approach to foreign policy include the American Enterprise Institute and the Project for the New American Century. The same approach is well represented in groups like the Ethics and Public Policy Center, the Heritage Foundation, the Claremont Institute, and the Hoover Institution.

The neoconservatives have worked hard to dispel the old prejudice among American conservatives against large, centralized government. The neoconservatives have argued that activist government is needed in large part because of the special moral status of the United States and its great mission in the world. American government must be bold and muscular, especially with regard to military power. In 2003, Irving Kristol, a self-described "neoconservative" and the reputed "godfather" of the movement, stated openly what had long been clear to informed observers, namely, that neoconservatism is attempting to transform and take the place of traditional American conservatism. According to Kristol, the "historical task and political purpose of neoconservatism would seem to be this: to convert the Republican party, and conservatism in general, against their respective wills" to a stance "more suitable to governing a modern democracy."[7]

William Kristol, Irving's son, and David Brooks have argued for what they call "a neo-Reaganite foreign policy of national strength and moral assertiveness abroad."[8] Foreign-policy expert Robert Kagan, who writes often in the *Washington Post,* sounds a ubiquitous theme when he asserts that Americans "believe in human perfectibility" and that "global security and a liberal order depend on the United States—that 'indispensable nation'—wielding its power."[9]

This view of America is not patriotic in the old sense of that word, for it does not spring from an attachment to the America of history, whose cultural identity is derived in large part from classical and Christian civilization and whose constitutionalism is especially influenced by English tradition. What the new Jacobins celebrate is an America of their own invention, America as an "idea," a nation defined by abstract, ahistorical principles. America's greatness does not lie in its distinctive, concrete historical reality, but rather in the alleged fact that it represents a new, noble conception of society. American principles liberate people from the past and show them the way to a better world. America is by virtue of its "founding principles" a revolutionary force—a clean break, specifically, with old Europe.

This theme has been stressed, for example, by Professor Harry Jaffa, an ardent and influential follower of Leo Strauss. "To celebrate the American Founding," Jaffa writes, "is . . . to celebrate revolution." For Jaffa, the American revolution was no mere separation of America from Britain. It was, he argues, only a milder version of the kind of radical revolutions that took place in France and later in Russia, China, and Cuba. "The American revolution represented the most radical break with tradition . . . that the world had seen."[10]

It should come as no surprise, then, that many of the new Jacobins have a radical leftist past. Some were Marxists of a Trotskyite type. They had a change of heart and moved in the direction of democratic capitalism as the way forward for mankind, but they retained a belief in a single model for all societies and in the need to revolutionize the world.

The new Jacobins regard their own principles as supranational and want them to supplant the traditions of old, nondemocratic societies. They are not inclined to respect or look for common ground with countries that do not share their preferences. Dedication to what they regard as noble American principles does not reduce but instead increases their desire to dictate terms to others. Although the new Jacobins regard their principles as belonging to no particular nation, they project their ideological universalism onto America, fostering a special kind of nationalism. America should dominate the world for the good of mankind. The new Jacobins attach themselves to America because they think it has the power to implement their plans and they think they are within reach of controlling that power.

In the United States, where the word "conservative" has a favorable ring in most ears, the new Jacobins are often called neoconservatives—despite the fact that most of them harbor a deep dislike for old traditions and civilizations, as distinguished from their own ahistorical, allegedly universal principles. One prominent neoconservative, Michael Ledeen, who was an advisor on national security in the Reagan White House, does not even attempt to hide the hostility to old ways that is typical of the fully fledged new Jacobin. Ledeen openly lauds America as a destroyer of inherited ways of life. The America that he admires annihilates whatever resists its historic cause:

> Creative destruction is our middle name, both within our society and abroad. We tear down the old order every day, from business to science, literature, art, architecture, and cinema to politics and the law. Our enemies have always hated this whirlwind of energy and creativity, which menaces their traditions (whatever they may be) and shames them for their inability to keep pace. . . . [We] must destroy them to advance our historic mission.[11]

Is there any wonder that countries around the world, especially non-Western ones, should fear and oppose an America thus conceived? It is indicative of great theoretical confusion in American public debate that ideas of this kind might be regarded as in some sense conservative.

The traditional American ethos that informed the making of the Constitution stressed the need for restraints on power. Flawed human beings need to be subject to external checks as well as to internal checks on impulse. Nobody can be trusted with unlimited power. The notion of moral universality that formed part of the older American ethos was indistinguishable from humility: Moral right exists and binds all human beings, but it does not unequivocally announce what is specifically required of them. Finding the right course usually involves struggle with conscience and difficulty ascertaining the relevant facts. Deciding what is politically best in particular situations is always demanding, and no individual or group can claim a monopoly on morality or wisdom—hence the need for self-restraint, open-mindedness, tolerance, and compromise.

The neo-Jacobin notion of universality, by contrast, makes its advocates feel morally and otherwise superior to others. It replaces humility with arrogance. To be in possession of political right is to be entitled to dictate to others. The notion that the United States and its values are models for all peoples implies the need for an ambitious exercise of American might. Whatever its other meanings and functions, neo-Jacobin ideology stimulates and unleashes the will to power, whether the power is expected to be wielded personally or enjoyed viscerally from a distance.

Neo-Jacobin universalism began to take shape among academics several decades ago. Many of them were self-identified followers of Leo Strauss, whose rejection of philosophical traditionalism and advocacy of ahistorical political right proved conducive to neo-Jacobin universalism. Another of the early heroes of neo-Jacobinism was the philosopher Sidney Hook (1902–89), a one-time defender of Stalin who became an anticommunist democratic socialist. Intellectuals with a leftist past boosted the revolutionary and activist temperament of the emerging neo-Jacobin movement. As the ideology spread from academia into practical politics, the will to dominate that was not so easily detected in abstract works on political right became more obvious, at least to observers with some philosophical and historical discernment.

By the 1980s, neo-Jacobin ideological nationalism had become widespread, indeed entrenched, in think tanks, the media, and politics, especially in the American foreign-policy establishment. It became more and more difficult for the will to power to keep up ideological appearances. For example, after the crumbling of the Soviet Union the writer and TV personality Benjamin Wattenberg wrote: "It's pretty clear what the global community needs: probably a top cop, but surely a powerful global organizer. Somebody's got to do it. We're the only ones who can." Feigning modesty, he explained, "Our goal in the global game is not to *conquer* the world, only to *influence* it so that it is hospitable to our values."[12] He did not hasten to add that, of course, those unwilling to adopt American values should be allowed to follow their own course. In the major media, TV commentator and columnist Charles Krauthammer was an early advocate of "a robust interventionism." "We are living in a unipolar world," he wrote. "We Americans should like it—and exploit it." "Where our cause is just and interests are threatened, we should act—even if . . . we must act unilaterally." Well before 9/11, Krauthammer asserted, "America is no mere international citizen. It is the dominant power in the world, more dominant than any since Rome. Accordingly, America is in a position to reshape norms, alter expectations and create new realities. How? By unapologetic and implacable demonstrations of will."[13]

Democratism has sometimes taken on a religious ardor. For the Roman Catholic writer Michael Novak, spreading democracy is a great religious cause that calls to mind God's Incarnation. One Christmas, Novak wrote that the "citizens of the world . . . demand the birth of democracy in history, in physical institutions: as physical as the birth at Bethlehem."[14]

Democratism has long had more than a foothold in American political thought and government. Irving Babbitt (1865–1933), the American sage and prophet who was also a Harvard professor of French and comparative literature, said in 1924 about the trend that President Woodrow Wilson represented: "We are rapidly becoming a nation of humanitarian crusaders." Leaders like Wilson viewed America as abjuring selfish motives and as being, therefore, above all other nations. By the time of the Wilson presidency the idea had long been common in America that in old Europe arrogant and heartless elites oppressed the common man. Wilsonian idealism reinforced and broadened the interventionist impulse previously seen in a president like Teddy Roosevelt. Wilson did not see himself as promoting partisan American national motives. America was no ordinary nation. It enjoyed a special moral status and was called to act for the good of the world. America would intervene internationally, Wilson said, to "serve mankind." Even before the start of the European war, Wilson stated that America's role was to serve "the rights of humanity." The flag of the United States, he declared, is "the flag, not only of America, but of humanity."[15] Babbitt commented that Wilson's simultaneously abstract and sentimental rhetoric revealed "a temper at the opposite pole from that of the genuine statesman." Wilson's humanitarian idealism made him "inflexible and uncompromising."[16]

Most American policymakers saw the Cold War as a defensive struggle against totalitarian tyranny, but some of the most dedicated cold warriors were strongly anticommunist because they were neo-Jacobin democratists who had their own universalistic plans for the world. They did not like to have competition. Even Ronald Reagan's rhetoric had at times a neo-Jacobin ingredient. With the disintegration of the Soviet Union, most American liberals and traditional conservatives felt that an acute political emergency was over and that America could now afford to limit its international commitments. Certain Cold War liberals had a much different idea. They believed that America should play an expanded role in the world. The United States had a historic opportunity to remake the world. Virtually all of these Cold War liberals, also known as neoconservatives, came from the Democratic Party, where they had been associated with politicians like Senators Hubert Humphrey (MN), Henry "Scoop" Jackson (WA), and Daniel Patrick Moynihan (NY). They were able to form an alliance with Republicans who liked the idea of a militarily strong and assertive America and would eventually even make the Republican Party receptive to democratism.

In both of the major parties, politicians and intellectuals spoke more and more frequently about U.S. foreign policy in the manner of the new Jacobinism. The rhetoric in the first Bush administration about a New World Order often had a distinctly democratist ring. President Bush's secretary of state, James Baker, declared that U.S. foreign policy should not serve specifically American interests but "enlightenment ideals of universal applicability." The United States should promote "common . . . universal values," first of all in a "Euro-Atlantic community that extends east from Vancouver to Vladivostok," and "indeed, elsewhere on the globe."[17] American power was there to be used. In 1992, a draft Pentagon planning document that had been produced under the supervision of then Undersecretary of Defense Paul Wolfowitz and leaked to the *New York Times* set forth the goal of a world in which the United States would be the sole and uncontested superpower. The draft gave the United States "the pre-eminent responsibility" for dealing with "those wrongs which threaten not only our interests, but those of our allies or friends, or which could seriously unsettle international relations." American world dominance would serve the spread of democracy and economic freedom. American military power should be so great that none of America's potential competitors would even think of trying to match or oppose it.[18] According to many commentators, this view of America's international role was wholly reasonable. In a lead editorial, the *Wall Street Journal* praised the draft plan and favored a "Pax Americana."[19]

In his 1992 presidential campaign, Bill Clinton declared that he would pursue a foreign policy similar to that of the Bush administration. An ideology that both sanctioned and generated an assertive, expansive use of American power had by this time become prevalent in the American foreign-policy establishment.

As already mentioned, President George W. Bush's rhetoric after 9/11 became distinctly neo-Jacobin. America was fighting for universal principle against the forces of evil. The president spoke of an "axis of evil," a phrase that originated with neoconservative speechwriter David Frum. The president often resembled Woodrow Wilson in assigning to the United States a great moral mission. He claimed that an attack upon the United States was not just an attack upon it but upon freedom: "Why would anybody want to fight a war with this nation? . . . The answer is because we love freedom. That's why. And they hate freedom."[20] Bush's rhetoric often recalled that of Wilson, who said in 1917 that the American flag stands "not only for our power, but for freedom."[21] An enemy or critic of the United States was an opponent of universal principle.

In September 2002, President Bush sent to the U.S. Congress the *National Security Strategy*, the yearly presidential statement on strategy. In that document it became clear that he had completely abandoned his earlier idea that U.S. foreign policy should be conducted with greater restraint and humility. "Sustained by faith in the principles of liberty and the value of a free society," America needed, on the contrary, to take on "unparalleled responsibilities, obligations, and opportunities." Her power in the world was "unprecedented" and "unequaled." America's military power should be so overwhelming as to discourage all other nations from challenging America's will and most especially deter them from developing weapons of mass destruction. The new strategy replaced the old doctrines of deterrence and containment and committed the United States to a greatly broadened understanding of security. The United States had to have the right to strike preemptively and unilaterally against *potential* threats. The report, which was released the day after the president asked the Congress to authorize the use of preemptive military force against Iraq, was presented as a strategy for fighting terrorism, but its stated objectives went far beyond responding to potential or imminent terrorist or military threats. The president proclaimed that it should be the goal of the United States to make the world "not just safer but better." America should advance freedom, democracy, and free trade. According to a *Washington Post* news article, the *Strategy* gave the United States "a nearly messianic role." The same story quoted a senior administration official as saying that the United States should preserve the peace, spread liberty and economic well-being by spreading American values, and promote good government around the world.[22]

In sum, the new *National Security Strategy* propounded a doctrine of armed American world hegemony. The *Strategy* entailed not just the acceptance but the extension of the 1992 Wolfowitz draft plan. Promoted to deputy secretary of defense in the George W. Bush administration, Wolfowitz was now an energetic and highly assertive proponent of American foreign-policy activism. After 9/11 he was quick to urge war against Iraq.

The first President Bush and Bill Clinton pursued a foreign policy with prominent Wilsonian and interventionist ingredients, but they never articulated and implemented a systematic strategy. President George W. Bush defined a bold new foreign policy whose explicit aim was American global supremacy.

He appointed the United States as the world's arbiter of good and evil and announced that, if needed, it would impose its judgments unilaterally.

The belief that America is morally superior to other powers and should bring its values to other peoples is by no means confined to the Republican Party; indeed, it is as widespread in the Democratic Party, the original home of the neoconservatives. Democratists in the Democratic Party disagree with their Republican counterparts mostly about the methods to be used by America in creating a better world. During the George W. Bush administration the Republicans have been more strongly prone to use confrontational military methods and to act unilaterally. Democrat democratists prefer to intervene in cooperation with other states and, if possible, with the approval of the United Nations. The belief in America's moral superiority and global mission is nonpartisan. It is shared, for instance, by Richard C. Holbrooke, who was American ambassador to the UN and American emissary to the Balkans in the Clinton administration. Holbrooke criticized the way in which the Bush administration prepared for war against Iraq but did not question America's special responsibility in the world. He said, "Over the past 60 years, the United States has consistently combined its military superiority with moral and political leadership."[23] The word "consistently" makes clear that America is above moral suspicion. Could a better justification be invented for not tolerating opposition?

Even as they disagree with Republicans about tactics and other specifics, many leading Democrats specializing in foreign policy, Madeline Albright being another example, are ready to employ military means nondefensively to advance America's ideological cause. Another sign among many that neo-Jacobin universalism is no Republican monopoly is that many of its strongest advocates—Robert Kagan and Charles Krauthammer among them—write often on the op-ed page of the *Washington Post*, a journalistic flagship for America's liberal and Democratic establishment. This is but one of many reasons why neo-Jacobinism is best understood as a militant, radical variant of modern American progressive liberalism.

Contrary to the old American belief in modesty and restraint on power, neo-Jacobinism justifies an unchecked, unapologetic exercise of American might. September 11 provided a strong boost for the neo-Jacobins, whose objectives could now masquerade as old-fashioned patriotism. They urged President Bush to be unyielding and uncompromising in implementing the new ambitious foreign policy. A representative neo-Jacobin voice was Robert

Kagan, who wrote in the *Washington Post* in 2002: "America, with its vast power, can sometimes seem like a bully on the world stage. But, really, the 1,200-pound gorilla is an underachiever in the bullying business."[24]

Considering that President Bush once called for greater American humility in foreign affairs, his signing on to the agenda of the new Jacobins must have seemed to them a great triumph. He began using their rhetoric, strongly asserted American power in the international arena, and gave the federal government a more intrusive role in the daily lives of U.S. citizens. His policies and universalistic language gained him the enthusiastic support of the architects of neo-Jacobinism, who had long advocated this kind of activist foreign policy, especially in the Middle East, and had long agitated, specifically, for intervention in Iraq.

That President Bush would be impatient with international opposition and dismiss criticism from other countries was suggested by his intimating more than once that America's cause in promoting liberty and fighting terrorism is also God's cause. When the president declared an end to major combat operations in Iraq on May 1, 2003, he thanked American soldiers for having taken up "the highest calling in history," which is to "bring liberty to others." American soldiers carried "a message of hope," he said, and he explained that message by quoting Scripture: "In the words of the Prophet Isaiah: To the captives, 'Come out,' and to those in darkness, 'Be free.'"[25] What theology has interpreted as a liberation from spiritual bondage, President Bush made to seem the work of the commander in chief and the armed forces of the United States.

The president revived and boosted considerably a type of American conceit that, though incompatible with the view of human nature that informed the Constitution, has asserted itself in American history with some regularity. George W. Carey, using a term from Eric Voegelin, has classified this way of thinking as one of the most important of the "derailments that have plagued the American tradition." It consists in the assumption that "[t]he Moses of the American people is Jehova himself." Carey describes this derailment in a way that is highly relevant to the present discussion of foreign policy: "God has appointed America, not as the suffering servant of mankind, but as the arbiter of mankind, the supreme judge of all people, with a special insight into Divine Providence that no other people can match." This, Carey argues, is one of the "false myths" that "produce the fanatics amongst us."[26]

Because the word "empire" does not, at least not yet, have a favorable ring in American ears, the new Jacobins often protest that, no, no, they do not want empire. But here they are playing with words. This is an era in which the United States is the only superpower. It has vast economic and political might, and it has intercontinental missiles, naval battle groups, military bases around the world, missile-equipped nuclear submarines, smart bombs, and an elaborate intelligence apparatus. In such circumstances, imperialism in the old-fashioned sense of occupying territory is an anachronism, and the new Jacobins know it. It is generally possible for the United States to force countries to do as they are told without invading their territory. The cost of opposing the will of the United States can be prohibitive. The neo-Jacobins are hoping that American imperialism will be easier to sell to the American people precisely because, for the most part, power can be projected without deploying troops in foreign lands.

Having become defensive about the charge of imperialism, President Bush said in April 2004, "We are not an imperial power. . . . We are a liberating power." It seemed not to have occurred to him that, from the point of view of a "liberated" people, the self-appointed liberators might be perceived as ruthless imperialists.[27]

Death and suffering of unexampled scope have been inflicted on mankind by power-seekers who have justified their power in terms of Jacobin ideology of one kind or another. Communism has crumbled, but another panacea seems to be taking its place. The neo-Jacobin plan for the redemption of humanity may not be as obviously utopian as that of communism. To many, it appears laudably benevolent and idealistic, but so did the communist vision. Communism and the new Jacobinism have important ideological differences, to be sure, but they resemble each other nevertheless in that they share a revolutionary spirit and a great conceit: that they, and they alone, know what is good for mankind.

The new Jacobins have worked diligently, notably through the propagation of their ideology, to clear away obstacles to their power. The main reason why they are strongly prejudiced against old traditions and deeply rooted institutions is that these stand in the way of the realization of their plans. The checks and balances of traditional American constitutionalism are major obstacles. This is one of the reasons why the new Jacobins have sought to redefine America as a virtuous democracy expressing its will through a strong national executive. The leaders of virtuous America have no reason to impose traditional restraints upon themselves.

It needs to be pointed out that, although America has in its history sometimes shown imperialistic inclinations—adorned, of course, with idealistic verbiage—the new Jacobinism represents a profound break with the older American political, moral, and cultural tradition. One of the most admirable achievements of that tradition, the Constitution of 1787, carefully circumscribed the will to power. It did so in large part because its authors had an acute awareness of original sin. The Constitution required and fostered self-restraint, humility, realism, prudence, and a willingness to compromise. The view of human nature that informed American constitutionalism had deep roots in Greek, Roman, and Christian civilization, as transmitted primarily through British culture.

The neo-Jacobin idea that the American "regime" has its sources in abstract, ahistorical principles rather than in historically evolved beliefs and practices is contradicted both by philosophical reflection and historical scholarship regarding the origins of the Constitution. No society or government can fail to be profoundly conditioned by its own past. To a far greater extent than we realize in the particular moment, our thoughts and actions carry forward assumptions and habits formed long ago. Though we can never be fully conscious of how the past is moving in our lives, history is always prominent in constituting the present. The American framers' strong preference in both theory and practice for limited, decentralized, constitutional government had everything to do with the long-standing habits and assumptions of British-American culture.

That the American Constitution was not the product of abstract theorizing but represented a continuation and creative adaptation of a living tradition to American circumstances has been amply and insightfully documented by George Carey. His close examination of central American political symbols and institutions has demonstrated and elucidated their deep historical roots in Western and especially British civilization. The American ideas of liberty and limited government cannot be properly understood without recognizing their antecedents across the Atlantic. The Bill of Rights is a poignant illustration of how the past animates American constitutionalism. These amendments to the Constitution are in large part a reaffirmation of the ancient "Rights of Englishmen."

Carey has shown that the Constitution of 1787 was inextricably connected with a historically evolved religious, moral, cultural, and social context and especially with particular personality traits. The framers understood the proposed political regime to be dependent on the people and its leaders exhibiting virtue. "The private sector—e.g., the family, churches, schools, communities—would cultivate and nourish the virtue necessary not only for the perpetuation of the regime, but for the pursuit of the collective good."[28] The traditional American stress on self-restraint, in government as well as in personal life, reflected the old Christian view of man's moral predicament.

The ascent of the new Jacobinism is a sign that traditional American virtues are weakening or disappearing. Under the cover of noble phrases, the will to power is throwing off inner and outer checks. The danger of conflict with other countries increases proportionally. Neo-Jacobinism is ultimately an ideological front for the desire to dominate others. The world needs the opposite of such self-serving and disingenuous universalism. Universal values there are, but, contrary to neo-Jacobin belief, they are not such as to demand adherence to a single political model or to the will of the United States. Universality is not the same as uniformity.

True universality—which used to be summarized as "the good, the true, and the beautiful"—delights in diversity. Because of the varying circumstances of time and place, universality must manifest itself differently in different societies and situations. Far from being an example of value nihilism or relativism, this view merely recognizes that for universality to be a force in human life it must adapt to and work through the infinite variety of human life. Universality becomes known to us in those potentialities inhering in given circumstances which can advance its purpose in the world. Universality forms a synthesis with historical particularity. This does not mean that, as ahistoricist universalism assumes, universality loses its universality and dissolves in a welter of circumstance. On the contrary, universality *manifests* itself in human experience by selectively aligning itself with particularity that it enlivens, ennobles, and orders.

Human existence can be elevated and enriched in an infinite number of ways. Diverse activities that are adjusted to time and place but have their inspiration in the same universal values harmonize with and support each other. There is unity in the diversity. The neo-Jacobin notion of a single model for all societies betrays a simplistic conception of the world and a truncated, merely abstract view of universality. The great arrogance with which neo-Jacobinism prescribes for all humanity shows that self-serving ideology, not philosophy, shapes its thinking.[29]

Our multicultural world does need a sharpened sense of universality so that the peoples of the world can cultivate their highest common ground. But to believe in the existence of the good, the true, and the beautiful is not the same as to claim to know just how these values can be realized in all particular circumstances. Different peoples and individuals must be credited with some ability to discern their own good. A notion of universality that does not recognize the opacity and infinite complexity of life is an ideological fiction. Differently put, a genuine sense of universality is indistinguishable from humility. Only an absurdly inflated ego will claim unimpeded access to the universal and a monopoly on political and other wisdom. It is disheartening to consider that, after ridding itself of the scourge of communism, humanity may now have to suffer the consequences of another homogenizing pseudo-universalism.

The world needs more cosmopolitanism, but not the pseudocosmopolitanism of the superficial Jacobin kind that is at home nowhere and everywhere. True cosmopolitanism is rooted in the traditions of a particular society. It is by becoming deeply and intimately familiar with the very best of his own culture that the civilized person is enabled to recognize the higher humanity of other peoples who are aspiring to the same within their own traditions. It is by cultivating their own distinctiveness at the highest level that representatives of different cultures find their common human ground and move closer to each other. Individuals and peoples are joined at that level in variations on a common theme.

The true cosmopolitan is very much at home in his own society, but, because of his openness to and interest in the achievements of the rest of mankind, he can be an enthusiastic traveler to or a welcome and respected guest in other societies. He does not assume that he is in all important respects superior to his hosts. He understands that the good life can be lived differently by different peoples and that all peoples, including his own, have strengths and weaknesses. The cosmopolitan is eager to expand his human range. He delights in the fact that the world is not a place of barren homogeneity. The universal has a depth and a richness beyond the grasp of neo-Jacobin ideologues.

To the extent that the spirit of true cosmopolitanism gains ground in different societies, their peoples can coexist in mutual respect and peace. They can recognize the admirable features of other societies as different instantiations of the higher strivings of humanity, even as they continue to argue about what kind of life is most deeply satisfying. Such cosmopolitanism is indistinguishable from love of one's own. Like the true patriot, the cosmopolitan cherishes, cultivates, and builds upon the highest achievements of his own society. But proper love of one's own nation contains no assumption that other societies should be remade in the image of one's own. The finest contribution a nation can make to the common life of humanity is to develop the best of its own heritage. To the extent that it succeeds, it will attract the admiration of other nations and will, in the area of its special strengths, be in a position to lead by example rather than by imposing its will.

Responsible nationhood requires genuine cosmopolitanism. It is characterized by pride in and love for a particular nation but also by respect for the attainments and legitimate interests of other societies. Ruthlessness and blatant partisanship are a chronic source of international tension, but responsible nationhood can reduce and tame conflict. The patriot is ready to take up arms to protect the society and culture that he loves, but war is for him a last resort, a sign that the belligerence of an opponent can no longer be contained.

Traditional American civilization is wholly compatible with the idea of responsible nationhood. When acting from within that moral and cultural inheritance, Americans can respect their competitors and seek common ground. Unilateralism in foreign policy, by contrast, is hard to reconcile with that same heritage—specifically with the spirit of American constitutionalism. According to the latter, it is necessary for particular interests to impose restraints on themselves and to accommodate other interests. The checks and balances of the Constitution were designed to enforce such restraints and to protect against the danger that a single interest would monopolize power and begin to tyrannize the American people.

What needs to be pointed out in the present context is that power needs checking and balancing no less in international than in domestic affairs. The neo-Jacobin idea that America is an exceptional, virtuous power that should be able to operate internationally without opposition radically contradicts the view of human nature and the world that shaped the U.S. Constitution. The neo-Jacobin myth of America the Virtuous offers a justification not for restraining but for unleashing the will to power. The triumph of this myth in American politics and public debate would mark the end of American constitutionalism.[30]

One has to hope that the world's only superpower will eventually come to its senses, reject neo-Jacobin universalism, and revive some of its traditional virtues. Only then will America be able to offer to the world of the twenty-first century an example of responsible nationhood.

Notes

EDITORS' INTRODUCTION

1. Charles S. Hyneman and George W. Carey, eds., *A Second Federalist: Congress Creates a Government* (New York: Appleton-Century Crofts, 1967; reprint, Columbia, SC: University of South Carolina Press, 1970).

2. Willmoore Kendall and George W. Carey, "Towards a Definition of Conservatism," *Journal of Politics* 26, no. 2 (May 1964), 406–22.

3. Willmoore Kendall and George W. Carey, "The 'Intensity' Problem and Democratic Theory," *American Political Science Review* 62, no. 1 (March 1968), 5–24.

4. Willmoore Kendall and George W. Carey, "The 'Roster Device': J. S. Mill and Contemporary Elitism," *Western Political Quarterly* 21, no. 1 (March 1968), 20–39.

5. Willmoore Kendall and George W. Carey, eds., *Liberalism Versus Conservatism: The Continuing Debate in American Government* (Princeton, NJ: Van Nostrand, 1966).

6. Willmoore Kendall and George W. Carey, "How to Read 'The Federalist,'" in *The Federalist Papers* (New Rochelle, NY: Arlington House, 1965).

7. Willmoore Kendall and George W. Carey, *The Basic Symbols of the American Political Tradition* (Baton Rouge, LA: Louisiana State University Press, 1970; new preface, Washington, DC: Catholic University of America Press, 1995).

8. *The Federalist: Design for a Constitutional Republic* (Urbana, IL: University of Illinois Press, 1989).

9. *In Defense of the Constitution*, revised and expanded edition (Indianapolis: Liberty Fund, Inc., 1995).

10. *A Student's Guide to American Political Thought* (Wilmington, DE: ISI Books, 2004).

11. George W. Carey and Bruce Frohnen, eds., *Community and Tradition: Conservative Perspectives on the American Experience* (Lanham, MD: Rowman and Littlefield, 1998).

12. George W. Carey, ed., *Freedom and Virtue: The Conservative/Libertarian Debate*, revised and updated edition (Wilmington, DE: ISI Books, 1998).

13. George W. Carey and George J. Graham Jr., eds., *The Post-Behavioral Era: Perspectives on Political Science* (New York: David McKay Co., 1972).

14. George W. Carey, ed., *The Political Writings of John Adams* (Washington, DC: Regnery, 2000).

15. George W. Carey and James McClellan, eds., *The Federalist: The Gideon Edition* (Indianapolis: Liberty Fund, 2001).

16. *Basic Symbols*, 10, 19, 85.

17. Ibid., 8.

18. Ibid., 22, 23.

19. Ibid., 79, 49.

20. Ibid., 145, 153, 147, 148, 149.

21. Ibid., 137.

22. Ibid., 145.

23. Ibid., 153.

24. Ibid., 95.

25. George W. Carey, "Traditions at War," *Modern Age* 36, no. 3 (Spring 1994), 237–43. See also Carey's "The 'New' American Political Tradition," *Modern Age* 15, no. 4 (Fall 1971), 358–69.

26. See, for example, Carey's "James Madison on Federalism: The Search for Abiding Principles," *Benchmark* 3 (January–April 1987), 27–57. This essay was reprinted as "James Madison and the Principle of Federalism," in *In Defense of the Constitution*, 77–121.

27. See Carey's "Natural Rights, Equality, and the Declaration of Independence," *Ave Maria Law Review* 3, no. 2 (Spring 2005), 45–67.

28. *In Defense of the Constitution*, 18–33.

29. Ibid., 17.

30. *The Federalist: Design for a Constitutional Republic*, xii.

31. Ibid.

32. *In Defense of the Constitution*, 55 and passim.

33. *The Federalist: Design for a Constitutional Republic*, 72, 53.

34. *The Federalist: The Gideon Edition*, No. 51, 270.

35. *The Federalist: Design for a Constitutional Republic*, 55.

36. Ibid., 26.

37. Ibid., 34, 36.

38. Ibid., 35–36.

39. *In Defense of the Constitution*, 47.

40. *The Federalist: Design for a Constitutional Republic*, 39.

41. *The Federalist: The Gideon Edition*, 44, 235 and 23, 113.

42. *The Federalist: Design for a Constitutional Republic*, 104–5.

43. Ibid., 111, 118, 104.

44. Ibid., 135–36.

45. For Carey's treatment of the limits of judicial review, see *The Federalist: Design for a Constitutional Republic*, 138–45; and *In Defense of the Constitution*, 132–35.

46. *In Defense of the Constitution*, 133.

47. "The Constitution and Community," in *Community and Tradition*, 64, 74.

48. "Federalism: Historic Questions and Contemporary Meanings, A Defense of Political Processes," in Valerie A. Earle, ed., *Federalism: Infinite Variety in Theory and Practice* (Itasca, IL: F. E. Peacock, 1968); and "Conservatism, Centralization and Constitutional Federalism," *Modern Age* 46 (Winter–Spring 2004), 48–60.

49. *The Federalist: Design for a Constitutional Republic*, 159.

50. "The Constitution and Community," 77.

51. Ibid., 77, 78.

52. Ibid., 79, 82.

53. *In Defense of the Constitution*, 47, 49.

54. Ibid., 49.

55. "The Constitution and Community," 63, 64.

56. "The Philadelphia Constitution: Dead or Alive?" in Kenneth L. Grasso and Cecilia Rodriguez Castillo, eds., *Liberty Under Law* (Lanham, MD: University Press of America, 1998), 72, 78. Carey draws here on the analysis of Hyneman, *The Supreme Court on Trial* (New York: Atherton, 1963).

57. "The Philadelphia Constitution: Dead or Alive?" 74.

58. Ibid., 73.

59. Ibid., 79, 80.

60. *In Defense of the Constitution*, 7.

61. Ibid., 80.

62. Ibid., 185, 187, 4.

63. Ibid., 188, 190.

64. Ibid., 191, 189. One also might argue that it makes such decision making extremely difficult on those occasions when the reality of intrinsic tensions between individual and social goods is inescapable, as in times of international conflict when the government's demand for security measures conflicts with traditional notions of procedural rights. In responding to such challenges under the conditions brought about by the Iraq War, for example, Congress has seemed utterly incapable of formulating a coherent response to executive actions. Having abandoned traditional conceptions of rights such as the right of the people to be secure in their homes and papers, it has been unable to formulate any alternative set of rights with sufficient legitimacy to cabin presidential power.

65. Ibid., 189.

66. For a discussion of contemporary political thought's tendency to reduce political issues to merely intellectual issues that are properly dealt with by those who possess the requisite specialized training, and thus in the American context by "permanent officials and Supreme Court Justices," see Willmoore Kendall and George W. Carey, "The 'Roster Device': J. S. Mill and Contemporary Elitism."

67. *In Defense of the Constitution*, 191, 190.

68. Ibid., 191, 188.

69. "The 'Intensity' Problem and Democratic Theory," 20.

70. Ibid., 21–22.

71. "How to Read 'The Federalist,'" in Willmoore Kendall, *Willmoore Kendall Con-*

tra Mundum, Nellie D. Kendall, ed. (New Rochelle, NY: Arlington House, 1971), 417.

72. "The 'Intensity' Problem and Democratic Theory," 14.

73. Ibid., 21, 22.

74. "How to Read 'The Federalist,'" 415.

75. "The 'Intensity' Problem and Democratic Theory," 21, 22.

76. See his "American Government Textbooks," *Political Science Reviewer* 1 (1971), 154–83; and "Religion and American Government Textbooks," *Teaching Political Science: A Journal of the Social Sciences* 10, no.1 (Fall 1982), 7–19.

77. George W. Carey, "Willmoore Kendall, 1963," *Modern Age* 26, nos. 3–4 (Summer–Fall 1982), 283–86; "Willmoore Kendall's Battle Line Metaphor," review of Willmoore Kendall, *The Conservative Affirmation in America*, *Modern Age* 30, nos. 3–4 (Summer–Fall 1985), 294–98; "Epilogue," in Willmoore Kendall and Mason Kendall, *Oxford Years: The Letters of Willmoore Kendall to His Father* (Wilmington, DE: Intercollegiate Studies Institute, 1993); "Willmoore Kendall and the Doctrine of Majority Rule," in John A. Murley and John E. Alvis, eds., *Willmoore Kendall: Maverick of American Conservatives* (Lanham, MD: Lexington Books, 2002).

78. George W. Carey, "Conservatives and Libertarians View Fusionism: Origins, Possibilities and Problems," *Modern Age* 26, no. 1 (Winter 1982), 8–18; *The Political Writings of John Adams* (Washington, DC: Regnery Publishers, 2000); "The Conservative Mission and Progressive Ideology," *Modern Age* 42, no. 1 (Winter 2000) 14–22.

79. See especially Carey's introduction to *Freedom and Virtue: The Conservative/Libertarian Debate*.

80. George W. Carey, "Who or What Killed the Philadelphia Constitution?" *Tulsa Law Journal* 36 (Spring 2001), 621.

81. *In Defense of the Constitution,* 199.

82. George W. Carey and James McClellan, eds., *The Federalist: Student Edition* (Dubuque, IA: Kendall/Hunt Publishers, 1990).

MAKING SENSE OF MAJORITARIANISM / *Paul Edward Gottfried*

1. George W. Carey and Willmoore Kendall, *The Basic Symbols of the American Political Tradition* (Baton Rouge, LA: Louisiana State University Press, 1970), especially chapters 1 and 5.

2. Ibid. Carey offered the description of the Constitution in conversation with the author on March 5, 1995.

3. See Kendall's essay "The Social Contract: The Ultimate Issue Between Liberalism and Conservatives," in *The Conservative Affirmation in America* (Chicago: Regnery Gateway 1985 [1963]), 83–99.

4. For Kendall's sympathies for Rousseau, see the introductions to his translations of *The Social Contract* (Chicago: Regnery Gateway, 1954) and *The Government of Poland* (Indianapolis: Hackett Publishing, 1985).

5. Willmore Kendall, "John Locke Revisited," *Intercollegiate Review* 2 (January–February 1966), 217–34; "Who Killed Political Philosophy?" *National Review,* March 12, 1960; and Kendall's panegyric to Strauss in *Philosophical Review* 75 (April 1966), 251–52.

6. George H. Nash, *The Conservative Intellectual Movement in America Since 1945,* updated edition (Wilmington, DE: ISI Books, 1996), 217.

7. George W. Carey, *The Federalist: Design for a Constitutional Republic* (Urbana, IL: University of Illinois Press, 1989), 81.

8. *The Federalist: Design for a Constitutional Republic,* 91.

9. Ibid., 143–44, 126–45. The key texts from *The Federalist Papers* for understanding the proper functions of the High Court are 78 and 81.

10. *The Federalist: Design for a Constitutional Republic,* 165.

11. Ibid., 172.

12. *The Conservative Affirmation in America,* xviii.

13. Christopher Lasch, *The Revolt of the Elites and the Betrayal of Democracy* (New York: W. W. Norton, 1995), 25–49.

14. Reprinted in George A. Panichas, ed., *Modern Age: The First Twenty-Five Years,* (Indianapolis: Liberty Press, 1988), 92; see also Paul Edward Gottfried, *After Liberalism: Mass Democracy in the Managerial State* (Princeton, NJ: Princeton University Press, 1999), 51–109.

15. See Willmore Kendall, *Contra Mundum* (New Rochelle, NY: Arlington House, 1971), 383.

16. Ibid., 383–84. It is hard for a historian looking at this essay, written in the fall of 1964, to conclude that its author is a right-wing observer of the American scene. Among the positions Kendall takes is that those pushing the civil-rights movement in a radical direction were making the "better case in logic and justice" but would not win in "public debate," because of the democratic process. Unless I have misread him grievously, Kendall wishes to convince us that civil-rights activists who are calling for more social justice have exhausted the public's goodwill but also hold the moral high ground. Although Kendall is apparently showing how a "civil rights crisis" will be averted, it is not clear whether he considers this upshot morally good (*Contra Mundum,* 282). A possible explanation for this view (although one that remains speculative) may be Kendall's absorption of the thinking of the left-Straussian George Anastapolo, who read some of his later published essays and is duly acknowledged in the forewords of his anthologies.

17. Jean-Jacques Rousseau, *Du Contrat Social* (Paris: Flammarion, 1966), 145.

18. Ibid., 146 *passim,* 47–59, 165–80. A source for this interpretation of Rousseau as an essentially reactionary communitarian, widely held in the eighteenth century, is Daniel Mornet's *Histoire de la littérature et de la Pensée Française* (Paris: P. Larousse, 1934).

19. *The Conservative Affirmation in America,* 83–99. Although Carey enters this anthology only by way of an oblique, misspelled reference to "George Casey" in the acknowledgments (267), he did offer critical comments on most of the essays chosen for inclusion.

20. See Kendall's scathing review of Harry V. Jaffa's *Crisis of the House Divided* in *The Conservative Affirmation in America*, 249–52.

21. *Contra Mundum*, 45–46. Despite his collaboration in some of the essays included here, Carey has never claimed any responsibility for the anti-Kirk diatribe. That outburst went into *Contra Mundum* presumably over Carey's objections.

22. Ibid., 53. The Straussian thrust of Kendall's argument is unmistakably present by the end of the essay: particularly the accusation that Kirk is "historicist" and "relativist" and not sufficiently enthusiastic about the Second World War and the Cold War as struggles for a universal vision of the Good. For a defense of this turn in Kendall's work, see John A Murley, *Willmore Kendall: Maverick of American Conservatism* (Lanham, MD: Lexington, 2002).

23. Two critical perspectives on "consensus history" that do not originate on the left can be found in Christopher Lasch's *The True and Only Heaven: Progress and its Critics* (New York: W. W. Norton, 1991), 112–19; and Clyde Wilson's incisive but neglected essay, "American Historians and their History," *Continuity* (Spring 1983), 1–16.

24. See for example, Harry V. Jaffa, "Lincoln and the Cause of Freedom," *National Review* (September 21, 1965), 827–28 and 842; and by the same author, *Equality and Liberty: Theory and Practice in American Politics* (Claremont Institute, 1999), especially 170–74.

25. Read Kendall's essay "What Is Conservatism?" in *The Conservative Affirmation*, 1–20.

26. See *Contra Mundum*, 476. The "intensity problem" in politics is equated here with deliberateness—or the lack thereof—in a "plebiscitary democracy," or an elastic, mass-based electorate that engages in token forms of self-government. This joint effort by Kendall and Carey was originally published in the *American Political Science Review* 62, no. 1 (March 1968).

27. See "Prolegomena to any Future Work on Majority Rule," *Contra Mundum*, 129–48.

28. See Carl Schmitt, *Verfassungslehre* (Berlin: Duncker and Humblot, 1928), particularly the introduction. See also Sandro Chignola's relevant discussion of the Schmittian argument about the groundings of real democracy in *Pratica del Limite* (Padua: Unipress, 1998), 28–30. Eric Voegelin, a postwar correspondent of Schmitt, had already elaborated on this constitutional principle as a young jurist in Austria, in the context of discussing Schmitt's legal theory. Note that Voegelin was highly skeptical of Schmitt's efforts to locate a vital ethical center in the people's will, a criticism that might be equally applied to Carey-Kendall. See also Aristotle, *Politica* (Oxford: Oxford Classical Texts, 1973), book 8, section 1237a and b.

29. *The Conservative Affirmation*, 118. In this famed essay, "Conservatism and the Open Society," Kendall registers a Burkean objection to Mill's belief that truth is always waiting to be uncovered. Such a reductionist approach to learning sacrifices "truth itself, with all its accumulated riches to date," 116.

30. *The Federalist: Design for a Constitutional Republic*, 171.

31. Plato, *Res Publica* (Oxford: Oxford Classical Texts, 1935) book 4, Section 440.

See also N. R. Murphy, *The Interpretation of Plato's Republic* (Oxford: Clarendon Press, 1951), especially 24–44.

32. See Philo of Alexandria, *De Specialibus Legibus* (Camridge, MA: Loeb Classical Library, 1929) book 4, section 15, 92–95. According to Philo, that which is *epithumetikon* participates in no way in our reasoning faculty (*hekista metaxousan logismou*). It is the most insatiable and least disciplined part of our nature (*panton aplestaton kai akolastaton*) and is like cattle that feeds in zones set apart for eating and copulation (*thremmaton emboskesthai topois en ohois trophai kai oxeia*). One may wonder whether the first-century Jewish Platonist had intimations of the character of American higher education two thousand years later.

33. *The Federalist,* 170.

34. Ibid., 156.

35. Ibid., 138.

36. See Plato, *Res Publica,* book 4, 423e for statement and elucidation of the maxim that "especially among friends are all things held in common [*hoti malista koina ta philon poieisthai*]." For a detailed discussion of this totalitarian form of political experimentation, see Paul Edward Gottfried, *Carl Schmitt: Politics and Theory* (Westport, NY: Greenwood Press, 1990), 102–22.

Carey on Constitutions, Constitutionalism, and Tradition / Bruce P. Frohnen

1. Portions of this essay appeared in an earlier form in my article, "Law's Culture: Conservatism and the American Constitutional Order," *Harvard Journal of Law & Public Policy* 27 (Spring 2004), 459.

2. George W. Carey, "The Philadelphia Constitution: Dead or Alive?" in Mitchell S. Muncy, ed., *The End of Democracy II: A Crisis of Legitimacy* (Dallas: Spence Publishing, 1999), 233.

3. George W. Carey, *In Defense of the Constitution* (Indianapolis: Liberty Fund, 1995), 4–5.

4. Willmoore Kendall and George W. Carey, *The Basic Symbols of the American Political Tradition* (Washington, DC: Catholic University of America Press, 1995), xxii–xxiii.

5. Ibid., xiv–xx.

6. Ibid., xviii–xx.

7. George Carey, "Who or What Killed the Philadelphia Constitution?" *Tulsa Law Journal* 36 (Spring 2001), 640.

8. *In Defense of the Constitution,* 16.

9. George W. Carey, *The Federalist: Design for a Constitutional Republic* (Urbana, IL: University of Illinois Press, 1994), xvi.

10. Ibid., 5–9.

11. *In Defense of the Constitution,* 54.

12. *The Federalist: Design for a Constitutional Republic,* 91.

13. Ibid., 89.

14. Ibid., 171.

15. Ibid., xii.

16. Ibid.

17. Ibid., 163.

18. *In Defense of the Constitution,* 47–48.

19. Ibid., 49.

20. *Basic Symbols,* ix.

21. *The Federalist: Design for a Constitutional Republic,* 165.

22. George W. Carey, "Natural Rights, Equality, and the Declaration of Independence," *Ave Maria Law Review* 3 (Spring 2005), 46.

22. Ibid., 66.

23. Ibid., 48.

24. Ibid., 64.

25. Ibid., 62.

26. Ibid., 57–61.

27. Ibid., 59.

28. Ibid., 76. On the founders' attachment to and reliance on virtue in the people as the foundation of free constitutional government, see also Graham Walker, "Virtue and the Constitution: Augustinian Theology and the Frame of American Common Sense" in Gary L. Gregg II, ed., *Vital Remnants: America's Founding and the Western Tradition* (Wilmington, DE: ISI Books, 1999).

29. On subsidiarity, see for example Kenneth L. Grasso, "Man, Society and the State: A Catholic Perspective," in Michael Cromartie, ed., *Caesar's Coin Revisited: Christians and the Limits of Government* (Grand Rapids, MI: Eerdmans, 1996).

30. *The Federalist: Design for a Constitutional Republic,* 160.

31. Ibid., 158.

32. Ibid.

33. Ibid., 159, citing *Federalist* 10, 51, and 48, respectively.

34. George W. Carey, "The Constitution and Community" in George W. Carey and Bruce Frohnen, eds., *Community and Tradition: Conservative Perspectives on the American Experience* (Lanham, MD: Rowman and Littlefield, 1998), 63.

35. Ibid., 63.

36. Ibid., 64.

37. Ibid., 63.

38. Ibid., 74.

39. Ibid., 83.

40. Ibid., 63.

41. Ibid., 78.

42. Ibid., 83.

43. Ibid., 83.

44. George W. Carey, "Traditions at War," *Modern Age* 36 (Spring 1994), 237. Citation omitted.

45. Ibid., 237.

46. Ibid., 241–42.

Locke, Our Great Founders, and American Political Life / *Peter Augustine Lawler*

1. George W. Carey, *The Federalist: Design for a Constitutional Republic* (Urbana, IL: University of Illinois Press, 1987).

2. Most of what I say here about Carey's thought is best supported by the impressive overview he provides in *A Student's Guide to American Political Thought* (Wilmington, DE: ISI Books, 2004).

3. Alexis de Tocqueville, *Democracy in America*, trans. Harvey C. Mansfield and Delba Winthrop (Chicago: University of Chicago Press, 2002), volume 2, part 2, chapters 1–15; volume 2, part 3, chapters 10–12.

4. Orestes A. Brownson, *The American Republic* (Wilmington, DE: ISI Books, 2003) and John Courtney Murray, *We Hold These Truths: Catholic Reflections on the American Proposition* (New York: Sheed and Ward, 1960). The overviews of Brownson and Murray presented here draw to some extent from my introduction to the ISI edition of Brownson and my introduction to the forthcoming new Sheed and Ward edition of Murray. My intention here is to show that this Catholic tradition in American political thought is real, still quite viable, and a supplement to Carey's wisdom.

5. Brownson, *The American Republic,* 222.

6. Ibid., 138.

7. Roger Scruton, *The Meaning of Conservatism*, 3rd ed. (South Bend, IN: St. Augustine's Press, 2002).

8. Murray, *We Hold These Truths*, 30.

9. Carey, *A Student's Guide*, 13.

10. Ibid., 27.

11. Ibid., 43.

12. Murray, *We Hold These Truths,* 309–10.

13. See Tocqueville, *Democracy in America*, volume 2, part 2, chapters 9–10.

14. Carey, *A Student's Guide,* 26.

15. Ibid., 72–74.

16. Wilmoore Kendall and George W. Carey, *Basic Symbols of the American Political Tradition* (Washington, DC: Catholic University Press, 1995).

17. See Pierre Manent, *The City of Man,* trans. Marc A. LePain (Princeton, NJ: Princeton University Press, 1998), chapter 4.

18. Wilson Carey McWilliams, "National Character and National Soul," in Peter Augustine Lawler, ed., *Democracy and Its Friendly Critics: Tocqueville and Political Life Today* (Lanham, MD: Lexington Books, 2004), 13; Harvey Mansfield, "Change and Bill Clinton," *Times Literary Supplement*, November 13, 1992.

19. Kennedy, opinion for the court, *Lawrence v. Texas* (2003).

20. Carey, *A Student's Guide*, 91

21. Ibid., 100.

22. Ibid.

23. Jonathan Rauch, *Gay Marriage: Why It Is Good for Gays, Good for Straights, and Good for America* (New York: Times Books, 2004).

24. Ibid., 71.

25. David Brooks, "The Power of Marriage," *New York Times,* November 22, 2003.

26. An earlier version of some of these comments on same-sex marriage are found in my "More Than a Contract," *National Review,* June 16, 2004.

27. Virginia Postrel, *The Substance of Style: How the Rise of Aesthetic Value is Remaking Commerce, Culture, and Consciousness* (New York: HarperCollins, 2003).

28. Tocqueville, *Democracy in America,* volume 2, part 3, chapters 6–7.

29. See Gregg Easterbrook, *The Progress Paradox* (New York: Random House, 2003).

30. David Brooks, *On Paradise Drive: How We Live Now (And Always Have) in the Future Tense* (New York: Simon and Schuster, 2004).

31. Tocqueville, *Democracy in America,* volume 2, part 1, chapter 8.

32. See, for example, Francis Fukuyama, *Our Posthuman Future: Consequences of the Biotechnology Revolution* (New York: Farrar, Straus, and Giroux, 2002).

33. Michael P. Zuckert, *The Natural Rights Republic: Studies in the Foundation of the American Political Tradition* (Notre Dame, IN: University of Notre Dame Press, 1996), 83. Zuckert, I think, is excellent on Locke, precisely because he thinks Locke teaches the truth. He is much less reliable as a guide on the American founding.

34. Zuckert, *The Natural Rights Republic,* 84.

35. Ibid., 84–85.

36. See especially Locke, *Second Treatise of Government,* chapter V, "Of Property."

37. Tocqueville, *Democracy in America,* volume 2, part 2, chapter 15.

38. The dispute between Michael Zuckert and Barry Shain on whether America rests on a Lockean or Calvinist foundation cannot be easily resolved, because they are both obviously partly right. See here Zuckert, *The Natural Rights Republic,* and Shain, *The Myth of American Individualism* (Princeton, NJ: Princeton University Press, 1994). But we must add that the American mixture of Lockeanism and Calvinism—although in some respects quite fortunate—is quite unstable. Even more fortunately, Locke and Calvin do not exhaust the American alternatives.

39. A fairly appreciative account of America from this view—given by two British observers—is John Micklethwait and Adrian Wooldridge, *The Right Nation: Conservative Power in America* (New York: Penguin Press, 2004).

40. James W. Ceaser and Daniel DiSalvo, "A New GOP," *Public Interest* 157 (Fall 2004), 15.

41. Phillip Longman, "Political Victory: From Here to Maternity," *Washington Post,* September 2, 2004.

42. See my *Postmodernism Rightly Understood: The Return to Realism in American Thought* (Lanham, MD: Rowman and Littlefield, 1999) and my *Aliens in America: The Strange Truth about Our Souls* (Wilmington, DE: ISI Books, 2002). Also, Walker Percy, *Lost in the Cosmos: The Last Self-Help Book* (New York: Farrar, Straus, and Giroux, 2003).

GEORGE CAREY AND THE ROOTS OF
AMERICA'S BASIC LIBERTIES / *Donald S. Lutz*

1. For what amount to my marching orders, see the introduction to George W. Carey, *The Federalist: Design for a Constitutional Republic* (Urbana, IL: University of Illinois Press, 1989), xxiii–xxv. See also Carey's "The Separation of Powers," in George Graham Jr. and Scarlett Graham, eds., *Founding Principles of American Government: Two Hundred Years of Democracy on Trial* (Bloomington, IN: Indiana University Press, 1976).

2. Donald S. Lutz, "Why Federalism?" a review essay in *William and Mary Quarterly,* series 3, 61 (2004), 587. The classic formulation "an indestructible Union, composed of indestructible States" was written by Justice Chase in *Texas v. White* 74 U.S. 700 (1868).

3. As an excellent example of how George Carey develops such questions as well as where he points us for answers, see chapter 1 in Kendall and Carey's *The Basic Symbols of the American Political Tradition* (Baton Rouge, LA: Louisiana State University Press, 1970), 3–29. The first four chapters of this book are taken from a series of lectures given by Wilimoore Kendall, but Carey revised them. Students of George Carey recognize his style and method of argumentation in this chapter, just as students of Willmoore Kendall recognize the differences from Kendall's distinctive style of developing an argument.

4. What follows is essentially a reprise of chapter 3 in Donald S. Lutz, *A Preface to American Political Theory* (Lawrence, KS: University Press of Kansas, 1992), 49–88.

5. I have relied upon the British texts as found in Richard L. Perry, ed., *Sources of Our Liberties* (New York: Associated College Presses for the American Bar Association, 1959), 11–22, 73–75, 245–50. See also Bernard Schwartz, *The Roots of the Bill of Rights,* volume 5 (New York: Chelsea House Publishers, 1980), 1204. Schwartz's comparison can be found in slightly emended form in Lutz, *A Preface to American Political Theory* (Lawrence, KS: University Press of Kansas, 1992), 52–53.

6. See for example Perry, *Sources of Our Liberties,* 23–24. For a lucid description of the development of English common law in general and the position of Magna Carta in particular, see Arthur R. Hogue, *Origins of the Common Law* (Indianapolis: Liberty Press, 1988), and I. F. Plucknett, *A Concise History of the Common Law* (Boston: Little, Brown, 1956).

7. See Bernard Schwartz, *The Great Rights of Mankind: A History of the Bill of Rights* (New York: Oxford University Press, 1977), 197; Irving Brant, *The Bill of Rights: Its Origin and Meaning* (Indianapolis: Bobbs-Merrill Company, 1965), chapters 5 and 6; William Nelson, *The Americanization of the Common Law: The Impact of Legal Change on Massachusetts Society, 1760–1830* (Cambridge, MA: Harvard University Press, 1975); Jack P. Greene, *Peripheries and Center: Constitutional Development in the Extended Politics of the British Empire and the United States, 1607–1788* (Athens, GA: University of Georgia Press, 1986); and Shannon C. Stimson, *The American Revolution in the Law* (Princeton, NJ: Princeton University Press, 1990).

8. *Annals of Congress,* 12 vols. (Philadelphia, 1804) 1:436.

9. The most accurate and accessible source for these ratifying convention records is Merrill Jensen, John P. Kaminski, Gaspare J. Saladino et al., eds., *The Documentary History of the Ratification of the Constitution* (Madison, WI: University of Wisconsin Press, 1976).

10. The state constitutions and their respective state bills of rights can be found in Francis N. Thorpe, ed., *The Federal and State Constitutions,* 7 vols. (Washington, DC: Government Printing Office, 1907); and also in William F. Swindler, ed., *Sources and Documents of the United States Constitutions,* 10 vols. (Dobbs Ferry, NY: Oceana Publications, 1973–79). Swindler published a second series of three volumes in 1982 that contains documents relating to the national Constitution.

11. Thorpe, *The Federal and State Constitutions* (Maryland), 1686–69 1 (Massachusetts), 1889–93, and (New Hampshire), 2453–57.

12. Thorpe, *The Federal and State Constitutions* (Virginia), 3812–14, and (Pennsylvania) 3082–84.

13. The complete historical story in Voegelinian terms, including the development of American rights, is the subject of Donald S. Lutz, *The Origins of American Constitutionalism* (Baton Rouge, LA: Louisiana State University Press, 1988). Most of the relevant colonial documents involved in this historical process can be found in Donald S. Lutz, ed., *Colonial Origins of the American Constitution: A Documentary History* (Indianapolis: Liberty Press, 1998).

14. The precise manner and extent to which this is the case is described in detail in Donald S. Lutz, *The Origins of American Constitutionalism,* chapters 8 and 12.

FEDERALISTS, ANTIFEDERALISTS, AND THE PHILADELPHIA CONSTITUTION / *Gordon Lloyd*

1. See "How to Read *The Federalist,*" reprinted in Nellie D, Kendall, ed., *Willmoore Kendall Contra Mundum* (New Rochelle, NY: Arlington House, 1971), 403–17.

2. See "Who or What Killed the Philadelphia Constitution?" *Tulsa Law Journal* 36 (Spring 2001), 621–40.

3. In *Federalist* 39, Madison suggests that the boundary between the federal and state governments is to be determined by the Supreme Court: "the tribunal which is ultimately to decide is to be established under the general government." In *Federalist* 46, however, Madison presents a political understanding that permits the people to switch from one level of government to another after due deliberation: "the people ought not surely to be precluded from giving most of their confidence where they may discover it to be most due." See Clinton Rossiter, ed., *The Federalist Papers* (New York: New American Library, 1961), 245 and 295, respectively.

4. The essential question in the ratification debate concerned the capacity of a people to govern themselves.

5. Carey cites the "superb article," written by Ralph Rossum, "that maintains the Seventeenth Amendment dealt a fatal blow to the framers' design of federalism."

Carey rejects Rossum's account because it tackles only the symptoms of the problem. There is indeed a problem with the Rossum thesis: equal representation rather than state election incorporates the central principle of federalism in the Philadelphia Constitution. This is confirmed in Article V of the United States Constitution.

6. See *Federalist* 37, 229.

7. See *Federalist* 39, 246. (Numbers added.) According to Madison, the five tests are foundation, sources, operation, extent of powers, and mode of amendment. He declares the Constitution to be national in operation and either mixed or federal in the other four. The Antifederalists were concerned that the mere enumeration of powers was insufficient because, with an ingenious interpretation of the necessary and proper clause, Congress could consolidate all power.

8. For an overview of the Convention as a four-act drama, see Gordon Lloyd, www.teachingamerica.org/convention. James Madison's notes are available here.

9. Ibid.

10. Max Farrand, ed., *The Records of The Federal Convention of 1787,* volume 2 (New Haven: Yale University Press, 1911) I, 52.

11. Ibid., 150.

12. Ibid., 196–204.

13. Ibid., 242–45.

14. Ibid., 322.

15. Ibid., 468.

16. Ibid., 468.

17. Ibid., 488–89.

18. Ibid., 510–76.

19. Ibid., 551.

20. Alexander Hamilton was not at the Philadelphia Convention during this critical discussion.

21. This interpretation is at odds with that of the greatest teachers on the American founding. Martin Diamond and Herbert Storing have been central to restoring the dignity of the founding enterprise, and much is owed to them. My central disagreement is that they see 1) the Connecticut Compromise as a validation of Madison's Virginia Plan rather than a derailment of the nationalist project; and 2) very little serious stuff going on during the last two months of the Convention because, for them, the central theoretical issue had been settled back in July. See Martin Diamond, *The Founding of the Democratic Republic* (Itasca, Illinois: Peacock Publishers, 1981), and Joseph M. Bessette, ed., *The Writings of Herbert J. Storing* (Washington, DC: AEI Press, 1995).

22. See www.teachingamericanhistory.org/convention

23. See Farrand, ed., *The Records of The Federal Convention of 1787,* volume 2, 493–528.

24. W. B. Allen and Gordon Lloyd, eds., *The Essential Antifederalist,* 2nd edition (Lanham, MD: Rowman and Littlefield, 2002), chapters 2 and 3.

25. See *Federalist* 33 and *Federalist* 44, 203 and 284. Emphasis in original.

26. Farrand, ed., *The Records of The Federal Convention of 1787,* volume 2, 27.

27. See Gordon Lloyd, www.teachingamericanhistory.org/convention, for a complete account of the debates.

28. Farrand, ed., *The Records of The Federal Convention of 1787,* volume 2, 28–29. Emphasis added.

29. Ibid.

30. Nor were the general welfare and common defense clauses viewed as expressing a wholly national disposition, since they were included in the Articles of Confederation.

31. Farrand, ed., *The Records of The Federal Convention of 1787,* volume 2, 21–36.

32. Farrand includes drafts of the Committee of Detail Report. Only Wilson's notes indicate that the following should be discussed: 1) "Powers which may, with Propriety, be vested" in Congress; and 2) "And to make all Laws that shall be necessary and proper for carrying into [full and complete] Execution [the foregoing Powers, and] all other powers vested, by this Constitution, in the Government of the United States, or in any Department or Officer thereof." See Farrand, ed., *The Records of The Federal Convention of 1787,* volume 2, 137–68.

33. Farrand, ed., *The Records of The Federal Convention of 1787,* volume 2, 177–89.

34. Ibid., 304.

35. The powers to tax and to regulate interstate commerce are now part of the congressional enumeration. Even the most ardent Antifederalists were in favor of their inclusion.

36. Kurland and Lerner have sixteen main entries on Article 1, Section 8, Clause 18. These are designed to help the modern reader grasp the original understanding of the necessary and proper clause. Regrettably, they have included none from the records of the Federal Convention. See Philip B. Kurland and Ralph Lerner, eds., *The Founders' Constitution,* III (Chicago: University of Chicago Press, 1987), 238–77.

37. Farrand, ed., *The Records of The Federal Convention of 1787,* volume 2, 344.

38. Ibid., 345.

39. Ibid. Emphasis added.

40. Alexander Hamilton was absent on August 20—he was absent for all of the critical discussions on the structural and powers dimensions of the national-federal deliberations. Thus, his remarks in *Federalist* 33 concerning why the necessary and proper clause was introduced are speculative:

> The answer is, that it could only have been done for greater caution, and to guard against all *caviling refinements* in those who might hereafter feel a disposition to curtail and evade the legitimate authorities of the union. The convention probably foresaw, what it has been the principle aim of these papers to inculcate, that the danger which most threatens our political welfare, is that the state governments will finally sap the foundations of the union; and might therefore think it necessary, on so cardinal a point, to leave nothing to construction. Whatever may have

been the inducement to it, the wisdom of the precaution is evident from *the cry* which has been raised against it; as that very *cry* betrays a disposition to question the great and essential truth which it is manifestly the object of that provision to declare. (Emphasis added.)

See *Federalist,* 203. For the Antifederalist "cry" about the necessary and proper clause, see William B. Allen and Gordon Lloyd, eds., *The Essential Antifederalist.*

41. Farrand, ed., *The Records of The Federal Convention of 1787,* volume 2, 321–65.

42. Ibid., 563–64.

43. Pierce Butler on August 30, 1787, noted in his diary: "The sweeping Clause absorbs everything almost by Construction." See James H. Hutson, ed., *Supplement to Max Farrand's The Records of the Federal Convention of 1787* (New Haven, CT: Yale University Press, 1987), 249.

44. Farrand, ed., *The Records of The Federal Convention of 1787,* volume 2, 632–33.

45. Ibid., 582–90.

46. Ibid., 612–20.

47. Ibid., 615–16. Emphasis added.

48. These exchanges anticipate the disagreement between Alexander Hamilton and Thomas Jefferson over the constitutionality of the First National Bank.

49. Farrand, ed., *The Records of The Federal Convention of 1787,* volume 2, 616–18.

50. Farrand, ed., *The Records of The Federal Convention of 1787,* volume 3, 362.

51. Ibid., 99.

52. Colleen Sheehan and Gary L. McDowell, eds., *Friends of The Constitution: Writings of the "Other" Federalists 1787–1788* (Indianapolis: Liberty Fund, 1998), 267.

53. Ibid., 493–94.

54. Ibid., 492.

55. Farrand, ed., *The Records of The Federal Convention of 1787,* volume 3, 99.

56. See Gordon Lloyd and Margie Lloyd, eds., *The Essential Bill of Rights* (Lanham, MD: University Press of America, 1998), chapter 6.

57. Ibid.

58. *Federalist* 37, 229.

59. See Madison's critique of Marshall's opinion (in contrast to his decision) in Marvin Meyers, ed., *Mind of the Founder* (Hanover, NH: University Press of New England, 1981), 357–93. Not even Hamilton dared to go so far.

JAMES MADISON AND THE EXTENDED REPUBLIC / *Quentin Taylor*

1. Alexander Hamilton, et al., *The Federalist,* ed., George W. Carey and James McClellan (Indianapolis: Liberty Fund, 2001). See also Walter Berns, "The Constitution as a Bill of Rights," in *In Defense of Liberal Democracy* (Chicago: Regnery, 1984), 3–28, and Ralph A. Rossum, "The Federalist's Understanding of the Constitution as a Bill of Rights," in Charles R. Kesler, ed., *Saving the Revolution:* The Federalist *and the American Founding* (New York: The Free Press), 219–33.

2. While Hamilton defended the absence of a bill of rights in *The Federalist*, Madison made a similar case in the Virginia Ratifying Convention and in a subsequent letter to Jefferson (October 15, 1788). See Robert A. Rutland and Charles F. Hobson, eds., *The Papers of James Madison* [hereafter PJM] (Charlottesville, VA: University Press of Virginia, 1977), XI:130–31, 175, 297–98.

3. See Forrest McDonald, *Novus Ordo Seclurom: The Intellectual Origins of the Constitution* (Lawrence, KS: University Press of Kansas, 1985) 205–9, and Harold S. Schultz, "James Madison: Father of the Constitution?" *Quarterly Journal of the Library of Congress* 37 (1980), 215–22.

4. "It is a delicious irony of history," writes Clinton Rossiter, "that the 'invention' of American federalism should have been the result of an ill-tempered struggle for power, and that the man, James Madison, who first celebrated publicly the beauties of this unique system should have been the most irreconcilable of nationalists and the last to surrender." *1787: The Grand Convention* (New York: W. W. Norton, 1966), 193–94.

5. See Jack N. Rakove, "Early Uses of *The Federalist,*" in *Saving the Revolution*, 234–49, and James G. Wilson, "The Most Sacred Text: The Supreme Court's Use of The Federalist Papers," *Brigham Young Law Review* 65 (1985), 65–135.

6. The pluralist school, which has been predominant in American political science since the 1950s, took its inspiration directly from Madison's No. 10. As one observer notes, "[t]hirty years later [after Beard] Madison's contention that internal divisions in a polity were inevitable—that a republic was preserved, indeed, not by its unity but by the multitudinousness of its divisions, by its possession of so many interests that no single interest could consume the rest—all this had moved into the very core of American political science." Daniel T. Rogers, *Contested Truths: Keywords in American Politics Since Independence* (New York: Basic Books, 1987) 185–86.

7. For the continuing influence of Antifederalist thought under the Constitution, see Saul Cornell, *The Other Founders: Anti-Federalism and the Dissenting Tradition in America, 1788–1828* (Chapel Hill, NC: University of North Carolina Press, 2001).

8. See Dennis J. Mahoney, "A Newer Science of Politics: The Federalist and American Political Science in the Progressive Era," in *Saving the Revolution*, 250–64.

9. New editions of *The Federalist Papers* were edited by Henry Cabot Lodge (1888) and Paul L. Ford (1898), and the papers were cited in the Legal Tender Cases (1871), Income Tax Cases (1895), and Federal Stamp Act Case (1901). See Charles W. Pierson, "*The Federalist* in the Supreme Court," *Yale Law Review* 33 (1924), 733.

10. Vernon Parrington, *Main Currents in American Thought: The Colonial Mind, 1620–1800* (New York: Harcourt, Brace, & World, 1927), 271–96. Parrington dedicated this volume to his teacher, J. Allen Smith. Richard Hofstadter, *The American Political Tradition and the Men Who Made It* (New York: Alfred Knopf, 1948), 3–55.

11. E. E. Schattschneider, *Party Government* (New York: Garrar and Rinehart, 1942); James MacGregor Burns, *The Deadlock of Democracy* (Englewood Cliffs, NJ: Prentice Hall, 1963).

12. While Bailyn, Wood, and Pocock are often grouped together, their methods, concerns, and findings are by no means univocal. The last two, however, do em-

phasize the break with the "classical conception of politics" signified by *The Federalist Papers* and share a certain nostalgia for "[w]hat might have been." Gordon S. Wood, *The Creation of the American Republic* (New York: W. W. Norton, 1969), 606; J. G. A. Pocock, "Cambridge Paradigms and Scotch Philosophy: A Study of the Relations Between the Civic Humanist and the Civil Jurisprudential Interpretation of Eighteenth-Century Social Thought," in Istvan Hont and Michael Ignatieff, eds., *Wealth and Virtue* (Cambridge: Cambridge University Press, 1985), 244.

13. For a survey of this literature and the well-worn debates surrounding early American political thought, see Robert E. Shalhope, "Toward a Republican Synthesis: The Emergence of an Understanding of Republicanism in American Historiography," *William and Mary Quarterly* 29 (1972), 49–80; "Republicanism and Early American Historiography," *William and Mary Quarterly* 39 (1982), 334–56; and Daniel T. Rogers, "Republicanism: The Career of a Concept," *Journal of American History* 79 (1992), 13–38.

14. See, in particular, Richard K. Matthews, who in one of the few full-length treatments of Madison's political thought charts the transmogrification of the Virginian's "liberal dream" into a "nightmare for increasing numbers of marginalized Americans" and calls on them to "reclaim their natural birthright to live the ideals of the Declaration of Independence. . . ." *If Men Were Angels: James Madison and the Heartless Empire of Reason* (Lawrence, KS: University Press of Kansas, 1995), 279.

15. The well-known phrase, "the most wonderful work ever struck off at a given time by the brain and purpose of man," was penned by William Gladstone in 1878, although nearly the same words had been used by Supreme Court Justice William Johnson in 1823.

16. For an exhaustive discussion of the difficulties involved in using original documents in determining the intent of the framers and interpreting the Constitution, see the series of articles by Jacobus tenBroek, "Admissibility and Use by the United States Supreme Court of Extrinsic Aids in Constitutional Construction," *California Law Review* 26 (1938), 287– , 437– , 664– ; 27 (1939), 165–81.

17. This expression of frustration issued from an Antifederalist in response to the long-winded Publius, but it certainly applies to the massive literature on *The Federalist Papers*, and especially No. 10.

18. Montesquieu was the most frequently cited author in the 1780s, and by Federalists and Antifederalists alike. See Donald S. Lutz, "The Relative Influence of European Writers on Late Eighteenth-Century American Political Thought," *American Political Science Review* 78 (1984), 189–97. For the French thinker's curious influence on the framers, *The Federalist Papers*, and the founding, see James W. Miller, "The American Framers' Debt to Montesquieu," in William J. Bennett, ed., *Revival of Constitutionalism* (Lincoln, NE: University of Nebraska Press, 1988), 87–102; "Montesquieu and Publius: The Crisis of Reason and *The Federalist Papers*," in Sheldon S. Wolin, *The Presence of the Past: Essays on the State and the Constitution* (Baltimore: The Johns Hopkins University Press, 1989), 100–119; and Anne M. Cohler, *Montesquieu's Comparative Politics and the Spirit of American Constitutionalism* (Lawrence, KS: University Press of Kansas, 1988).

19. Madison would also "bandy quotations" from Montesquieu in extolling "the advantages of a confederate republic" (*Federalist* 43), and not just Hamilton, as Douglas Adair maintained. "The Intellectual Origins of Jeffersonian Democracy" (Ph.D. diss., Yale University, 1943).

20. Adair's "discovery" of Madison's sources for *Federalist* 10 has had a similar impact on the study of that essay as Beard's economic and Dahl's pluralist reading. "'That Politics May be Reduced to a Science': David Hume, James Madison, and the Tenth Federalist," *Huntington Library Quarterly* 20 (1957), 343–60.

21. Wills's effort to interpret the American founding through the lens of the Scottish Enlightenment represents a hypertrophy of Adair's approach to *Federalist* 10. The results in his volumes on the Declaration of Independence (*Inventing America*, 1978) and *The Federalist* (*Interpreting America*, 1981) are admittedly ingenious but have not escaped critical censure. See George W. Carey, "On Inventing and Explaining America," *Modern Age* 26 (1982), 122–35; and Edmund S. Morgan, "Safety in Numbers: Madison, Hume, and the Tenth Federalist," *Huntington Library Quarterly* 95 (1986), 95–112.

22. While Madison was apparently squeamish about crediting Hume, others such as Hamilton pronounced him "a celebrated author," "an ingenious and sensible writer," and praised "the profound and ingenious Hume." Harold C. Syrett, ed., *The Papers of Alexander Hamilton* (New York: Columbia University Press, 1961), I:94, III:77, IV:217. He also, as Publius, cites Hume in No. 85.

23. It was, however, offered as a refutation. Even before Madison published *Federalist* 10 on November 22, 1787, a number of critiques of the proposed Union faulted its extensiveness for one reason or another. The need to refute (indeed invert) these criticisms is clear in No. 9, where Hamilton dismisses the Antifederalist reading of Montesquieu as "the novel refinements of an erroneous theory." In the following paper the refutation is largely implicit, but Madison does settle the question of size with "obvious considerations," whereas in No. 14 he confronts head-on "the prevailing prejudice with regard to the practical sphere" of a republic. Though claiming to have already "refuted" this prejudice, he provides fresh supports for "unmixed and extensive republics." The spirit of confutatio is also present in the two other papers that deal explicitly with extensiveness, Nos. 27 and 51. For a summary of the Antifederalist position on "small republics" see Herbert J. Storing, *What the Anti-Federalists Were* For (Chicago: University of Chicago Press, 1981), 15–23.

24. An even earlier adumbration appears in a letter to Jefferson (August 20, 1784), where in considering the position of Spain in North America, Madison observes that its "security lies in the Complexity of our federal govt. and the diversity of interests among the members of it which render offensive measures, improbable in Council, and difficult in execution." Accordingly, instead of seeking to hinder the growth of American states, Spain should "wish to see the number enlarged . . ." *PJM*, VI, 106. The clear implication is that a divided government composed of a multiplicity of interests and covering an extensive territory is ill-suited for "offensive" action. Spanish policy was also the occasion for Madison's first explicit rejection of "the interest of

the majority [as] the political standard of right and wrong," particularly in matters of "property and wealth," where it "would be the interest of the majority in every community to despoil & enslave the minority . . ." Madison to James Monroe (October 5, 1786) *PJM*, IX, 141.

25. "Memorial and Remonstrance Against Religious Assessments" (June 20, 1785) *PJM*, VI, 295–306.

26. In between writing the "Memorial" and "Vices" Madison offered suggestions on a constitution for Kentucky in response to a request from a friend who had migrated there. This first effort at constitution making contains a number of provisions he would press for in Philadelphia, including strictly limiting the number of representatives and providing for a council of revision. Madison to Caleb Wallace (August 23, 1785) *PJM*, VI, 350–58.

27. "Vices of the Political System of the United States" (April 1787) *PJM*, IX, 345–58. The contents of "Vices" were largely the result of Madison's intensive study of "Ancient and Modern Confederacies," which occupied much of his spare time in the mid-1780s. (April–June 1786) *PJM*, IX, 3–24. His notes of these studies would serve him in the federal and Virginia conventions, and provide much of the material for *Federalist* 18–20.

28. Madison to Edmund Pendleton (February 24, 1787) *PJM*, IX, 295.

29. Madison to Washington (April 16, 1787), *PJM*, IX:382–85. He had called for the "negative" on state laws in earlier letters to Jefferson (March 19, 1787) and Edmund Randolph (April 10, 1787). *PJM*, IX, 316, 370.

30. Charles F. Hobson is almost alone in emphasizing the indispensability of the "negative" in Madison's republican theory and its relation to the principle of extensiveness. "The Negative on State Laws: James Madison, the Constitution, and the Crisis of Republican Government," *William and Mary Quarterly* 36 (1979), 215–33.

31. Max Farrand, ed., *Records of the Federal Convention of 1787*, 4 vols. (New Haven, CT: Yale University Press, 1966).

32. *Federalist* 62; Madison to Jefferson (October 24, 1787) *PJM*, X, 209.

33. Farrand, *Records*, I:464; 416. Even writing as Publius, Madison could not quite suppress his deep disappointment in the composition and election of the Senate. In *Federalist* 62 he implies that "every district ought to have a proportional share in the government," and he suggests that the standard of equality proposed by the Convention was "evidently the result of compromise. . . ." Similarly, the proposed appointment of senators by the state legislatures was not owing to principle or policy, but was "probably the most congenial with the public opinion."

34. Madison to Jefferson (September 6, 1787) *PJM*, X, 163.

35. Madison to Pendleton (September 20, 1787) *PJM*, X, 171.

36. Madison to Jefferson (October 24, 1787) *PJM*, X, 205–20.

37. The quote is from Hamilton in *Federalist* 15, but Madison qua Publius would also use the "monster" metaphor in Nos. 19 and 44.

38. Madison to Jefferson (October 24, 1787), *PJM*, X:214.

39. The sincerity of Madison's "conversion" has been the subject of much speculation

ever since Jefferson "discover[ed] that the author [Publius] means only to say what may best be said in defense of opinions in which he did not concur." Jefferson to Madison (November 18, 1788), *PJM*, XI:216. Among recent observers, Lance Banning maintains that Madison quickly reconciled himself "to positions he had earlier opposed" and "confessed his reconciliation" in *The Federalist Papers*. "The Practicable Sphere of a Republic: James Madison, the Constitutional Convention, and the Emergence of Revolutionary Federalism," in Richard Beeman et al., eds., *Beyond the Confederation: Origins of the Constitution and American National Identity* (Chapel Hill, NC: University of North Carolina Press, 1988), 164. At the other end of scale, Hobson claims that the post–Convention Madison was "highly dissatisfied with, not to say contemptuous of, the proposed government," and that he was forced to improvise in *The Federalist Papers* in order to salvage something for a system he privately considered "crazy." "The Negative on States Laws," 233.

40. Madison did mention in passing "all the errors in the System positive & negative" in a letter written after ratification, but even as an advocate for the Constitution he acknowledged that its authors were "forced into some deviations," namely in the composition and election of the Senate. Madison to Jefferson (October 17, 1788), *PJM*, XI:297; *Federalist* 37, 62.

41. Madison to Jefferson (October 24, 1787) *PJM*, X, 212.

42. The tendency to confute the functions of extensiveness with those of the structure and operations of government accounts for much of the distortion in readings of Madison. Shattschneider, for example, claimed that "Madison's defense of federalism [in *Federalist* 10] annihilates his defense of the separation of powers. If the multiplicity of interests in a large republic makes tyrannical majorities impossible, the principal theoretical prop of the separation of powers has been destroyed." *Party Government*, 9. Yet as Carey has shown, "separation of powers was primarily intended to perform a function other than controlling majorities. That function . . . was to prevent tyranny and to prevent the governors . . . from ruling arbitrarily and capriciously to abuse and oppress the governed." In *Defense of the Constitution* (Indianapolis: Liberty Fund, 1995) 54. See also Carey, *The Federalist: Design for a Constitutional Republic* (Urbana, IL: University of Illinois Press, 1989), passim. Some have found this distinction overdrawn, but Madison settles the matter in favor of Carey. "In our Government the real power lies in the majority of the Community, the invasion of private rights is chiefly to be apprehended, not from acts of Government contrary to the sense of its constituents, but from acts in which the Government is the mere instrument of the major number of the constituents." Madison to Jefferson (October 17, 1788) *PJM*, XI, 298. Separation of powers is designed to prevent a betrayal of the "sense" of the community, while extensiveness aims to prevent government from becoming the "mere instrument" of a tyrannical majority.

43. While Madison would cite "the enlargement of the sphere [as] a cure for many of the evils inseparable from the popular forms in small communities" as late as 1833, shortly after ratification he appears to have abandoned the theory of factions that the remedy of extensiveness presupposed. Quoted in Saul K. Padover, ed., *The Forging of American*

Federalism: Selected Writings of James Madison (New York: Harper & Rowe, 1965), 63. Theodore Draper notes that after making the extended republic a centerpiece in *The Federalist Papers*, "Madison does not seem to have had any more use for it; and . . . he even began to move away from it the following year." "Hume and Madison: The Secrets of *Federalist Paper* No. 10," *Encounter* 58 (1982), 43. Others have charged Madison with "inconsistency" in condemning the factional politics of the 1790s and have found a "great contradiction" in his emphasis on a homogeneity of interests as the guarantor of republicanism. John Zvesper, "The Madisonian Systems," *Western Political Science Quarterly* 37 (1984), 236–56. See also Douglas W. Jaenicke, "Madison v. Madison: The Party Essays v. *The Federalist Papers*," in R. Maidment and J. Zvesper, eds., *Reflections on the Constitution: The American Constitution after Two Hundred Years* (Manchester: University of Manchester Press, 1989), 116–47. Madison may have temporarily jettisoned the extended republic in favor of ideological orthodoxy, but Hamilton would continue to champion "republics of large extent" well into the 1790s. "Hamilton's Original Major Draft," in Victor H. Paltsits, *Washington's Farewell Address: In Facsimile, with Transliterations of all the Drafts of Washington, Madison, & Hamilton, Together with their Correspondence and Other Supporting Documents* (New York, 1935), 189–90.

44. *PJM*, XI, 163. Of course, this begs the question of how a society ensures an adequate degree of virtue and intelligence in its people. The alleged failure to answer this question—by way of establishing "a regime without a regimen"—has been called "the paramount failure of the Founding Fathers." Paul A. Rahe, *Republics, Ancient and Modern,* volume 3, *Intentions of Prudence: Constituting the American Regime* (Chapel Hill, NC: University of North Carolina Press, 1994), 235; Paul Eidelberg, *The Philosophy of the American Constitution* (New York: The Free Press, 1968), 248. The focus on "virtue" (or lack thereof) in the American founding has been a particular concern of the "Straussian school" of political theory.

The Virtue of Education / *Jeffry Morrison*

1. Parts of this essay are taken from chapter 3 of my *John Witherspoon and the Founding of the American Republic* (Notre Dame, IN: University of Notre Dame Press, 2005).

2. Thomas Jefferson to P. S. Dupont de Nemours, April 24, 1816, in Merrill D. Peterson, ed., *Thomas Jefferson: Writings* (New York: Library of America, 1984), 1387.

3. George W. Carey, *In Defense of the Constitution* (Indianapolis: Liberty Fund, 1995), 4.

4. "Pinckney Plan," May 29, 1787, in Max Farrand, ed., *The Records of the Federal Convention of 1787*, volume 3 (New Haven, CT: Yale University Press, 1966), 598.

5. See Washington's eighth annual message to Congress, December 7, 1796; Washington to Thomas Jefferson, March 15, 1795; Washington to Alexander Hamilton, September 1, 1796; Last Will and Testament, July 9, 1799. Available online at www.gwpapers.virginia.edu.

6. Richard Brookhiser, *Founding Father: Rediscovering George Washington* (New York: Free Press, 1996), 141.

7. Benjamin Rush to Richard Price, May 25, 1786, in L. H. Butterfield, ed., *Letters of Benjamin Rush,* volume 2 (Princeton, NJ: Princeton University Press, 1951) II:388–89.

8. John Adams, diary entry of August 27, 1774, in L. H. Butterfield, ed., *The Diary and Autobiography of John Adams,* volume 2 (Cambridge, MA: Harvard University Press, 1961), 112.

9. In Thomas Jefferson Wertenbaker, *Princeton: 1746–1896* (Princeton, NJ: Princeton University Press, 1946), 19–20.

10. Charter of the College of New Jersey (1746), in Richard Hofstadter and Wilson Smith, eds., *American Higher Education: A Documentary History,* volume 1 (Chicago: University of Chicago Press, 1961), 83.

11. Witherspoon, "Address to the Inhabitants of Jamaica, and Other West-India Islands in Behalf of the College of New-Jersey (1772)", in *The Works of John Witherspoon,* volume 8 (Edinburgh: Ogle & Aikman et al., 1804–5), 328, 329 [hereinafter *Works*].

12. *New-Jersey Gazette,* April 23, 1783, n.p. This toast was raised on April 19, 1783, in Princeton, during a celebration after peace was declared.

13. In Jack Scott, ed., "Introduction," *An Annotated Edition of John Witherspoon's Lectures on Moral Philosophy* (Newark, DE: University of Delaware Press, 1982), 16 [hereinafter *Lectures on Moral Philosophy*].

14. Garry Wills, *Explaining America: The Federalist* (Garden City, NY: Doubleday, 1981), 18.

15. "On the Religious Education of Children (1789)", in *Works,* volume 4, 139.

16. Witherspoon, "Address to the Inhabitants of Jamaica," *Works,* volume 8, 309.

17. "Recapitulation," in *Lectures on Moral Philosophy,* 187. See also Jack Scott's helpful appendix, which he titles Witherspoon's "Bibliography of Chief Writers on Ethical and Political Thought," in ibid., 189–91.

18. "Lecture I," in *Lectures on Moral Philosophy,* 64.

19. Ibid., 65.

20. See Scott, "Introduction," in *Lectures on Moral Philosophy,* 27.

21. "The outline of Hutcheson's *System* is virtually identical to Pufendorf's *On the Law of Nature and Nations.*" Frank D. Balog, "The Scottish Enlightenment," in Allan Bloom and Steven J. Kautz, eds., *Confronting the Constitution* (Washington: AEI Press, 1990), 503n.

22. See *Federalist* 5 by Jay, and *Federalist* 22, 29, 31, 83 and 84 by Hamilton. Number 83 alone contains four references to "common sense."

23. "Let all, therefore, who wish or hope to be eminent, remember, that as the height to which you can raise a tower depends upon the size and solidity of its base, so they ought to lay the foundation of their future fame deep and strong in . . . *plain common sense.*" Witherspoon, "Druid IV (1781?)", in *Works,* volume 9, 266–67 [emphasis in original]; see also, *Works,* volume 9, 252.

24. "The truth is, the immaterial system, is a wild and ridiculous attempt to unsettle the principles of common sense by metaphysical reasoning, which can hardly produce any thing but contempt in the generality of persons who hear it, and which I verily

believe, never produced conviction even on the persons who pretend to espouse it."
See "Lecture II," in *Lectures on Moral Philosophy,* 76.

25. Thomas Jefferson to Peter Carr, August 10, 1787, in Julian P. Boyd et al., eds.,
Papers of Thomas Jefferson, volume 12 (Princeton, NJ: Princeton University Press,
1950–), 15.

26. Thomas Jefferson to Thomas Law, June 13, 1814, in Andrew A. Lipscomb and Al-
bert Ellery Bergh et al., eds., *The Writings of Thomas Jefferson,* volume 14 (Washington:
Thomas Jefferson Memorial Association of the United States, 1904–5), 139, 142.

27. "Lecture III," in *Lectures on Moral Philosophy,* 78.

28. "Lecture IV," in *Lectures on Moral Philosophy,* 90.

29. Jefferson originally wrote "sacred & undeniable," then changed it to read "self-
evident." See "Original Rough Draft" of the Declaration in *Papers of Thomas Jefferson,*
volume 1, 423, 427–28n. Although the change is sometimes attributed to Benjamin
Franklin, the editors of Jefferson's *Papers* say the attribution "rests on no conclusive
evidence, and there seems to be even stronger evidence that the change was made by
TJ." See editor's note, *Papers of Thomas Jefferson,* volume 1, 427–28n.

30. Thomas Jefferson to John Adams, March 14, 1820, in *The Writings of Thomas
Jefferson,* volume 15, 239–40. I am indebted to Professor Daniel N. Robinson of the
University of Oxford for bringing this passage to my attention.

31. "Even Jefferson, who never used a plow, would take extreme pride in his one truly
original invention, the formulae for a moldboard's 'curve of least resistance'; and, like
Thomas Reid, he used 'a ploughman' as his test of the moral sense that is equal in all
men." Garry Wills, *Inventing America: Jefferson's Declaration of Independence* (New York:
Random House, 1978), 100.

32. "Lectures on Eloquence," in *Works,* volume 7, 165.

33. "Aristides," in *Works,* volume 9, 91.

34. Ibid.

35. Alexander Hamilton, ["The Farmer Refuted'" (1776)] in Michael Novak, *On
Two Wings: Humble Faith and Common Sense at the American Founding* (San Francisco:
Encounter Books, 2002), 3.

36. Caroline Robbins has traced the transatlantic influence of the moral-sense epistemology in "'When It Is That Colonies May Turn Independent': An Analysis of
the Environment and Politics of Francis Hutcheson (1694–1746)," *William and Mary
Quarterly,* third series, 11 (1954): 214–51.

37. See Novak, *On Two Wings,* 43.

38. See I. Woodbridge Riley, *American Philosophy: The Early Schools* (New York: Russell & Russell, 1958 [1907]), 483–96; and Herbert W. Schneider, *A History of American
Philosophy* (New York: Columbia University Press, 1946), 246–50. Elizabeth Flower
and Murray G. Murphey have attempted to revise this singularly "jaundiced" view
of Scottish realism in America, as well as Witherspoon's part in it. See their *History of
Philosophy in America,* volume 1 (New York: Putnam's Sons, 1977), 203–73. The authors "hold that so far from being a drag on the American Enlightenment, Common
Sense Realism was a part of it." See ibid., 204.

39. Schneider, *History of American Philosophy,* 246.

40. John E. Bentley, *An Outline of American Philosophy* (Totowa, NJ: Littlefield, Adams & Co., 1965), 40.

41. Vincent Buranelli, "Colonial Philosophy," *William and Mary Quarterly,* third series, 16 (1959), 353–54. Conspicuously absent from this list are the more "philosophical" of the founders like Jefferson and Franklin.

42. Eric Voegelin, *Autobiographical Reflections,* ed. Ellis Sandoz (Baton Rouge, LA: Louisiana State University Press, 1987), 28–29.

43. See Douglass Adair, "'That Politics May be Reduced to a Science': David Hume, James Madison and the Tenth Federalist," in Trevor Colbourn, ed., *Fame and the Founding Fathers* (New York: W. W. Norton, 1974), 93–106. Adair saw Hume especially clearly in Madison's formulation of the extended republic, and he quoted from Hume's "Idea of a Perfect Commonwealth" as follows: "[t]hough it is more difficult to form a republican government in an extensive country than in a city; there is more facility, when once it is formed, of preserving it steady and uniform, without tumult and faction." See ibid., 98.

44. Frank D. Balog, "The Scottish Enlightenment," in Allan Bloom and Steven J. Kautz, eds., *Confronting the Constitution,* 504n. The "work" to which Balog refers is Adams's *Discourse on Davila.*

45. See Ashbel Green, *Life of the Revd. John Witherspoon,* ed. Henry Lyttleton Savage (Princeton, NJ: Princeton University Press, 1973), 132–33. Witherspoon's essay was "Remarks on an Essay on Human Liberty," *Scots Magazine* 15 (April 1753), 165–70, which does indeed predate much of Reid's published work, but his claim, particularly to have anticipated "any other author of their views" (e.g., Shaftesbury or Hutcheson), has been brought into serious question.

46. "The Berklean [sic] system of Metaphysics was in repute in the college when he entered on his office. The tutors were zealous believers in it, and waited on the President, with some expectation of either confounding him, or making him a proselite [sic]. They had mistaken their man. He first reasoned against the System, and then ridiculed it, till he drove it out of the college." Green, *Life of the Revd. John Witherspoon,* 132.

47. The phrase "century and a half" is used because the pragmatists of the early twentieth century can be seen as the legitimate heirs of Scottish realism. See Elizabeth Flower and Murray G. Murphey, *A History of Philosophy in America,* volume 1, 216, for the assertion that "the Common Sense Realists were a bridge between the Enlightenment and the pragmatists, not least because they helped determine the way the Kantian philosophy was to be utilized."

48. Ibid., 178.

49. Thomas Jefferson to Peter Carr, August 10, 1787, in *Papers of Thomas Jefferson,* volume 12, 15. Note that Jefferson repeats the "bungling" language about the creator in his letter to Thomas Law on June 13, 1814; see *The Writings of Thomas Jefferson,* volume 14, 142.

50. Thomas Jefferson to John Witherspoon, January 12, 1792, in *Papers of Thomas Jefferson,* volume 23, 40.

51. "Recapitulation," in *Lectures on Moral Philosophy*, 186.

52. Thomas Jefferson to Henry Lee, May 8, 1825, in Adrienne Koch and William Peden, eds., *The Life and Selected Writings of Thomas Jefferson* (New York: The Modern Library, 1993), 656–57.

53. Morton White, *The Philosophy of the American Revolution* (Oxford: Oxford University Press, 1978), 3.

54. Frederick Mayer, *A History of American Thought: An Introduction* (Dubuque, IA: Wm. C. Brown Co., 1951), 1.

55. Thomas Jefferson to John Trumbull, February 15, 1789, in *Papers of Thomas Jefferson*, volume 14, 561.

56. Alexis de Tocqueville, *Democracy in America*, trans. George Lawrence, ed. J. P. Mayer (New York: Harper & Row, 1969), 429.

57. Adams to Jefferson, July 16, 1814, in Lester J. Cappon, ed., *The Adams-Jefferson Letters*, volume 2 (Chapel Hill, NC: University of North Carolina Press, 1959), 437.

58. Thomas Jefferson to Peter Carr, August 10, 1787, in *Papers of Thomas Jefferson*, volume 12, 15.

59. Frederick Copleston, *A History of Philosophy*, volume 5 (Garden City, NY: Doubleday, 1962–77), 140.

60. Alexis de Tocqueville, *The Old Régime and the French Revolution*, trans. Stuart Gilbert (New York: Doubleday, 1955), 153.

No Presidential Republic / *Gary L. Gregg II*

1. See Willmoore Kendall and George W. Carey, *The Basic Symbols of the American Political Tradition* (Baton Rouge, LA: Louisiana State University Press, 1970).

2. *The Federalist Papers* were written by Alexander Hamilton, James Madison and John Jay under the pseudonym of "Publius." I adopt their pseudonym here as they intended, as I find there to be no essential differences between the authors on the central questions of our concern. For a solid and critical consideration of Publius's supposed "split personality," see George W. Carey, *In Defense of the Constitution* (Indianapolis: Liberty Fund, 1995).

3. Cincinnatus IV (Arthur Lee), "To James Wilson, Esquire, New York Journal, 22 November 1787," reprinted in John P. Kaminski and Richard Leffler, eds., *Federalist and Anti-Federalist: The Debate over the Ratification of the Constitution* (Madison, WI: Madison House, 1989), volume 1, 72.

4. Richard Henry Lee, "To Governor Edmund Randolph, 16 October 1787, New York." Reprinted in Kaminski and Leffler, *Federalist and Anti-Federalist*, 154.

5. All subsequent quotations from *The Federalist* are from George W. Carey and James McClellan, eds., *The Federalist* (Indianapolis: Liberty Fund, 2001). They will be cited parenthetically in the text.

6. Gary L. Gregg II, *The Presidential Republic: Executive Representation and Deliberative Democracy* (Lanham, MD: Rowman and Littlefield, 1997).

7. On the electoral process becoming "the foundation and measure of representation,"

see Gordon S. Wood, *The Creation of the American Republic, 1776–1787* (New York: W. W. Norton, 1972), 447.

8. On all three branches of the government being representative, see Gordon S. Wood, *Representation in the American Revolution* (Charlottesville, VA.: University of Virginia Press, 1969). "Indeed since all governmental power in a republic, whatever its nature or function, was something of a delegation by the people, all parts of a republican system now seemed representative, essentially indistinguishable in their character"(53).

9. On Publius's *realistic* view of human nature, see James P. Scanlan, "*The Federalist* and Human Nature," *Review of Politics* 21 (1959), 657–77.

10. There seems to be a convincing argument that the arena of government in which parochial interests were to be actively voiced and promoted were the state legislatures. The federal structure serves as a "double representation" of the people dividing the functions of representatives between those in the state and those in the national governments. See Robert J. Morgan, "Madison's Theory of Representation in the Tenth *Federalist*," *Journal of Politics* 37 (1974), 860–61; see also William Kristol, "The Problem of the Separation of Powers *Federalist* 47–51," in Charles R. Kesler, ed., *Saving the Revolution: The Federalist Papers and the American Founding* (New York: The Free Press, 1987), 126–27.

11. On the representatives "reporting" the particular interests see David F. Epstein, *The Political Theory of* The Federalist (Chicago: University of Chicago Press, 1984).

12. George W. Carey, *The Federalist: Design for a Constitutional Republic* (Urbana, IL: University of Illinois Press, 1989), 42.

13. United States Constitution, Article I, Section 7.

14. See Alexis de Tocqueville, *Democracy in America* (New York: Vintage Books, 1990) volume 2, book 4, chapter 7, 325–26. For an important contemporary consideration of the importance of constitutional forms, see Harvey C. Mansfield Jr., *America's Constitutional Soul* (Baltimore: Johns Hopkins University Press, 1991).

15. On this point, see Harvey C. Mansfield Jr., *Taming the Prince: The Ambivalence of Modern Executive Power* (New York: The Free Press, 1989), 279–91.

16. Joseph Bessette, "Deliberative Democracy: The Majority Principle in Republican Government," in Robert Goldwin and William A. Schambra, eds., *How Democratic Is the Constitution?* (Washington, DC: American Enterprise Institute, 1980), 105.

17. Samuel H. Beer makes a similar point in *To Make A Nation: The Rediscovery of American Federalism* (Cambridge, MA: Harvard University Press, 1993). "For a government which attempts to coordinate the interests of the many, a separation of powers, each of which represents the same social body, the people at large of the nation, heightens the probability that discussion and decision will realize the economies of generalization by focusing on common interests requiring similar treatment" (287).

18. Willmoore Kendall, "The Two Majorities in American Politics," reprinted in Kendall, *The Conservative Affirmation in America* (Chicago: Gateway Editions, 1985), 42.

Rights in a Federalist System / *Francis Canavan*

1. George W. Carey, "Judicial Activism and Regime Change," in Kenneth L. Grasso and Robert P. Hunt, eds., *A Moral Enterprise: Politics, Reason and the Human Good* (Wilmington, DE: ISI Books, 2002).

2. Carey, "Judicial Activism and Regime Change," 313. The author quotes Rebecca L. Brown, "Accountability, Liberty and the Constitution," in John H. Garvey and T. Alexander Aleinikoff, eds., *Modern Constitutional Theory: A Reader* (St. Paul: West Publishing, 1999), 240.

3. Carey, "Judicial Activism and Regime Change," 313.

4. Ibid., 313–14.

5. Ibid., 317.

6. H.R. Doc. No. 398, 69th Cong. 1st Sess., 1927 (hereafter *Documents Illustrative*).

7. Ibid., 114–15.

8. Ibid., 117.

9. Ibid., 391–92.

10. *Black's Law Dictionary*, 4th ed. (1951), 1316–17.

11. *Documents Illustrative,* note 6, 934 (from papers of Dr. James McHenry, a delegate from Maryland).

12. *A Century of Lawmaking for a New Nation: U.S. Congressional Documents and Debates, The Congressional Globe*, 39th Cong. (1774–1875), 1034. Available online at http://memory.loc.gov/ammem/amlaw.

13. *A Century of Lawmaking for a New Nation*, 2542–43.

14. Ibid., 2766.

15. *The Slaughter House Cases*, 83 U.S. (16 Wall). 36, 78 (1872).

16. Alfred H. Kelly and Winifred Harbison Kelly, *The American Constitution: Its Origin and Development* (New York, W. W. Norton, 1955).

17. *Allgeyer v. Louisiana*, 165 U.S. 578, 589 (1897).

18. *West Coast Hotel v. Parrish,* 300 U.S. 379, 391 (1937).

19. *Gitlow v. New York*, 268 U.S. 552 (1925).

20. *Griswold v. Connecticut*, 381 U.S. 479 (1965).

21. Ibid., 482.

22. Ibid., 484–85.

23. Ibid., 509–10.

24. Ibid., 479.

25. *Eistenstadt v. Baird*, 405 U.S., 438 (1972).

26. *Roe v. Wade*, 410 U.S. 113 (1973).

27. *Planned Parenthood v. Danforth*, 428 U.S., 52 (1976).

28. *Bowers v. Hardwick*, 478 U.S., 52 (1986).

29. Ibid., 191.

30. Ibid., 191–92.

31. Ibid., 192.

32. Ibid., 204–5.

33. Ibid., 205.

34. *Romer, Governor of Colorado v. Evans,* 517 U.S., 620 (1996).

35. Ibid., 632.

36. George F. Will, *Statecraft as Soulcraft: What Government Does* (New York: Simon & Shuster, 1983), 158.

37. *Washington v. Glucksberg,* 521 U.S., 702 (1997); *Vacco v. Quill,* 521 U.S., 621 (1997).

38. Ibid., 702.

39. Ibid., 720.

40. Ibid., 755, n. 4.

41. Ibid., 764.

42. Ibid.

43. Ibid., 767.

44. *Black's Law Dictionary,* 345–46.

45. *Lawrence v. Texas,* 539 U.S., 558 (2003).

46. Ibid., 513.

47. Ibid., 514.

48. Ibid., 526.

49. *Planned Parenthood v. Casey,* 505 U.S., 833 (1992).

50. James Howard Graham, *Everyman's Constitution* (Madison: State Historical Society of Wisconsin, 1968), vii.

51. Sheldon S. Wolin, *Politics and Vision: Continuity & Innovation in Western Political Thought* (Boston: Little & Brown, 1960), 293.

52. John Locke, *The Works of John Locke,* ed. Thomas Tegg (Darmstadt: Scientia Verlag, 1963 [1823]). All subsequent references will be to the book, chapter, and subsection in Locke's work, plus the volume and page number in the 1963 edition.

53. Ibid., 52, *Essay on Understanding,* IV, 5, 11; III, 7.

54. Ibid., II, 23, 32; II, 30.

55. Ibid., III, 3, 20; II, 185.

56. Ibid., III, 3, 11; II, 172.

57. Ibid.

58. Ibid., III, 32, 11–12; II, 140–1.

59. Ibid., II, 20, 2; I, 231.

60. Ibid., II, 28, 8; II, 98.

61. Ibid., IV, 3, 18; II, 168. A similar thought lies behind Spinoza's work, *Ethics Demonstrated in the Manner of Geometry.*

62. John Dunn, *The Political Thought of John Locke* (Cambridge: Cambridge University Press 1969), 187.

63. Thomas Hobbes, *Leviathan: or the Matter, Forme, and Power of a Commonwealth, Ecclesiastical and Civil,* ed. Michael Oakeshott (Oxford: B. Blackwell, 1946).

64. Ibid., iv.

65. Ibid., 63–64.

66. Ibid., 66.

67. Ibid., 82.

68. Ibid.

69. Ibid., 83.

70. Ibid.

71. Ibid.

72. Ibid., 84.

73. Ibid.

74. Ibid., 98.

75. Ibid., 104.

76. Ibid.

77. Fredrick Copleston, S.J., *A History of Philosophy* (New York: Doubleday Image Books, 1963) volume 3, part 1, 59.

78. Philotheus Boehner, O.F.M., *Philosophical Writings of William of Ockham* (Indianapolis: Hackett Publishing, 1990), xviii. My statements about Ockham are based on this and the previous source.

79. George H. Sabine, "The Two Democratic Traditions," *Philosophical Review* 61, no. 4 (Fall 1952), 467.

RELIGIOUS PLURALISM AND THE AMERICAN
EXPERIMENT / *Kenneth L. Grasso*

1. *The Basic Symbols of the American Political Tradition* (Baton Rouge, LA: Louisiana State University Press, 1970; reprint, Washington, DC: Catholic University of America Press, 1995), 154. On the distinction between religion and politics in the American political tradition, see 73–74 and 137–154, passim.

2. It "is perhaps all to the good," they write, that the authors of the Mayflower Compact began with the words "In the name of God," rather than "In the name of the Father, the Son, and the Holy Ghost," because "there will come a day when at least some of the heirs of the Compact . . . would take vigorous exception to any reference to the Trinity." *Basic Symbols*, 31.

3. For an introduction to the subject of interreligious conflict in American history, see Robert N. Bellah and Frederick E. Greenspahn, eds., *Uncivil Religion* (New York: Crossroad, 1987).

4. James Davison Hunter, *Culture Wars: The Struggle to Define America* (New York: Basic Books, 1991). "Arguably," he writes, "our national identity and purpose has not been more of a source of contention since the Civil War." Ibid., 50.

5. "American Conservatism and the 'Prayer' Decisions," in *Willmoore Kendall Contra Mundum*, ed. Nellie D. Kendall (New Rochelle, NY: Arlington House, 1971; reprint, Lanham, MD: University Press of America, 1994), 336.

6. Murray, *We Hold These Truths: Catholic Reflections on the American Proposition* (Kansas City, MO: Sheed & Ward, 1960), x.

7. Ibid., 84, 72–73.

8. Ibid., 9, 80–81.

9. Ibid., 45, x.

10. For an overview of this philosophy, see ibid., viii–ix, 27–43.

11. Ibid., 46, 47, 54, 66.

12. Ibid., 73.

13. Ibid., 56, 69, 49.

14. Ibid., 27, 74–60

15. Ibid., xi, 69, 49, 54.

16. Ibid., 48, 49.

17. "Beyond Murray's Articles of Peace and Faith," in Robert P. Hunt and Kenneth L. Grasso, eds., *John Courtney Murray and the American Civil Conversation* (Grand Rapids, MI: William B. Eerdmans Publishing Co., 1992), 181–204.

18. Murray, *We Hold These Truths*, 64, 66.

19. Ibid., 64, 65, 202.

20. Bradley, "Beyond Murray's Articles," 194, 195, 196, 199.

21. Os Guinness, introduction to James Davison Hunter and Os Guinness, eds., *Articles of Faith, Articles of Peace: The Religious Liberty Clauses and the American Public Philosophy* (Washington, DC: Brookings Institution, 1990), 13.

22. *Democracy in America*, ed. J. P. Mayer, trans. George Lawrence (New York: Harper & Row, 1969), volume 1, part 2, chapter 9, 292; and volume 2, part 1, chapter 1, 432.

23. Ibid., volume 1, part 2, chapter 9, 288–89; and volume 1, part 1, chapter 2, 35–36.

24. Ibid., volume 1, part 2, chapter 9, 290–91.

25. Hunter, *Culture Wars*, 68–69.

26. Ibid., 69–71.

27. Francis Canavan, *The Pluralist Game: Pluralism, Liberalism and the Moral Conscience* (Lanham, MD: Rowman and Littlefield, 1995), 65, 63, 110.

28. Thus, as Carey observes, Publius was able to focus "on means principally," rather than ends, because in his America "substantial agreement existed . . . about the meaning, priority, and desirability" of these ends. "Despite the difficulties confronting him," Publius enjoyed "the luxury of advancing his positions in a society with shared moral foundations, convictions, and outlooks." *The Federalist: Design for a Constitutional Republic*, 163. Indeed, as he points out, Publius's treatment of the problem of faction "presumes that there exists among the people . . . a moral consensus" encompassing "generally shared notions of what is 'unjust' and 'dishonorable.'" "The Constitution and Community," in George W. Carey and Bruce Frohnen, eds., *Community and Tradition* (Lanham, MD: Rowman and Littlefield, 1998), 76–77.

29. *Basic Symbols*, 55.

30. *In Defense of the Constitution*, rev. and exp. (Indianapolis: Liberty Fund, 1995), 35.

31. Samuel Cooper, "A Sermon on the Day of the Commencement of the Constitution," in Ellis Sandoz, ed., *Political Sermons of the Founding Era* (Indianapolis: Liberty Fund, 1991), 637.

32. *The Federalist: Design for a Constitutional Republic*, 10.

33. Letter to John Adams, October 12, 1813, in *Jefferson's Extracts from the Gospels*, Dickinson W. Adams, ed., *The Papers of Thomas Jefferson: Second Series* (Princeton, NJ: Princeton University Press, 1983), 352.

34. Thomas A. Spragens Jr., *The Irony of Liberal Reason* (Chicago: University of Chicago Press, 1981), 200.

35. Canavan, *The Pluralist Game*, 110.

36. Henry F. May, *The Enlightenment in America* (Oxford: Oxford University Press, 1976), 360.

37. *Catholicism and the Renewal of American Democracy* (New York: Paulist Press, 1989) 199, 212.

38. *In Defense of the Constitution*, 49.

39. *Faith and Order: The Reconciliation of Law and Religion* (Atlanta: Scholars Press, 1993), 226, 229.

40. Canavan, *The Pluralist Game*, 70.

41. Alexander Hamilton, James Madison, and John Jay, *The Federalist: The Gideon Edition*, ed. George W. Carey and James McClellan (Indianapolis: Liberty Fund, 2001), No. 39, 198.

42. Joseph Story, *Commentaries on the Constitution of the United States* (Boston: Hilliard, Gray and Company, 1833) volume 3, 371.

43. Kendall, *Contra Mundum*, 343.

44. Canavan, *The Pluralist Game*, 12.

45. George W. Carey, "America's Founding and Limited Government," *Intercollegiate Review* 39 (Fall 2003/Spring 2004): 21.

46. Kendall, *Contra Mundum*, 342.

47. On the limits of "cultural federalism," see Richard Samuelson, "Can Federalism Solve America's Culture Wars?" at http://www.realclearpolitics.com/articles/2006/04/states_rights_and_wrongs.html (accessed November 18, 2006).

48. David Gelernter, "Back to Federalism," *Weekly Standard*, April 10, 2006, 24.

49. For helpful recent overviews of the origin and history of the religion clauses, see John Witte Jr., *Religion and the American Constitutional Experiment*, 2nd ed. (Boulder, CO: Westview Press, 2005); and Philip Hamburger, *Separation of Church and State* (Cambridge, MA: Harvard University Press, 2003).

50. Witte, *Religion and the American Constitutional Experiment*, 117, 118.

51. Ibid., 118.

52. Ibid.

53. George W. Carey, "Conservatism, Centralization and Constitutional Federalism," *Modern Age* 46 (Winter-Spring 2004): 58.

54. Charles S. Hyneman, *The Supreme Court on Trial* (New York: Atherton Press, 1963), 250, 263, 253.

55. Ibid., 249–55. Such support is critically important because, as Kendall and Carey have shown in their classic analysis of the "intensity" problem in democratic theory, a sufficiently intense minority opposed to a law can create a situation in which a law is

effectively unenforceable or in which the social costs—in terms of both resources and civic amity—of enforcement are unacceptably high. "The 'Intensity' Problem and Democratic Theory," *American Political Science Review* 62, no. 1 (March 1968), 5–24.

56. Ballard C. Campbell, *The Growth of American Government: Governance From the Cleveland Era to the Present* (Bloomington, IN: Indiana University Press, 1995), 1.

57. *In Defense of the Constitution*, 14.

58. "The Constitution and Community," 79.

59. Gelernter, "Back to Federalism," 22.

60. "The Constitution and Community," 81–82.

61. Gelernter, "Back to Federalism," 22–23.

62. Robert F. Nagel, "Nationhood and Judicial Supremacy," in Christopher Wolfe, ed., *That Eminent Tribunal* (Princeton, NJ: Princeton University Press, 2004), 32–33. For an extended discussion of the dangers of nationalizing the whole range of issues confronting the American polity, see Nagel's *The Implosion of American Federalism* (Oxford: Oxford University Press, 2001).

63. Edward S. Corwin, "The Supreme Court as National School Board," *Law and Contemporary Problems* 14, no. 1 (Winter 1949), 3–22.

64. Hyneman, *The Supreme Court on Trial*, 243.

65. *In Defense of the Constitution*, 179.

66. Ibid.

67. Hyneman, *The Supreme Court on Trial*, 249–55.

68. Hunter, *Culture Wars*, 73.

69. Ibid., 75–76.

70. Ibid., 128, 42, 44.

71. Ibid., 132, 124–25, 119–20.

72. Ibid., 131–32.

73. Ibid., 76.

74. Alasdair MacIntyre, *After Virtue*, 2nd ed. (Notre Dame, IN: University of Notre Dame Press, 1984) 11, 12, 72.

75. *In Defense of the Constitution*, 189, 188, 4.

76. Hunter, *Culture Wars*, 42. This would seem to be true even of the Civil War. However bitterly divided the two sides were, both, as Lincoln noted, read "the same Bible and pray[ed] to the same God." "Second Inaugural Address," in John Gabriel Hunt, ed., *The Inaugural Addresses of the Presidents* (New York: Gramercy Press, 1995), 200.

77. Hunter, *Culture Wars*, 42, 131, 128.

78. Ibid., 130, 129.

79. Ibid., 132.

80. David Novak, *Jewish Social Ethics* (New York: Oxford University Press, 1992), 46–59.

81. George M. Marsden, *Religion and American Culture*, 2nd ed. (Fort Worth: Harcourt, 2001), 43.

82. For studies that emphasize what I have called the conservative character of the

Anglo-American Enlightenment, see May; and Gertrude Himmelfarb, *The Roads to Modernity: The British, French and American Enlightenments* (New York: Alfred Knopf, 2004).

83. For accounts of the underlying unity of Enlightenment thought and of the radical (and largely unanticipated) consequences of the core philosophical premises informing it, see Spragens; and Lester G. Crocker, *Nature and Culture: Ethical Thought in the French Enlightenment* (Baltimore: Johns Hopkins University Press, 1963).

HORIZONTAL AND VERTICAL CONSOLIDATION OF THE UNITED STATES INTO AN ADMINISTRATIVE STATE / *John S. Baker, Jr.*

1. For a concise discussion of the challenges to federalism and separation of powers, see George W. Carey, *In Defense of the Constitution* (Richmond, VA: James River Press, 1989).

2. See Woodrow Wilson, *Congressional Government* (New York: Houghton Mifflin Co., 1885).

3. See e.g., *Carter v. Carter Coal Co.*, 298 U.S. 238 (1936)

4. See John S. Baker, "Nationalizing Criminal Law: Does Organized Crime Make it Necessary or Proper?" *Rutgers Law Journal* 16 (1983), 495, 523 n. 12.

5. 74 U.S. 700 (1869).

6. Ibid., 725.

7. John C. Calhoun, *A Disquisition on Government*, ed. K. Cralle, (New York: Peter Smith, 1943).

8. Const., Article IV, Section 2.

9. See *Federalist* 39, James Madison, John Jay, and Alexander Hamilton, *The Federalist,* eds. George W. Carey and James McClellan (Indianapolis, Liberty Fund, 2001), 193–99.

10. See *A. L. A. Schechter Poultry Corp. v. United States*, 295 U.S. 495 (1935); *Panama Refining Co. v. Ryan*, 293 U.S. 388 (1935).

11. 14 U.S. 304 (1815).

12. 22 U.S. 1 (1816).

13. 17 U.S. 316 (1819).

14. *Federalist* 31, 154–57.

15. 312 U.S. 52 (1941).

16. 430 U.S. 519 (1977).

17. 350 U.S. 497 (1956).

18. See, e.g., *Landgraf v. USI Film Products*, 511 U.S. 244 (1994).

19. "In the final analysis, there can be no one crystal clear distinctly marked formula." *Hines v. Davidowitz*, 312 U.S. 52, 67 (1941).

20. *Federalist* 23.

21. *Federalist* 32, 155.

22. *Federalist* 10, 48.

23. 505 U.S. 144 (1992).

24. 521 U.S. 98 (1997).

25. *See Alden v. Maine*, 527 U.S. 706 (1999).

26. The Constitution is not a "compact" among the states. *McCulloch v. Maryland*, 4 Wheat (17 U.S), 316, 402–403 (1819).

27. The subject of conflicts of laws covers 1) jurisdiction; 2) choice of law (i.e., choice of which state law to apply on a particular issue); and 3) recognition and enforcement of judgments. Symeon C. Symeonides, Wendy Collins Perdue, and Arthur T. von Mehren, *Conflict of Laws: American, Comparative, International* (St. Paul: West Publishing, 1998), 3.

28. William Prosser, "Interstate Publication," *Michigan Law Review* 51 (1953), 971, quoted in Michael H. Gottesman, "Draining the Dismal Swamp: The Case for Federal Choice of Law Statutes," *Georgetown Law Journal* 90 (1991), 1.

29. What the entire field of conflicts seems to have done over the last century is move from a set of purportedly rigid, black-letter rules that were covertly manipulable to a modernized set of flexible principles that are overtly manipulable. Linda S. Mullenix, "Federalizing Choice of Law for Mass Tort Litigation," *Texas Law Review* 70 (1992), 1623, 1648.

30. Joseph Story, *Commentaries on the Conflict of Laws* 9–12 (Boston: Hilliard, Gray, and Company, 1834; emphasis added):

> it is an essential attribute of every sovereignty, that it has no admitted superior, and that it gives the supreme law within its own dominions on all subjects appertaining to its sovereignty. What it yields, it is its own choice to yield; and it cannot be commanded by another to yield it as matter of right. And accordingly it is laid down by all publicists and jurists, as an incontestable rule of public law, that one may with impunity disregard the law pronounced by a magistrate beyond his own territory.
>
> The jurisprudence, then, arising from the conflict of the laws of different nations, in their actual application to modern commerce and intercourse, is a most interesting and important branch of public law. *To no part of the world is it of more interest and importance than to the United States, since the union of a national government with that of twenty-six distinct States, and in some respect independent States, necessarily creates very complicated private relations and rights between the citizens of those States, which call for the constant administration of extra-municipal principles.* This branch of public law may, therefore, be fitly denominated private international law, since it is chiefly seen and felt in its application to the common business of private persons, and rarely rises to the dignity of national negotiations, or of national controversies.

31. See Symeonides, *Conflict of Laws*, 440.

32. Douglas Laycock, "Equal Citizens of Equal and Territorial States: The Constitutional Foundations of Choice of Law," *Coorado Law Review* 92 (1992), 249, 251.

33. Ibid., 251.

34. The Extradition Clause and the nullified Fugitive Slave Clause. Article IV, Section 2, 4. 2 and 3.

35. Laycock, "Equal Citizens," 301 (footnotes omitted).

36. *Federalist*, 413–14.

37. Laycock, "Equal Citizens," 279.

38. Ibid. (emphasis added).

39. 28 U.S.C. 1738(C) provides:

> No State, territory, or possession of the United States, or Indian tribe,
> shall be required to give effect to any public act, record, or judicial
> proceeding of any other State, territory, possession, or tribe respecting
> a relationship between persons of the same sex that is treated as a mar-
> riage under the laws of such other State, territory, possession, or tribe,
> or a right or claim arising from such relationship.

40. David P. Currie, "Full Faith & Credit to Marriages," *Green Bag* 1 (1997), 7, 11–12.

41. Robert H. Jackson, "Full Faith and Credit: The Lawyer's Clause of the Constitution," *Columbia Law Review* 45 (1945), 1, 26 ("the mutual limits of the states' powers are defined by the Constitution").

42. "No State shall, without the Consent of the Congress . . . enter into any Agreement or Compact with another State." Article I, Section 10, Clause 3.

43. See *Federalist* 10 and 51.

44. 95 U.S. 714 (1877).

45. Charles Wright, Arthur Miller and Mary Kane, *Federal Practice and Procedure* (St. Paul: West Publishing Company, 1986), 1064, 231 (emphasis added).

46. Story, *Commentaries*, 30, 538, 883. (footnote omitted.)

47. "Considered in an international point of view, jurisdiction, to be rightfully exercised, must be founded either upon the person being within the territory, or upon the thing being within the territory; for, otherwise, there can be no sovereignty. . . . On the other hand, no sovereignty can extend its process beyond its own territorial limits, to subject either persons or property to its judicial decisions." Ibid., 539, 883–84 (footnote omitted).

48. 5 Otto (95 U.S) , at 733.

49. Wright et al., *Federal Practice and Procedure*, 1067, 248–49.

50. "The fundamental view that essentially local crime is, with rare exception, a matter principally for the states to attack has been strained in practice in recent years. Congressional activity making more individual, and essentially local, conduct a federal crime has accelerated greatly, notably in areas in which existing state law already criminalizes the same conduct. This troubling federalization trend has contributed to a patchwork of federal crimes often lacking a principled basis." "ABA Task Force, Report on the federalization of Criminal Law" 10 (J. Strazella, Reporter) (1998), 5. (Hereafter "ABA Task Force Report.")

51. Ibid., 7.

52. Ibid., 11.

53. Ibid.,10, fn. 11. See also John S. Baker, "Measuring the Explosive Growth of Federal Crime Legislation." Federalist Society, May, 2004, www.fed-soc.org.

54. This author does not agree that statutes with civil penalties are crimes.

55. "ABA Task Force Report," 10.

56. Ibid., 13. "A Congress's decision to create a federal crime confers jurisdiction upon other federal entities and results in the involvement of others in different federal government branches. . . . Federal executive departments . . . assume broad supervisory responsibility and power over newly created crimes. This activates powerful federal investigatory agencies (such as the FBI, Treasury Department agencies, or Postal Inspectors) to investigate citizen activity for possible federal criminal violations. The scope of federal prosecutors' interest widens, resulting in power to act in a broader range of citizen conduct and intervene in more local conduct."

57. See L. Hall, "The Substantive Law of Crimes—1887–1936," *Harvard Law Review* 50 (1937), 616, 622–31 (discussing antitrust statutes, banking, and security regulations).

58. Interstate Commerce Act, chapter 104, 24 Stat. 379 (1887) (codified as amended at 49 U.S.C. 301 *et seq.* (1998)).

59. See generally Sherman Antitrust Act, chapter 647, 26 Stat. 209 (1890) (codified as amended at 15 U.S.C. 1–7 (1998)), William L. Letwin, "Congress and the Sherman Antitrust Law, 1887-1890," *University of Chicago Law Review* 23 (Winter 1956); Limbaugh, "Historic Origins of Anti-Trust Legislation," *Missouri Law Review* 18 (1953), 215.

60. Distinguishing between "true" crimes and other noncriminal or regulatory offenses is problematic. See generally J. Hall, "Prolegomena to a Science of Criminal Law," *University of Pennsylvania Law Review* 89 (1941), 549, 563–75. The *malum in se* –*malum prohibitum* distinction (crimes by nature–crimes by convention) has proven analytically ambiguous. Ibid., 566. The distinction has also been made between "public welfare offenses" and "real crimes." Sayre, "Public Welfare Offenses," *Columbia Law Review* 33 (1933), 55. For the purpose of designating a category of offenses that need not carry a *mens rea*, see *Morissette v. United States*, 342 U.S. 246 (1952). The distinction between regulatory offenses and "true" crimes reflects the distinction made by Professor Henry Hart in "The Aims of the Criminal Law," *Law and Contemporary Problems* 23 (1958), 401.

61. *See In Re Rapier*, 143 U.S. 110, 134 (1892).

62. 188 U.S. 321 (1903).

63. But see *Hammer v. Dagenhart*, 247 U.S. 251 (1918), which was an exception to this trend. Later reversed by *U.S. v. Darby*, 312 U.S. 100 (1941), *Hammer* found a congressional law excluding from interstate commerce the products of child labor unconstitutional in that it exerted power over a purely local matter.

64. See Baker, "Nationalizing Criminal Law," 520–26.

65. See *Perez v. United States*, 402 U.S. 146 (1971).

66. Stern, "The Commerce Clause Revisited—The Federalism of Intrastate Crime," *Arizona Law Review* 15 (1973), 271, 276–85.

67. 301 U.S. 1 (1937).

68. 514 U.S. 549 (1995).

69. It did not declare federal criminal statutes unconstitutional, but instead tended to construe them narrowly in order to avoid constitutional problems.

70. 402 U.S. 146 (1971).

71. But see Kurt A. Schlichter, "Locked and Loaded: Taking Aim at the Growing Use of the American Military in Civilian Law Enforcement Operations," *Loyola of Los Angeles Law Review* 26 (1993), 1291.

72. U.S. Constitution, Article IV, Section 4. See Jay S. Bybee, "Insuring Domestic Tranquility: Lopez, Federalization of Crime, and the Forgotten Role of the Domestic Violence Clause," *George Washington Law Review* 66 (1997), 1, 75–76.

73. Sara Sun Beale, "Too Many and Yet Too Few: New Principles to Define the Proper Limits for Federal Criminal Jurisdiction," *Hastings Law Journal* 46 (1995), 979, 997. ("Dual federal-state criminal jurisdiction is now the rule rather than the exception. Federal law reaches at least some instances of each of the following state offenses: theft, fraud, extortion, bribery, assault, domestic violence, robbery, murder, weapons offenses, and drug offenses. In many instances, federal law overlaps almost completely with state law." Citations omitted.)

THE RULE OF MEN / *William Gangi*

1. See George W. Carey, "The Philadelphia Constitution: Dead or Alive?" in Kenneth L. Grasso and Cecilia Rodriguez Castillo, eds., *Liberty Under Law* (Lanham, MD: University Press of America, 1998), 75. For Carey's critique of noninterpretivism and account of the implications of its ascendancy for the future of our constitutional republic, see "The Philadelphia Constitution: Dead or Alive?" 71–84; "Judicial Activism and Regime Change," in Kenneth L. Grasso and Robert P. Hunt, eds., *A Moral Enterprise: Politics, Reason and the Human Good* (Wilmington, DE: ISI Books, 2002), 305–20; and *In Defense of the Constitution*, revised and expanded edition (Indianapolis: Liberty Fund, 1995), 122–94.

2. Carey, "Judicial Activism and Regime Change," 305.

3. Carey, "The Philadelphia Constitution: Dead or Alive?" 72, 75.

4. For more detailed accounts of the nature of interpretivism and noninterpretivism, and of damage inflicted on our constitutional order by the latter, see William Gangi, *Saving the Constitution From the Courts* (Norman, OK: University of Oklahoma Press, 1995).

5. Wallace Mendelson, "Raoul Berger's Fourteenth Amendment—Abuse by Contraction vs. Abuse by Expansion," *Hastings Constitutional Law Quarterly* 6 (1979), 437, 443.

6. Willmoore Kendall and George W. Carey, *The Basic Symbols of the American Political Tradition* (Baton Rouge, LA: Louisiana State University Press, 1970), 145.

7. *Brown v. Board of Education,* 349 U.S. 294 (1954).

8. See Samuel G. Freedman, "Still Separate, Still Unequal," *New York Times Book Review,* May 16, 2004.

9. Walter Schaefer, "Federalism and State Criminal Procedure," *Harvard Law Review* 70 (1956), 29.

10. The linchpin for these decisions has been the imposition of the exclusionary rule, which some scholars defend on the basis of "judicial integrity," which is but another name for an expanded idea of judicial review. See Thomas Schrock and William Welsh, "Up from Calandra: The Exclusionary Rule as a Constitutional Requirement," *Minnesota Law Review* 59 (1974), 312. For an alternative perspective, *see* William Gangi, "The Exclusionary Rule: A Case Study in Judicial Usurpation," *Drake Law Review* 34 (1984–85), 33.

11. *United States v. Mendenhall,* 446 U.S. 544, 565 (1980). But see *City of Indianapolis v. Edmond,* 148 L Ed 2d 333.

12. As Justice Jackson advised: "[The] Bill of Rights [is not] a suicide pact." *Terminiello v. City of Chicago,* 337 U.S. 1, 37 (1949).

13. The third leg, of course, would be the right of privacy.

14. See Leonard Levy, *Freedom of Speech and Press in Early America: Legacy of Suppression* (Cambridge: MA: Belknap Press of Harvard University, 1960); Lawrence J. Adams, "The Reality of Seditious Libel in America: Zenger to the 1798 Sedition Act" (M.A. thesis, St. John's University, 1998). As originally understood, Adams writes, the constitutional guarantee of freedom of speech "certainly permitted prosecutions for seditious libel (not to mention such items as obscenity and blasphemy)—that is, things that people considered licentious and not liberty."

15. *Texas v. Johnson,* 491 U.S. 397 (1989).

16. See also *United States v. Eichman,* 496 U.S. 310 (1990) and *Virginia v. Black,* 155 L Ed 2nd 535 (2003). In the latter case, the Supreme Court struck down a Virginia statute that provided that any person burning a cross on another person's property, highway, or public place, was presumed to have an intent to intimidate another person or group.

17. The oral arguments before the Supreme Court in *Virginia v. Black* initially showed promise of discussing symbol utilization. Justice Clarence Thomas observed that cross burnings are "intended to cause fear and to terrorize a population" (*New York Times,* December 12, 2002). That observation was rooted in an experiential *fact*—one of concern to any government—rather than some historically ungrounded *theory* of the First Amendment. It raised the question of what the citizens of Virginia were entitled to do about symbol usage that created a societal issue for some of its citizens. When *Virginia v. Black* was decided, however, it fell short of any principled discussion of these issues. Instead, it focused on the implications of the principles enunciated by the Court in the course of previous cases involving the First Amendment. Justice Thomas's dissent came closest to raising the relevant issues.

18. Kendall and Carey, *The Basic Symbols of the American Political Tradition,* 23, 22.

19. Another obvious instance where judicial interpretations of the First Amendment

have diminished governmental competence is the whole area of freedom of the press, or what the media like to call "the people's right to know." Not a day passes where the media do not publish some diagram describing, for instance, New York City's water system, where there is little or no security. Or, to take another example from television, the media reported that an Oregon town stores our biological and chemical weaponry (yes, they provided a map and a picture of the building), and as if oblivious of recent events, noted that if a fully fueled plane crashed into that building, it would release enough biological and chemical weapons to kill some 10,000 nearby residents. Here again, obvious questions include whether or not judicial decisions have reduced the government's ability to secure public safety, and who is better equipped—the courts or the legislature—to strike the proper balance between the "people's right to know" and public safety.

20. Carey, *In Defense of the Constitution*, 179.

21. James Willard Hurst, *Dealing with Statutes* (New York: Columbia University Press, 1982). Too often noninterpretivists focus on cases where legislatures have failed, rather than on their overall record of success.

22. See Willmoore Kendall and George W. Carey, "The 'Intensity' Problem and Democratic Theory," *American Political Science Review* 62, no. 1 (March 1968): 5–24.

23. Ibid., 5.

24. Ibid., 21–22.

25. Ibid,. 22.

26. Kendall and Carey, "How to Read 'The Federalist,'" in *Willmoore Kendall Contra Mundum,* ed. Nellie D. Kendall (New Rochelle, NY: Arlington House, 1971), 415.

27. Kendall and Carey, *The Basic Symbols of the American Political Tradition*, 147.

28. Carey, "The 'Intensity' Problem and Democratic Theory," 8.

29. Kendall and Carey, "How to Read 'The Federalist,'" 414.

30. Carey, *In Defense of the Constitution*, 179.

31. Ibid.

32. Such polls consist of questions that include phrases like "on a scale of 1 to 5" (or "1 to 10," or "very satisfied to very dissatisfied"), what are your preferences on A, B, or C. See "The 'Intensity' Problem and Democratic Theory," 9 n.7.

33. Alexander Hamilton, James Madison, and John Jay, *The Federalist: The Gideon Edition*, ed. George W. Carey and James McClellan (Indianapolis: Liberty Fund, 2001), *Federalist* 10, 46; and 63, 327. Again, it should be stressed that an essential part of the deliberative process—this process of refining and enlarging public views—is the gauging of the intensity with which various views are held, so it can be taken into account in the crafting of legislation.

34. *Federalist* 78, 403.

35. Carey, *In Defense of the Constitution*, 135. *Marbury v. Madison*, Carey points out, reflects the understanding of the nature, scope, and limits of judicial review propounded in *Federalist* 78.

36. Ibid., 129; my emphasis.

37. Ibid., 134.

38. *Federalist* 78, 402.

39. Carey, *In Defense of the Constitution*, 135.

40. *Federalist* 78, 404.

41. See *The Basic Symbols of the American Political Tradition*.

42. For the full text of this document, see Robert B. Morris, ed., *Basic Documents of American History* (Princeton, NJ: D. Van Nostrand, 1956), 13–14. As Carey observes "the Massachusetts Constitution is generally conceded to be the most 'advanced' or sophisticated of the early State Constitutions." George W. Carey, "Liberty and the Fifth Amendment: Original Intent," *Benchmark* 4 (1990), 301.

43. Kendall and Carey, *The Basic Symbols of the American Political Tradition*, 59, 58.

44. Ibid., 53, 59–60.

45. Ibid., 52.

46. Morris, *Basic Documents of American History*, 13–14.

47. *Federalist* 51, 269.

48. For Kendall and Carey's account of the concepts of individual rights and self-government in the key documents of the founding era, see Kendall and Carey, *The Basic Symbols of the American Political Tradition*, 61–136.

49. The First Amendment guarantee of freedom of speech, for example, was historically understood as consistent with laws proscribing various types of speech (e.g., seditious speech, obscenity, "fighting words," etc) deemed by the legislature to be destructive of the general good.

50. See, for example, Zechariah Chafee, *Free Speech in the United States* (New York: Harcourt, Brace and Howe, 1948), 1–35. I should stress that I am not suggesting that scholars past or present are guilty of committing intentional fraud. What I am suggesting is that every age has its climate of opinion, its own distinctive set of common—and uncritically accepted—assumptions; and that these assumptions may distort scholarship. We must thus strive to understand what these assumptions are and how they may have influenced their works. We should also recognize that we are probably guilty of doing the very same thing (i.e., of allowing the commonplaces of our day to influence our work).

51. For an example of such an approach, see Clinton Rossiter, *Seedtime of the Republic* (New York: Harcourt, Brace and Company, 1953).

52. Kendall and Carey offer this crucial and practical rule of thumb: "Unless we can see a correspondence between the symbols we have in hand and the people's action in history, the symbols we have in hand do not in fact represent that people and we must look a second time for the symbols that do in fact represent them." *The Basic Symbols of the American Political Tradition*, 26. Put another way: if scholars claim that particular words in a document mean one thing, but the people's actions are inconsistent with that meaning, the presumption has to be that the scholars have not understood what the people meant when they used the words they did. To simply conclude without further investigation that the people in question are being hypocritical is, at a minimum, premature.

53. Larry Kramer, "We the People: Who has the Last Word on the Constitution?" *Boston Review* (March 17, 2004), at http://www.bostonreview/BR29.1/kramer.

html.

54. See Carey, "The Philadelphia Constitution: Dead or Alive?" 79; and Carey, "Judicial Activism and Regime Change," 308.

55. Kramer, "We the People," 11–12.

56. Maurice Holland explains that Felix Frankfurter was one of the formulators of "Robert La Follette's platform plank in 1924 which called for a constitutional amendment giving Congress power to override Supreme Court invalidation of federal statutes by a two-thirds vote. Frankfurter even advanced the modest proposal of excising the due process clause from the fourteenth amendment." See Maurice Holland, "American Liberals and Judicial Activism: Alexander Bickel's Appeal from the New to the Old," *Indiana Law Journal* 51 (1976): 1025, 1036 n.23. The quotation from Frankfurter appears in Jesse Choper, "The Supreme Court and the Political Branches: Democratic Theory and Practice," *University of Pennsylvania Law Review* 122 (1974): 810, 815n.13, citing *AFL v. American Sash & Door*, 335 U.S. 538, 556 (Frankfurter, concurring).

57. Richard H. Fallon Jr. "'The Rule of Law' As a Concept in Constitutional Discourse," *Columbia Law Review* 97 (1997): 1.

58. On the dangers of such "appeals to the people" as a means of remedying usurpations by one or more branches of government of powers that properly belong to the other branch or branches, see *Federalist* 48–50, 256–67.

The Crisis of the American Political Tradition / *E. Robert Statham, Jr.*

1. George W. Carey, "Who or What Killed the Philadelphia Constitution?" *Tulsa Law Journal* 36, no. 3 (Spring 2001): 621.

2. E. Robert Statham Jr., *The Constitution of Public Philosophy: Toward a Synthesis of Freedom and Responsibility in Postmodern America* (Lanham, MD: University Press of America, 1998); see also George W. Carey, "On the Degeneration of Public Philosophy in America: Problems and Prospects," in E. Robert Statham Jr., ed., *Public Philosophy and Political Science: Crisis and Reflection* (Lanham, MD: Lexington Books, 2002), 43–56.

3. Walter Lippmann, *The Public Philosophy* (New York: Mentor Books, 1955), 11; see also Sir Ernest Barker, *Traditions of Civility* (Cambridge: Cambridge University Press, 1948).

4. Ibid., 19.

5. See José Ortega y Gasset, *The Revolt of the Masses* (New York: W. W. Norton & Company, 1957); E. Robert Statham Jr., "Ortega y Gasset's 'Revolt' and the Problem of Mass Rule in the 21st Century," *Modern Age* 46, no. 2 (Spring 2004).

6. Lippmann, *The Public Philosophy*, 19.

7. Robert Brown, ed., *Classical Political Theories* (New York: Macmillan, 1990), 99.

8. Willmoore Kendall and George W. Carey, *The Basic Symbols of the American Political Tradition* (Baton Rouge, LA: Louisiana State University Press, 1970), 8, 85.

9. Ibid., 7.

10. Robert Brown, *Classical Political Theories,* 118.

11. Alexander Hamilton, John Jay, and James Madison, *The Federalist: The Gideon Edition*, ed. George W. Carey and James McClellan (Indianapolis: Liberty Fund, 2001) *Federalist* 51, 268–69.

12. George W. Carey, "Restoring Popular Self-Government," *Modern Age* 40, no. 1 (Winter 1998), 50–51; George W. Carey, "The Conservative Mission and Progressive Ideology," *Modern Age* 42, no. 1 (Winter 2000), 14.

13. Eric Voegelin, *The New Science of Politics* (Chicago: University of Chicago Press, 1987), 27.

14. Ibid., 31.

15. Carey, "The Conservative Mission and Progressive Ideology," 16; Carey, "Traditions at War," *Modern Age* 36, no. 3 (Spring 1994), 238.

16. Carey, "Traditions at War," 242–43; Carey, "The Conservative Mission and Progressive Ideology," 14.

17. Carey, "The Conservative Mission," 16–17; see also Lippmann, *The Public Philosophy*, 54–71.

18. Carey, "The Conservative Mission," 16–17.

19. Lippmann, *The Public Philosophy*, 60–61.

20. Alexis de Tocqueville, *Democracy in America,* volume 1 (New York: Vintage Books, 1990), 53.

21. Ibid., 95, 97.

22. Carey, *In Defense of the Constitution*, 51.

23. Ibid.

24. George W. Carey, "The Constitution and Community," in George W. Carey and Bruce Frohnen, eds., *Community and Tradition: Conservative Perspectives on the American Experience* (Lanham, MD: Rowman and Littlefield, 1998), 63.

25. Alexis de Tocqueville, *Democracy in America,* volume 1 (New York: Vintage Books, 1990), 322–23.

26. Alexander Hamilton, John Jay, and James Madison, *The Federalist*, Michael Loyd Chadwick, ed., (Springfield, VA: Global Affairs Publishing, Co., 1987), xxii; 11–13; See also *The Federalist,* George W. Carey and James McClellan, eds., 268–69; David Hume, *An Enquiry Concerning Human Understanding* (New York: Prometheus Books, 1988), 20, 77–78.

27. Carey, *In Defense of the Constitution*, 52.

28. Statham, *The Constitution of Public Philosophy*, 29.

29. Ibid.

30. Note that Alexander Hamilton did not consider that a bill of rights should be amended to the original Constitution, but that such should have been drafted into an ethical treatise. See Alexander Hamilton, John Jay, and James Madison, *The Federalist*, George W. Carey and James McClellan, eds., 442–51.

31. Carey, "The Constitution and Community," 75.

32. Ibid., 77.

33. George W. Carey, *The Federalist: Design for a Constitutional Republic* (Urbana, IL: University of Illinois Press, 1994), 156.

34. Ibid., 157.

35. Ibid., 158.

36. Ibid., 160.

37. E. Robert Statham Jr., "Carl Schmitt, Leo Strauss, and Heinrich Meier: A Dialogue Within the 'Hidden Dialogue,'" *Political Science Reviewer* 27 (1998): 225.

38. Ibid.

39. See Giovanni Sartori, "Liberty and Law," in Kenneth S. Templeton Jr., ed., *The Politicization of Society* (Indianapolis: Liberty Press, 1979), 251–311.

40. Leo Strauss, *What Is Political Philosophy?* (Chicago: University of Chicago Press, 1959), 17.

41. Statham, "Carl Schmitt, Leo Strauss, and Heinrich Meier," 226.

42. Ibid.; see also Leo Strauss, *Natural Right and History* (Chicago: University of Chicago Press, 1953), 314.

43. Leo Strauss, "Political Philosophy and the Crisis of Our Time," in George J. Graham Jr. and George W. Carey, *The Post-Behavioral Era: Perspectives on Political Science* (New York: David McKay Company, 1972), 239.

44. Ibid., 222.

45. Statham, "Carl Schmitt, Leo Strauss, and Heinrich Meier," 228; see also Erich Fromm, *Escape From Freedom* (New York: Avon Books, 1965), 155.

46. Statham, "Carl Schmitt, Leo Strauss, and Heinrich Meier," 228.

47. Carey, "Constitution and Community," 78.

48. Ibid., 78–79.

49. George W. Carey, "Who or What Killed the Philadelphia Constitution?" 632–33; see also Jeffrey C. Isaac, *The Poverty of Progressivism: The Future of American Democracy in a Time of Liberal Decline* (Lanham, MD: Rowman and Littlefield, 2003).

50. Carey, "Who or What Killed the Philadelphia Constitution?" 633–34.

51. Ibid., 637.

52. Ibid., 638.

53. Ibid., 636; see also Theodore J. Lowi, *The End of Liberalism: The Second Republic of the United States* (New York: W. W. Norton & Co., 1979).

54. Leo Strauss, "Progress or Return?" in Thomas L. Pangle, ed., *The Rebirth of Classical Political Rationalism* (Chicago: University of Chicago Press, 1989), 270.

55. Carey, "The Constitution and Community," 83.

56. Alexis de Tocqueville, *Democracy in America,* volume 2, 20.

57. Ibid.

58. Ibid., 21.

59. Ibid., 22.

60. George W. Carey, "Political Science: A Split Personality," *Perspectives on Political Science* 24, no. 3 (Summer 1995), 145.

61. Ibid.

62. Ibid., 142, 145–46.

63. Mordecai Roshwald, "Socrates Today," *Modern Age* 41, no. 2 (Spring 1999), 149.

64. Robert Nisbet, *The Quest for Community* (San Francisco: Institute for Contemporary Studies, 1990), 42–43.

65. Ibid., 48.

66. Ibid., 62.

67. See *Federalist* 10, 42–49.

68. Nisbet, *The Quest for Community*, 176–77.

69. Bertrand de Jouvenel, *On Power: The Natural History of Its Growth* (Indianapolis: Liberty Fund, 1993), 282.

70. Ibid., 284. See also Baron de Montesquieu, *The Spirit of the Laws*, book 11, in Robert Brown, ed., *Classical Political Theories*, 313–25.

71. Jouvenel, *On Power*, 306.

72. Ibid., 284.

73. Ibid., 285.

74. Ortega y Gasset, *The Revolt of the Masses*, 11.

75. Ibid., 11, 17.

76. Ibid., 17.

77. Ibid., 116.

78. Ibid., 18.

79. Ibid., 20.

80. Jouvenel, *On Power*, 306.

81. Ortega y Gasset, *The Revolt of the Masses*, 13.

82. Ibid., 73–74

83. Ibid., 69–73.

84. Carey, "On the Degeneration of Public Philosophy in America," 51–52.

85. Ibid., 52; see also John Courtney Murray, *We Hold These Truths* (New York: Sheed and Ward, 1960), 111, 120.

86. Carey, "On the Degeneration of Public Philosophy in America," 52.

87. Ibid., 54.

88. Walter Berns, "Constitutionalism and Multiculturalism," in Arthur M. Melzer, Jerry Weinberger, and M. Richard Zinman, eds., *Multiculturalism and American Democracy* (Lawrence, KS: University Press of Kansas, 1998), 102–3.

89. See Strauss, "Progress or Return," 227–70.

90. Friedrich Nietzsche, "The Madman," in Walter Kaufmann, ed., *Existentialism From Dostoevsky To Sartre* (New York: Meridian Books, 1975), 126–27.

91. Allan Bloom, *The Closing of the American Mind* (New York: Simon & Schuster, 1987), 25.

92. Ibid., 381.

93. Ibid., 382.

94. Roshwald, "Socrates Today," 149.

95. Ibid., 150.

96. Ibid.

97. Carey, "On the Degeneration of Public Philosophy in America," 53; see also Jerry

L. Martin and Anne D. Neal, "Losing America's Memory: Historical Illiteracy in the 21st Century," a report by the American Council of Trustees and Alumni, February 16, 2000, Washington, DC, 3.

98. Carey, *The Federalist: Design for a Constitutional Republic*, 165.

99. Ibid.

100. See Edward B. McLean, "A Public Philosophy: Dangers, Possibilities, and Probabilities," in Statham, ed., *Public Philosophy and Political Science*, 57–71.

101. Carey, "On the Degeneration of Public Philosophy in America," 53.

102. Carey, *The Federalist: Design for a Constitutional Republic*, 166.

103. Kendall and Carey, *The Basic Symbols of the American Political Tradition*, 3.

104. Plato, *The Apology of Socrates*, Benjamin Jowett, trans. (Danbury, CT: Grolier Enterprises Corp., 1980), 26.

105. Bloom, *The Closing of the American Mind*, 381.

106. Plato, *Crito*, Benjamin Jowett, trans. (Danbury, CT: Grolier Enterprises Corp., 1980), 31–44.

Neo-Jacobin Nationalism or Responsible Nationhood? / *Claes G. Ryn*

1. Statement to the U.S. Congress, June 18, 2002, www.whitehouse.gov/news/releases/2002/06.

2. Jean-Jacques Rousseau, *The Basic Political Writings* (Indianapolis: Hackett, 1987) *Social Contract*, book 1, chapter 1, 141.

3. William Kristol and David Brooks, "What Ails Conservatism," *Wall Street Journal*, September 15, 1997.

4. Woodrow Wilson, speech to the U.S. Congress, Apr. 2, 1917.

5. Allan Bloom, *The Closing of the American Mind* (New York: Simon and Schuster, 1987), 153.

6. Remarks by President George W. Bush in taped interview with Bob Woodward, *Washington Post*, November 19, 2002, excerpted from Woodward, *Bush at War* (New York: Simon and Schuster, 2002).

7. Irving Kristol, "The Neoconservative Persuasion: What It Was and What It Is," *Weekly Standard*, August 25, 2003.

8. Kristol and Brooks, "What Ails Conservatism," *Wall Street Journal*, September 15, 1997.

9. Robert Kagan, "The U.S.-Europe Divide," *Washington Post*, May 26, 2002.

10. Harry Jaffa, "Equality as a Conservative Principle," in William F. Buckley and Charles R. Kessler, eds., *Keeping the Tablets* (New York: Harper and Row, 1970), 86.

11. Michael Ledeen, *The War Against the Terror Masters* (New York: St. Martin's Press, 2002), 213.

12. Benjamin Wattenberg, "Showdown Time . . . Wake-up Slap," *Washington Times*, August 8, 1990, and "To Sow Seeds of Freedom," *Washington Times*, August 1, 1990 (emphasis added).

13. Charles Krauthammer, "Bless Our Pax Americana," *Washington Post*, March 22, 1991 and *Time,* March 5, 2001.

14. Michael Novak, "Human Rights at Christmas," *Washington Times*, December 23, 1988.

15. Woodrow Wilson, Thanksgiving Proclamation, November 7, 1917, *The Papers of Woodrow Wilson*, Arthur S. Link, et al. (Princeton, NJ: Princeton University Press, 1966–93), 44, 525; and Address at Independence Hall, Philadelphia, *Papers*, 30, 254. For an in-depth study of Woodrow Wilson and his notion of America as servant of mankind, see Richard M. Gamble, "Savior Nation: Woodrow Wilson and the Gospel of Service," *Humanitas* 14, no. 1 (2001).

16. Irving Babbitt, *Democracy and Leadership* (Indianapolis: Liberty Fund, 1979), 314.

17. Secretary of State James A. Baker, speech to the Aspen Institute in Berlin, Germany, June 18, 1991.

18. Patrick E. Tyler, "U.S. Strategy Plan Calls for Insuring No Rivals Develop," *New York Times*, March 8, 1992.

19. *Wall Street Journal*, lead editorial, March 16, 1992.

20. Remarks of President to United Brotherhood of Carpenters and Joiners of America 2002 Legislative Conference, June 19, 2002, www.whitehouse.gov/news/releases/2002/06; Peter Slevin, "The Word at the White House: Bush Formulates His Brand of Foreign Policy," *Washington Post*, June 23, 2002.

21. Remarks of President to West Point Commencement, June 1, 2002, www.whitehouse.gov/news/releases/2002/06. The same kind of imagery had been used by General George C. Marshall at the commencement exercises in 1942, and the president began his speech by quoting Marshall, who had expressed the hope that "our flag will be recognized throughout the world as a symbol of freedom on the one hand, and of overwhelming power on the other."

22. *National Security Strategy of the United States of America*, September 17, 2002, http://www.whitehouse.gov/nsc/nss.html, and Karen DeYoung and Mike Allen, "Bush Shifts Strategy From Deterrence to Dominance," *Washington Post*, September 21, 2002.

23. Richard C. Hoolbrooke, "It Did Not Have to Be This Way," *Washington Post*, February 23, 2003.

24. *Washington Post*, November 3, 2002.

25. George W. Bush, speech to the nation, "America is Grateful for a Job Well Done," *Washington Post*, May 2, 2003.

26. George W. Carey and Willmoore Kendall, *The Basic Symbols of the American Political Tradition* (Baton Rouge, LA: Louisiana State University Press, 1970), 152–54.

27. President George W. Bush, opening statement at press conference on April 13, 2004.

28. George W. Carey, *The Federalist* (Urbana, IL: University of Illinois Press, 1989), 160. See also Carey and Kendall, *Basic Symbols*, and Carey, *In Defense of the Constitution* (Cumberland, VA: James River Press, 1989). For related and largely compatible explorations of the historical origins of American social and political thought, see Rus-

sell Kirk, *The Roots of American Order* (La Salle, IL: Open Court, 1974) and Forrest McDonald, *Novus Ordo Seclorum* (Lawrence, KS: University Press of Kansas, 1985).

29. For an in-depth discussion of universality and particularity with special reference to the issue of peace among individuals, peoples, and cultures, see Claes G. Ryn, *A Common Human Ground: Universality and Particularity in a Multicultural World* (Columbia, MO: University of Missouri Press, 2003).

30. For a study of neo-Jacobinism and the myth of America the Virtuous and how these relate to large moral, political, and cultural trends in the United States and the Western world, see Claes G. Ryn, *America the Virtuous: The Crisis of Democracy and the Quest for Empire* (New Brunswick, NJ: Transaction Publishers, 2003).

About the Contributors

John S. Baker, Jr., is Dale E. Bennett Professor of Law at the Louisiana State University Law Center. Among his books are *An Introduction to the Law of the United States* (with A. A. Levasseur) and *The Intelligence Edge* (with George Friedman, Meredith Friedman, and Colin Chapman). His articles have appeared in journals such as the *Cornell Law Review, Boston College Law Review,* and the *Notre Dame Journal of Law, Ethics, & Public Policy.*

Francis Canavan, S.J., is retired from teaching political science at Fordham University. He has authored numerous articles and essays on topics ranging from the thought of Edmund Burke to the role of morality in politics to American pluralism. Among his books are *Edmund Burke: Prescription and Providence, The Pluralist Game,* and *Freedom of Expression: Purpose as Limit.*

Bruce P. Frohnen is Visiting Associate Professor of Law at Ohio Northern University College of Law, editor of the *Political Science Reviewer,* and senior fellow at the Russell Kirk Center for Cultural Renewal. His books include *Virtue and the Promise of Conservatism: The Legacy of Burke and Tocqueville* and *American Conservatism: An Encyclopedia* (edited with Jeremy Beer and Jeffrey O. Nelson). His articles have appeared in many journals, including the *Harvard Journal of Law & Public Policy,* the *George Washington Law Review,* and the *American Journal of Jurisprudence.*

William Gangi is Professor of Government and Politics at St. John's University. He is the author of *Saving the Constitution from the Courts* and numerous essays and articles in academic journals and law reviews, including the *Washington University Law Review, Benchmark,* and the *Catholic Lawyer.*

Paul Edward Gottfried is Raffensperger Chair in Humanities at Elizabethtown College. A former Guggenheim Fellow, he is the author of many books, including *Conservatism in America: Making Sense of the American Right, Multiculturalism and the Politics of Guilt: Toward a Secular Theocracy,* and *After Liberalism: Mass Democracy in the Managerial State.*

Kenneth L. Grasso is Professor of Political Science and director of the Project on American Constitutionalism at Texas State University, San Marcos. He is editor, with Robert P. Hunt, of *A Moral Enterprise: Essays in Honor of Francis Canavan* and *John Courtney Murray and the American Civil Conversation.* His articles have appeared in journals such as the *American Political Science Review* and the *Review of Politics.*

Gary L. Gregg II holds the Mitch McConnell Chair in Leadership and is director of the McConnell Center at the University of Louisville. He is the author of *The Presidential Republic: Executive Representation and Deliberative Democracy.* His edited volumes include *Thinking About the Presidency: Documents and Essays from the Founding to the Present* and, with Mark Rozell, *Considering the Bush Presidency.* His articles have appeared in such outlets as *Presidential Studies Quarterly* and *Perspectives on Political Science.*

Peter Augustine Lawler is Dana Professor of Government and International Studies at Berry College and executive editor of *Perspectives on Political Science.* Among his books are *Homeless and at Home in America, Stuck with Virtue: The American Individual and our Biotechnological Future,* and *Postmodernism Rightly Understood.* His many articles have appeared in such journals as *First Things,* the *American Political Science Review,* the *Journal of Politics,* and the *Review of Politics.*

Gordon Lloyd is a professor in the School of Public Policy at Pepperdine University. His articles have appeared in journals from the *Political Science Reviewer* to *Leviathan: A Journal of Politics and the Arts.* Among his books are *The Essential Antifederalist* (edited with W. B. Allen) and *The Essential Bill of Rights* (edited with Margie Lloyd).

Donald S. Lutz is Professor of Political Science at the University of Houston. Among his books are *The Origins of American Constitutionalism* and *Prin-*

ciples of Constitutional Design. His articles have appeared in such periodicals as the *American Political Science Review, Publius: The Journal of Federalism,* and the *Emory Law Journal*.

Jeffry Morrison is an associate professor in the Department of Government at Regent University. He is the author of *John Witherspoon and the Founding of the American Republic* and the editor, with Daniel L. Dreisbach and Mark David Hall, of *The Founders on God and Government*. His *The Political Philosophy of George Washington* will be published in 2009.

Claes G. Ryn is Professor of Politics at the Catholic University of America, chairman of the National Humanities Institute, and editor of *Humanitas.* Among his books are *America the Virtuous: The Crisis of Democracy and the Quest for Empire* and *A Common Human Ground: Universality and Particularity in a Multicultural World*. His work has appeared in numerous journals in the United States, Sweden, and China, where he served as Distinguished Foreign Scholar at Peking University in 2000.

E. Robert Statham, Jr., is a fellow at Liberty Fund, Inc. Among his books are *The Constitution of Public Philosophy: Toward a Synthesis of Freedom and Responsibility in Postmodern America* and *Public Philosophy and Political Science: Crisis and Reflection* (editor). His articles have appeared in a number of journals, including *Modern Age* and the *Journal of Legislative Studies*.

Quentin Taylor is Associate Professor of History and Political Science at Rogers State University. Among his books are *The Essential Federalist: A New Reading of The Federalist Papers* (editor) and *The Republic of Genius: A Reconstruction of Nietzsche's Early Thought*. His articles have appeared in such journals as *Humanitas* and the *Independent Review*.

Index

A

abortion, 21–22, 46, 161, 193, 194

Adair, Douglas, xiii, 107, 132

Adams, John, 123, 132, 133, 136

"Address to the Inhabitants of Jamaica" (Witherspoon), 125

administrative state: horizontal and vertical federalism and, 202–10; police power and, 215–19; Senate, U.S. and, 201–2, 204–7; states, horizontal balance among and, 210–15; Supreme Court, U.S. and, 201

affirmative action, 225

Albright, Madeline, 275

America: divided soul of, 50–53; philosophy in, 138

American Bar Association, 216

American Enterprise Institute, 268

American Philosophical Society, 136

American Political Science Association, ix, 105

American Political Science Review, ix

American political tradition: alternative interpretations of, xi–xii; American morality and, xxiii; Bill of Rights, U.S. and, x–xi, x; consensus and, xi, xii, xxi; Constitution, U.S. and, x–xi, x, xii, 3, 18, 19; crisis of, 245–62;

Declaration of Independence and, x–xi, x, xii, 27, 28; Enlightenment and, x, 253–54; equality and, ix, xi; fanaticism and, xi, xii; federalism and, xviii, 22; *The Federalist* and, xii; founders and, xii–xiii; freedom and, ix, xi; human nature and, xi; judiciary, new role of and, xxi; limited government and, 22; Locke, John and, 37–53; majoritarianism and, 3–15; moderation and, xi; official literature on, ix, x; origin of, ix, x–xi; progressivism and, 35; public philosophy and, 260–62; reason and, 257–60; religion and, 25–26; republicanism and, 22; rights and, ix, xi, 236–37; self-government and, x, xi; separation of powers and, 22; symbols of, 246–47, 261; virtue and, xviii, xx, 252

The American Republic (Brownson), 38

American Revolution, 63, 100, 117, 125, 130, 131, 269

American Spectator, ix

anticommunism, 11. *See also* communism

Antifederalists, 6, 105; Bill of Rights, U.S. and, 60, 64, 84, 103; central government and, 260; Constitution,

U.S. and, 64; necessary and proper clause and, 88; Philadelphia Constitution of 1787 and, 79; ratification debates and, 103; representation and, 140, 142; states and, 203

anti-sodomy laws, 44

Apology (Plato), 262

Appeal to Common Sense in Behalf of Religion (Oswald), 127

Aquinas, St. Thomas, 40, 169

Aristotle, 12, 42, 58, 119, 170, 246, 252

Articles of Confederation, 83, 85, 87, 95, 96, 100, 102, 109, 154, 204

B

Babbitt, Irving, 272

Bailyn, Bernard, 105

Baker, James, 273

Baldwin, Abraham, 87

Balog, Frank, 132

The Basic Symbols of the American Political Tradition (Carey and Kendall), viii, ix–x, xii, 3–4, 10, 19, 25–26, 58, 78, 177

Beard, Charles, 103, 104, 105

Beatty, James, 132

Bennett, William, 267

Bentham, Jeremy, xxii

Berkeley, George, 128, 132, 135

Berman, Harold J., 187

Bible, 50–51, 128, 184, 190

bicameralism, 4–5, 112

Bill of Rights, U.S.: American political tradition and, x, x–xi; Antifederalists and, 60, 64, 84; Congress and, 77; English common law and, 60–61, 63–64, 74–76; *The Federalist* and, 99–100; founders and, 99; freedom and, 99; Madison, James and, 60, 63, 64, 65–69 (table), 69–70, 70–74 (table), 74–75, 156; origin of, 60–76; penumbras and emanations and, 160;

rights, roots of and, 59, 60–76; state bills of rights and, 70–74 (table), 74–75; state constitutions and, 60; state ratifying conventions and, 65–69 (table), 69–70. *See also* rights

Bingham, John A., 157

Black, Hugo, 160

Blackmun, Harry, 161–62

Bloom, Allan, 259, 267

Bowers v. Hardwick, 161, 164–65

Bradley, Gerard V., 182

Brave New World, 48

Brearley, David, 87

Brearley Committee, 87

Brooks, David, 47, 48, 266, 267, 268

Brownson, Orestes, 38–42, 43, 53

Brown v. Board of Education, 225, 226, 227

bureaucracy, 201

Burke, Edmund, 34

Burnham, James, 151

Burns, James MacGregor, 104

Burr, Aaron, 125

Bush, George H. W., 273, 274

Bush, George W., 52, 264–65, 266, 267, 273–75, 277

Butler, Pierce, 87

C

Calhoun, John C., 97, 151, 203

Calvin, John, 199

Calvinism, 51, 135

Campbell, Ballard C., 192

Canavan, Francis, 184, 186, 187, 188

Carey, George W.: American political tradition and, ix–xviii, xxvi–xxvii, 185, 236, 237, 246–47, 248–50, 251; background of, vii–ix; commerce clause and, 193; communities and, 30–31, 32–33; conservatism and, vii, xxvi–xxvii, 37, 43; Constitution, U.S. and, 17–19, 221; constitutional morality and, xix–xxiii, 18, 23–25, 122; constitutions and, 18–23; democratic theory and, xxiii–xxviii; education of, vii–viii; *The Federalist* and, 3, 13–14, 18, 41; human sociability and, vii; judicial activism and, 153–54; judicial review and, 5, 38; Kendall, Willmoore and, vii, viii, xxvii, 3; Locke, John and, 37; majoritarianism and, 3–15; non-interpretivism and, 224, 229, 231, 232, 233; Philadelphia Constitution of 1787 and, 79–80, 96; politics and, vii; religion and education and, 122; religious pluralism and American Experiment and, 177, 187, 192; rights, roots of and, 59, 78; as scholar, xxvii–xxx, 3; as teacher, viii, xxix; tradition and, 33–35; virtue and constitutional limits and, 29–31; as writer, viii–ix

Carroll, Daniel, 87

Catholicism, Catholics, 184, 196; founding and, 38–42; Kendall, Willmoore and, 4

Ceaser, James W., 52

Champion v. Ames, 217

Chase, Salmon, 202

checks and balances, xiv–xv, xiv, 99, 100

Cheney, Richard, 265

China, 269

Chisholm v. Georgia, 137

Christianity, 38, 40, 51–52, 182–83

Citizen of New Haven Letters (Sherman), 94

citizenship, 59, 60

civil rights, 8, 157–58, 205, 225

Civil Rights Act of 1866, 157

Civil Rights Act of 1964, 225

Civil War, U.S., xi, 38–39, 103, 157, 202, 205, 216

Claremont Institute, 268

Clay, Henry, 151

Clinton, Bill, 44, 274

The Closing of the American Mind (Bloom), 267

Colden, Cadwallader, 131

Cold War, 11, 267, 268, 272

College of New Jersey. *See* Princeton University

Commentary, 268

Common Sense (Paine), 127, 130

communism, 6, 11, 267, 276–77

The Communist Mind (Kirk), 11

community, 80, 87; constitutions and, 30–31; good and, 246; ordered liberty and, 139; Supreme Court, U.S. and, 33–34

Community and Tradition: Conservative Perspectives on the American Experience (ed. Carey), ix

confederation, 14, 79, 203

Conflicts of Law (Story), 211, 215

Congress: bicameralism and, 4–5; Bill of Rights, U.S. and, 77; Constitution, U.S. and, 9; extended republic and, xv–xvi; faction and, xv–xvi; *The Federalist* and, 3; judicial review and, xvi–xvii; necessary and proper clause and, 87–94; rights and, 59; supremacy of, 3, 9

Connecticut, 94

Connecticut Compromise, 84–85, 86–87, 88, 112

consensus: American political tradition and, xi, xii, xxi; Christianity and, 182–83; civic unity and, 178–79; conditions of, 181; faction and, 26; founders and, xiii; fragmentation of, 6; majoritarianism and, 9–12; multiculturalism and, 10; religious pluralism and, 178–79, 181–83, 197; self-government and, 9–10, 15

conservatism: Carey, George W. and, vii, xxvi–xxvii, 37, 43; challenges confronting, xxiii; character of, xxvii; congressional supremacy and, 9;

consensus and, 11–12; Constitution, U.S. and, xxx; *The Federalist* and, 148; libertarianism vs., xxvii; Locke, John and, 52; national government and, xxvii; natural law and, xxvii; nature of, xxiii; neo-, 37, 268–70; progressivism and, 43; tradition and, xxvii; virtue and, xxvii

Conservatism versus Liberalism (Carey and Kendall), 10

The Conservative Intellectual Movement in American Since 1945 (Nash), 4

Constitution, U.S.: abortion and, 22; American political tradition and, x–xi, xii, 3, 18, 19, 257; articles of peace and, 180–81, 182–85; Bill of Rights, U.S., 99, 156; checks and balances and, xiv–xv, 99; commerce clause of, 193, 217–18; as compact, 57–58, 77; constitutional morality and, xiii–xiv, 23; Declaration of Independence and, 11, 19, 20, 26, 28–29; due process clause of, 158–60, 163; equality and, 19; equal protection clause of, 163; extended republic and, 116; federalism and, xvi, 22, 99, 210–11; *The Federalist* and, 37, 106; Fifth Amendment, 166; First Amendment, 156, 159–60, 180–81, 182, 188–89, 190–91, 227–28; Fourteenth Amendment, 104, 157–58, 159, 162, 163–66, 215, 225; freedom and, 31, 250–51; full faith and credit clause of, 211–13; general-welfare clause of, 81; interstate-commerce clause of, 81; judicial review and, xvii, 99; judicial supremacy and, xx–xxi; majoritarianism and, 3, 4, 14–15; "manifest tenor" of, xvii, xx, 5; meaning of, 17, 159; natural law and, 28–29; nature of, 17, 18–19; necessary and proper clause of, xvi, 81, 82, 83, 87–94; Ninth Amendment, 156; as organic act, 57–58, 77; original understanding of, viii, 19; partly federal, partly national concept and, 87; penumbras and emanations and, 160, 223; police power and, 218–19; preamble to, xxiii, 155–56; preemption doctrine and, 207–10; privileges and immunities clause of, 211–13; progressivism and, 20, 26, 43, 251–52; purpose of, 17, 20–21, 22–23, 154, 155–56; ratification of, 95–96, 106; republican government and, 31, 57; republicanism and, xxii, 22; rights and, 59, 99, 156–66; self-government and, 23; separation of powers and, xiv–xv, 22, 99; Seventeenth Amendment, 80–81, 201; supremacy clause of, 207, 208–9; Supreme Court, U.S. and, xxi, 44, 78, 81, 97, 157, 159, 221; Tenth Amendment, 95, 156; Thirteenth Amendment, 157; virtue and, 23, 252. *See also* Constitutional Convention of 1787; Philadelphia Constitution of 1787; *The Federalist*

Constitutional Convention of 1787, 81, 97; bill of rights and, 88; Connecticut Compromise and, 204; federalism and, xviii; Madison, James and, 88–91; national university and, 94, 122; necessary and proper clause and, 87–94; New Jersey Plan and, 85; Virginia Plan and, 84, 86, 87, 88–90, 96, 110, 112. *See also* Constitution, U.S.; Philadelphia Constitution of 1787

constitutionalism, 17, 21, 30, 122, 250

constitutional law: destruction of, 221–43; non-interpretivism and, 222–34; refounding of, 222, 234–40

constitutional morality, 18; Constitution, U.S. and, xiii–xiv; constitutional structure and, 24–25; elements of, 23–24; *The Federalist* and, xiii–xiv, xviii, 23, 80, 122; founders and, 80,

249; judicial review and, xiv; Kirk, Russell and, 11; ordered liberty and, 24; Philadelphia Constitution of 1787 and, 82; self-government and, 80

constitutions: character of people and, 18; community and, 30–31, 32–33; government and, 18; as laws, 18; natures of, 18–21; politics and, 18; purposes of, 21–23, 29; rights and, 19–20; self-government and, 25–29; structures of, 18, 19, 24–25; virtue and limits of, 29–31

contraception, 160–61, 193

cosmopolitanism, 264, 280–81

Croly, Herbert, 81

Cuba, 269

culture war, religious pluralism and, 178, 192–93, 198

D

Dahl, Robert, 104, 105

Dallas, University of, viii

Darwin, Charles, 42

Darwinism, 42

Davie, Jonathan, 86

Declaration of Independence, 11, 103, 123, 185; "all men are created equal" clause of, xii, 20; American political tradition and, x–xi, x, xii, 27, 28; Constitution, U.S. and, 11, 19, 20, 26, 28–29; culture and, 257; equality and, 19, 20, 26; freedom and, 48; historical context of, xii; independence and, 26; individual rights and, 26; Locke, John and, 134; natural law and, 28–29; new interpretation of, xi; political theory of, xii; purpose of, 26–27; rights and, 76–77; social-contract theory and, 28; Supreme Court, U.S. and, 44

Defense of Marriage Act (DOMA), 213, 215

Delaware, bill of rights of, 71–74 (table)

deliberation, xi, xxiv, 13, 146, 148–49, 151

democracy: contemporary theory of, xxiii–xxv; deadlock of, 20; deliberation and, xxiv; elections and, xxiv; equality and, 247–48; *The Federalist* and, xxiv; freedom and, 38; hyper-, 255–56; intensity problem and, xxv, 229–34; Madison, James and, xxiv–xxv, 230–34; majority and, xxv; meaning of, xxiii; organic, 9; plebiscitary, xiv, xxii, xxiii–xxv, 79; pluralism and, 6; populistic, xxiii, xxiv; unanimity and, xxv; U.S. foreign policy and, 271

Democracy in America (Tocqueville), 183, 248

Democratic Party, Democrats, 44, 268, 275

democratism, 271, 272

Descartes, Rene, 136

desegregation, 225

Diamond, Martin, 9

Dickinson, John, 85, 87, 94–95

DiSalvo, Daniel, 52

"Dissertation on Liberty and Necessity, Pleasure and Pain" (Franklin), 136

divorce, 45–46

Documents Illustrative of the Formation of the Union of the American States (Tansill), 154

DOMA. *See* Defense of Marriage Act

domestic tranquility, xxiii, xxvi

Dred Scott v. Sandford, 158

Dunn, John, 169–70

E

Eco, Umberto, 173

An Economic Interpretation of the Constitution (Beard), 103

education: founders and, 121–38; ordered

liberty and, 122; political, 122; religion and, 121–22; religious pluralism and, 192–93; self-government and, 121–22; virtue and, 122–23; Witherspoon, John and, 122–38

Edwards, Jonathan, 123, 127, 128, 131, 132, 133

egalitarianism, 248; malleability of, 251; permissive, 251; secular liberalism and, xxii, xxiii. *See also* equality

election: democracy and, xxiv; of House of Representatives, U.S., 82–83; of president, 83, 87, 145; of Senate, U.S., 80–81, 82–83, 111–12

Electoral College, 82–83, 144, 145

Ellsworth, Oliver, 85–86, 90, 91, 94, 95

English Bill of Rights (1689), 60, 61 (table), 63

English common law: Bill of Rights, U.S. and, 60–61, 63–64, 74–76; Madison, James and, 63; rights and, 78

English Petition of Right (1628), 60, 63

Enlightenment, xi, 48, 135, 196, 198–99; American, 131; American political tradition and, 247, 253–54; Constitution, U.S. and, 3; progressivism and, 35; religion and, 260; Scottish, 107, 127, 131, 199; secularism of, x; tradition and, 34–35

equality: American political tradition and, ix, xi; of condition, xxii; Constitution, U.S. and, 19; Declaration of Independence and, 19, 20, 26; democracy and, 247–48; destructive nature of, viii; freedom and, 38; as ideal, viii; legal, 22; liberalism and, 162; majoritarianism and, 13; overvaluation of, 247–48; political, viii. *See also* egalitarianism

An Essay Concerning Human Understanding (Locke), 168

Ethics and Public Policy Center, 268

European Commission, 210

European Union (EU), 209, 210

Exodus, Book of, 177

extended republic: Constitution, U.S. and, 116; faction and, xv–xvi, 102, 104, 107–11; *The Federalist* and, xv–xvi, 5–6, 103–4, 107, 111, 260; freedom and, 99; legislature and, xv–xvi; Madison, James and, 5–6, 107–19; majoritarianism and, 260; pluralism of, xv–xvi; president and, 145; size of, xv–xvi

F

Fabius Essay VIII (Dickinson), 95

faction: bicameralism and, 4–5; Congress and, xv–xvi; consensus and, 26; constitutional structure and, 24; extended republic and, xv–xvi, 102, 104, 107–11; federalism and, 37; *The Federalist* and, xv–xvi, xix–xx, 24, 26; Madison, James and, 102, 104, 107–11; pluralism and, 10; power, abuse of and, xiv; republicanism and, xiv, 5, 102; separation of powers and, xiv; state laws and, 109; Union and, 107

family, 162

fanaticism, xi

federalism, xiv; American political tradition and, xviii, 22; Constitution, U.S. and, xvi, 22, 99, 210–11; Constitutional Convention and, xviii; faction and, 37; *The Federalist* and, xvi, 187; founders and, 81; freedom and, 99; Hamilton, Alexander and, 88; horizontal, 201, 202–10; horizontal-vertical balance of, 202–10; original understanding of, 45; religious pluralism and, 187–89, 193–94; rights and, 59; Senate, U.S., democratization of, 204–7; Seventeenth Amendment and, 81; states and, 45;

vertical, 201, 202–10

The Federalist, viii; bicameralism and, 5; Bill of Rights, U.S. and, 99–100; Carey, George W. and, 3, 13–14, 18, 41; checks and balances and, xiv–xv, 100; coherence of, xiii; common sense and, 127; congressional supremacy and, 3; conservatism and, 148; Constitution, U.S. and, 37, 106; constitutionalism and, 250; constitutional morality and, xiii–xiv, xviii, 23, 80, 122; constitutional order and, xiii–xiv; constitutions, purposes of and, 30; contemporary understanding of, xiv; democracy and, xxiv; extended republic and, xv–xvi, 5–6, 103–4, 107, 111, 260; faction and, xv–xvi, xix–xx, 24, 26; federalism and, xvi, 187; Hamilton, Alexander and, xiii, 103; House of Representatives, U.S. and, 142–43; human nature and, 143; Jay, John and, 103; judicial review and, xvi–xvii, 5; justice and, 185; Madison, James and, xiii, 102–3; majoritarianism and, 13; modern critique of, 104–6; necessary and proper clause and, xvi, 88; president and, 145–49; privileges and immunities clause and, 212; representation and, 140–42; republicanism and, xxii, 80; Senate, U.S. and, 143–45; separation of powers and, xiv–xv, 139–40; state vs. federal governments and, xvi; Supreme Court, U.S. and, 104; virtue and, 14, 29. *See also* Constitution, U.S.

The Federalist: Design for a Constitutional Republic (Carey), viii, xiii, 5, 9

Federalists, 79, 95, 96, 104

The Federalist: The Gideon Edition (ed. Carey), ix

feminism, 42, 256

Fifth Amendment, 161, 166

First Amendment, 156, 159–60, 180–81, 182, 188–89, 190–91, 227

founders: Bill of Rights, U.S. and, 99; consensus and, xiii; constitutional morality and, 80, 249; education and, 121–38; federalism and, 81; freedom and, 37; human nature and, xii–xiii, 37; importance of, xii–xiii; individual rights and, 153–54; judicial review and, xiv, xvi, 234–35; Locke, John and, 38, 39; natural rights and, 43; ordered liberty and, xiii; popular government and, xiv; republicanism and, xiv; rule of law and, 249; self-government and, xiii, 15; virtue and, 14, 30

Founding Fathers. *See* founders

Fourteenth Amendment, 104, 157–58, 159, 161, 162, 163–66, 215, 225

framers. *See* founders

France, 52, 53, 269

Franklin, Benjamin, 86, 93, 134, 135, 136

freedom: American political tradition and, ix, xi; Bill of Rights, U.S. and, 99; checks and balances and, 99; Constitution, U.S. and, 31, 250–51; Declaration of Independence and, 48; democracy and, 38; equality and, 38; extended republic and, 99; federalism and, 99; founders and, 37; judicial review and, 99; libertarianism and, xxvii; limited government and, 99; Locke, John and, 48–49; pursuit of happiness and, 49–50; of religion, 40; rights and, 99; self-government and, xi; separation of powers and, 99; of speech, 28. *See also* ordered liberty

Freedom and Virtue: The Libertarian/Conservative Debate (ed. Carey), ix

French *philosophes,* x, 34

French Revolution, 34, 40, 48, 247, 265

Fundamental orders of Connecticut, x

G

gambling, 202, 203
gay marriage, 44, 46–47, 163, 165, 213
Gelernter, David, 189, 193, 194
Georgetown University, viii, 57
German Basic law, 20
Gerry, Elbridge, 86–87, 92
Gerry Committee Report. *See* Connecticut Compromise
Gibbons v. Ogden, 207
Gilman, Nicholas, 87
Glorious Revolution of 1688, 26
gnosticism, 43
God, xi, 25, 27, 40, 42, 50, 169, 173, 177, 271
Goldman, Eric, 11
Gore, Al, 52
Gorham, Nathaniel, 90
government: constitutions and, 18; education and, 121–22; energy in, 100; limited, xiv, 22, 40, 99; national, xvii–xviii; ordered liberty and, 18; people and, 249–50; popular, xiv; positive, 5; rights and, 59; society vs., 14. *See also* republican government; self-government
governmental tyranny, xiv
Great Britain, 26
Great Compromise. *See* Connecticut Compromise
Great Society, 81, 192
Great Tradition, 4
Greeks, 21, 277
Green, Ashbel, 132
Griswold v. Connecticut, 160
Guinness, Os, 182

H

Hamilton, Alexander, 86, 108, 118; American Revolution and, 131; common sense and, 127; Constitutional Convention of 1787 and, 94; extended republic and, 107; faction and, 110–11; federalism and, 88; *The Federalist* and, xiii, 103; privileges and immunities clause and, 212; rights and, 130–31
Hamilton, Sir William, 131
Hartz, Louis, 41
Hegel, Georg Wilhelm Friedrich, 48
Heritage Foundation, 268
Hines v. Davidowitz, 207
Hiroshima, Japan, 11
historicism, historicists, 78
Hobbes, Thomas, 143, 167, 170–72
Hofstadter, Richard, 104, 105
Holbrooke, Richard C., 275
homosexuality, 46, 161, 163, 165
Hook, Sidney, 271
Hoover Institution, 268
House of Representatives, U.S.: election of, 82–83; *The Federalist* and, 142–43; horizontal and vertical federalism and, 203; representation in, 142–43
Howard, Jacob M., 158
How Democratic Is the American Constitution? (Dahl), 105
Hughes, Charles Evans, 159
humanism, xxi–xxiii
human nature, 80; American political tradition and, xi; Constitution, U.S. and, 276; *The Federalist* and, 143; founders and, xii–xiii, 37; limitations and imperfections of, xi; Locke, John and, 37; self-government and, 100; transformation of, 81
Hume, David, 107–8, 127, 128, 132, 135, 137, 168
Humphrey, Hubert, 272
Hunter, James Davison, 177, 184, 195, 198
Hutcheson, Francis, 126, 133

Hyneman, Charles, vii, viii, xx, 191, 194

I

Illinois, University of, viii
Incarnation, 271
In Defense of the Constitution (Carey), viii, xiii
Indiana University, viii
individualism, xxvii, 37, 40; Christianity and, 51–52; Locke, John and, 51; marriage and, 46; Tocqueville, Alexis de and, 47–48, 51–52
intensity, xxv, 229–34
"The 'Intensity' Problem in Democratic Theory" (Carey and Kendall), viii, 12
Intercollegiate Review, ix
Intercollegiate Studies Institute (ISI), ix
interpretivism, 222–28
Interstate Commerce Act, 217
Isaiah, Prophet, 276
ISI. *See* Intercollegiate Studies Institute

J

Jackson, Henry "Scoop," 272
Jacobinism, French, 247, 265
Jaffa, Harry, 269
Jay, John, 5, 103, 108
Jefferson, Thomas, xii, 44, 105, 115, 116, 136, 137; Declaration of Independence and, 257; education and, 121; morality and, 186; philosophy of, 127, 128–29, 130, 133–34, 135
Jesus Christ, 186, 252
Jews, 184
"John Locke Revisited" (Kendall), 4
Johnson, Samuel, 131, 132
Jones v. Rath Packing Co., 207
Journal of Politics, ix
Jouvenel, Bertrand de, 255

Judaism, 196
judicial activism, xx
"Judicial Activism and Regime Change" (Carey), 153
judicial review: centralization and, 38; civil rights and, 157–58; Constitution, U.S. and, xvii, 99; constitutional morality and, xiv; *The Federalist* and, xvi–xvii, 5; founders and, xiv, xvi, 234–35; freedom and, 99; legislative power and, xvi–xvii; noninterpretivism and, 240; rights and, 158; state vs. federal governments and, xvi; Supreme Court, U.S. and, xvii, 5, 235
judicial supremacy, xx–xxi, 235
judiciary: American political tradition and, xxi; constitutional interpretation by, xvii; judicial activism and, xx; judicial review and, xvi–xvii; judicial supremacy and, xx–xxi; legislative power and, xvi–xvii; legitimacy of, xxi; Philadelphia Constitution of 1787 and, 96–97; public policy and, 221–28, 228–34; republicanism and, xxi; transformation in the role of, xx–xxi. *See also* Supreme Court, U.S.
Judiciary Act of 1789, 59
justice, xi, xxiii, 7, 185

K

Kagan, Robert, 267, 268, 275–76
Kant, Immanuel, 135
Kendall, Nellie, viii
Kendall, Willmoore, 19, 150, 151; American political tradition and, 185, 236, 237; *The Basic Symbols of the American Political Tradition* and, x, 3; Carey, George W. and, vii, viii, xxvii, 3; Catholicism and, 4; federalism and, 188; majoritarianism and, 4, 6–13;

Mill, John Stuart and, 6, 12; non–interpretivism and, 224, 229, 231, 232; open society and, 6–7; Philadelphia Constitution of 1787 and, 79–80, 96; relativism and, 8; religion and education and, 122; religious pluralism and American Experiment and, 177, 178, 188, 189; rights, roots of and, 78; socialism and, 4; Strauss, Leo and, 4
Kennedy, Anthony, 43–44, 164
Kennedy, John F., xii
King, Rufus, 86, 87, 93, 111
Kirk, Russell, 11
Kneir, Charles, viii
Kramer, Larry, 240, 241
Krauthammer, Charles, 267, 271, 275
Kristol, Irving, 267, 268
Kristol, William, 266, 267, 268
kulturkampf, 194, 198, 199

L

Lasch, Christopher, 6
law, rule of, 22, 248–49
Law, Thomas, 129
Lawrence v. Texas, 164
Laycock, Douglas, 211
Lectures on Moral Philosophy (Witherspoon), 126, 127, 128, 133, 135, 136, 137, 138
Ledeen, Michael, 267, 270
Lee, Richard Henry, 140
Left, 6, 8, 11, 57
legislature. *See* Congress
Leuchtenberg, William, 11
Leviathan (Hobbes), 170
Levy, Leonard W., 167
liberalism, liberals, vii, xxi–xxiii, 162
Liberalism Versus Conservatism: The Continuing Debate in American Government (ed. Carey and Kendall), viii
libertarianism, xxvii, 4, 42, 43–44, 51
libertinism, 47

liberty. *See* freedom
Liberty Fund, Inc., ix
limited government, xiv; American political tradition and, 22; Christianity and, 40; Constitution, U.S. and, 22, 99; constitutionalism and, 30; freedom and, 99
Lincoln, Abraham, xi, xii, 10, 11, 20, 43, 202
Lippmann, Walter, 245, 247, 248
Locke, John, x, 4, 137; American divided soul and, 50–53; American political tradition and, 37–53; autonomous individual and, 42, 43; Carey, George W. and, 37; Catholicism and, 38–42; conservatism and, 52; Constitution, U.S. and, 44; Declaration of Independence and, 134; family and, 39; founders and, 38, 39; freedom and, 48–49; French Revolution and, 48; human nature and, 37; individualism and, 51; libertarianism and, 4; majoritarianism and, 4; marriage and, 39, 45–47; nominalism and, 167–70; philosophy of, 167–70; progress and, 47–50; pursuit of happiness and, 49–50; religion and, 48; sovereignty and, 39
logistikon, 13
Longman, Phillip, 52
Lowi, Theodore J., ix
Luther, Martin, 199

M

McCulloch v. Maryland, 207
MacIntyre, Alasdaire, 197
McWilliams, Carey, 43
Madison, James, 125, 153–54, 246; Bill of Rights, U.S. and, 60, 63, 64, 65–69 (table), 69–70, 70–74 (table), 74–75, 156; Constitution, U.S. and, 102–3; Constitutional Convention

of 1787 and, 88–91; democracy and, xxiv–xxv, 230–34; education and, 121; English common law and, 63; extended republic and, 5–6, 107–19; faction and, 102, 104, 107–11; *The Federalist* and, xiii, 102–3; modern critique of, 104–6; necessary and proper clause and, 88–91; Philadelphia Constitution of 1787 and, 83–84, 87; republicanism and, 88; states, representation of and, 86

"The Madman" (Nietzsche), 258

Magna Carta (1215), 26, 60–61, 61–62 (table), 63, 64

majoritarianism: American political tradition and, 3–15; Carey, George W. and, 3–15; consensus and, 9–12; Constitution, U.S. and, 3, 4, 14–15; democracy and, xxv; equality and, 13; extended republic and, 260; *The Federalist* and, 13; Kendall, Willmoore and, 6–13; natural law and, 28; progressivism and, 25; secular liberalism and, xxii; self-government and, 4, 28; virtue and, 13

"Majority Rule Revisited" (Carey), 6

managerial state, 7

Mansfield, Harvey, 43

marriage: individualism and, 46; Locke, John and, 39, 45–47; Philadelphia Constitution and, 45; same-sex, 44, 46, 163, 165, 213

Marsden, George, 199

Marshall, John, 5, 81, 94, 97, 207

Martin, Luther, 89, 155

Martin v. Hunter's Lesee, 207

Marx, Karl, 48, 104

Maryland, bill of rights of, 70, 71–74 (table)

Mason, George, 86, 88, 92, 93

Massachusetts: bill of rights of, 70, 71–74 (table); necessary and proper clause of, 83

Massachusetts Body of Liberties, x–xi

Massachusetts Body of Liberties (1641), 61, 61–62 (table), 76, 236–37

Massachusetts Declaration of Rights (1780), 76

May, Henry, 186

Mayer, Frederick, 135

Mayflower Compact, x, 3, 236

media, 266–67

"Memorial and Remonstrance" (Madison), 108

Mendelson, Wallace, 224

messianism, xi

Middle Ages, 21, 172

Mill, John Stuart, 6, 12

Modern Age, ix, 6

monarchy, 109–10

Montesquieu, Charles de Secondat, 107, 139

morality. *See* constitutional morality

Morris, Gouverneur, 87, 89, 91, 94

Moynihan, Daniel Patrick, 272

multiculturalism, 6, 10, 256

Muravchik, Joshua, 267

Murray, John Courtney, 38–42, 43, 48, 53, 178–80, 181–82, 257

N

Nagel, Robert F., 194

The Name of the Rose (Eco), 173

Nash, George H., 4

National Council on the Humanities, ix

national government, xvii–xviii, xxi

National Review, ix, 268

National Security Strategy, 274

National University, 94, 122, 125

natural law: conservatism and, xxvii; Constitution, U.S. and, 28–29; Declaration of Independence and, 28–29; majority rule and, 28; morality and, 186; prudence and, vii; rights and, 28; self-government and, 29; Western civilization and, vii

natural rights. *See* rights

The Nature of True Virtue (Edwards), 133

necessary and proper clause, xvi

neoconservativsm, 37, 52, 268–70

neo-Jacobinism, U.S. foreign policy and, 265–81

neo-Marxism, 103

Neo-Platonism, 13

neutrality, 110, 116

New Deal, xix, 159, 192, 201, 217

New Hampshire, 71–74 (table)

New Jersey Plan, 85

New Jerusalem, xii

New Republic, 268

Newsweek, 268

Newton, Isaac, 135

New World Order, 273

New York, 76

New York Times, 273

New York v. United States, 210

Nietzsche, Friedrich, 48, 198, 258

Ninth Amendment, 156

Nisbet, Robert, 254

NLRB v. Jones & Laughlin Steel, 218

nominalism, 167–70, 172–73

non-interpretivism, 221–34

North Carolina, bill of rights of, 71–74 (table)

Northwestern University School of Law, vii

Northwest Ordinance of 1787, 121, 122

Novak, David, 198–99

Novak, Michael, 267, 271

O

Oakeshott, Michael, 19, 27, 59, 78, 170, 172

obscenity, 191

On Paradise Drive (Brooks), 48

On the Law of Nature and Nations (Pufendorf), 126

open society, critique of, 6–7, 12

ordered liberty, 223; community and, 139; Constitution, U.S. and, 22–23; constitutional morality and, 24; education and, 122; founders and, xiii; government and, 18; republican government and, 22–23; secular liberalism and, xxiii. *See also* freedom

The Origins of American Constitutionalism (Lutz), 77

Ortega y Gasset, José, 245, 255–56

orthodoxy, 12–13

Oswald, James, 127

P

Paine, Thomas, 127, 130

Parrington, Vernon, 104

Paterson, William, 85, 86

patriotism, 113

Paul, St., 247

Pax Americana, 273

Pendleton, Edmund, 115

Penn, William, 76

Pennoyer v. Neff, 215

Pennsylvania, 95; bill of rights of, 70, 71–74 (table), 76; necessary and proper clause of, 83

Pennsylvania Declaration of Rights (1776), 76

Pennsylvania v. Nelson, 207

people: American political tradition and, xxvi; constituent will of, xvii; government and, 249–50; Philadelphia Constitution and, xxi; political will of, xvii; self-understanding of, x; state vs. federal governments and, xvi

Perez v. United States, 218

Perle, Richard, 267

Pfeffer, Leo, 161

Philadelphia Constitution of 1787, 21; Articles of Confederation vs., 96; bill of rights and, 95; Carey, George W. and, 79–80; constitutional morality and, 82; as dead, 80–81, 96–97, 245; judiciary and, 96–97; Madison, James and, 83–84; marriage and, 45; meaning of, 80; necessary and proper clause and, 83, 87–94; partly federal, partly national concept and, 82–87, 90–91, 94–95; people and, xxi; progressives and, 81, 96–97; ratification of, 83; representation and, 85–86; republicanism and, 79; republicanism of, 88; revolutionary character of, xxi; states, representation of and, 85–86; structure of, 80–81. *See also* Constitution, U.S.; Constitutional Convention of 1787

Philadelphia Convention, xiii. *See* Constitutional Convention of 1787

philosophes, x, 34

physician-assisted suicide, 163

Pinckney, Charles Cotesworth, 86, 87, 91, 93

Planned Parenthood, 160

Planned Parenthood v. Casey, 166–67

Plato, 13, 252

Platonism, 13

plebiscitary democracy, xiv, xxii, xxiii–xxiv, 79

pluralism, 117; dangers of, 8; democracy and, 6; of extended republic, xv–xvi; faction and, 10; Kendall, Willmoore and, 6–7; religious, 177–200; self-government and, 6

Pocock, John, 105

Podhoretz, Norman, 267

police power, 155, 190–91, 202, 215–19

political science, xxiii, xxvi, 4

Political Science Reviewer (PSR), ix, 9, 58

The Political Writings of John Adams (ed. Carey), ix

politics: Carey, George W. and, vii; constitutions and, 18; religion and, 177;

study of, xxvi

Politics (Aristotle), 58, 246

popular government. *See* government

populism, 4

The Post-Behavioral Era: Perspectives on Political Science (ed. Carey), ix

postmodernism, 257

Postrel, Virginia, 47

Preface to Democratic Theory (Dahl), 105

president: election of, 83, 87, 145; extended republic and, 145; *The Federalist* and, 145–49; legislative power and, 147–49; representation and, 142; veto power and, 147–49

Princeton University, 123, 124–26, 131–33

Printz v. United States, 210

progress, 47–50

progressivism, progressives, xxvii, 103; American political tradition and, 35; conservatism and, 43; Constitution, U.S. and, 20, 26, 43, 251–52; Enlightenment and, 35, 196; French Revolution and, 247; majoritarianism and, 25; Philadelphia Constitution of 1787 and, 81, 96–97; religious pluralism and, 196–97

Prohibition, 203–4

Project for the New American Century, 268

Promised Land, xi, 255

Protestantism, Protestants, x, 50–51, 184, 196

providence, 38–42

prudence, vii, 29, 38

The Public Philosophy (Lippmann), 245

Publius. *See The Federalist*

Pufendorf, Samuel, 126

Puritanism, Puritans, x, 124

R

radicalism, xxvii

Randolph, Edmund, 88, 90, 92, 154
Rauch, Jonathan, 46–47
Reagan, Ronald, 270, 272
reason: American political tradition and, 257–60; morality and, 186; prudence and, 29; religious pluralism and, 185–87; virtue and, 252
Reconstruction, 81, 104, 157
Rehnquist, William, 163, 164
Reid, Thomas, 127, 128, 129, 130, 131, 132, 135, 137
relativism, 8, 248
religion: American political tradition and, 25–26; civil, 4, 20, 40; education and, 121–22; Enlightenment and, 260; freedom of, 40; Locke, John and, 48; politics and, 177; state governments and, 187–88; states and, 190. See also religious pluralism
religious pluralism: articles of peace and, 180–81, 182–85, 200; civic unity and, 178–81; consensus and, 178–79, 181–83, 197; culture war and, 178, 192–93, 198; education and, 192–93; federalism and, 187–89, 193–94; morality and, 185; political and constitutional preconditions and, 187–92; problem posed by, 177–78; progressivism and, 196–97; reason, tradition of and, 185–87; religious integrity and, 178–81. See also religion
representation: Philadelphia Constitution of 1787 and, 85–86; in Senate, U.S., 94; virtue and, 149–50
republican government, xiv; Constitution, U.S. and, 31; constitutional restraint and, 57; neutrality and, 110, 116; ordered liberty and, 22–23; virtue and, xviii, xxiii, xxvii. See also government; republicanism
republicanism, xiv; American political tradition and, 22; Constitution, U.S. and, xxii, 22; faction and, xiv, 5, 102;

The Federalist and, xxii, 80; founders and, xiv; judiciary, new role of and, xxi; Madison, James and, 88; Philadelphia Constitution of 1787 and, 79, 88; plebiscitary democracy and, xxii; power, abuse of and, xiv; subsidiarity and, 261; virtue and, 122. See also republican government
Republican Party, Republicans, 44, 158, 268, 272, 275
responsible nationhood, 263, 264, 281
Review of Politics, ix
Revolt of the Elites (Lasch), 6
Revolt of the Masses (Ortega y Gasset), 245
Revolutionary War. See American Revolution
Right, 4, 11, 57
rights: abortion, 21–22; American political tradition and, ix, xi, 236–37; civil, 205, 225; Congress and, 59; Constitution, U.S. and, 59, 99, 156–66; constitutions and, 19–20; contraceptive, 160–61; covenant theology and, 76; Declaration of Independence and, 26, 76–77; English common law and, 78; federalism and, 59; founders and, 153–54; freedom and, 99; government and, 59; human, 10; judicial review and, 158; Judiciary Act of 1789 and, 59; natural, 43; natural law and, 28; roots of, 59–78; secular liberalism and, xxii, xxiii; state bills of rights and, 60; state codes of law and, 60; state constitutions and, 20, 59, 60, 70, 74–75, 77; state courts and, 60; state of nature and, 171–72; Supreme Court, U.S. and, 157; U.S. legal code and, 59–60. See also Bill of Rights, U.S.
Riley, I. Woodbridge, 131
Rittenhouse, David, 136
Robespierre, Maximilien, 266

Roe v. Wade, 21–22, 161
Romans, 277
Romer v. Evans, 162
Roosevelt, Franklin D., xii, 11
Roosevelt, Theodore, xii, 272
Rorty, Richard, 43, 198
Roshwald, Mordechai, 254, 259–60
"The 'Roster Device': J. S. Mill and Contemporary Elitism" (Carey and Kendall), viii
Rousseau, Jean-Jacques, 4, 9–10, 42, 265–66
rule of law, 22, 248–49
Rush, Benjamin, 122–23, 127
Russia, 269
Rutledge, John, 86, 90, 91

S

Sabine, George H., 173
same-sex marriage, 44, 46–47, 163, 165, 213
Schicksalsgemeinshaft, 6
Schlesinger, Arthur, 11
Schmitt, Carl, 6, 12
Schneider, Herbert, 131
school vouchers, 225
Schwartz, Bernard, 60
Schwarzenegger, Arnold, 44
Scott, Jack, 126
Scottish Enlightenment, 107, 127, 199
Scottish philosophy, 127–32
Scruton, Roger, 39
secession, 38–39, 81
A Second Federalist: Congress Creates a Government (Carey and Hyneman), viii
secularism, Enlightenment, x
secular liberalism, xxi–xxiii; egalitarianism and, xxii, xxiii; individual rights and, xxii, xxiii; majority rule and, xxii; natural rights theory and, xxi–xxii; ordered liberty and, xxiii; plebiscitary democracy and, xxii

segregation, 225
Seinsgrund, 12
self-government: American political tradition and, x, xi; consensus and, 9–10, 15; Constitution, U.S. and, 23; constitutional morality and, 80; constitutions and, 25–29; deliberation and, 13; education and, 121–22; founders and, xiii, 15; freedom and, xi; human nature and, 100; majoritarianism and, 4, 28; national government and, xvii–xviii; natural law and, 29; pluralism and, 6; prudence and, 29; social-contract theory and, 27–28. *See also* government
Senate, U.S.: administrative state and, 201–2; democratization of, 204–7, 210; election of, 25, 80–81, 82–83, 111–12; *The Federalist* and, 143–45; horizontal and vertical federalism and, 203; national character of, 144–45; people and, 143–44; representation in, 94, 142; superiority of, 112; Supreme Court, U.S. and, 202
separation of powers, xiv; American political tradition and, 22; checks and balances and, xiv; Constitution, U.S. and, xiv–xv, 22, 99; faction and, xiv; *The Federalist* and, xiv–xv, 139–40; freedom and, 99; state constitutions and, 118
September 11, 219, 227, 264, 265, 266–67, 271, 275
Seventeenth Amendment, 80–81, 201
Shattschneider, E. E., 104
Shays' rebellion, 100
Sherman, Roger, 85, 87, 89, 93, 94, 95
Sherman Anti-Trust Act, 217
slavery, 157, 202, 203–4
Smilie, John, 96
Smith, Adam, 132, 135
Smith, James Allen, 104
Smith, Samuel Stanhope, 125

sociability, vii

social contract, 4

The Social Contract (Rousseau), 9, 265

social-contract theory, 27–28

socialism, 4, 48

social justice, 7

society: government vs., 14; open, 6–7, 12

Socrates, 119, 136, 252, 253–54, 259, 262

sodomy laws, 161, 191

Souter, David, 163–64

South, secession and, 38–39

Soviet Union, 11, 272

Sparta, 21

speech, freedom of, 28

The Spirit of American Government (Smith), 104

Spragens, Thomas A., 186

Stalin, Joseph, 271

Stalinism, Stalinists, 6

state: administrative, 201–20; managerial, 7; welfare, 7, 192

state constitutions, 58; Bill of Rights, U.S. and, 60; bills of rights in, 20; necessary and proper clause and, 83; rights and, 20, 59, 60, 70, 74–75, 77; separation of powers and, 118

state governments: federal vs., xvi; national vs., xvii–xviii, xxi; religion and, 187–88

states: Constitution, U.S. and, 154–55, 202; faction and, 109; federalism and, 45; horizontal balance among, 210–15; Philadelphia Constitution of 1787 and, 85–86; police power and, 155, 215–19; religion and, 190; representation of, 85–86; secession and, 39; sovereignty of, 82

stem-cell research, 193

Stewart, Dugald, 129, 131, 135, 137

Storing, Herbert, 9

Story, Joseph, 187, 211, 215

Strauss, Leo, xxviii, 4, 267, 269, 271

Straussians, 9, 11, 14

A Student's Guide to American Political Thought (Carey), viii–ix, xxix

subsidiarity and, 261

suicide, physician-assisted, 163

Supreme Court, U.S.: abortion and, 21–22, 194; administrative state and, 201; centralization and, 33; choice-of-law issues and, 212; community and, 33–34; Constitution, U.S. and, xxi, 44, 78, 81, 97, 157, 159, 221; contraception and, 160; Declaration of Independence and, 44; due process and, 158–60, 163–66; equal protection clause and, 163; *The Federalist* and, 104; First Amendment and, 227–28; general-welfare clause and, 81; interstate-commerce clause and, 81; judicial activism and, 153–54, 166–67; judicial review and, xvii, 5, 235; judicial supremacy and, 235; jurisdiction of, 158–60; nominalism and, 173; police power and, 215–18; policy making and, 221–28; public policy and, 228–34; rights and, 157; same-sex marriage and, 44; Senate, U.S. and, 202; state laws and, 207–9; supremacy clause and, 207. *See also* judiciary

System of Moral Philosophy (Hutcheson), 126, 133

T

Taft, Robert, 11

Tansill, Charles C., 153–54

Ten Commandments, 184, 190

Tenth Amendment, 95, 156

Texas, 44

Texas v. Johnson, 227–28

Texas v. White, 202

Thirteenth Amendment, 157

Thomas Aquinas, St., 40, 169
thumoeides, 13
Time magazine, 268
Tocqueville, Alexis de, 38, 206; communities and, 32; democracy and equality and, 247–48; individualism and, 47–48, 51–52; philosophy in America and, 136, 138; religion and, 252–53; self-government and, xvii
"Towards a Definition of Conservatism" (Carey and Kendall), viii
Tracy, Destutt de, 129
tradition: conservatism and, xxvii; Enlightenment and, 34–35; prudence and, 29; of reason, 185–87; recovery of, xxix
transcendence, xi
Truman, Harry S., 11
truth, xi
"The Two Majorities" (Kendall), 9, 12

U

UN. *See* United Nations
unanimity, xxv
Union, 58, 107, 116, 202
United Nations (UN), 275
United States. *See* America
United States v. Lopez, 218
U.S. foreign policy: Bush, George W. and, 264–65, 273–75, 277; democracy and, 271; imperialism and, 276–78; media and, 266–67; neoconservativsm and, 268–70; neo-Jacobinism and, 265–81; peace and, 263; responsible nationhood and, 263
U.S. News and World Report, 268
University Bookman, ix
utopianism, xi

V

Vanderbilt University, viii

"Vices of the Political System of the United States" (Madison), 108–9, 110, 111
Virginia: bill of rights of, 70, 71–74 (table), 76; necessary and proper clause of, 83
Virginia Declaration of Rights (1776), 62 (table), 76
Virginia Plan, 84, 86, 87
virtue: American political tradition and, xviii, xx, 252; conservatism and, xxvii; Constitution, U.S. and, 23, 252; constitutional limits and, 29–31; education and, 122–23; *The Federalist* and, 14; founders and, 14, 30; majoritarianism and, 13; reason and, 252; representation and, 149–50; republican government and, xviii, xxiii, xxvii; republicanism and, 122
Voegelin, Eric, viii, x, 58, 59, 77, 131–32, 246–47

W

Wall Street Journal, ix, 268, 273
Ward, Nathaniel, 76
Washington, George, xii, 110, 122, 125, 134
Washington Post, 268, 274, 275, 276
Wattenberg, Benjamin, 267–68, 271
Webster, Daniel, 151
Weekly Standard, 268
We Hold These Truths (Murray), 38
Weigel, George, 186
welfare state, 7, 192
Western Political Science Quarterly, ix
White, Byron, 161
White, Morton, 134–35
Whitefield, George, 123
Whitehill, Robert, 95–96
"Who or What Killed the Philadelphia Constitution?" (Carey), 80
Will, George F., 162

William and Mary Quarterly, 131
William of Ockham, 167, 172–73
Williamson, Hugh, 86, 87, 169
Wills, Garry, 107, 125
Wilson, James, 86, 87, 90, 91, 93–96, 110, 112, 136, 137
Wilson, Woodrow, 11, 124, 201, 267, 272, 273–74
Witherspoon, John, 122, 123–28; background of, 123–24; moral philosophy of, 127–30, 134–36; Princeton University and, 123, 124–26, 131–33; Scottish philosophy and, 127–32
Witte, John, 190

Wolfowitz, Paul, 268, 273, 274
Wolin, Sheldon, 167
Wood, Gordon, 105
World War II, 223, 267

Y

Yale University, 6, 132
Yates, Robert, 86, 113

Z

Zuckert, Michael, 48